European Administrative Decisions

Europa Law Publishing, Groningen 2009

European Administrative Decisions

How the EU Regulates Products on the Internal Market

Dr. Andrea M. Keessen

European Administrative Law Series (2)

Europa Law Publishing is a publishing company specializing in European Union law, international trade law, public international law, environmental law and comparative national law.
For further information please contact Europa Law Publishing via email: info@europalawpublishing.com or visit our website at: www.europalawpublishing.com.

Typeset in Scala and Scala Sans, Graphic design by G2K Designers, Groningen/Amsterdam

NUR 828; ISBN 978-90-8952-056-2

The *European Administrative Law Series* hosts academic publications related to the development of European administrative law. The series aims to cover all aspects of European administrative law, reflecting the role of the European Union, the role of domestic legal orders and their mutual relation and influence.

Mixed Sources
Productgroep uit goed beheerde bossen, gecontroleerde bronnen en gerecycled materiaal.
FSC www.fsc.org Cert no. CU-COC-803615
© 1996 Forest Stewardship Council

Abbreviations

CEN	European Committee for Standardization
CENELEC	European Committee for Electrotechnnical Standardization
CFI	Court of First Instance
CHMP	Committee for Medicinal Products for Human Use
CIS	Customs Information System
CITES	Convention on International Trade in Endangered Species
EC	European Community
ECHR	European Convention of Human Rights
ECtHR	European Court of Human Rights
ECJ	European Court of Justice
EFSA	European Food Safety Authority
EMEA	European Medicines Agency
ETSI	European Telecommunications Standards Institutes
EU	European Union
EU-TWIX	European Union-Trade in Wildlife Information Exchange
FVO	Food and Veterinary Office
GMO	Genetically Modified Organism
IPPC	Integrated Pollution and Prevention Control
POP	Persistent Organic Pollutant
RAPEX	Rapid Alert System for Dangerous Consumer Products
RASFF	Rapid Alert System for Food and Feed
REACH	Registration, Evaluation, Authorization and Restriction of Chemicals
SPS Agreement	Sanitary and Phytosanitary Agreement
TBT	Technical Barriers to Trade Agreement
+	positive
-	negative
?	doubtful
*	not present

Curriculum Vitae

Dr. Andrea Keessen is post-doc at the Institute for Constitutional and Administrative Law at the Utrecht University and a member of the research school Ius Commune. She graduated with honours (*cum laude*) in Dutch Law – specialising in European Law – at Utrecht University in 2001. Subsequently she worked as a lawyer at the Amsterdam office of Allen & Overy. From September 2003 she was PhD researcher at the Institute for Constitutional and Administrative Law at the Utrecht University and in this book she presents the results of her research. She currently participates in the research project European Environmental Quality Requirements and Emission Ceilings: Towards Effective Implementation. Her general research interest lies in the field of European administrative law, with a focus on the implementation of European law in general and of environmental law and water law in particular.

CHAPTER I

Introduction

Imagine that a manufacturer of a new medicine wants to market it in the European Union. Surprisingly, even today he has to request a marketing authorization in each Member State. However, he does not need to ask permission from all individual Member States due to the European integration. Instead, he can file an application with the Dutch authorities and know that a positive decision will ensure access to the entire internal market, as the other Member States will recognize the Dutch decision on his request and base their marketing authorizations on it, unless they have good reason to question the decision of the Dutch authorities. And even if they have such doubts, this will not result in fragmentation of the internal market, since the Commission settles disputes between the Member States about the authorization of medicines. The Commission can restore uniformity by issuing a marketing authorization or rejecting the application. Such decisions are examples of European administrative decisions.[1]

The complex reality of European administrative decisions has defeated the classical distinction between direct and indirect administration of Community law. In the classical view, indirect administration refers to the application and enforcement of Community legislation by the national authorities of the Member States in accordance with their national laws, subject to compliance with the Community law standards of effectiveness and equivalence (the so-called procedural autonomy).[2] At the other end of the spectrum stands direct administration of Community law, which means that the Commission implements Community law in accordance with Community administrative law. When intensive administrative cooperation between the Commission and the administrative authorities of the Member States makes it hardly possible to distinguish between direct and indirect administration, the administration of Community law is better described as integrated or mixed administration.[3] This qualification is particularly apt where European integration has proceeded so far that Community law imposes both vertical and horizontal administrative cooperation duties.

The creation of the internal market of goods is inextricably linked with integrated administration, since the sheer volume of trade makes national control of all goods impossible. Instead, the open borders of the internal market imply Community-wide responsibilities for national authorities, since the goods they authorize gain free access throughout the EU and the results of their surveillance affect consumers in the internal market[4] and in other countries. For this reason, the European Court of Justice ('ECJ') established that Article 10 EC imposes on the Member States the obligation to enforce Community law with the same diligence as if it were their national law and – in the absence of

1 See section 2 of this chapter.

2 Van Gerven (2000), pp. 501-502; Jans *et al.* (2007), pp. 40-59.

3 Schmidt-Aßmann (2004), p. 383; Schmidt-Aßmann and Schöndorf-Haubolt (2005), p. 1; Hofmann and Türk (2007), pp. 253-271; Jans *et al.* (2007), pp. 29-31, Chiti (2004), pp. 37-38 and 45.

4 Sutherland report (1992), p. 58.

Community law sanctions – impose sanctions that are equivalent, effective, proportionate and dissuasive.[5]

The 1992 Sutherland Report firmly placed the importance of application and enforcement of the legal framework of the internal market of goods on the Community agenda. It recommended that the Community legislator establish a framework to promote administrative partnerships, so that Member States can effectively apply and enforce Community rules and the Commission can act as a facilitator to ensure their effectiveness.[6] Ever since, the improvement of application, enforcement and administrative cooperation are priorities of every Internal Market Strategy.[7] The issue gained further significance as the Enlargement created a larger and more diverse European Union.[8] It is surprising that apart from the preliminary ruling procedure, judicial cooperation that would match the administrative cooperation,[9] for instance through mutual recognition of administrative court judgments, does not exist and is not a priority of any Internal Market Strategy.

1 Research question

In view of the alleged democratic deficit at the European level, it is all the more important that the administration of Community law suffers neither from an application or enforcement deficit nor from a judicial deficit.[10] Since the Member States are primarily responsible for the implementation of Community law, this concern is particularly acute where the administration of Community law is integrated through a division of competences between the Member States, because that makes their administration efforts interdependent. That raises the question how Community law ensures that the integrated administration does not suffer from a deficit concerning its effectiveness or the respect for procedural guarantees. This book aims to answer this question

5 C-68/88 *Commission* v *Greece (Greek maize)* [1989] ECR 2965.

6 Sutherland report (1992), pp. 8 and 56.

7 Report from the Commission to the Council and the European Parliament on Cooperation between administrations for the enforcement of internal market law, COM (1996) 20 final; Communication from the Commission to the Council and the European Parliament, the European Economic and Social Committee and the Committee of the Regions, Internal Market Strategy, COM (1999) 464, and its follow-ups: 'Review of the Internal Market Strategy', COM (2001) 198, 'Internal Market Strategy, Priorities 2003-2006', COM (2003) 238 final, 'A Europe of Results: Applying Community law', COM (2007) 502 final and 'A Single Market for the 21st century', COM (2007) 724 final.

8 Lazowski (2007), pp. 401-430.

9 Informal networks exist between administrative courts, e.g. the Network of Councils of State. See: Prechal *et al.* (2005).

10 Van Gerven (2005), p. 63. The democratic deficit falls outside the scope of the central question of this book. See *inter alia*: Curtin (2007), pp. 523-541; Craig (2006 A), pp. 315-345 and Harlow (2002), pp. 108-143.

through legal research in the field of Community product regulation, more precisely in four reference areas that represent various forms of European administrative decisions and thus various approaches to integrated administration.[11] Therefore, the central research question is:

How can Community product regulation that produces European administrative decisions with potentially EU-wide effect be shaped effectively and offer sufficient procedural guarantees?

It is well known that the Treaty leaves the administration of Community law primarily in the hands of the Member States, without offering a general legal basis for the harmonisation of procedural administrative law. Therefore, the point of departure is constituted by national implementation of Community product regulation with procedural autonomy. Procedural autonomy means that in the absence of Community action or rules, the Member States implement Community law in accordance with national procedural laws, provided that these rules observe the principle of equivalence (or non-discrimination) and the principle of effectiveness.[12] Consequently, only when national administrative law is perceived to hinder the effective implementation of Community law, the 'Europeanization' of national administrative law occurs through the Community court's case law[13] and through many Regulations and Directives. That leads to piecemeal harmonization, especially since the potentially harmonizing effect of the effectiveness standard on procedural autonomy is mitigated by the procedural rule of reason.[14] This rule provides that when a national provision renders application of Community law impossible or excessively difficult, the national court has to strike a balance between the protection of Community rights of individuals and the justification for the national rule, such as the principle of legal certainty or the proper conduct of procedure.[15]

The consequence of the choice to allow the Member States to maintain reasonable national procedural rules[16] and to limit Community intervention to what is considered essential for the effective implementation of Community law[17] is that procedural administrative law is only harmonized to the extent

---

[11] Since the EEA Agreement extends the principles of the internal market to the EFTA countries (Norway, Iceland and Liechtenstein) and allows for the incorporation of secondary legislation, the findings of this research may apply to those countries as well. This book does not specifically take their position into account, however, because they are not EU Member States.

[12] Prechal (1998), p. 682.

[13] Kapteyn Verloren van Themaat (2003), p. 451.

[14] C-312/93 *Peterbroeck* v *Belgian State* [1995] ECR I-4599, Joined Cases C-430/93 and C-431/93 *Van Schijndel and Others* [1995] ECR I-4705. See: Van Gerven (2000), p. 525 and Prechal (1998), p. 681.

[15] Jans *et al.* (2007), pp. 55-56.

[16] Widdershoven (1996), p. 111; Widdershoven (2004 A),p p. 322-326. See also: Lenaerts (2004), pp. 317-343.

[17] Jans *et al.* (2007), p. 59.

that it is necessary to achieve the substantive aims of a particular Community policy.[18] It is assumed that harmonization, Community action and administrative cooperation between the Member States are necessary for the implementation of Community legislation that produces European administrative decisions with potential EU-wide effect, in order to overcome the limitations of the territoriality principle and prevent the division of the Community along territorial lines by unilateral actions of Member States. Therefore, the hypothesis is that in the area of Community product regulation, Community rules and actions will increasingly govern and enable the coordination of European administrative decision-making, enforcement and judicial review. Since these procedural rules serve to facilitate implementation of the substantive rules of a policy, they can be based on the same legal basis as the substantive rules of the policy. In addition, in a Community based on the rule of law, Community rules should also ensure sufficient respect for procedural guarantees in the implementation of Community law. In other words, the evaluation criteria of effectiveness and procedural guarantees serve to assess the legitimacy of the creation, enforcement and judicial review of European administrative decisions that arise from the integrated administration of Community product regulation.

The chapters of this book are organized by phase of the implementing activity, with the exclusion of transposition: one for application, which is called decision-making, one for enforcement and two for judicial review. Since the focus of the book is on the regulatory activities of the administration, punitive enforcement will hardly be considered in the enforcement chapter. Each chapter starts with a general introduction, then analyzes the European rules in each reference area and assesses and compares the findings in order to answer the research question for that particular phase of the implementing activity. Therefore, this question is split up in the questions: how competences are divided, how differences are prevented or solved and which procedural guarantees Community law offers to individuals, in order to understand the qualities and the gaps of the Community rules and the similarities and differences between the various European administrative decisions, as they occur in the reference areas. The concluding chapter will assess to what extent national implementation with procedural autonomy is superseded by implementation in cooperation between the Member States and the Community institutions and bodies and to what extent Community regulation can be effective and observe procedural guarantees. It will give recommendations towards the improvement of the effectiveness and respect for procedural guarantees of Community law, insofar as it produces European administrative decisions with potentially EU-wide effect.

18 Jans *et al.* (2007), p. 366. Chiti (2004), pp. 51-52.

2 Key concepts

For the purpose of this research, a European administrative decision is defined as a decision of a Community or national administrative authority taken on the basis of secondary Community legislation that is binding on those to whom it is addressed.[19] This definition builds on Article 249 EC, which states that a decision is binding in its entirety on those to whom it is addressed. The ECJ has interpreted Article 249 EC by establishing that a decision is binding if it was intended to have legal effects (of whatever nature and form)[20] and has a legitimate legal basis.[21] It is assumed that most Member States use similar elements for their definition of administrative decisions.[22] The definition applies irrespective of their form. This means that both the decision to include an active substance in an Annex to the Plant Protection Products Directive, which is taken in the form of a Commission or Council Directive, and the refusal to do so, which is taken in the form of a Commission or Council decision, fall within the scope of the definition used in this book.[23] European administrative decisions can be addressed to Member States or to individuals. Their effect can be limited to one Member State, like an IPPC permit issued by the Dutch authorities for a Dutch factory, but they can also have EU-wide effect, like the marketing authorization for medicines seen above. This research only concerns European administrative decisions that can have EU-wide effect.

The focus of this research is on the administration of Community law, or in other words, the European law of the first pillar. The administration of Community law is usually distinguished into direct administration, which refers to administration by the Commission, and indirect administration, which refers to administration by the Member States, but it is also possible that administration occurs by Community institutions and bodies and the Member States on the basis of the principle of loyal cooperation of Article 10 EC, which is called integrated administration.[24] The administration of Community law should not be confused with the implementation of Community law, which refers to the process of transposition, application and enforcement.[25] Transposition (or incorporation) refers to the creation of national legislation to implement Community legislation. Application refers to the correct application of Community law in specific cases by the administrative authorities, e.g. by issuing a CITES import

---

19 Cf. the definition adopted by Bignami (2004), p. 62 of an administrative proceeding, which is defined as any determination of rights and duties made individually by the Commission or the Council in furtherance of powers conferred by the EC Treaty or by European laws.

20 C-22/70 *Commission* v *Council* [1971] ECR I-263 and C-325/91 *France* v *Commission* [1993] ECR I-3283.

21 T-113/89 *Nefarma* v *Commission* [1990] ECR II-816. See: Lenaerts and Arts (1999), p .197.

22 See: Seerden and Stroink (2002).

23 Administrative decisions with cross-border effects taken by a national authority are also called transnational decisions. See *inter alia*: Ruffert (2001), pp. 453-487; Neßler (1995), pp. 863-866.

24 Schmidt-Aßmann (2004), p. 384; Hofmann and Türk (2007), pp. 262-263.

25 Curtin and Mortelmans (1994), p. 426.

permit on request.[26] Enforcement, more specifically public enforcement, refers to the actions by the authorities that force parties to comply with Community law, respectively national law transposing Community law.[27] Albeit generally not included as part of the implementation process, judicial protection is added as an important element, because judicial control of the administration guarantees that the rule of law is observed in the implementation process.

The first evaluation criterion is effectiveness. It is used only to evaluate *legal* effectiveness, because this is a legal research. Other aspects on which the effectiveness of regulation depends, such as political willingness and capacity, will not be analyzed. Legal effectiveness means that the available rules are adequate to enable the administration to achieve the aims of the legislation.[28] The effectiveness of Community product regulation is measured by assessing whether the aims of ensuring both the free movement of the EC regulated products and the protection of public health or the environment at a sufficiently high level can be met.[29] Although it is assumed that the prescribed scientific risk assessment sufficiently covers the latter aspect, tension can still arise between these two aims, because different balances can be struck between free movement and the protection of public health or the environment.[30] Both are shared competences of the Community and the Member States, but whereas free movement of goods is a pillar of the internal market and requires a high degree of uniformity, the protection of public health or the environment leaves the Member States some room for discretion. Nevertheless, if disagreement occurs as to which decision should be taken or how intensive enforcement efforts should be, the differences between the Member States should neither endanger the free movement of products nor result in the free movement of dangerous, flawed or illegal products. This means that the focus of this book is on the regulatory activities of the administration. Punitive enforcement falls outside its scope because its main aim is to punish the offender, even though that arguably may contribute to achieve the aims of the legislation.

The second evaluation criterion is sufficient respect for procedural guarantees. It is measured because the Community is a community governed by the rule of law and therefore procedural guarantees should constrain administrative discretion.[31] Measuring compliance with this evaluation criterion depends on the answer to the question which interested parties should enjoy which procedural guarantees. For the purpose of this research, sufficient procedural guarantees are offered when the right to be heard and the right to judicial protection are respected. These rights constitute the core of the rights of defence and to a fair trial.[32] This means that a person who is adversely affected by a decision

[26] Curtin and Mortelmans (1994), p. 428.

[27] Curtin and Mortelmans (1994), p. 428.

[28] Cf. Blomberg and Michiels (1997), p. 32.

[29] Cf. Weatherill (2002), p. 51.

[30] Dougan (2000), pp. 853-885.

[31] Shapiro (1999), pp. 30-34.

[32] See: Jans *et al.* (2007), p. 187 et seq. and p. 241 et seq.

should be given the opportunity to make his views known to the administration and have access to a court, which can offer him a remedy to ensure compliance with the law.[33] It follows from Community case law that the applicant or the addressee of the decision is entitled to respect of these fundamental rights.[34] There is some debate on whether and under what conditions these rights should be extended to other interested parties.[35] In this research, it is evaluated to what extent it is and should be extended to so-called third parties, which are those who are not directly involved in the decision, but whose interests might be affected by it.

A source of inspiration for the (desired) Community approach is the European Convention of Human Rights ('ECHR') and the case law of the European Court of Human Rights ('ECtHR') on the rights of defence and the right to a fair trial.[36] Even though the EU itself is not a Party to the ECHR and does not have the competence to accede,[37] the Court of Justice established in its case law that the ECHR has become a part of Community law and can be invoked as such both in the Community courts and in the national courts where Community law is at issue.[38] Another source of inspiration is the Aarhus Convention, which applies to the broad area of Community and national environmental law and is therefore relevant for some reference areas.[39] Although its provisions on public participation are limited to decisions about the physical environment, its provisions on judicial review harmonize the standing conditions for individuals and environmental organisations that want to bring an action against acts or omissions of national authorities or institutions and bodies of the European Union in the general interest of protection of the environment.[40] It has been signed and ratified by all EU Member States and by the EU, which implemented it into the Aarhus Regulation and the Aarhus Directives.[41] Only the Aarhus Directive about judicial review is still a proposal and therefore this part of the Aarhus Convention is directly implemented by the Member States.[42]

---

33 Cf. Arnull (2006), p. 47.

34 E.g. C-28/05 *G.J. Dokter et al.* v *Minister van Landbouw, Natuur en Voedselkwaliteit* [2006] ECR I-5431. See: Jans *et al.* (2007), pp. 187-196 and 241-317.

35 E.g. Tridimas (2000), pp. 296-297; Bignami (2004), pp. 73 and 82, Prechal (2008), pp. 155-182.

36 E.g. Groussot (2006), pp. 215-267.

37 Opinion 2/94 [1996] ECR I-3425.

38 E.g. C-112/00 *Schmidtberger* [2003] ECR I-5659; Art. 6 (2) EU and Art. 47 and 48 of The Charter of Human Rights, OJ 2000 C 364/01. See *inter alia*: Costello (2006), pp. 87-130 and Canor (1998), p. 137.

39 The Aarhus Convention, available at www.unece.org/env. See for the (desired) impact of the Aarhus Convention on situations similar to the Greenpeace case: De Lange (2003), pp. 227-248.

40 De Sadeleer, Roller and Dross (2005), p. 178 et seq.

41 Council Decision 2005/370/EC; Regulation 1367/2006 ('Aarhus Regulation'), Directive 2003/4/EC on public access to environmental information and Directive 2003/35/EC on public participation.

42 Proposal for a Directive of the European Parliament and of the Council on access to justice in environmental matters COM (2003) 624 final.

3 Research methods

This book presents legal research that is qualitative in nature, as the object of research is to acquire a better understanding of the legal framework that organizes European administrative decisions by analyzing and comparing the applicable rules in a number of reference areas. In order to gain a better understanding of the legal rules in legislation and case law, legal literature has been consulted. Choosing reference areas with established administrative cooperation ensures that the applicable rules reflect actual practice. Moreover, Commission communications were analyzed in order to ground the research on data collected by the Commission regarding the implementation of the relevant Community legislation. Finally, Dutch experts working in one of the reference fields were consulted in order to gain insight into everyday practice. The main issues discussed below are the way in which legislation and case law are studied and analysed, the approach towards Community and national law and the selection of reference areas.

3.1 Qualitative research

European and national legislation and case law, in particular regarding the selected reference areas, will be analysed and interpreted in this book. Arguably, national law cannot be ignored. In the absence of European law and for the implementation of European law, national law applies insofar as it is in conformity with European law standards. As such, national law has a complementary function. However, in order to understand the functioning of the Community regulatory system as a whole, the focus is on how European law finds solutions to problems that arise in the implementation of Community law and not on how national law finds solutions to implementation problems.[43] Instead of comparing the legislation of States, the focus is on the comparison of reference areas. The study of legislation will answer the question of how systems of regulation have been set up, while the study of case law will answer the question which issues may cause disputes and which rules have been developed in case law. For this purpose, qualitative case-law research is used. Cases were therefore selected on the basis of their characteristics, for instance because in a particular case a new line of reasoning was used, a new legal rule was formulated or an existing legal rule was improved.

3.2 Reference areas

General administrative law interacts with specific areas of administrative law. On the one hand, specific areas of administrative law can provide general rules (induction). On the other hand, general rules can be clarified and tested in specific areas of administrative law (deduction). Specific areas

---

[43] See for example: Van de Gronden (1998).

of administrative law can demonstrate the functioning of regulatory models established for the weighing of various interests. The different areas of administrative law both reflect regulatory needs and offer reservoirs of solutions.[44] The advantage of taking a comparative approach is that a comparison involving more than one system widens the perspective of possible problems and solutions.[45] It is expected that a comparison of decision-making, enforcement and judicial protection offered in specific areas of administrative law will reveal similar conflicts for which various solutions were adopted, thus offering insight into the pros and cons of each solution.

Various selection approaches are possible. The selection of reference areas can be made on the basis of extreme variation or minimal variation and it is possible to select typical cases at random or critical cases by information-oriented sampling.[46] Since the aim of this research is to provide insight into integrated administration of Community law, the selection was limited to reference areas where the administrative authorities would take European administrative decisions with potential EU-wide effect. In order to study various approaches to regulation while all other factors remain equal, a choice was made for minimal variation and critical cases. This means that all reference areas originate from a similar area of law and that each distinct type of European administrative decisions with potential EU-wide effect is represented. The field of product legislation was chosen to provide the reference areas, because both vertical and horizontal administrative cooperation is well established in this field.

Instead of choosing a product regulated by national law, such as liquors, a product regulated by New Approach legislation, such as toys, and a product regulated by Community legislation, such as medicines, only the latter type of products were selected, i.e. products that require an authorisation in accordance with an operational procedure established by Community law before they may be placed on the market. The reason is that the Europeanization of the regulation of other products is limited, with the exception of the coordination of enforcement via rapid alert mechanisms.[47] By contrast, the regulation of the latter products is firmly based on Community legislation. Therefore, they can provide insights on how regulation that produces European administrative decisions with potential EU-wide effect can be shaped effectively and offer sufficient procedural guarantees for other areas of Community law where administrative cooperation has started developing more recently. The following list demonstrates that many reference areas could have been selected from the field of Community product regulation:

- plant protection products
- biocides

---

44 Schmidt-Aßmann (2004), pp. 8-10.

45 Zweigert and Kötz (1998), nos 2-11.

46 Baarda and De Goede (2001), pp. 76-78.

47 Council Regulation 2679/98.

- chemicals
- CITES
- waste
- dual use goods
- cultural goods
- weapons
- genetically modified organisms
- food and feed additives
- food supplements
- novel food
- cosmetics
- medicines for human use
- veterinary medicines
- medical devices

The selected reference areas are endangered wildlife (CITES), medicines for human use, plant protection products and genetically modified organisms (GMOs). The critical cases selection criterion required finding reference areas that present a variable mix of Community decisions, national decisions, mutual recognition and single licence decisions, as will become clear in the chapter on decision-making. On grounds of procedural similarity, the inclusion of one area led to the exclusion of other areas with a similar type or mix of European administrative decisions. The minimal variation selection criteria further reduced the choice to Community regulation driven by environmental protection or public health concerns. These interests are not far apart, as environmental policy is partly driven by health considerations,[48] while health policy considers environmental impact a major health determinant.[49] Moreover, in the context of the internal market, both environmental policies and health policies have to be compatible with the aim of removing barriers to free trade.

48 Art. 174 EC; Communication from the Commission to the Council, the European Parliament and the European Economic and Social Committee – A European Environment and Health Strategy COM (2003) 338 final, p. 2. Communication from the Commission to the Council, the European Parliament and the European Economic and Social Committee: 'The European Environment and Health Action Plan 2004-2010', COM (2004) 416 final, implements this strategy. It is also visible in Decision 1600/2002 of the European Parliament and of the Council laying down the Sixth Environmental Action Programme OJ 2002 L242/1, where the goal is set that EU environmental policy contributes to a high level of quality of life and social well-being for citizens by providing an environment where the level of pollution does not give rise to harmful effects on human health and the environment.

49 Decision 1786/2002 Community Action Programme on public health (2003-2008) OJ 2002 L271/1.

4 Introduction to the reference areas

In order to gain a basic understanding of the selected reference areas, each area will be introduced, but first, they will be placed within the perspective of the internal market and the creation of Community product regulation. The realization of the internal market is one of the main achievements of European integration. It is essentially based on three pillars. The first pillar is the free movement of goods of Article 28 EC, which prohibits quantitative restrictions on imports and exports within the EU and other measures having equivalent effects, thus removing barriers created by tax and quota. The barriers created by border controls were removed when the Community abolished internal border controls in 1992. However, Article 30 EC prevented the removal of obstacles arising from differences in national regulation provided they protect public interests such as human health or the environment. The other two pillars of the internal market are mutual recognition and harmonization, because they integrated the market despite the legal obstacles presented by rules which protect legitimate public interests.

4.1 Product regulation

Two instruments removed the legal obstacles to the realization of the internal market and thus stood at the basis of Community product regulation: mutual recognition and harmonization.[50] The rule of mutual recognition was introduced in the *Cassis de Dijon* judgment as an instrument to remove trade barriers created by slightly divergent national regulations.[51] Through mutual recognition, goods lawfully marketed in one Member State (home state) can be lawfully marketed in all other Member States (host states), unless an obstacle resulting from disparities between the various national law systems is justified on the basis of a ground described in Article 30 of the EC Treaty or a mandatory requirement recognized in ECJ case law, because it is both necessary and proportionate to the aim in view.[52] If similarity is sufficient to allow for mutual recognition, the rules of the Member State of origin prevail. Otherwise compliance with the rules of more than one Member State would be required.

Mutual recognition has the limitation that court intervention may be required to settle disputes caused by a lack of trust in the similarity of the rules.[53] Such disputes signal the need for harmonisation,[54] as that offers the

---

50 Cf. Leebron (1996), pp. 91-94.

51 C-120/78 *Rewe-Zentral AG* v *Bundesmonopolverwaltung für Branntwein (Cassis de Dijon)* [1979] ECR p. 649.

52 Mandatory requirements were introduced by C-120/78 *Rewe-Zentral AG* v *Bundesmonopolverwaltung für Branntwein (Cassis de Dijon)* [1979] ECR p. 649, and expanded and elaborated in later case law, e.g. C-302/86 *Commission* v *Denmark (Danish bottles)* [1988] ECR p. 4607. Member States must notify exceptions to the Commission under Decision 3052/95.

53 Weiler (1999), p. 368.

54 Armstrong (1999), p. 227.

certainty of common standards that eliminate substantial and justifiable obstacles to the free movement of goods.[55] This instrument is available because the EC Treaty provides for a host of legislative competences, which are based on a high level of protection of health, safety, the environment and consumers.[56] When the Community legislator replaces national regulatory regimes (deregulation) by a common framework for the regulation of these products (re-regulation), interests such as environmental protection remain protected, but at a Community rather than a national level.[57] However, harmonization may not be easy to achieve due to the complexities of the subject matter.[58]

Both instruments stood at the basis of two types of Community product legislation. The first type consists of harmonization of technical standards.[59] Initially, detailed technical standards for specific products, such as motor vehicles and tractors, replaced national technical standards. As the proposed rules were detailed and unanimity required in the decision-making process, it was not very easy to accomplish harmonisation of product standards.[60] After the breakthrough of the *Cassis de Dijon* judgment for the deregulation of products such as foodstuffs, the progress in the harmonization of safety requirements was stepped up through the adoption of a 'New Approach' to harmonisation, which combined harmonization and mutual recognition.[61] New Approach legislation contains essential safety requirements that products must meet before being placed on the market if they are to benefit from free movement.[62] Manufacturers may place the CE mark on products to declare their conformity with harmonised standards, as developed by CEN, CENELEC and ETSI, or any other technical solution that provides compliance with the essential requirements established

55 Communication from the Commission concerning the consequences of the judgment given by the Court of Justice on 20 February 1979 in Case 120/78 (*Cassis de Dijon*), OJ C 256 of 3 October 1989, 'Cassis de Dijon' Judgment ECR 1979, p. 649; White Paper on Completing the Internal Market, from the Commission to the European Council COM (85) 310 final, of 14 June 1985.

56 This represents the main difference between the EU and the WTO legal regime. See: Weiler (2000), pp. 201-232. See also: Trebilcock and Howse (2005).

57 Weatherill (1995), p. 225.

58 Weatherill (2002), pp. 41-74.

59 Cf. the Technical Barriers to Trade (TBT) and Sanitary and Phytosanitary (SPS) agreements complementing the GATT in the WTO Treaty.

60 White Paper from the Commission to the European Council: 'Completing the Internal Market', COM (1985) 310 final, p. 21.

61 Armstrong (1999), p. 227. See also: Guide to the Implementation of Directives based on the New Approach and the Global Approach, European Communities 2000, available at: http: //europa.eu.int/comm/enterprise/newapproach/newapproach.htm.

62 Examples are: Directive 90/396/EEC Appliances burning gaseous fuels; Directive 95/16/EC Lifts; Directive 98/37/EC Machinery safety; Directive 88/378/EEC Toys safety. For a complete list, see http://europa.eu.int/comm/enterprise/newapproach/standardization/harmstds/reflist.html. The New Approach was not extended to products for which European product legislation was already in place before 1985.

by a New Approach Directive.[63] The national authorities must not hinder the marketing of CE products, unless the manufacturer wrongly used the CE marking or a certain hazard was not covered.[64] The New Approach legislation was complemented by Global Approach legislation, which allowed for mutual recognition of conformity assessments.[65]

The second type of product regulation consists of risk regulation.[66] Since the risks involved with certain products are such that they cannot be regulated by technical standards but require a case-by-case assessment, the New Approach could not be extended to these products.[67] However, if individual Member States were to take divergent measures with respect to a product or a class of products, they could create different levels of protection and thereby create obstacles that would prevent products from moving freely within the Community.[68] Therefore, Community legislation provides that such products may not be placed on the (internal) market without a marketing authorization, which is issued by administrative authorities on the basis of a risk assessment by experts. The administrative authority that issues such a decision can be a national authority – and then its decision can or must be recognized by national authorities in other Member States – or a Community institution or body. Secondary legislation thus amended national administrative law to enable the free movement of 'risky' products and produced European administrative decisions with EU-wide effect.

4.2 Genetically modified organisms

Legislation	Decision-making	Enforcement	Judicial Review
Regulation 1829/2003 (Artt. 37 and 95 EC) and Directive 2001/18 (Art. 95 EC)	Community authorization and Single licence	Community inspection service; National monitoring and sanctioning	Community courts National courts

The first genetically modified organism ('GMO') to be introduced onto the US market in 1994 was a tomato,[69] while the first GMO to be introduced onto the EU market in 1996 was a soybean tolerant to glufosinate.[70] Other, more

63 Chiti (2000) pp. 318-320; Ladeur (1999).

64 Guide to the implementation of directives based on the New Approach and the Global Approach, p. 9.

65 Council Decision 90/636/EEC, Decision 93/465/EEC.

66 No WTO counterpart exists. Instead, specific international conventions, such as the Stockholm Convention on POPs, constitute international counterparts of European regulations and directives.

67 Guide to the Implementation of directives based on the New Approach and the Global Approach, European Communities 2000, p. 8.

68 A series of cases, in particular tobacco cases, highlight the scope of Art. 95 EC. See: Gutman (2006), pp. 147-187.

69 Christoforou (2004), p. 637.

70 A list of authorized GMOs is available at: http://www.gmo-compass.org/eng/gmo/db/.

common types of GMO plants on the market are maize, soybean, oil-seed rape, flowers and cotton varieties. GMOs have been created for agricultural, industrial and medicinal use. It is the fear of harmful consequences for human health or the environment that makes GMOs controversial. Specific international rules on GMOs concern food safety and environmental safety. The UN Codex Alimentarious contains principles of human health risk analysis, which also cover GMO food safety. These principles recommend a pre-market assessment, performed on a case-by-case basis, including an evaluation of direct effects (nutritional effects and stability of the inserted gene) and unintended effects (toxicity and tendency to provoke allergenic reactions). The Cartagena Protocol on Biosafety to the Convention on Biodiversity ('Cartagena Protocol') specifically covers GMO environmental risks.[71] It established an advance informed agreement procedure for transboundary movements and the Biosafety Clearing House to facilitate information exchange.[72]

Community legislation

Community GMO legislation was first established in the early 1990s. The marketing of GMOs is regulated by Regulation 1829/2003 and Directive 2001/18, which also regulates their cultivation.[73] The Cartagena Protocol gave legitimacy to these rules and resulted in Regulation 1946/2003 on transboundary movement of genetically modified organisms, which regulates the intentional and unintentional movements between Member States and third countries, with the exception of intentional movements within the EU.[74] Community legislation defines a genetically modified organism as 'an organism, with the exception of human beings, in which the genetic material has been altered in a way that does not occur naturally by mating and/or natural recombination.'[75] Therefore, a tulip with genetically modified carnation is a GMO. Genetically modified food or feed is regulated if it contains, consists of or is produced from a GMO, for example genetically modified maize and popcorn made from GMO maize. This definition excludes meat from a pig fed with GMO maize, which therefore does not require labelling under Regulation 1930/2003. The same applies to other products as well, when the level of GMOs is below the threshold for labelling.

After the EU authorization procedures for GMOs grinded to a halt in 1998 because Member States failed to reach agreement on the safety of GMOs, the United States, Canada and Argentina filed a complaint before the WTO. In the 2006 Biotech Ruling, the WTO Panel established a violation of the undue delay

71 The Cartagena Protocol to the Convention on Biosafety was adopted in 2000 and is available at: http://cbd.int/biosafety/. The Protocol was concluded on behalf of the Community by Council Decision 2002/628/EC and its provisions were implemented mainly by Regulation 1946/2003/EC.

72 Art. 1 Cartagena Protocol.

73 The EU does not regulate the co-existence of GMOs with conventional and biological plants and seeds.

74 Regulation 1946/2003.

75 Art. 2 (2) Directive 2001/18/EC.

provision of the SPS Agreement.[76] The Panel did not condemn the establishment of a marketing authorisation procedure, nor did it order the Community to approve GMOs. It condemned the de facto moratorium on the approval of GMOs, the delay on the approval of specific GMOs and the safeguard measures (bans) of some Member States against approved GMO varieties, because these measures could not be justified by sound scientific evidence. As the de facto moratorium had already ceased to exist in 2004, the EU had time to act in compliance with the Biotech Ruling before the deadline expired in November 2007 by ensuring that decisions were taken within the strict time-limits established by the new secondary legislation. In addition, the EU has to enforce the rules on safeguard measures, thus avoiding unjustified permanent national safeguard measures.

Directive 2001/18 Part C applies to the placing on the market of all GMOs,[77] but Regulation 1829/2003 restricted the scope of the Directive by establishing a Community procedure for the placing on the market of GMOs for food and feed use. This means that Directive 2001/18 Part C only applies when national authorities issue authorizations for the placing on the market of GMOs for other uses (than food or feed use), such as GMO flowers.[78] A GMO is 'placed on the market' when it is made 'available to third parties, whether in return for payment or free of charge.'[79] An operation does not qualify as placing on the market if a GMO is deliberately released into the environment, which means that it has received authorization for cultivation in the EU,[80] or if a GMO is used for research and development in the EU.[81] In the event of disputes between Member States concerning authorizations issued under the Directive, the Commission settles these disputes by issuing an authorization in accordance with the regulatory procedure, which it also follows when issuing authorizations under the Regulation. The Member States that oppose authorization of a GMO can be overruled in this procedure, which led some to ban GMOs as a safeguard measure.[82]

---

76 Dispute DS291(the Biotech Ruling) is available at: http:// www.wto.org/english/tratop_e/dispu_e/cases_e/ds291_e.htm

77 A number of infringement procedures were directed against late transposition of Directive 2001/18, e.g. C-416/03 *Commission* v *Greece* OJ 2005 C-106/7 and C-422/03 *Commission* v *the Netherlands* OJ 2005 C 6/16.

78 Directive 2001/18 entered into effect in October 2004.

79 Art. 2 (4) Directive 2001/18/EC.

80 Art. 2 (3) Directive 2001/18/EC, regulated by Part B of Directive 2001/18/EC.

81 Regulated by Directive 90/219/EEC.

82 See the section on GMOs in the chapter on decision-making.

4.3 Medicines

Legislation	Decision-making	Enforcement	Judicial Review
Directive 2001/83 Regulation 726/2004 (Art. 95 EC)	Community authorization and mutual recognition authorization	Community information exchange and emergency measures National monitoring and sanctioning	Community courts National courts

Ever since the scandal involving Thalidomide in the early sixties, the regulation of medicines is considered indispensable to ensure the safety, efficacy and quality of medicines. Yet there is no international treaty that sets common standards for the regulation of medicines. International cooperation in this field has a bilateral character, as illustrated by the International Conference on Harmonisation of Technical Requirements for Registration of Pharmaceuticals for Human Use ('ICH'). Within this organization, the authorities of the European Union, the United States and Japan are developing an international pharmacopoeia, which is a book about the preparation and identification of medicines. The EU Member States cooperate with neighbouring countries in the Council of Europe, which has resulted in a European pharmacopoeia. The World Health Organisation ('WHO'), the United Nations specialized agency for health, has assisted States in the development of a medicines policy since 1975. It does not prescribe a regulatory framework, but it sets norms and standards that are widely followed.[83]

Community legislation

Although the EU only has limited competence in the field of health care, it has had a medicines Directive since 1965 on the basis of Article 95 EC. However, Article 152 EC leaves the competence for health care matters primarily in the hands of the Member States,[84] as it explicitly states that Community action will complement national policies and actions and excludes any harmonisation whatsoever of the laws and regulations of the Member States.[85] Hence, Article 152 EC does not seem to allow for Community regulation of medicines for human use. Nevertheless, Article 95 EC may provide a legal basis for Community medicines legislation because the conditions for recourse to Article 95 EC as a legal basis are met, even though protection of public health is a decisive factor in the choices to be made.[86] The dual aim of safeguarding public

83 See: www.who.int; Sands and Klein (2001), pp. 96-98.

84 Lonbay (2000), p. 47.

85 Art. 152 (4) (c) EC. By contrast, Art. 152 (4) (b) EC provides the legal basis for the regulation of veterinary medicines.

86 C-376/98 *Germany* v *Parliament and Council (Tobacco Advertising)* [2000] ECR I-8419 and C-74/99 *British American Tobacco (Investments) and Imperial Tobacco* [2000] ECR I-8599, as confirmed in C-210/03, *Swedish Match* [2004] ECR I-11893.

health and removing barriers that hinder the free movement of medicines, allow the harmonisation of the medicines legislation to be based on Article 95 EC.[87]

The Medicines Directive and Regulation apply to medicines[88] for human use which are intended to be placed on the market in the Member States.[89] Medicines[90] may only be sold in a Member State of the EU after the Commission or a national authority has issued a marketing authorisation, in accordance with the procedure of the Medicines Regulation and the procedure of the Directive, respectively.[91] A medicine is defined as '(a) any substance or combination of substances presented as having properties for treating or preventing disease in human beings; or (b) any substance or combination of substances which may be used in or administered to human beings either with a view to restoring, correcting or modifying physiological functions by exerting a pharmacological, immunological or metabolic action, or to making a medical diagnosis'.[92] A product is a medicine if it meets the first or the second of those two definitions.[93] A product that falls under the definition of a medicine and also under the definition of a product covered by other Community legislation[94] falls within the scope of the medicines legislation.[95] The REACH Regulation neither applies to medicines nor to substances in medicines.[96]

---

87 See: Barnard (2004), pp. 493-504 and Van Ooik (1999), in particular p. 58 and pp. 312-315.

88 The Directive and the Regulation use another term, namely 'medicinal product'.

89 Art. 2 Regulation 726/2004; Art. 2 (1) Directive 2001/83. Art. 3 Directive 2001/83 explicitly states a few exceptions, e.g. medicines prepared in a pharmacy in accordance with a medical prescription for an individual patient.

90 For the purpose of this book, medicines refers to medicines for human use and not to veterinary medicines, which are regulated by Regulation 726/2004 and Directive 2001/82/EC.

91 Intellectual property issues fall outside the scope of this research, even though marketing authorisations for medicines are closely linked to patents. Patents are important for research-based companies that develop medicines, because they protect their invention. A patent is issued before the quality, side effects and therapeutic effectiveness of the medicine are thoroughly tested. Therefore, after obtaining a patent, it may take many years of research before the medicine is authorised to be placed on the market. Since a patent expires 20 years after registration, marketing authorisations offer some additional protection against competitors. The research data that underlies the marketing authorisation is protected for at least 8 years after the first registration in the European Union. See on this subject, e.g. Hancher (2000), pp. 76-93.

92 Art. 1 (1) Directive 2001/83, e.g. ABRvS 22-03-1996 JGR 2000/1, about a dandruff shampoo not falling under either (a) or (b), thus not being a medicinal product.

93 Joined Cases C-211/03, C-299/03 and C-316/03 to C-319/03 *HLH Warenvertriebs, Orthica* v *Deutschland*, [2005] ECR I-5141.

94 Art. 2 (2) Directive 2001/83. E.g.: C-227/82 *Van Bennekom* [1983] ECR 3883, C-369/88 *Delattre* [1991] ECR I-1487, C-112/89 *Upjohn (Upjohn I)* [1991] ECR I-1703 and Joined Cases C-211/03, C-299/03 and C-316/03 to C-319/03 *HLH Warenvertriebs, Orthica* v *Deutschland* [2005] ECR I-5141.

95 Joined Cases C-211/03, C-299/03 and C-316/03 to C-319/03 *HLH Warenvertriebs, Orthica* v *Deutschland*, [2005] ECR I-0000.

96 Art. 2 REACH Regulation 1907/2006, OJ 2006 L 396/1.

There is a difference between proprietary medicines and generics: generics are produced after the patent protecting a proprietary medicine has expired. The names of generics are usually based on the active substance and they are much cheaper than proprietary medicines because it does not require expensive research to produce them and because a simplified authorization applies to generics once the applicant is able to demonstrate essential similarity with a reference medicine for which the data protection period of the risk assessment has expired. There is also a difference between medicines that require prescription by a doctor and non-prescription medicines. The individual Member States decide to which category a medicine belongs and determine the reimbursement of its costs to consumers. Costs are lowered by the use of generics and by parallel trade, which refers to the import of medicines from one Member State into another in order to place it on the market there, outside the manufacturer's or its licensed distributor's formal channels.[97] It is motivated by price differences between the Member States and facilitated by ECJ case law.

4.4 CITES

Legislation	Decision-making	Enforcement	Judicial Review
Regulation 338/97 (Art. 175 EC)	Community listing decision and single licence	Community registration and emergency measures National monitoring and sanctioning	Community courts National courts

The urge to regulate international trade in wildlife led in 1973 to the signing of the Convention on International Trade in Endangered Species of Wild Flora and Fauna ('CITES').[98] After ratification by 15 states, the CITES Convention entered into effect in 1975. Nearly every state in the world is now party to the CITES Convention, including all EU Member States. The scope of the CITES Convention is limited to the species listed on the Appendixes (I to III) to the Convention. The main criticism regarding the CITES convention is that it only aims at protecting wild flora and fauna against overexploitation as a result of international trade and that it does not prevent the loss of habitat. Yet this should not stop the attempts to prevent extinction caused by overexploitation as a result of international trade. The threat of uncontrolled trade in animals and plants is best clarified by taking the trade in shark as an example. Shark fins are used as an ingredient for fin soup, which is considered a delicacy in Asia. It is ironic that while sharks usually attract attention following attacks on humans, these

97 Commission Communication on parallel imports of proprietary medicinal products for which marketing authorisations have already been granted, COM (2003) 839(01).

98 The CITES Convention is available at: http://www.cites.org/eng/disc/text.shtml.

are extremely rare events. In contrast, humans kill millions of sharks each year. This puts shark populations at risk from overexploitation.[99]

Community legislation

In the European Union, the CITES Convention has been applied through the CITES Regulations since 1984. Regulation 338/97 on the protection of species of wild fauna and flora by regulating trade therein ('CITES Regulation')[100] is a compromise between the need to regulate the international trade in endangered species and the need to respect the (European) fundamental freedom of free movements of goods on the internal market.[101] This led to the creation of a single licence system: CITES documents regarding the import, export and status of listed species are issued by the authorities of one Member State and have effect in all Member States. These decisions are based on a common decision-making procedure and on Community decisions concerning the listing of species on the Annexes to the Regulation and emergency measures. The Member States have some discretion in the implementation of the CITES Regulation. Since Article 175 (1) EC provides the legal basis of the Regulation, the Member States may take more stringent measures. The Regulation particularly allows this for holding live animals, subject to the requirement that the national rules are in compliance with the Treaty, which generally boils down to passing the free movement test.[102]

The main concepts in the CITES regulation are defined in the Regulation. *Species* refers to any species, subspecies or geographically separate population thereof. The CITES Regulation only applies to species that are listed on one of the Annexes to the Regulation. *Annex A* contains all Appendix I species, plus some Appendix II and II species, for which the EC has adopted stricter measures, and some non-CITES species. Inclusion means that all trade is forbidden, unless a specimen is born and bred in captivity. *Annex B* contains all other Appendix II species, plus some Appendix III species and some non-CITES species. Inclusion means that trade must be regulated by import and export permits. *Annex C* contains all other CITES Appendix III species. Inclusion here means that a State wants to monitor the export of a species from its country. *Annex D* contains species for which the EU monitors their import levels, including some CITES Appendix III species for which the EU Member States hold a reservation. A *specimen* means an animal or plant, whether live or dead, and any readily recognizable part or derivative thereof.

---

99 George Burgess, director of the Florida Program for Shark Research, World environment news, 27 October 2003, www.planetark.org.

100 Council Regulation 338/97 on the protection of species of wild fauna and flora by regulating trade therein, OJ 1997 L 61/1, as amended.

101 http://ec.europa.eu/environment/cites/pdf/diff_between_eu-cites.pdf.

102 E.g. ABRvS 22-08-2007 *Stichting de Grieze tegen de Minister van Landbouw, Natuur en Voedselkwaliteit*, 200701364/1.

International trade refers to import, export, re-export and introduction from the sea, i.e. the landing of specimens of a species taken in the marine environment outside the jurisdiction of any state.[103] For the purpose of CITES, the term 'trade' is broadly defined. Therefore, the concept of trade in the sense of CITES covers the crossing of any national border of a specimen of a CITES-listed species. The motivation for the movement of the specimen is not important. Moreover, it does not matter if the exporting country is not the country of origin of the species. This type of export is named *re-export* and is specifically included in the definition of trade. It is defined as the export of any specimen that has previously been imported. The purpose of including re-export is to try to eliminate the possibility of individuals seeking to circumvent the provisions of the convention by shipping the specimens through a number of countries until its origins become lost in a tangle of paperwork.[104]

4.5 Plant Protection products

Legislation	Decision-making	Enforcement	Judicial Review
Directive 91/414 (Art. 37 EC) Proposal for a Regulation concerning the placing of plant protection products on the market COM (2006) 388 (Artt. 37 (2) and 152 (4) (b) EC)	Community listing decision and national authorization, optional mutual recognition Community listing decision and mutual recognition within zones	National monitoring and sanctioning Idem	Community courts National courts Idem

Plant protection products are pesticides used for agricultural purposes.[105] Their use mainly benefits farmers, as these products kill weed or insects. Environmental organisations take an interest in plant protection products because they are also associated with serious risks to human health, especially children's health, and the environment. They affect people, animals and plants via their contamination of groundwater, soil, food and even the air.[106] The main international convention is the 2001 Stockholm Convention on Persistent Organic Pollutants (POPs),[107] which aims to eliminate production, use, emissions and

[103] Art. 1 (c, d, e) CITES Convention.

[104] Favre (1989), p. 25 et seq.

[105] Biocides are pesticides for other uses, e.g. disinfectants, in-can preservatives, antifouling products.

[106] Carson (1962).

[107] The text of the Stockholm Convention on Persistent Organic Pollutants (2001) can be found on www.pops.int. It was preceded by the 1979 Convention on Long-Range Transboundary Air Pollution on Persistent Organic Pollutants and the Protocol on Persistent Organic Pollutants (1998) to this Convention, to which the Community is a Party as well. Other important Conventions include the Rotterdam Convention on Prior Informed Consent (1998) (preceded by a voluntary prior informed consent

discharges of chemicals and pesticides with the characteristics of POPs. Both the European Union and the Member States are parties to this Convention. Currently, this Convention is of limited significance to the EU, because it only targets twelve chemicals and pesticides. It does not completely ban these POPs, it allows the use of DDT to fight malaria, for example. Its relevance might increase in the coming years, however, because it contains criteria for the evaluation of chemicals and pesticides in use, it regulates their disposal and it obliges the parties to prevent the development of new POPs. It even allows for the introduction of a POP review committee that would issue recommendations for the evaluation of chemicals and pesticides.[108]

Community legislation

The European Union is ahead of international developments. It has banned the active substances that the Stockholm Convention forbids from being used in plant protection products via Regulation 850/2004,[109] which also lists other active substances whose presence is forbidden in plant protection products to be marketed within the EU.[110] In addition, the EU regulates the marketing of pesticides,[111] the maximum level of pesticide residues on food[112] and the classification, packaging and labelling of pesticides.[113] For the time being, the regulation of the use of pesticides still belongs to the competences of the Member States. However, the Commission has developed a Community strategy and action plan to reduce the use of pesticides. This includes a proposal for a Directive on the sustainable use of pesticides, which relies on national action plans as a means to reduce pesticide use.[114]

---

procedure, in effect since 1989) and the Basel Convention on the Control of Transboundary Movements of Hazardous Wastes and their Disposal (1989). For an overview of these three Conventions and their inter-relationship, please see: www.pops.int/documents/background/hcwc.pdf.

108 This international review committee may operate in the context of the Strategic Approach to International Chemicals Management (SAICM) within the United Nations Framework.

109 Regulation 850/2004 on persistent organic pollutants.

110 Council Directive 79/117.

111 Council Directive 91/414 EC concerning the placing of plant protection products on the market and Directive 98/8/EC concerning the placing of biocidal products on the market. Directive 98/8/EC was based on Directive 91/414/EC.

112 Directive 90/642 on the fixing of maximum levels for pesticide residues in and on certain products of plant origin, including fruit and vegetables.

113 Directive 99/45 concerning the approximation of the laws, regulations and administrative provisions of the Member States relating to the classification, packaging and labelling of dangerous preparations.

114 Communication from the Commission to the Council, the European Parliament, the European Economic and Social Committee and the Committee of the Regions, 'A Thematic Strategy on the Sustainable Use of Pesticides', COM (2006) 373 final, as proposed in Decision 1600/2002/EC of the European Parliament and of the Council of 22 July 2002, laying down the Sixth Environmental Action Programme, OJ 2002 L242/1, Art. 8 (c) and (d). See also: Communication from the Commission to the Council, the Parliament, the Economic an Social Committee and the Committee of the Regions on the

Within the European Union, the marketing of plant protection products is regulated by Directive 91/414/EC on the placing on the market of plant protection products.[115] This Directive harmonises the legal regimes of the Member States for the authorisation of plant protection products[116] by introducing common authorisation criteria.[117] It established a dual authorization procedure. The Commission reviews the active substances used in plant protection products,[118] while the Member States implement the outcome of this review in their authorisation for the marketing of these products. Since the Directive entered into effect before any active substances were listed on Annex I, a transition regime allows the Member States to maintain authorisations of plant protection products that contain unlisted active substances until all active substances have been evaluated at Community level.[119] Therefore, not all plant protection products are covered by a national authorisation issued in accordance with the dual authorization procedure of the Directive.[120] The regulatory system of the Directives may be replaced by a Proposal for a Regulation, which will combine Community decisions with compulsory mutual recognition decisions within three authorization zones (North, Centre and South).[121] The REACH Regulation does not apply to substances authorized or in the process of being authorized in accordance with the Plant Protection Product Directive.[122]

sixth environmental action programme of the European Community, 'Environment 2010: Our future, Our choice', COM (2001) 31 final, pp. 43-45.

[115] Council Directive 91/414 EC.

[116] In the Netherlands: the Pesticides Act ('Bestrijdingsmiddelenwet'), which regulates plant protection products and biocides. See: Backes *et al.*. (2004), pp. 252-259; Vogelezang-Stoute (2004).

[117] Art. 8 Directive 91/414/EC.

[118] In accordance with Commission Regulation 3600/92 laying down the detailed rules for the implementation of the first stage of the programme of work referred to in Art. 8 (3) of Directive 91/414.

[119] According to Artt. 8 (2) and (3) Directive 91/414/EC, the transition period was supposed to end twelve years after notification of the Directive. Case law has shown that the ECJ has accepted an extension of this period, e.g. C-443/02 *Schreiber* [2004] ECR I-7275. See for a critical review of Dutch practice: Rutteman (2002), pp. 312-317.

[120] C-316/04 *Stichting Zuid-Hollandse Milieufederatie* v *College voor de toelating van bestrijdingsmiddelen*, [2005] ECR I-0000. Cf. C-125/88 *Nijman* [1989] ECR 3533.

[121] Proposal for a Regulation concerning the placing of plant protection products on the market.

[122] Art. 15 REACH Regulation.

CHAPTER 2

Decision-Making

The authorization for a product to be placed on the internal market can serve the dual interest of protecting the environment and/or public health on the one hand and of enabling the free movement of products as regulated by Community product legislation on the internal market on the other hand. The EU-wide effect of such an authorization depends on administrative cooperation between the national authorities and the Commission (vertical cooperation) and between the national authorities of the various Member States (horizontal cooperation). The question is whether the procedural rules that govern the creation of European administrative decisions enable effective administration by enhancing uniformity while also complying with procedural guarantees. In order to answer that question, first the various types of European administrative decisions will be analyzed below. Subsequently, their appearance and the European procedural rules governing these decisions will be analyzed in the context of the reference areas, in order to understand how decisions are taken, how competences are divided, disputes are resolved and uniformity is promoted and which procedural guarantees are recognized concerning the applicant and interested third parties. Finally, conclusions will be drawn about the qualities and gaps in the creation of the various types of European administrative decisions as they occur in the reference areas process concerning both the effectiveness and the procedural guarantees offered.

1 Four types of decisions

In the area of product legislation, European administrative decisions are taken to authorize the placing of products on the single market, to settle disputes between the Member States or to amend the Annex to a Regulation or a Directive. These decisions are binding decisions, which create rights and duties for individuals. They are either taken by a competent authority of a Member State or by a Community institution, in particular the Commission or the Council. Their legal basis is either a Regulation or a transposed Directive. Their effect can be EU-wide or limited to one Member State. The procedural rules that determine their creation offer rights to individuals, in particular to the applicant, but these rules differ as well. Yet it will be seen below that it is possible to group the various decision into a typology.

1.1 Classification

Four types of European administrative decisions can be distinguished on the basis of the Community or national administrative authority issuing them and on the basis of the division of competence between the Member States.[1] These decisions are called: Community decisions, national

---

1 Sydow (2004), p. 123.

decisions, mutual recognition decisions and single licence decisions.[2] In a Community decision system, the Commission or the Council takes a decision with EU-wide effect. In a national decision system, an administrative authority takes a decision that is valid in its own territory. In a mutual recognition system, an administrative authority from one Member State takes a decision whose validity is limited to its own territory, but which can acquire validity in other Member States when their national authorities recognize it in their own decision. By contrast, in a single licence system, an administrative authority from one Member State takes a decision, which is valid in all other Member States without any further implementation being necessary.[3]

Figure 2.1 The relationship between the four types of decisions

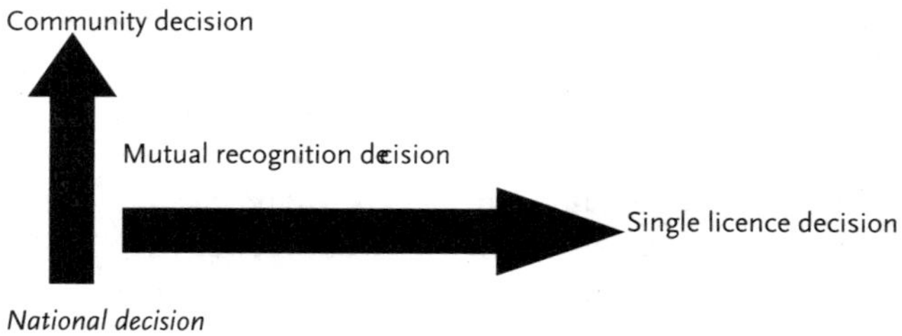

Seen from the position where the national decision is situated, both the Community decision and the single licence decision are examples of centralisation, the former vertically, the latter horizontally. At the horizontal – Member State – level, the mutual recognition decision is placed as an intermediary between a national decision and a single licence decision. This is because a mutual recognition decision depends on recognition before it acquires effect in other Member States, while a single licence decision has EU-wide effect once it is issued. As will be seen in the reference areas, each type of decision can occur in combination with another type of decision or become similar to another type of decision.

1.2 Decisions taken by national authorities

Whereas the national decision system means that each Member State takes a decision regarding its own territory, both the mutual recognition system and the single licence system leave it to the applicant to choose which Member State will assess the application and issue an authorization that is, or may be, valid in all Member States. A mutual recognition system means that each Member State has to recognize the decision of the reference Member State and thus allows the applicant not only to choose their own reference Member State, but also the Member States where they will request recognition of the

[2] The German terminology used by Sydow (2004) is Direktvollzugsmodell, Einzelvollzugsmodell, Referenzentscheidungsmodell and Transnationalitätsmodell.

[3] Sydow (2004), pp. 122-123.

decision. In the mutual recognition system non-recognition can hinder the achievement of uniformity unless a dispute settlement procedure ensures uniformity. A single licence system does not present this choice, because all Member States are bound by the single licence. Both systems offer the advantage that uniformity can be achieved through administrative cooperation, which also reduces bureaucracy when compared to a national decision system, because the Member States do not have to assess each application themselves.

Procedural rules

When the Member States implement Community product legislation, the applicable rules of procedure differ depending on the Member State where the decision is taken, because there is no such thing as a 'Community Administrative Law Code' containing the procedural rules applicable to the decisions taken by the Member States. However, secondary legislation and case law provide for many Community rules regarding the decision-making procedure, including the right to be heard.[4] It follows from the *Dokter* case that administrative authorities may only adopt decisions without a hearing, if they have to act promptly and effectively in the general interest and interested parties are given the opportunity to contest the measures and make their views known in subsequent proceedings.[5] The right to be heard applies to those who are adversely affected by a decision. They should be heard before a decision is taken on the elements on which the decision is based. This includes the applicant but not necessarily third parties, because they are not directly involved even though they might be affected by a decision.

Sectoral secondary legislation elaborates the right to be heard and contains more specific procedural rules, e.g. time limits for the stages in a decision-making procedure. In addition, it provides rules that establish a division of competences between the Member States and administrative cooperation duties vis-à-vis the Commission and between the Member States. The authorization of products falls outside the scope of the right to public participation in decision-making even when an environmental assessment of the product is mandatory, because the right to public participation is limited to proposed activities that directly and significantly affect the environment.[6] The authorization of products falls within the scope of the right to access to information, which concerns not only the authorizations themselves but also the reports underlying the application. While the authorizations are made public, access to the reports – even to environmental assessment reports – may be refused because Community legislation gives the applicant the right to confidentiality of this commercially sensitive information, as a competitor could use the environmental research for his

4 Since C-269/90 *Hauptzollamt München-Mitte* v *Technische Universität München* [1991] ECR I-5469, the right to be heard has applied to adverse (individual) decisions in general and not only to decisions imposing sanctions. See: Lenaerts and Vanhamme (1997), pp. 533-539; Craig (2006), pp. 314-316.

5 C-28/05 *Dokter* [2006] ECR I-5431.

6 Cf. Art. 6 (1) (a) and Annex I Aarhus Convention; Directive 2003/35 on public participation.

own application. Yet this ground for refusal should be interpreted in a restrictive way and be weighed against the public interest served by disclosure.[7] In line with disclosure of summaries of other research, the authorities may publish a summary of the environmental assessment report to inform the public.[8] This summary does not give competitors sufficient information to gain authorization, because it only presents the outcome of the research and does not give full information about the quality of the underlying research.[9]

1.3 Decisions taken by Community institutions

Secondary legislation usually enables the Commission to take implementing measures.[10] The Commission's implementing powers can be far reaching, since they include both measures of general scope, such as amending Annexes to Regulations or Directives, and measures of individual scope, such as issuing marketing authorizations for medicines and genetically modified organisms. When the Commission takes its decisions to implement secondary legislation in accordance with the Comitology procedures, occasionally, the Council takes implementing measures as well.[11] For this reason, these European administrative decisions are called Community decisions. The advantage of Community decisions is that a uniform decision is taken with the participation of representatives of all Member States through the Comitology procedure.

Community decisions can be further distinguished into general implementing rules or amendments to the Annexes to Directives or Regulations, and the application of rules to specific cases by means of acts of individual application.[12] The decisions of individual application include decisions on the authorization of placing products on the market, on disputes between the Member States or on the invocation of safeguard clauses. They can be further distinguished on the basis of their effect. There are decisions that require implementation by the Member States (comparable with a mutual recognition decision) and decisions that do not require implementation (comparable with a single licence). They can also be distinguished into Community decisions addressed to a single, to several or to all Member States.[13] Finally, they can be distinguished into decisions taken in accordance with the Comitology procedure and decisions taken

7 Artt. 3, 4 and 7 Directive 2003/4/EC.

8 See: Montforts and Keessen (2007).

9 See: Montforts and Keessen (2007).

10 See Artt. 202 and 212 EC. By way of exception, the Council can exercise certain implementing powers itself. See (Opinion AG Geelhoed in) C-378/00 *LIFE* [2003] ECR I-937.

11 See section 2.4 below.

12 C-16/88 *Commission* v *Council (Delegation)* [1989] ECR p. 3457; C-122/04 *Commission* v *Parliament and Council* [2006] ECR I-2001.

13 The chapter on judicial protection before the national courts will show that this distinction between various Community decisions makes a difference for third parties that seek judicial review.

without the use of the Comitology procedure, which occurs when the Council or the Commission exercises autonomous decision-making powers.

When the Commission takes Community decisions implementing secondary legislation, it has to observe the requirements imposed by the Council in the transfer of implementing powers to the Commission,[14] with the exception of areas where the Treaty conferred the Commission its own decision-making power.[15] Instead of drafting detailed provisions,[16] the Council relies on committees composed of representatives (officials or scientists) from the Member States to monitor the Commission's implementation measures. In this way, the Commission is assisted by national experts in matters with a high technical content,[17] while the Member States can exert some control over the way in which the Commission implements Community law.[18] The European Parliament may also exert influence in the so-called Comitology procedures, provided that the basic law is adopted under co-decision.[19] Secondary legislation may provide for agencies to assist the Commission in order to meet its need for specialised technical expertise and for independent and visible public action.[20] The involvement of an agency does not rule out the role of committees.[21] An agency can incorporate a scientific committee in order to enable the agency to issue a recommendation to the Commission on the basis of scientific advice, while regulatory committees continue to assist the Commission in accordance with the Comitology Decision.[22]

---

14 Art. 202 EC; C-25/70 *Einfuhr- und Voratstelle für Getreide und Futtermittel* v *Köster, Berodt and Co.* [1970] ECR 1161.

15 E.g. the Commission's powers in the area of Competition: the decisions it takes in that field are Commission decisions.

16 C-240/90 *Germany* v *Commission* [1992] ECR I-5383.

17 Cf. C-212/91 *Angelopharm* v *Freie und Hansestadt Hamburg* [1994] ECR I-171.

18 See Vos (1999), pp. 33-37.

19 See Artt. 7 and 8 Comitology Decision. For reasons to be sceptical about the contribution of parliamentary control to the legitimacy of Comitology proceedings, see Dehousse (1999), pp. 117-120.

20 Report by the Working Group 'Establishing a framework for decision-making regulatory agencies' (Group 3A) – Annex to White Paper on European Governance, COM (2001) 428, p. 9.

21 Note that the same division between regulatory and management committees applies to regulatory and management agencies. See Art. 3 Draft Interinstitutional Agreement on the operating framework for the European regulatory agencies, COM (2005) 59.

22 The involvement of agencies is in line with the Meroni doctrine (C-9/56 *Meroni* [1958] ECR 133) if the delegated implementation tasks do not require discretion, implying policy choices. Interestingly enough, some agencies implement Community legislation by taking decisions, e.g. the Office for Harmonisation in the Internal Market and Community Plant Variety Office, while Others only issue recommendations to the Commission, e.g. the European Medicines Authority and the European Food Authority. See: Dehousse (2002) pp. 220-224. See for a typology of agencies: Chiti (2000), pp. 309-343.

Procedural rules

Community decisions implementing Community product legislation are taken in accordance with the regulatory and advisory decision-making procedures of the Comitology Decision as prescribed and supplemented by secondary legislation.[23] The Comitology Decision does not provide for procedural guarantees for interested parties,[24] but that does not mean that they do not exist.[25] Decisions should observe the rights to proper and transparent administration, as developed in the case law of the Community courts and enshrined in the Treaty, Articles 41 and 42 of the (non-binding) Charter and the (non-binding) European Code of Good Administrative Behaviour.[26] This means that the applicant is entitled to have its affairs handled impartially, fairly and within a reasonable time by the institutions and bodies of the Union. This includes the right of every person to be heard before any individual measure is taken which would affect him adversely, the right of access to information (Article 255 EC) and the obligation of the administration to state the reasons for its decisions (Article 253 EC).[27] In addition, sector specific sectoral legislation elaborates the right to be heard, as stated above. In so far as Community law does not prescribe that third parties be heard in the decision-making procedure, they may not be involved in the decision-making procedure, as the public participation provisions do not apply to Community product legislation (as stated above).[28] They can only exercise their right to access to information, which is further elaborated in Regulation 1049/2001 on access to documents and Regulation 1367/2006 on access to environmental information.[29]

1.4 The Comitology Decision

The Comitology Decision, based on Article 202 EC, governs both the establishment of committees and their decision-making procedures.[30] Community product legislation refers to the advisory and the regulatory

23 The management procedure is not used in the area of Community product regulation.

24 Dehousse (1999), p. 121.

25 C-269/90 *Technische Universität Munchen* [1991] ECR I-5469.

26 The European Code of Good Administrative Behaviour is available at: http://ombudsman.europa.eu/code/en/default.htm.

27 Franchini (2004), pp. 184-190.

28 See: Art. 9 Regulation 1367/2006.

29 Art. 3 to 8 Regulation 1049/2001 on Public Access to Documents held by Institutions of the European Community and Regulation 1367/2006; Green Paper Public Access to Documents held by Institutions of the European Community, A review, COM (2007) 185 final, pp. 13-14.

30 Council Decision 1999/468 laying down the procedures for the exercise of implementing powers conferred on the Commission. It is referred to as the Comitology Decision, although it is the second Comitology Decision, as it replaced the first Comitology decision (Council Decision 87/373). See: Lenaerts and Verhoeven (2000), pp. 645-686. For extensive references to literature on Comitology, see footnote 2 to that article.

procedures of the Comitology Decision in cases where the Commission takes decisions or settles disputes.[31] The advisory procedure is followed for scientific advice.[32] A scientific advisory committee consists of scientific experts appointed by the Member States, chaired by a Commission representative. The opinion of an advisory committee does not bind the Commission. This does not mean that the Commission need not attach great value to it. According to the ECJ, a scientific opinion serves to enable the Community institutions to determine which measures are necessary from a fully informed position.[33]

The Commission may also need to consult a scientific committee if there is no provision on the consultation of a scientific committee.[34] In *Angelopharm*, the ECJ explained that the Cosmetics Directive could not be interpreted as allowing for optional consultation of a scientific committee instead of mandatory consultation, because the purpose of consulting the scientific committee is to ensure that the measures adopted at Community level are necessary and geared to the objective of protecting human health pursued by the directive.[35] However, the ECJ left it to the Commission to refer a matter twice if the relevant legislation confers discretion on the Commission in that regard.[36] When the Commission has consulted a scientific committee it is not obliged to follow the opinion. The ECJ established in the *Beef Hormones* case[37] that the Community institutions may deviate from the opinion of a scientific committee in order to give priority to the interests of consumers.[38] Probably, the Community institutions may also deviate in order to give priority to environmental protection or to the protection of public health.[39] In those circumstances, the statement of reasons must explain why the opinion was disregarded.[40]

---

31 Art. 2 Comitology Decision. For the record, Art. 2 (a) Comitology Decision states that management measures, such as those relating to the application of the common agricultural and common fisheries policy or for the implementation of programmes with substantial budgetary implications (e.g. Structural Funds), should be adopted using the management procedure.

32 Artt. 2 (c), 4, 7 and 8 Comitology Decision. It can also be followed to obtain advice in other, appropriate fields.

33 C-212/91 *Angelopharm* v *Freie Hansestadt Hamburg* [1994] ECR I-171.

34 Cf. C-41/93 *France* v *Commission* [2994] ECR I-1829 and C-6/99 *Greenpeace* v *Ministere de l'Agriculture et de la Peche and Others* [2000] ECR I-1651. See: Hervey (2001), p. 321-333 and Abraham and Lewis (2000), in particular chapters 1, 5 and 7.

35 C-212/91 *Angelopharm* v *Freie Hansestadt Hamburg* [1994] ECR I-171.

36 T-105/96 *Pharos* v *Commission* [1998] ECR II-285 upheld on appeal in C-151/98 *P Pharos* v *Commission* [1999] ECR I-8157 and T-199/96 *Bergaderm and Goupil* v *Commission* [1998] ECR II-2805 upheld on appeal in C-352/98 P *Bergaderm and Goupil* v *Commission* [2000] ECR I-5291,T-13/99 *Pfizer Animal Health* v *Council* [2002] ECR II-3305.

37 C-68/86 *United Kingdom* v *Council* [1988] ECR 855.

38 Hervey (2001), p. 329.

39 Cf. C-213/96 *Outokumpu Oy* [1998] ECR I-1801.

40 T-13/99 *Pfizer Animal Health* v *Council* [2002] ECR II-3305.

The regulatory procedure is followed in order to assist the Commission in taking measures of general scope designed to apply essential provisions of basic instruments, including measures concerning the protection of the health or safety of humans, animals or plants, as well as measures designed to adapt or update certain non-essential provisions of a Regulation or a Directive.[41] This includes safeguard measures as well. Regulatory committees are composed of national officials from the Member States and chaired by a representative of the Commission. The opinion of a regulatory committee on a draft Commission decision binds the Commission.[42] The opinion must be delivered by the majority laid down in Article 205 (2) of the Treaty. The chairman has no vote. If the committee approves the draft measures, the Commission adopts them (without prejudice to a resolution from the European Parliament).[43]

Sometimes, in exceptional cases, a regulatory committee does not approve the draft measures or does not deliver an opinion.[44] The Commission then has to submit it without delay to the Council and inform the European Parliament. If the European Parliament finds that the draft measures exceed the implementing powers provided for in the basic instrument, it will inform the Council of its position. The Council may act by qualified majority, within a period to be laid down in each basic instrument but which never exceeds three months from the date of referral. If the Council neither adopts the draft measures nor indicates its opposition to them by qualified majority before the expiry of the given period, the Commission can adopt its proposed implementing act (the 'filet mechanism'). If the Council opposes the draft measures by qualified majority before the expiry of the given period, the Commission cannot adopt its draft measure but has to re-examine it (the 'contre-filet mechanism'). However, the Commission is neither defeated by a negative opinion of a regulatory committee nor by a negative qualified majority in the Council, because it can always resubmit its draft measure, amended or not, or present a legislative proposal on the basis of the Treaty.[45]

The dispute settlement procedure

Disputes between Member States can be solved in various ways. The first step is always consultation between the Member States concerned. If that does not solve the dispute, it depends on the applicable legislation which options are open. If the applicable secondary legislation contains a dispute settlement provision that declares the regulatory procedure applicable, it gives the Commission,

---

41 Art. 2 (b), 5, 7 and 8 Comitology Decision. See: C-378/00 *Commission* v *Parliament and Council (LIFE)* [2003] ECR I-937 and C-122/04 *Commission* v *Parliament and Council* [2006] ECR I-2001.

42 This might be the reason why the Commission prefers to abolish regulatory (and management) committees. See: European Governance, A White Paper, COM (2001) 428 final, p. 31.

43 Art. 8 Comitology Decision.

44 Commission Staff Working Document, Annex to the Report from the Commission on the working of committees during 2004 Com (2005) 554 final. See: Ciavarini Azzi (1999), p. 53.

45 C-5/77 *Tedeschi* v *Denkavit Commerciale* [1977] ECR 1555.

and in last resort the Council, the competence to settle disputes through a binding Community decision. In the absence of such a dispute settlement provision, the Commission and the Council lack the competence to settle disputes through a binding Community decision. That raises the question how disputes between Member States can then be settled. Perhaps the easiest option is to persuade the Commission to become involved and if necessary start the infringement procedure of Article 228 EC, but there also other means to settle disputes informally.

Inspiration on informal dispute settlement can be found in the case law of the ECJ, although it is not certain that solutions can be transplanted from one area to another. The ECJ suggested in the *Banks* case, a dispute over the validity of a single licence social security document, that the Member States concerned should submit their disputes to the regulatory committee established by the applicable secondary legislation.[46] It further suggested that if the relevant committee did not succeed in reconciling the two Member States, they could either allow their national authorities to use national remedies in the Member States concerned or consider using the infringement procedure of Article 227 EC.[47] Perhaps Member States may also use the procedure of Article 239 EC to submit a dispute between them to the ECJ.[48] The Member States rarely use court proceedings to settle disputes, to which they seem to prefer arbitration. However, it follows from the *MOX Plant* case that the Member States cannot solve their disputes about the application or interpretation of Community law through arbitration because they must submit Community law disputes to the ECJ.[49] This means that Member States that do not want to go to court themselves, need to request the Commission to start the infringement procedure of Article 228 EC against the allegedly defecting Member State.

2 Genetically modified organisms

Theoretically, the authorization for the marketing of a GMO includes a mix of a single licence and a Community procedure, but it is more properly characterized as an example of a regulation based on Community decisions. Even though national authorities may issue authorizations for the placing on the market of GMOs as or in products in accordance with the procedure of Directive 90/220,[50] now replaced by Directive 2001/18 Part C,[51] few authoriza-

46 C-178/97 *Banks* [2000] ECR I-2005.

47 C-178/97 *Banks* [2000] ECR I-2005.

48 Widdershoven (2005), pp. 30-32.

49 C-459/03 *Commission* v *Ireland (MOX Plant)* [2006]ECR I-4635. See: Lavranos (2006), pp. 456-469.

50 The replacement did result in any change to the procedural rules. See for the old substantive rules: Jans (2000), pp. 382-385.

51 Part C Directive 2001/18 is further elaborated by Council Decision 2002/811 and Council Decision 2002/812 on the summary information format, Commission Decision 2002/204 on operation of the

tions have actually been issued by them.[52] Whereas in other areas, consensus is the rule,[53] in the area of GMOs it is the exception. This means that it is usually the Commission that takes the decision on the authorization of the placing on the market of GMOs, especially since the de facto moratorium was lifted in 2004.[54] Indeed, a national procedure has been omitted altogether in Regulation 1829/2003, which applies to GMOs for food and feed use.[55] Another striking feature here is that every stage in the decision-making procedure is subject to strict time limits in order to prevent any foot-dragging by Member States that are against the authorization of GMOs.

2.1 The single licence procedure

The single licence procedure of Directive 2001/18 part C applies to GMOs that are to be placed on the market. Since the introduction of the Regulation, it only applies to GMOs that are not for food or feed use, such as flowers with genetically modified carnations. It is interesting that the Directive's authorization procedure confers consultation duties on the Member States, because that makes this single licence procedure similar to a mutual recognition procedure. The procedure starts when a trader who wants to market a GMO or a combination of GMOs (not for food or feed use) submits a notification to the competent authority of the Member State where the product will be placed on the market for the first time.[56] This Member State will act as the reference Member State. It has to notify the competent authorities of all other Member States and the Commission of the application and prepare an assessment report,[57] which indicates whether the GMO can be placed on the market. The object of this risk assessment is to identify and evaluate potential adverse effects of the GMO, either direct or indirect, immediate or delayed, on human health or the environment which the placing on the market of this GMO may have.[58] If necessary, the reference Member State can ask the applicant for further information.[59]

The reference Member State does not take its decision on its own, as might be expected in a single licence procedure. It forwards the assessment report to

---

registers for recording information and Commission Decision 2004/204 on guidance notes for the environmental risk assessment.

52 See: www.gmo-compass.org/eng/gmo/db/.

53 Dehousse (1999), p. 112.

54 www.gmo-compass.org/eng/gmo/db/.

55 Regulation 1829/2003 is further elaborated by Commission Regulation 65/2004 and Commission Regulation 641/2004.

56 Art. 13 Directive 2001/18 lists the (research) materials that must be submitted with the notification.

57 Art. 14 Directive 2001/18.

58 Section A Annex II to Directive 2001/18.

59 Art. 14 (4) Directive 2001/18.

the other competent authorities and the Commission for approval.[60] After receiving the dossier, the Commission makes the summary of the dossier available to the public. The public can then submit comments to the Commission, but the legislation does not impose that these comments should be reflected in the statement of reasons that will accompany the final decision. The Commission then sends the dossier with the national assessment report to the other authorities. The national authorities and the Commission can request the applicant for additional information. The national authorities can send comments or present reasoned objections to the Commission.[61] In the hypothetical situation that the competent authority of the reference Member State decides that the product may be placed on the market and no objections are raised or they have been resolved, the Commission gives the notifier written consent to place the product on the market and informs the other authorities and the Commission.[62] The same procedure applies in case of a refusal to which no objections have been raised or maintained. In that case, the reference Member State has to explain the refusal in the assessment report.[63]

Both consent and rejection have EU-wide effect without any further implementing measures. This means that a GMO can be used without further notification throughout the Community after obtaining a single national consent.[64] However, this does not imply that it makes no difference in which Member State the GMO is marketed. The decision may impose specific conditions for use, which may concern different rules for certain environments or geographical areas.[65] Consequently, the applicable rules may vary from one Member State to another. This 'mutual recognition feature' is possible due to the consultation between the Member States during the decision-making procedure. The legislation regarding GMOs also offers procedural guarantees to the public, as it obliges all Member States to take all necessary measures to ensure that the written consent is made accessible to the public.[66]

The public participation provisions of the Aarhus legislation do not apply to GMOs until the specific regime of the GMO amendment to the Aarhus Convention has been ratified and implemented. The GMO amendment renders the provisions on public participation – which provide for access to court as well – applicable to decisions about the deliberate release into the environment of GMOs.[67] Third parties such as Greenpeace may then no longer need to limit themselves to lobby in order to ensure that the other, qualified parties take their

---

[60] Art. 13 Directive 2001/18.

[61] Art. 15 Directive 2001/18.

[62] Art. 15 (3) Directive 2001/18 and Art. 18 (2) Directive 2001/18.

[63] Art. 15 (2) Directive 2001/18.

[64] Art. 19 (1) Directive 2001/18.

[65] Art. 19 (1) Directive 2001/18.

[66] Art. 19 (4) Directive 2001/18.

[67] Art. 6 (11) Aarhus Convention.

interests into account.[68] However, it is not certain whether these provisions apply to the marketing authorization procedure for GMOs and what effect they will have on access to the Community courts.[69] Perhaps the public participation provisions that prescribe access to court will not apply to GMO marketing authorizations, but only to decisions regarding the growing of GMOs, because that constitutes deliberate release into the environment and can have a direct impact on the quality of living in the vicinity of the location where the GMOs are grown.

2.2 The dispute settlement procedure

Member States may raise objections or comments regarding the risks of a GMO to human health or the environment. These objections or comments must be sent to the Commission, which sends them to the other Member States. First, informal discussion takes place with the aim of achieving consensus. If this is unsuccessful, the dispute will be settled by the Commission under the regulatory procedure as described above.[70] The Commission will request the European Food Safety Authority ('EFSA') to provide its opinion, focusing on the points of divergence between the Member States. The Commission takes its decision in accordance with the regulatory procedure. The Community decision is implemented as a consent issued by the national authority of the reference Member State, which informs the notifier of its decision.[71]

This means that if Member States are unable to reach a qualified majority in favour of or against authorization in the regulatory committee and in the Council, the Commission can adopt its draft decision at the end of the dispute settlement procedure on the basis of the assessment report of the reference Member State and the opinion of the scientific committee regarding the questions raised by objections or comments.[72] The frequent invocation of safeguard clauses shows that the dispute settlement procedure is unable to solve all disputes between Member States.[73] This can be explained by the procedure's bias towards the issuance of authorization: the Directive allows the applicant to choose which reference Member State is to assess the application, and of course they will

68 E.g.:http://www.greenpeace.org/international/campaigns/genetic-engineering

69 Council Decision 2006/957/EC on the conclusion, on behalf of the European Community, of an amendment to the Convention on access to information, public participation in decision-making and access to justice in environmental matters.

70 Art. 18 and 30 (2) Directive 2001/18. Art. 30 Directive 2001/18 provides that the dispute settlement procedure applies in accordance with Art. 5 and 7 of Decision 1999/468/EC, having regard to Art. 8 of that Decision. The period is set at three months. The dispute settlement procedure also applies in case of objections during the renewal procedure or during the procedure followed after new information has become available, provided respectively in Art. 15 and Art. 20 Directive 2001/18.

71 Art. 18 (2) Directive 2001/18.

72 Art. 28 Directive 2001/18.

73 E.g. C-236/01 *Monsanto* [2003] ECR I-8105.

choose a willing Member State. Any ensuing dispute will then be ended by a Community decision, which will be positive, as it is based on a positive scientific assessment.[74] The other Member States will be forced to accept this outcome, since a single consent issued by the reference Member State suffices and the free movement clause states that the Member States should refrain from prohibiting, restricting or impeding the placing on the market of GMOs which comply with the requirements of the Directive.[75]

2.3 The safeguard procedure

The safeguard procedure of the GMO Directive may have been designed as an emergency procedure, as it requires new evidence, but it is used in this reference area to avoid the placing on the market of a Community authorized GMO in a Member State by imposing a national ban.[76] A Member State may also base a ban on Article 95 EC, the safeguard clause of the Treaty, which requires that new evidence be established and that the risk be specific to one Member State. The invocation of either safeguard clause requires approval by the Commission, which takes a decision in accordance with the regulatory Comitology procedure.[77] Consequently, an unjustified ban can remain in place if a Member State musters sufficient support to reach a qualified majority in the regulatory committee or in the Council. The safeguard procedure does not grant any participation rights to the marketing authorization holder. Six Member States had bans in place in 2007, despite EFSA opinions that the bans are not justified and despite Commission requests to lift the bans.[78]

The ECJ established in *Association Greenpeace* that the reference Member State is obliged to implement the Commission decision in a national marketing authorization without retaining any margin of discretion.[79] However, in the same judgment, the ECJ allowed the reference Member State to decide to implement the Commission decision but suspend its application by using the safeguard procedure of the Directive, when new information resulted in a different risk assessment.[80]

---

74 Ostrovsky (2007), pp. 114-116.

75 Art. 22 Directive 2001/18. See: Ostrovsky (2007), pp. 113-126.

76 Art. 23 Directive 2001/18.

77 Art. 23 Directive 2001/18. The same applies in case of invocation of the safeguard clause of Regulation 1829/2003.

78 See: the Second Report from the Commission to the Council and the European Parliament on the experience of Member States with GMOs placed on the market under Directive 2001/18, COM (2007) 81 final.

79 C-6/99 *Association Greenpeace France and Others* v *Ministere de l'Agriculture et de la Peche and Others* [2000] ECR p. I-01651.

80 C-6/99 *Association Greenpeace France and Others* v *Ministere de l'Agriculture et de la Peche and Others* [2000] ECR p. I-01651.

Austria and one of its regions brought proceedings against the Commission's refusal – on the basis of an opinion of the EFSA – of its request for a regional ban on GMOs on the basis of Article 95 EC.[81] Since Austria and its region failed to show new evidence of risks or the existence of a specific problem, they lost in both instances.[82] Nevertheless, Austria did not lift the ban. Since a decision regarding the invocation of the safeguard clause under Directive 2001/18 is taken via the regulatory Comitology procedure, the Member States, or their officials, can agree in the regulatory committee or in the Council to prevent the Commission from acting against an unwilling Member State by issuing an approval. This occurred twice in the case of Austria. This frustrated the Commission, as it can hardly resort to the infringement procedure in case of a Council approval of a national ban. It therefore reproposed the order that Austria lift the ban on GMOs for a third time and this time it did not require Austria to lift the ban on cultivation and it was backed by the threat of the USA that it would take retaliatory measures if the EU failed to act in compliance with the WTO ruling before the expiry of the deadline.[83] As the Member States were then unable to reach a qualified majority in the committee or the Council, the Commission could finally order Austria to open its borders to authorized GMOs.[84]

2.4 The Community procedure

Regulation 1829/2003 provides for a Community authorization procedure for GMOs for food or feed use, which prescribes the use of the regulatory Comitology procedure and the duty to base decisions on the scientific opinions of the European Food Safety Authority ('EFSA'), whose members are scientific experts appointed by the Member States and some Community officials.[85] Applicants whose application for authorization of a GMO for food or feed use is pending under Directive 2001/18 can withdraw their application and apply under this new procedure as well. The procedure begins when a party sends an application for the marketing of a GMO food or feed to the national authorities of a Member State of their choice.[86] The Member State then sends the application and any supplementary information supplied by the applicant to the EFSA.[87] Without delay, the EFSA informs the other Member States and the Commission by sending them the application and the supplementary informa-

81 Commission Decision 2003/653 OJ 2003 L 230/34.

82 Joined Cases T-366/03 and T-235/04 *Land Oberosterreich and Austria* v *Commission* [2005] ECR II-4005, on appeal Joined Cases C-439/05 P and C-454/05 P *Land Oberosterreich and Austria* v *Commission* [2007] ECR I-0000.

83 See the section on GMOs in Chapter 1.

84 Commission decision 2008/495, OJ 2008 L 172/25.

85 The EFSA was established by Regulation 178/2002.

86 See Commission Regulation 641/2004.

87 Art. 5 and 15 Regulation 1829/2003.

tion. In addition, EFSA makes a summary of the dossier available to the public.[88] If the application is not complete, the EFSA, or a national authority through the EFSA, may request the applicant for additional information.

The risk assessment takes place at the European level. It is carried out by experts from the GMO panel in a Community reference laboratory of a Member State, under supervision of the Scientific Committee, which operates under the final responsibility of the EFSA.[89] On the basis of the risk assessment, the EFSA gives its opinion on the application. The EFSA forwards its opinion to the Commission, the Member States and the applicant, including a report describing its assessment of the food and stating the reasons for its opinion and the information on which the opinion is based. The EFSA makes its opinion public, after deleting all confidential information.[90] After publication of the opinion, the public may submit comments to the Commission.[91] Perhaps these provisions will be adapted to comply with the public participation provisions of the Aarhus Regulation after implementation by the EU of the amendment to the Aarhus Convention concerning GMOs, but it is not certain that the amendment applies to GMO marketing authorizations.[92]

The Commission then takes a decision, assisted by the Standing Committee on the Food Chain and Animal Health, in accordance with the regulatory procedure as described above.[93] The draft decision has to accommodate the EFSA's opinion, any relevant provisions of Community law and other legitimate factors relevant to the matter at hand. If the draft decision is not in accordance with the opinion of EFSA, the Commission has to explain the differences.[94] The Commission sends the draft decision to the Standing Committee on the Food Chain and Animal Health and – if approval has not been given – to the Council. When both are unable to reach a qualified majority in the decision about the draft Commission decision,[95] the Commission can adopt its draft decision, taken on the basis of the EFSA's opinion.[96] Its decision will be valid in the EU (without any further implementation) for ten years, after which it is renewable.[97] It can be challenged by invocation of the safeguard clause of Regulation 1829/2003[98] or Article 95 EC, as set out above.

---

88 Art. 5 and 17 Regulation 1829/2003.

89 The supervision of the EFSA – an independent authority – should increase public confidence in the assessment. See: Vos (2005), pp. 117-127.

90 Art. 6 18 Regulation 1829/2003.

91 Art. 6 and 18 Regulation 1829/2003 (the time limit is 30 days).

92 See above at section 3.1.

93 Art. 35 Regulation 1829/2003 refers to Art. 5, 7 and 8 Council Decision 1999/468/EC.

94 Art. 7 (1) and 19 (1) Regulation 1829/2003.

95 Art. 5 (2) Decision 1999/468/EC in conjunction with Art. 205 (2) EC.

96 Art. 7 (3), 19 (3) and 35 Regulation 1829/2003 in conjunction with Art. 5 Decision 1999/468/EC.

97 Art. 7 Regulation 1829/2004.

98 Art. 34 Regulation 1829/2003.

Reducing controversiality

The Member States are divided into two GMO camps, pro and con, and neither can muster enough support to reject or approve an application by qualified majority voting. Since the regulatory procedure provides for a legal default mechanism if Member States fail to agree, applications will eventually be decided by the Commission on the basis of the EFSA opinion. As a consequence, the Member States are unable to influence the decision-making procedure – apart from causing delay, which is minimised by the fixed periods for decision-making. These Community decisions have created unease, which is enhanced by the bans on certain GMO varieties that some Member States – most notably Austria – still have in place despite infringement procedures. This is possible because Directive 2001/18 allows Member States to ban a GMO in its territory (temporarily) by invoking the safeguard clause.[99] In order to change this situation, several Member States have called for the GMO voting system to be changed. This is not an easy task, since it implies changing the regulatory Comitology procedure, which operates satisfactorily where it concerns other subjects.

The Commission has therefore proposed practical improvements to the way in which the European GMO legislative framework is implemented, in order to increase scientific consistency and transparency of decisions regarding GMOs within the existing framework.[100] For example, it has invited the EFSA to cooperate more closely with national scientific bodies, with a view to resolving possible diverging scientific opinions among Member States and it will ask applicants and EFSA to include more explicit data on potential long-term effects and bio-diversity issues in their risk assessment. In addition, it has proposed to fully exercise its regulatory competences as foreseen in GMO legislation, to specify the legal framework in which EFSA assessment is to be carried out. It has promised to address specific risks identified in the risk assessment or substantiated by Member States by introducing additional, proportionate risk management measures in draft marketing authorizations. Finally, it has proposed to suspend procedures if the Commission finds that a Member State's comments raise important new scientific questions not properly or completely addressed by the EFSA's opinion, such in order to refer the question back for further consideration. In this way, it hopes to meet the objections by certain Member States that currently these aspects are not fully considered in the risk assessment.[101]

---

[99] Cf. C-236/01 *Monsanto* [2003] ECR I-8105.

[100] See: IP/06/498, Brussels, 12 April 2006.

[101] Second Report from the Commission to the Council and the European Parliament on the experience of Member States with GMOs placed on the market under Directive 2001/18/EC on the deliberate release into the environment of genetically modified organisms, COM (2007) 81 final, pp. 5-7.

2.5 Conclusions

The prevailing type of decision in the area of GMOs is the Community decision, but single licences may occur as well. In that case, the authorities of the reference Member State take a decision that binds the other Member States as it has effect in all Member States without requiring implementation into a national decision. Interestingly, the single licence authorization of GMOs somewhat resembles the mutual recognition decision, because the reference Member State has to consult the other Member States before it takes a final decision. There is a strong centralisation trend, as Community decisions have superseded the single licence decision. Community decisions are taken when the Commission settles a dispute between the Member States about the draft single licence decision by taking a Community decision on the authorization of a GMO for other uses in accordance with the dispute settlement procedure of the Directive and when the Commission authorizes GMOs for food and feed use in accordance with the Community authorization procedure. The Member States are involved in the dispute settlement procedure of the Directive and in the Community procedure of the Regulation through the regulatory Comitology procedure. However, they are usually unable to agree and decide by qualified majority, which allows the Commission to take its decisions on its own, based on the draft decision of the reference Member State and the EFSA's opinion.

The authorization procedures may seem effective in achieving uniformity, but discontented Member States can strike back at the so-called rubberstamped authorizations issued by the Commission. They can use the safeguard procedure of the Treaty or of the GMO legislation to impose a national ban on an authorized GMO, thus disrupting the unity of the internal market and reducing the EU-wide effect of an authorization. As regards procedural guarantees, they are not necessarily observed at all stages and regarding all individuals concerned. The authorization procedures observe procedural guarantees with regard to the applicant and even include the feature that the public may comment on draft decisions, thus anticipating on the new GMO provisions in the Aarhus Convention. However, the legislation does not state that the comments of the public should be taken into account. Another shortcoming is that the safeguard procedure does not grant the holder the right to participate in the national procedure and subsequent Community procedure other than by filing comments to the draft Community decision as a member of the public.

3 Medicines

Initially, Community medicines legislation only provided for national marketing authorizations issued on the basis of Community legislation.[102] This system has now developed into a mix of Community decisions and

[102] Directive 65/65/EEC.

mutual recognition decisions. European medicines legislation and policy documents[103] ensure that all national competent authorities base their decisions on the same set of standards and protocols for the performance of tests and trials on medicines for human use and on common assessment criteria: risk-benefit balance, quality, safety (for humans) and efficacy.[104] It does not prescribe a comparative assessment.[105] Since 1998, the mutual recognition procedure has been applicable to new and existing authorizations, while a simplified procedure has applied to the authorization of parallel trade and generics.[106] Since 2004, a Community procedure has applied to the authorization of innovative, highly technological medicines. The Commission takes its decisions in accordance with the regulatory Comitology procedure and on the basis of the opinions of the European Medicines Agency ('EMEA'). This procedure applies as well to settle disputes between the Member States about mutual recognition decisions. In addition, the ECJ attempted to add a decision-making procedure in its case law about the free movement of authorized medicines. All legislative procedures contain time limits.

The medicines legislation also provides for a licence system directed at the manufacturer or the importer of the medicines to control the quality of medicines produced within the EU. The EU cooperates with third countries to allow quality control to take place prior to export, to ensure that imported medicines are high-quality products, without placing a burden on the importer.[107]

3.1 The Community procedure

The Community procedure for the authorization of medicines is intended for innovative and highly technological medicines. Accordingly, it is compulsory for biotechnology medicines,[108] orphan medicines[109] and medi-

---

[103] The Notice to the Applicants is a Guideline adopted by the Commission in consultation with the competent authorities of the Member States and the European Agency for Medical Products pursuant to Annex I to Directive 2001/83. It presents the harmonised views of the Member States and EMEA, but it has no legal force.

[104] See Artt. 19, 26 and 117 and cons. 2, 7, 11 and 12 in the Preamble to Directive 2001/83/EC. See : Joined Cases C-211/03, C-299/03 and C-316/03 to C-319/03 *HLH Warenvertriebs, Orthica* v *Deutschland* [2005] ECR I-5141; T-13/99 *Pfizer* v *Council* [2002] ECR II-3305 and T-70/99 *Alpharma* v *Council* [2002] ECR II-3945.

[105] Member States may use comparative assessments for their decision on the price of the medicine and its possible inclusion in the list of medicines that will be reimbursed under their national health system.

[106] For this reason, inconsistencies still exist, e.g regarding indications, where only minor differences may remain, such as the name and the packaging of the medicine. See: Notice to the Applicants, Volume 2A, p. 3.

[107] Art. 40 et seq. Directive 2001/83 and Art. 18 et seq. Regulation 726/2004.

[108] Rec. 6 Regulation 726/2004.

[109] Orphan medicines are intended for diseases that occur so infrequently that the costs of developing a medicine would not be recovered by its expected sales and are therefore eligible for incentives. See Rec. 1 and 4 and Art. 2 (2) and 3 Regulation 141/2000 on orphan medicines.

cines which appear in the Annex to the Regulation. In addition, the Community procedure applies on request of the applicant if: (a) the medicine contains a new active substance which was not previously authorized in the EU,[110] or (b) the medicine constitutes a significant therapeutic scientific or medical innovation, or the granting of a central authorization is in the interests of patients or animal health at European level.[111] When the centralized procedure is an option, more applicants prefer to use this procedure to using the mutual recognition procedure.[112] The scope of the Community procedure can be further extended to medicines containing a new active substance with a therapeutic indication included in the Annex.[113] The Member States may authorize generics of a Community-authorized reference medicine, although the applicant should submit the relevant application to EMEA.[114] Parallel distribution of a Community-authorized medicine should be reported to EMEA.[115]

The Community authorization procedure starts when the applicant submits an application to EMEA.[116] EMEA will then ask the opinion of the Committee for Medicinal Products for Human Use ('CHMP').[117] The CHMP assigns two Member States the task of rapporteur and co-rapporteur, which means that they will prepare the assessment report. They submit their report to the CHMP for discussion. Then the CHMP issues its opinion to EMEA, which informs the applicant. If the applicant states objections against the opinion, the CHMP may review it. After that, EMEA sends the definitive CHMP opinion to the Commission, the Member States and the applicant.[118] The Commission takes a draft decision on the basis of the opinion. The draft decision is passed to the Standing Committee for approval[119] and sent to the Member States, so they can send comments and questions about the draft decision to the Commission. If a question requires further advice from the CHMP, the procedure is suspended.[120] The additional consultation of the CHMP can be reflected in an amendment to the draft decision.

---

110 See also Rec. 7 Preamble Regulation 726/2004.

111 Art. 3 (1) and (2) Regulation 726/2004.

112 Report from the Commission on the experience acquired as a result of the operation of the procedures for granting marketing authorizations for medical products as laid down in Regulation (EEC) No 2309/93, Chapter III of Directive 75/309/EEC and Chapter IV of Directive 81/851/EEC. Report on the basis of Art. 71 of Regulation (EEC) No 2309/93 ('Review 2001') COM 2001 yyy final.

113 Rec. 8 Regulation 726/2004.

114 Art. 3 (3) and 4 Regulation 726/2004 and Art. 10 Directive 2001/83.

115 As proposed in Review 2001, p. 17.

116 Art. 3 (1) and (2) Regulation 726/2004.

117 Art. 6 (3) Regulation 726/2004.

118 Art. 9 Regulation 726/2004.

119 Art. 10 Regulation 726/2004, which refers to Art. 87 (3) Regulation 726/2004, which declares the procedure of Art. 4 and 7 Decision 1999/468 applicable.

120 Art. 10 (4) Regulation 726/2004.

If the Standing Committee is unable to agree by qualified majority or disagrees with the Commission about the draft decision, the draft decision is sent to the Council, which votes by qualified majority. If the Standing Committee approves the draft decision by qualified majority, the Commission finalises the decision and makes it publicly available.[121] The Commission also makes the decision publicly available if it issues a refusal or if the applicant withdraws the application.[122] If an authorization is granted, EMEA makes the assessment report and the reasons for its decision publicly available.[123] Medicines that have acquired a central authorization may be traded in all Member States,[124] as the authorization will be valid in all Member States without transposition for five years, after which it is eligible for renewal.[125] The Commission grants conditional authorizations only by way of exception. A conditional authorization is valid for one year and must be renewed.[126]

Biotechnology medicines

Specific rules apply to biotechnology medicines. Medicines containing or consisting of genetically modified organisms are subject to both the centralised authorization procedure and to the procedure of Part B of Directive 2001/18 in order to establish the environmental risk of the deliberate release into the environment of the biotechnological medicine.[127] The environmental risk assessment is conducted in parallel with the evaluation of the quality, safety and efficacy of the product under a single Community procedure.[128] The applicant has to send research data and a monitoring plan to all competent national authorities. These authorities are responsible for the environmental risk assessment. For each case, they will assess the risk that introduction poses to public health and the environment in their Member State.[129] Under this procedure, each Member State takes

[121] Art. 13 Regulation 726/2004.

[122] Respectively Art. 11 and Art. 12 (3) Regulation 726/2004.

[123] Art. 13 (3) Regulation 726/2004.

[124] The name and packaging of a Community authorized medicine are generally identical in all Member States, but differences may occur if this is justified by exceptional circumstances, see T-123/00 *Dr Karl Thomae* [2002] ECR II-5193.

[125] Art. 13 (1) Regulation 726/2004.

[126] Art. 14 Regulation 726/2004.

[127] Art. 6 (2) Regulation 726/2004. This Article refers to the procedure under B of Directive 2001/18, which regulates deliberate release of GMOs into the environment. Art. 6 Regulation 726/2004 and Art. 5 Directive 2001/18 provide that the procedure of part B applies to medicines that consist of one or more GMOs or contain GMOs, until the European medicines legislation provides for a specific procedure for biotechnological medicines. Regulation 726/2004 declares the procedure under Part C of Directive 2001/18 not applicable. The reason could be that Regulation 726/2004 regulates the marketing of GMO medicines.

[128] Rec. 36 Regulation 726/2004. This procedure has not been used yet, so any expected difficulties might be purely theoretical.

[129] Art. 4 (3) Directive 2001/18.

a decision, after taking into account the opinion of other Member States and the Commission.[130]

It is not clear from the wording of the Regulation whether the issuance of a marketing authorization for a biotechnology medicine requires the express consent of the national authorities of each Member State. This does not seem to be the case though, because the Regulation only states that the opinion of the CHMP should respect the environmental protection rules of Directive 2001/18, as the CHMP opinion can be delivered after a rapporteur of the CHMP has consulted with the national authorities that are competent on the basis of Directive 2001/18.[131] Since the environmental risk is not framed as a ground for refusal,[132] a positive assessment of the quality, safety and efficacy of the medicine will result in a Community authorization. Thus, it seems that the environmental risk assessment only serves to limit the risks for the environment caused by the authorization of the medicine, e.g. by establishing appropriate conditions for use.[133]

3.2 The national and the mutual recognition procedure

Applicants submit an application to the Member States where they want to market their medicine.[134] From these so-called 'concerned' Member States, the applicant selects the 'reference' Member State. The national authority from the reference Member State is responsible for the assessment of the application (and for subsequent regulatory activities).[135] This authority examines whether the conditions for issuing a marketing authorization are met.[136] For this purpose, it may submit the medicine, its starting materials and its intermediate products or other constituent materials for testing by an Official Medicines Control laboratory or another specialized laboratory.[137] Although the word 'may' suggests that the national authorities are not obliged to seek scientific advice before taking a decision, they seem to have little choice in this matter. It follows from the Community court's case law that they need scientific advice to base

[130] Art. 6 (5) and 11 Directive 2001/18.

[131] Art. 6 (3) Regulation 726/2004. The Regulation does not provide for similar rules in case of renewals.

[132] Cf. the combined authorization procedure of Regulation 1829/2003 and Directive 2001/18 Part B applicable to authorizations for the cultivation and marketing of GMOs for food and feed use.

[133] Art. 20 (4) Regulation 726/2004. See: Montforts *et al.* (2006).

[134] Theoretically it is still possible to file an application in one Member State only. Then only one Member State will carry out the procedure, under the harmonised conditions of Directive 2001/83.

[135] See Art. 17 and 19 Directive 2001/83. The procedure has to be completed within 210 days, under Art. 17 (1) Directive 2001/83.

[136] Cf. Art. 26 Directive 2001/83, which refers to Artt. 8, 10, 10a, 10b and 10c Directive 2001/83, which list the relevant documents and particulars to be submitted by the applicant. See also the Notice to the Applicants, Volume 2B, concerned with the presentation and content of the application dossier, June 2004.

[137] Art. 19 (2) Directive 2001/83.

their decision on sound reasoning.[138] If any uncertainties persist, the authorities can ask the applicant for more information.[139]

If the application meets the requirements of the medicines legislation, the conclusion of the assessment report will be to grant the authorization to place the medicine on the market of the relevant Member State. This decision is valid for five years and can then be renewed for an unlimited period of time.[140] When the competent authority takes its decision, it will inform the applicant of its decision and of the approved summary of the product characteristics. Then it will make the authorization and the summary of the product characteristics publicly available and the assessment report publicly accessible, together with the reasons for their opinion, after deleting all commercially sensitive information.[141] Only in exceptional cases, after consultation with the applicant, will the competent authorities grant an authorization subject to specific conditions, in particular concerning the safety of the medicine. A conditional authorization is only valid for one year. It is then renewed annually after reassessment of these conditions.[142]

If the application is filed in more than one Member State (simultaneous mutual recognition), the other national authorities will wait for the reference Member State to send them, and the applicant, a draft assessment report, a draft summary of product characteristics and a draft of the labelling and package leaflet. If the application concerns a medicine that has already received authorization in another Member State (consecutive mutual recognition), the marketing authorization holder has to request the marketing authority of that Member State to act as reference Member State and to send the original version or an update of the assessment report to the Member States to whom the applicant has submitted an application.[143] A Member State may also recognize an authorization on its own initiative. It then needs to notify the marketing authorization holder and the Member State where the product has already been authorized or where the application for authorization was assessed and request the latter to send a copy of the assessment report.

The mutual recognition procedure facilitates the work of national authorities that receive an application for a medicine that is already under examination or has been authorized in another Member State, because they only have to review the assessment of the reference Member State.[144] If the authorities from the

138 See above, in the section on Comitology.

139 Art. 19 (3) Directive 2001/83, which also stipulates that the time that lapses between the request for additional information and the receipt of it is not included in the 210-day limit.

140 Art. 24 Directive 2001/83.

141 Art. 21 Directive 2001/83.

142 Art. 22 and Annex I Directive 2001/83.

143 Since the applicant is not obliged to file an application in all Member States at once, it is possible that a national authority receives an application for authorization of a medicine already authorized in one or more other Member States.

144 This procedure has applied since 1998.

Member States concerned reach the same decision regarding the underlying documents, they will adopt the same authorization decision,[145] if not, they will have to use the dispute settlement procedure.[146] Consequently, applicants will prefer reference Member States whose decision is issued quickly and is of such quality that it is immediately recognized by other Member States.[147] A coordinating group consisting of representatives from the Member States facilitates this process.[148] When the Member States concerned agree that the application should be rejected, they inform the applicant, stating the reasons for the rejection.[149] They do not have to make rejections and the reasons for rejection publicly available.[150] If they agree to authorize the medicine, they inform the applicant of their decision. Subsequently, they will make the marketing authorization and the summary of the product characteristics publicly available and the final assessment report and comments on the file publicly accessible, together with the reasons for their opinion, after deleting all commercially sensitive information.[151] The Member States should also notify the Commission, as it registers all national authorizations.

3.3 The simplified procedure

A generic medicine is authorized via the simplified procedure,[152] if the applicant applies for authorization of a medicine on the basis of the dossier of an authorized medicine to which it is essentially similar (the so-called reference medicine) after expiry of the patent protection period and the marketing exclusivity period of the proprietary medicine, which is copied.[153] The ECJ established in the Generics case that a generic medicine is essentially similar to a reference medicine when three criteria are met: (a) they have the same qualita-

---

[145] See Art. 28 Directive 2001/83, which also establishes the time limits for mutual recognition.

[146] See section 4.4 below.

[147] See: See Cameron Mc Kenna and Andersen Consulting, Cameron-Mc Kenna-Anderson Report 2000 and the EFPIA Survey on the Mutual Recognition Procedure, both available at: http: //pharmacos.eudra.org.

[148] Art. 27 and 30 Directive 2001/83.

[149] Art. 26 Directive 2001/83 describes the grounds for rejection.

[150] As yet, the authorities are under no obligation to publish rejections or rejected indications. The increasing availability of information about medicines may lead to publication of information about rejections and rejected indications, according to Lisman (2004) p. 899.

[151] Art. 21 Directive 2001/83. It follows from Directive 2003/4 that a summary of the environmental assessment should also be made public. See: Montforts and Keessen (2007).

[152] The terminology used in the medicines legislation is 'abridged procedure'.

[153] According to Art. 10 (1) Directive 2001/83, the data protection period is 10 years after the first authorization in an EU Member State, but it can be extended. It compensates for the costs and the time spent – thus reducing the usefulness of patent protection – on the tests (which cannot be protected by intellectual property rights) required to obtain a marketing authorization for a new medicine. See: Dodds-Smith (2000), pp. 93-136.

tive and quantitative composition in terms of active substances, (b) they have the same therapeutic form and (c) where necessary, bio-equivalence between the two products has been established in appropriate bio-availability studies.[154] The Directive has codified these criteria in its definition of essential similarity.[155] This means that the applicant only needs to establish essential similarity in order to be exempted from the duty to submit documentary evidence concerning the quality, safety and efficacy of the medicine.[156]

The authorization of generics through the simplified procedure is facilitated by administrative cooperation and mutual recognition. If an applicant submits an application for a generic to a Member State where the reference medicine has not been authorized, the Member States have to cooperate. At the request of the authority that has to assess the essential similarity between the generic and the reference medicine, the competent authority of the Member State that authorized the reference medicine sends the authority a confirmation that it has authorized the reference medicine, together with the full composition of the reference medicine and other relevant information.[157] The national authority may then use this information for its assessment of the essential similarity.[158] If the applicant refers to a generic that has already been authorized by another Member State, the Member State where the applicant applies for an authorization does not have to assess essential similarity, but should recognize the decision of the reference Member State, unless it fears that authorization may pose a serious risk to public health.[159]

The *Seroxat* case illustrates the complications that can arise due to mutual recognition. GSK had obtained a Dutch marketing authorization for the proprietary medicine Seroxat. Genthon applied for a Danish authorization for a generic, called Euplix. The Danish authorities authorized Euplix in accordance with the simplified procedure, using Seroxat as a reference medicine and hence the Dutch dossier, because Genthon had established the essential similarity of Euplix and Seroxat. GSK did not agree that Euplix was essentially similar and started administrative proceedings in Denmark, during which the Danish

[154] C-368/96 *Generics* [1998] ECR I-7967. The criteria developed in the Generics case are applied in a whole series of cases. See in particular: C-106/01 *Novartis* [2004] ECR I-4403 and C-112/02 *Kohlpharma* [2004] ECR I-3369. Cf. Dutch Council of State 23-02-2005, JGR 2005/22, Dutch Council of State 28-04-2005, JGR 2005/23 and Dutch Council of State 18-06-2003, JGR 2003/23.

[155] Art. 10 (2) (b) Directive 2001/83.

[156] Note that the environmental assessment report is not mentioned among the reports to which the applicant may refer. See: Montforts *et al.* (2006).

[157] Art. 10 Directive 2001/83.

[158] Dutch Council of State 18 December 2002, AB 2003/276, JGR 2003/1 and Dutch Council of State 01-07-2004, AB 2005/19, JGR 2004/41. This is in line with its earlier case law, e.g. Dutch Council of State 22-08-2001, AB 2001/310.

[159] C-452/06 *The Queen on the application of Synthon* v *Licensing Authority of the Department of Health* [2008] ECR I-0000.

judge asked the ECJ questions about essential similarity.[160] This did not prevent Genthon from filing an application in the Netherlands requesting mutual recognition of the Danish authorization. The Dutch authorities recognized the Danish authorization despite the ongoing European and Danish court proceedings. Recognition would not have been prevented by suspension of the decision because that does not constitute a ground for non-recognition.[161] Following this, another competitor obtained an authorization in the Netherlands for a generic through the simplified procedure by reference to Genthon's dossier. GSK started administrative proceedings in the Netherlands against both authorizations. The Dutch court had to decide (twice!) about the question whether mutual recognition was possible without conducting an independent assessment on the issue of essential similarity.[162] As could have been expected, it held that European legislation allowed for this approach.[163] The dispute fizzled out when the ECJ ruled that the medicines could be considered essentially similar.[164]

3.4 Non-recognition

The mutual recognition procedure has been streamlined to the extent that once one State has authorized a medicine, the other Member States are nearly obliged to follow suit.[165] A Member State may only refuse recognition if there are grounds to assume that authorization presents a potential serious risk to public health.[166] However, a Member State cannot refuse recognition without being confronted with Community intervention. In order to reach a uniform decision in case of disagreement, the medicines legislation provides for a binding dispute settlement procedure.[167] The Member States involved have to refer issues to the CHMP if they fail to reach agreement during the (simultaneous) mutual recognition procedure ('mutual recognition referral') or if divergent decisions occur due to consecutive mutual recognition ('divergent decisions referral').[168] The latter referral option can also be used to promote harmonisation of authorizations issued prior to the establishment of the mutual recognition

---

160 C-74/03 *SmithKline Beecham plc* v *Laegemiddelstyreisen* [2005] ECR I-595.

161 See the chapter on judicial review before the national courts.

162 Dutch Council of State 18/12/2004, AB 2003/276 and Dutch Council of State 21 July 2004, AB 2005/19.

163 It became clear in C-452/06 *The Queen on the application of Synthon* v *Licensing Authority of the Department of Health* [2008] ECR I-0000 that the Dutch approach was correct.

164 C-74/03 *SmithKline Beecham plc* v *Laegemiddelstyreisen* [2005] ECR I-595 and C-452/06 *The Queen on the application of Synthon* v *Licensing Authority of the Department of Health* [2008] ECR I-0000.

165 See Directive 2001/83 as amended, See also Notice to Applicants Volume 2A Chapter 1 p. 2.

166 Art. 29 Directive 2001/83. Joined Cases C-211/03, C-299/03 and C-316/03 to C-319/03 *HLH Warenvertriebs, Orthica* v *Deutschland* [2005] ECR I-5141.

167 Arbitration is also used when Member States are unable to agree on the variation, suspension or withdrawal of an authorization, see: Art. 35-37 Directive 2001/83.

168 C-452/06 *The Queen on the application of Synthon* v *Licensing Authority of the Department of Health* [2008] ECR I-0000.

procedure.[169] Finally, it is also possible that the Community's interest prompts a referral ('Community interest referral').[170] The two latter referral options allow the Commission and the (prospective) holder of the authorization to request a referral.

The Community referral was created after Review 2001 revealed that the option to withdraw an application at any time in any Member State where it had been submitted was used by applicants to withdraw applications from Member States that filed objections in order to avoid the referral. Not only did they thus avoid the risk of a negative outcome, but they also saved the time spent waiting for its outcome, during which the medicine could not be marketed.[171] For this reason, the referral procedure was changed, so that arbitration would always take place when Member States were unable to solve their dispute in the informal phase.[172] Even if an application is withdrawn from the Member State that objected, a Community referral is accepted by the CHMP if this is in the Community's interest.[173] The Community interest covers the interests set out in the EC Treaty, e.g. the creation of the internal market, the attainment of a high level of health protection, the strengthening of consumer protection, avoidance of distortion of competition and environmental protection.[174]

It is not certain whether the Member States can also use the dispute settlement procedure if they disagree on points that fail to justify non-recognition. Indeed, the Commission complained in the Review 2001 that the Member States too often resorted to dispute settlement, as the notion of 'risks to public health' was invoked in a number of situations where it did not appear to be consistent with the idea of mutual recognition.[175] However, the formulation in the Notice to the Applicant is inviting enough, as it states that any concern about the quality, safety and efficacy of the medicine may be a legitimate reason for referral.[176] Moreover, the Notice to the Applicant allows for broad use of the Community referral procedure by stating that the CHMP accepts a Community referral if the referring party demonstrates that a Community interest is at stake.[177] The advantage of a broad use of the procedure is that the Member States

---

[169] Lisman (2006), pp. 33-34.

[170] These referral procedures are also called the Article 29, Article 30 and the Article 31 referral, after the Articles of Directive 2001/83 in which they have been codified.

[171] Review 2001, pp. 18 and 19.

[172] Lisman (2006), p. 43.

[173] Notice to the Applicants, Vol. 2A, Chapter 3, February 2004, p. 6.

[174] Notice to the Applicants, Vol. 2A, Chapter 3, February 2004, p. 6.

[175] Review 2001, p. 18.

[176] For interpretation of 'the grounds of potential serious risk to public health', Art. 29 (2) Directive 2001/83 refers to the Guidelines to be adopted by the Commission. The Commission has indeed specified these grounds in the Notice to Applicants, Vol. 2A, June 2004, Chapter 1, p. 5 and Vol 2A, February 2004, Chapter 3, pp. 2 and 3. Please note that the interpretation given in the Notice to Applicants does not constitute a binding rule.

[177] Notice to the Applicants, Vol. 2A, Chapter 3, February 2004, p. 6.

use the available procedural means in order to arrive at a uniform application of Community law.[178]

3.5 The dispute settlement procedure

If an authority has concerns during the mutual recognition procedure, it should send a detailed account of the reasons for its position to the reference Member State, the other Member States involved and the applicant.[179] It should also indicate what action may be necessary to correct any defects in the application.[180] The relevant Member States will discuss the points of disagreement in the coordination group,[181] which consists of representatives from the Member States.[182] Only in case of a Community referral, arbitration is not necessarily preceded by such informal discussions. During this informal phase, the applicant has the opportunity to explain his point of view to the Member States. The Member States have 60 days to use their best endeavours to reach an agreement.[183] If the Member States reach an agreement, the mutual recognition procedure can be continued. If the coordination group is unable to reach an agreement, the Member States concerned inform EMEA and the applicant that they are moving on to arbitration.

Despite any objections from other Member States leading to the use of the dispute settlement procedure, the Member States that approve the application may authorize the medicine.[184] However, the validity of their decisions will be affected by the outcome of the dispute settlement procedure, as all Member States concerned must implement the Community decision.[185] The formal dispute settlement procedure starts when the referring party informs EMEA,[186] the Member States concerned, the Commission and the applicant that the case is subject to arbitration. The referring party and the Member States concerned send a report to EMEA and to the applicant in which they explain on which matters they were unable to agree.[187] The applicant needs to send EMEA a copy

---

178 Opinion AG Geelhoed in Joined Cases C-211/03, C-299/03 and C-316/03 to C-319/03 *HLH Warenvertriebs, Orthica* v *Deutschland* [2005] ECR I-5141, JGR 2005/40. The dispute was about the classification of a product as a medicinal or a cosmetic product.

179 Art. 29 (1) Directive 2001/83. Notice to Applicants, Vol. 2A, February 2004, Chapter 3, p. 3.

180 Notice to the Applicants, Volume 2A Notice to the Applicants, Chapter 3, Feb. 2004, p. 2.

181 Also called: the Coordination group for Mutual recognition and Decentralised procedures (human), abbreviated to CMD(h). It is the successor of the informal Mutual Recognition Facilitation Group.

182 The coordination group was established pursuant to Art. 27 Directive 2001/83. It consists of representatives from each Member State. It was set up to settle disputes informally, but it also meets to discuss general issues, in order to facilitate the mutual recognition procedure.

183 Artt. 29 (3) and (4) Directive 2001/83.

184 Art. 29 (6) Directive 2001/83.

185 Art. 34 Directive 2001/83.

186 Notice to the Applicants, Vol. 2A, Chapter 3, February 2004, p. 10.

187 Notice to the Applicants, Vol. 2A, Chapter 3, February 2004, p. 7.

of the dossier that he submitted to the Member States involved.[188] EMEA will ask the opinion of the CHMP, which gives the applicant the opportunity to be heard before it gives its opinion.[189] Only in case of a Community referral, the CHMP is not obliged to hear the applicant or the marketing authorization holder, but it generally hears the applicant as well as a matter of good administrative practice.[190]

The CHMP issues an opinion on the points of discussion. If the applicant submits objections to this opinion to EMEA, the CHMP will review its opinion. After this, the opinion is sent to the Member States concerned, the Commission and the applicant. On the basis of the opinion of the CHMP, the Commission will take a draft decision, which it sends to the Member States involved and the applicant. If the Commission disagrees with this opinion in its draft decision, it has to attach an annex to its decision in which it justifies the differences.[191] The draft decision is then submitted for approval to the Standing Committee on Medicinal Products for Human Use ('Standing Committee') in accordance with the regulatory procedure.[192] The Commission sends its final decision to the Member States concerned and to the applicant. The Member States concerned implement the decision into a national decision.[193] The Commission also informs the other Member States, so they will be able to follow this Community decision if necessary.[194]

The dispute settlement procedure may result in a Community decision forcing a Member State to allow a medicine that it would not have authorized otherwise.[195] It can no longer postpone the authorization of the medicine by Member States that have approved all relevant documents, as they may grant a temporary authorization at the request of the applicant while arbitration is pending.[196] Arbitration can therefore result in confirmation, suspension, amendment or revocation of the authorizations that have already been issued.[197] That is possible in particular in cases of repeated use of the mutual recognition procedure,[198] because then arbitration may take place after an authorization has been granted by one or more Member States. The Regulation does not preclude

188 Art. 29 (5) Directive 2001/83.

189 The Committee has to issue its opinion within 60 days.

190 Notice to the Applicants, Vol. 2A, Chapter 3, February 2004, p. 11.

191 Art. 33 (3) Directive 2001/83.

192 The Standing Committee should not be confused with the CHMP, which consists of scientific experts. Instead, the Standing Committee is a regulatory committee, consisting of national civil servants, established in accordance with Artt. 5 and 7 Decision 1999/468, taking Art. 8 Decision 1999/468 into account. See Art. 34 (1) and (2), which refers to 121 (2) and (3) Community Code.

193 Artt. 31-34 Directive 2001/83.

194 Notice to the Applicants, Vol. 2A, February 2004, Chapter 3, p. 15.

195 Abraham and Lewis (2000), pp. 152-155.

196 Art. 29 Directive 2001/83.

197 Abraham and Lewis (2000), p. 205.

198 See Notice to Applicants, Volume 2A, June 2004, Chapter 2, p. 3.

that arbitration takes place twice. However, issues that are challenged in the first procedure must not be taken up again.[199] This does not constitute undue influence on Member States that had no concerns about the application and hence do not have to implement the Community decision, because all Member States can be involved in the arbitration procedure due to the use of the regulatory Comitology procedure.

3.6 Free movement of authorized medicines

The ECJ established that the principle of free movement of goods also applies to authorized medicines and that it is therefore forbidden for national authorities to obstruct parallel trade.[200] Parallel traders do not need to apply for a regular authorization in the Member State of destination, because they only need a parallel trade authorization in the Member State of destination for the import of a product already covered by a marketing authorization in that particular Member State.[201] The ECJ created the parallel trade authorization in the *De Peijper* case, because the documents and information prescribed by the Community Code hinder the free movement of goods and are only justified by the objective of safeguarding public health when a product is placed on the market for the first time.[202]

At first, authorization of the reference medicine in the Member State of destination remained a prerequisite, because medicines must not be placed on the market unless a marketing authorization has been issued.[203] However, the ECJ established in *Rhone-Poulenc* that if a Member State revokes the authorization of a proprietary medicine at the holder's request – because the holder has obtained authorization for a newer version and prefers to market only that – the national authorities of that Member State cannot refuse to grant (or withdraw) a parallel trade authorization for the old version on that ground.[204] As long as the 'old' version is legally marketed in one Member State, it may be marketed in all Member States. In other words, a single authorization suffices as reference for a parallel trade authorization.

The ECJ confirmed this point of view in *Ferring*[205] and in *Paranova*,[206] by stating that a Member State acts contrary to Article 28 EC if it automatically

---

[199] See Notice to Applicants, Volume 2A, June 2004, Chapter 2, p. 3.

[200] Berendschot and De Wit (2005), pp. 13-23. See also: Hancher (2000).

[201] C-32/80 *Officier van Justitie* v *Kortmann* [1981] ECR 250. See: Lasok (1998), p. 62. Note that temporary derogations may apply regarding new Member States.

[202] C-104/75 *De Peijper* [1976] ECR 613.

[203] C-322/01 *Deutscher Apothekerverband eV* v *0800 DocMorris and Jacques Waterval* [2003] ECR I-14887. See Art. 6 (1) Community Code.

[204] C-95/98 *Rhone-Poulenc*, ECR I-4835.

[205] C-172/00 *Ferring* v *Eurim Pharma* [2002] ECR I-6891.

[206] C-15/01 *Paranova* [2003] ECR I-4175, NJ 2004/17 and C-113/01 *Paranova* [2003] ECR I-4243, with a Joined Opinion of AG Jacobs.

revokes an authorization for parallel trade as a consequence of the revocation of the authorization for the reference medicine, unless the ground for revocation was that the medicine presented a health risk. The ECJ ignored the recommendation of AG Geelhoed that the parallel importer should be obliged to apply for a marketing authorization in the Member State of destination within a reasonable time on penalty of revocation of his parallel import authorization in order to maintain effective pharmacovigilance.[207] The ECJ may have taken into account that a parallel importer – whose activities resemble those of a wholesaler – would not be happy (or able) to take over the pharmacovigilance duties of the previous authorization holder.[208] Consequently, if the authorities of the Member State of destination issue or maintain a parallel trade authorization for the old version of a medicine, they do so on the basis of the marketing authorization for the old version issued by the authorities of the reference Member State where the old version is still legally marketed, and will cooperate with the latter authorities in order to maintain effective pharmacovigilance.

The ECJ has gradually extended the scope of the parallel trade authorization.[209] In *Kohlpharma*, it extended the scope of the parallel trade procedure so far that it resulted in an overlap with the simplified procedure for generics.[210] It held that a parallel trade authorization must not be refused to a generic product if the reference product is a proprietary medicine. It held that the applicant, who may not have all information, should at least make it plausible that the two medicines do not differ significantly for the purpose of assessing their safety and efficacy. As the ECJ transferred the duty to establish essential similarity from the applicant to the competent authority, it seemed to remove the need to request authorization for a generic.[211] However, an authorization must still be applied for because the medicines legislation does not allow national authorities to authorize applications for parallel trade of generics, unless the applicant establishes essential similarity with a reference medicine during the parallel trade authorization procedure.[212]

3.7 Conclusions

The prevailing types of decisions in the area of medicines are Community authorizations and mutual recognition authorizations. The transition period from national decisions to mutual recognition decisions will soon end. The subsequent mutual recognition referral procedure is a last reminder of different national decisions, but it can also be used if an applicant has not filed

---

[207] Opinion AG Geelhoed in C-172/00 *Ferring* v *Eurim Pharma* [2002] ECR I-6891.

[208] Lisman, annotation to C-112/02 Kohlpharma, JGR 2004/29. See Chapter 3, section 3.3 about pharmacovigilance.

[209] C-201/94 *Smith and Nephew and Primecrown* [1996] ECR I-5819.

[210] C-112/02 *Kohlpharma* [2004] ECR I-3369.

[211] This appears from C-201/06 *Commission* v *France* [2008] ECR I-0000. See section 6.4 of this chapter.

[212] E.g. the Dutch policy, available at: www.cbg-meb.nl/NL/reghoudr/parimp.htm#beleid.

an application for authorization in all Member States at once, as he may choose not only the reference Member State but also the recognizing Member States. It is important to note that although mutual recognition suggests that non-recognition is possible, non-recognition is not a final decision, but is solved through the binding dispute settlement procedure. This results in a Community decision if informal discussions did not produce agreement between the Member States concerned. Only the Member States concerned will implement the Community decision, but Member States where the applicant subsequently applies for authorization are also bound by it, although they may use the dispute settlement procedure for disputes about other aspects.

There seems to be a trend towards centralization in the division of tasks between the Commission and the Member States. The Commission authorizes high-tech proprietary medicines, while the Member States authorize ordinary proprietary medicines, variations on existing medicines and generics.[213] First and foremost, the possible future extension of the Community procedure to other proprietary medicines creates the impression of a centralization trend.[214] This would reduce the significance of the mutual recognition procedure, but not oust the Member States from the authorization procedure entirely, as they participate in the regulatory Comitology procedure.[215] In addition, centralisation is also on the rise at the Member State level, as the ECJ reduced the room for discretion concerning non-recognition and facilitated parallel trade. Its attempt to merge the parallel trade and the simplified authorization procedure was unsuccessful because it misinterpreted the Medicines Directive when it thought that a merger was possible and therefore parallel trade has not become as easy as the ECJ thought it could be. In principle, it is still prohibited to market a medicine in a Member State without having obtained a marketing authorization there, although it is possible to market a medicine that is only covered by a parallel trade authorization, provided that someone holds a marketing authorization for that medicine in one of the Member States.

Both authorization procedures provide uniformity, but the mutual recognition procedure is inherently weaker in guaranteeing uniformity. Since the applicant is not obliged to apply for an authorization in all the Member States, it is possible that a medicine is authorized in one Member State and unauthorized in another. However, uniformity is not threatened by non-recognition, as the dispute settlement procedure guarantees that disputes between Member States are settled by a binding Community decision, which restores uniformity. Both authorization procedures offer procedural guarantees to the applicant. The only drawback for applicants may be that they cannot choose between the two authorization procedures. The applicants' interests are even protected in the dispute settlement procedure, because it prescribes that he be heard before a decision is taken and the procedure does not suspend a marketing authorization issued by

213 Review 2001, pp. 8 and 9.

214 Review 2001, pp. 8 and 9.

215 The difficulties in the area of GMOs are the exception that prove the rule.

willing Member States. The procedural guarantees offered to third parties in the medicines legislation are limited to the duty to inform the public when decisions are issued and to make the decisions and the summaries of assessment reports public.

4 CITES

The CITES Regulation features a combination of Community decisions and single-licence decisions. At first sight, the European implementation of the Convention of international trade in endangered species (CITES) into the CITES Regulation constitutes an example of a single licence system.[216] This is because only the national CITES management authorities are responsible for issuing import, export and re-export permits and certificates of origin for individual specimens of listed species. Their decision is valid in all Member States without any further implementing measures being necessary. However, national decisions may complement the single licence decisions. Moreover the single licence decisions are part of a dual authorization procedure, as they are based on Community decisions. The Commission decides on whether or not to include species in the Annexes to the CITES Regulation and on emergency measures. The Commission does not have the competence to take a Community decision to settle disputes between the Member States.

4.1 The Community procedure

The CITES Regulation provides the general framework of rules regulating trade in various species of fauna and flora. The Commission takes implementing measures in accordance with the regulatory committee procedure, with the assistance of the Committee on Trade in Wild Fauna and Flora[217] and the Scientific Review Group.[218] The Commission is responsible for the implementing provisions to be established in an implementing Regulation.[219] The CITES Regulation stipulates general conditions for the issuance of permits and certificates, which are elaborated by the Commission in the implementing Regulation as systems for how to draw up authorizations, certificates, notifications and labels, even including the colour and size of the paper to be used for these documents. Any permit or certificate issued in accordance with the Regulation may stipulate conditions and requirements imposed by the issuing authority to ensure compliance with the relevant provisions, as national authori-

---

216 Regulation 338/97/EC on the protection of species of wild fauna and flora by regulating trade therein

217 Artt. 2 (a) and 18 Regulation 338/97.

218 Rec. 19 Preamble to Regulation 338/97 and Art. 17 Regulation 338/97.

219 Commission Regulation 865/2006 laying down detailed rules concerning the implementation of Council Regulation 338/97/EC.

ties may adapt CITES documents to the situation at hand.[220] Only where such conditions or requirements require incorporation into the design of authorizations or certificates, are the Member States obliged to inform the Commission of the conditions or requirements they have set.[221] This notification obligation is part of the provision on the validity of and special conditions for authorizations and certificates. Insofar as these conditions and requirements are not technical requirements, they can probably be applied even before they have been duly notified to the Commission.[222]

The Commission also takes trade measures in accordance with the regulatory committee procedure.[223] First of all, it is responsible for the listing of species in the Annexes to the Regulation. Species are listed in one of the four Annexes to the Regulation on the basis of objective criteria.[224] The Commission adopts the amendments to Annex A to D on the basis of information sent by the competent authorities of the Member States to the Commission.[225] In addition, it is an exclusive Community competence to impose (temporary) general restrictions on imports of specimens of species with an Annex A or B listing or to ban trade with a certain country.[226] Such a measure can be established following an international recommendation of the CITES Secretariat. It can take the form of a Commission Regulation prepared in accordance with the regulatory Comitology procedure,[227] but also of a Commission Recommendation. The form does not change the Member States' obligation to reject import authorizations following general restrictions established by the Commission.[228] In the *Bolivian Wildcat Skins* case,[229] the Court held that Commission recommendations must be taken into account by the national authorities in their decision-making process. A Member State is not allowed to take unilateral measures. National authorities should inform the Commission if they believe that trade measures should be taken.[230] Once introduction of specimens of a certain species into the Community is restricted, the Commission may also restrict the rules on keeping and transporting live specimens of this species.[231]

---

220 Art. 11 (3) Regulation 338/97.

221 Art. 11 (3) Regulation 338/97.

222 Cf. C-194/94 *CIA Security* [1996] ECR I-2201.

223 Art. 18 Regulation 338/97.

224 Rec. (4) Preamble and Art. 3 Regulation 338/97.

225 Art. 15 (5) Regulation 338/97.

226 See C-182/89 *Commission* v *France (Bolivian wild-cat skins)* [1990] ECR I-04337.

227 E.g. Commission Regulation (EC) No 349/2003, based on Artt. 19 (2) and 4 (6) Regulation 338/97.

228 Art. 4 (6) Regulation 338/97.

229 C-182/89 *Commission* v *France (Bolivian wildcat skins)* [1990] ECR I-4337, to be further elaborated in paragraph 5.3 of this chapter. See also the Opinion of Advocate General Mischo in this case.

230 Artt. 4 (6), 5 (7) and 19 (2) and (4) Regulation 338/97.

231 Artt. 19 (2) jo 9 (6) Regulation 338/97.

4.2 The single licence procedure

The holder of a specimen of a species listed in the Annexes to the CITES Regulation must always be able to present a certificate demonstrating its legal origin.[232] The holder of animals born and bred in captivity or artificially propagated plants needs a CITES certificate (and possibly other proof, e.g. a chip or a ring) in order to be granted treatment in accordance with Annex B, which means that commercial use of the specimen is no longer prohibited.[233] Certificates for specimens that are born and bred in captivity or for artificial propagation are issued at the breeder's request by the management authorities of the Member States, on the condition that the breeder meets the requirements imposed by the implementing Regulation.[234] Scientific institutions and zoos in particular benefit from these exemptions.[235] These certificates are valid in all Member States – and in third countries – without any further implementing measures being necessary.

For imports into the EU of specimens of an Annex A or B listed species, the trader needs an import permit before the shipment arrives at a port of entry into the EU. The application must be submitted to, and will be assessed by, the management authority of the Member State of destination, i.e. the Member State where the specimen will normally be kept after its introduction into the European Union.[236] The applicant must present documentary evidence of the legal origin of the specimen. For import from a third country this is an export permit and, in case of re-export, a re-export certificate.[237] The national management authority takes its decision on the basis of the opinion of the national scientific authority, which states whether the shipment has a harmful effect on the conservation status or the extent of the territory occupied by the relevant population of the species, also taking into account the opinions of the Scientific Group on these subjects.[238] The management authority should also approve the accommodation and with the purpose of import into a Member State. For Annex A listings, the management authority must also be satisfied that the specimen is not to be used for primarily commercial purposes.[239]

When a shipment with specimens of listed species arrives at a designated customs office of one of the EU Member States, the import procedure for

---

[232] Art. 9 Regulation 338/97.

[233] Artt. 7 and 10 Regulation 338/97, further elaborated in Regulation 865/2006.

[234] Artt. 8 (3) and 10 Regulation 338/97, further elaborated in Regulation 865/2006.

[235] Artt. 7 (4) and 8 (3) Regulation 338/97.

[236] Art. 2 (h) and (k) Regulation 338/97.

[237] A re-export certificate is required when a specimen does not originate from the exporting state, but was previously imported into that state. This requirement aims to avoid the 'laundering' of specimens through trade. If a state does not observe this requirement, the CITES Secretariat may recommend the Parties to the Convention to impose a trade ban on that state.

[238] Art. 19 and Art. 4 Regulation 338/97.

[239] Art. 4 Regulation 338/97.

specimens of Annex A or B listed species is followed, but not necessarily by the authorities of the Member State which issued the CITES documents. The customs authorities at the port of entry need to check the shipment in order to ensure that it complies with the accompanying CITES documents, including the import permit.[240] The authorities at the port of entry should recognize the import authorization issued by the management authority of the Member State of destination. The customs authorities at the port of entry are also responsible for legal import of specimens of species with an Annex C or D listing, as these imports should be notified on arrival at a designated customs office. For Annex C listings, the importer should present an export permit if the specimen originates in the State that listed the species on Appendix III of the CITES Convention, or a certificate of origin and, where appropriate, a re-export certificate.

Rejections

The competent national management authority has to reject an application for an import permit if the proposed shipment fails to meet the conditions imposed by the CITES Regulations. It does not matter whether the exporting country has already granted an export permit, because the management authorities of the Member States are obliged to make an independent assessment before granting an import permit.[241] Even if all import requirements are considered fulfilled, the management authority can still choose to reject the application, after consulting with the scientific authority, if it finds that other factors oppose issuance of an import authorization. This ground can be used, for example, to reject an application for an import authorization filed by a trader with a bad reputation. Late submission of an application constitutes a procedural ground for rejection of an import permit, since authorizations should be applied for in sufficient time to allow their issuance prior to the introduction of specimens into the Community instead of on arrival of the shipment.[242] The CITES Regulation does not allow the national management authorities to take safeguard measures. Even in urgent situations, only the Commission can impose a trading ban relating to certain countries or species.[243]

National authorities are not obliged to consult each other before issuing or rejecting an import permit. They fulfil their tasks independently. This may lead to different outcomes. In order to prevent 'forum shopping', a rejection of an application has EU-wide effect. In this respect, three rules are significant.[244] First of all, only in cases that are significantly relevant to the objectives of the CITES Regulation, the management authority is obliged to immediately inform the Commission of the rejection and the reasons for rejection. The Commission

[240] Art. 12 Regulation 338/97.

[241] Art. 4 Regulation 338/97.

[242] Art. 4 Regulation 338/97, as elaborated in Art. 8 Regulation 865/2006. Cf. Dutch Council of State 12-11-2003, LJN: AN 7892.

[243] Art. 4 (6) Regulation 338/97.

[244] Art. 6 and 11 Regulation 338/97.

communicates the information received to the other Member States to ensure uniform application of the CITES Regulation. Secondly, the applicant should inform the authority of any previous rejections. Finally, although Member States have to recognize the rejection of applications for authorizations and certificates by the competent authorities of other Member States, where such rejection is based on the provisions of this Regulation, this obligation does not apply where circumstances have changed significantly or where new evidence to support an application has become available. In such cases, if a management authority issues an authorization or certificate, it must inform the Commission of its decision and explain the reasons for issuance. These rules give traders the opportunity to play the Member States off against one another. Therefore, although Member States should normally recognize the rejection of an application, forum shopping still occurs in practice.

In Dutch case law, examples can be found of traders who object to a rejection by stating that the application would not have been rejected in another country. One applicant substantiated the claim that double standards were applied.[245] This party argued that the Dutch authority should authorize the import, because Germany issued import authorizations for Guayacan timber originating from Mexico. However, from the evidence, a letter from the German authorities, it became clear that they had refused to issue import authorizations for some time and had only recently decided to issue import authorizations for old stocks of Guayacan timber (an Annex B listed species). Concerning the argument of the double standards, the Dutch court stated that a letter from the German authorities is not equal to a German import authorization. Therefore, the applicant had failed to show that the German authorities would have issued an import authorization for this consignment if they had applied for one. Even if the applicant had managed to prove that the German authorities could have issued an import permit, the Dutch authorities still would not be obliged to issue an import permit. As the court added, if another Member State may have failed to apply European law correctly, this does not create a legally enforceable right for the applicant to have the Dutch authorities convert to that policy. Applicants will therefore be unsuccessful when trying to invoke double standards, as long as the national court is convinced that the national authorities applied the CITES Regulation correctly.

4.3 Non-recognition

Even though it provides for a single licence, the CITES Regulation allows the Member States to impose stricter measures, in particular to prohibit any commercial use of Annex A listed species.[246] Since the regulation of use falls outside the scope of the CITES Regulation,[247] this provision of the Reg-

[245] Raad van State 11-02-2004, LJN AO3387, not published.

[246] Art. 8 Regulation 338/97. Confirmed by the ECJ in: C-510/99 *Tridon* [2001] ECR I-7777.

[247] Cf. C-473/98 *Toolex Alpha* [2000] ECR I-5681. See: Weatherill (2002), p. 52.

ulation signals a use of the minimum harmonization clause of Article 176 EC compatible with the Treaty obligations of the Member States, which in this case would particularly refer to the free movement of specimens covered by CITES documents issued by one of the Member States.[248] Consequently, the CITES Regulation allows for the imposition of additional requirements regarding the use of specimens covered by a certificate that they are born and bred in captivity or that they are artificially propagated. When the CITES certificates were issued by another Member State, this amounts to de facto non-recognition.

The following Dutch case illustrates the complications that arise if one Member State prohibits commercial use and another does not. The Dutch owner of a hawk (Accipiter gentiles, listed in Annex A) was prosecuted for having brought his bird into Dutch territory in violation of Dutch legislation.[249] He justified himself by pointing out that a German CITES certificate, which stated that the bird was born and bred in captivity in Germany, accompanied the bird and that it had a matching, closed ring on its leg. The Dutch authorities recognised the CITES certificate and did not dispute the 'born and bred in captivity status' of the bird. However, they insisted that the owner should have applied for a hunting licence. Since birds of prey could only be kept in the Netherlands with a hunting licence, the owner of the bird had violated Dutch legislation. Thus, despite the CITES certificate, the Dutch Supreme Court convicted the owner for not having brought the bird into Dutch territory in conformity with Dutch legislation.

Inspection may also reveal that the Member State of destination issued a CITES document on the false premise that the conditions for its issuance had been met.[250] It is debatable whether non-recognition in this situation is possible in case of a single licence. Arguably, only the administration of the Member State that issued the authorization is entitled to reconsider it.[251] However, a Member State should not be obliged to accept a decision that is manifestly invalid and can therefore be considered void and thus as having no effect in any Member State.[252] That is problematic insofar as it could lead to fragmentation of the market if a decision is accepted in one Member State but not in another.[253] This issue is addressed in the enforcement chapter.

4.4 The dispute settlement procedure

The CITES Regulation allows a Member State to question the validity of a CITES document and declare it void after consultation with the Member State that issued the decision. It is conceivable that the authorities from

[248] See: Dougan (2000), p. 865; Van Ooik (2007), pp. 21-27.

[249] HR 21-05-2002, NJ 2002, 404.

[250] See the CITES section in the chapter on enforcement.

[251] Sydow (2004), p. 148.

[252] Ruffert (2001), p. 453 et seq.

[253] Sydow (2004), p. 149.

the Member States involved have consulted each other, but still disagree on the validity of the CITES document. In this case, the statement that the CITES document is void will have a unilateral character and may not be followed by a revocation from the competent authority. While this may not be problematic in a single case, because CITES documents can be unilaterally replaced by new CITES documents, it is problematic when the failure seems systematic and a change of policy is required. In the absence of a dispute settlement procedure provision, the Commission cannot take a Community decision to settle disputes in accordance with the regulatory Comitology procedure. Instead, the Member States can discuss the issue in a CITES committee meeting or persuade the Commission to intervene by bringing an infringement procedure.

4.5 The national procedure

Despite the single licence character of the regulatory system established by the CITES Regulation, national decisions also occur in order to monitor trade within the EU of specimens of Annex A listed species. These requirements may have been introduced due to international concern about the traceability of CITES-regulated wildlife within the EU. The single licence system, the free movement of goods and the elimination of internal border controls made the movement of CITES specimens within the European Union difficult to monitor and report, because only trade with non-EU states is monitored and reported. This caused some tension with the requirements of the CITES Convention for Appendix I listed species, which should be monitored by import authorizations.[254] It even led to a resolution at the fifth Conference of the Parties to the Convention. The resolution recommended that in their annual reports, members of a regional trade agreement include information on trade in CITES specimens with other member states of the regional trade agreement, unless the record-keeping and reporting duties of Article VIII CITES are in direct and irreconcilable conflict with the provisions of the regional trade agreement.[255]

Whether or not as a result of international pressure, CITES Regulation 338/97 introduced a specific certificate for the movement within the EU of Annex A listed species, with the sole exception of movement of a live animal for the purpose of urgent veterinary treatment followed by immediate return to the authorized location.[256] The holder needs to apply for a certificate prior to any movement within the Community of a live specimen of a species listed in Annex A from the location indicated in the import authorization or in another CITES certificate. They should apply for a movement certificate to the management authority of the Member State of location.[257] This authority may only grant the certificate if the competent scientific authority of the Member State

[254] Reeves (2002), pp. 113-114; Favre (1989) pp. 239-240.

[255] Res. Conf. 5.5.

[256] Art. 9 Regulation 338/97.

[257] Art. 9 Regulation 338/97.

of location is satisfied that the intended accommodation is adequate. In case of movement to another Member State, the competent scientific authority of the Member State of future location has to approve the intended accommodation as satisfactory. If the national authority of the Member State of location then issues the certificate, it will communicate this immediately to the management authority of the Member State of future location.

4.6 Conclusions

The prevailing decisions in the area of CITES are the Community decision on the listing of a species and the single licence decision on the authorization of a shipment. The combination of Community decisions for the listing of species in the Annexes and emergency measures and a single licence for the import of specimens that are listed in the Annexes to the CITES Regulation guarantees uniformity at the level of the rules that apply to a single shipment of CITES-listed specimens. However, this does not guarantee that each Member State will take the same decision, because the Member States are not obliged to consult each other on their decisions, be they positive or negative. They may not even be aware of a rejection, as Member States should only report serious infringements to the Commission. Since an applicant is free to choose the Member State that issues a CITES authorization, the lack of coordination between the Member States involves the risk that applications are filed in the Member State that least checks the application before issuing an authorization.

The risk to overall uniformity is mitigated by the CITES Regulation, because it prescribes a national residency document for Annex A listed species and because it allows to restrict trade in endangered species between the Member States through the imposition of more stringent measures. This is permitted because the Regulation is based on Article 175 EC, although a Member State may come into conflict with the free movement rules if it fails to recognize CITES documents issued by another Member State. The Regulation shows the way, as it explicitly allows Member States to regulate the possession of CITES-listed species, in particular in case of Annex A listed species. As regards the observance of procedural guarantees, it is a serious shortcoming that the CITES Regulation does not prescribe any procedural guarantees for individuals in any of its decision-making procedures. This is only mitigated in the authorization and residency procedures concerning the applicant, because these decisions are based on the information and evidence filed by him.

5 Plant protection products

The regulation of the marketing of plant protection products is currently developing from a national decision-making system into a combination of Community decisions and mutual recognition decisions. Two Directives determine the discretionary room that national authorities have in taking decisions. Directive 79/117 determines that national authorities may not authorize the placing on the market of plant protection products containing substances prohibited from being used in plant protection products by their listing in the Annexes to Council Directive 79/117. By contrast, Directive 91/414 ('Plant protection products Directive') determines that they may authorize plant protection products containing substances that are listed in Annex I to the Directive and provides for a transition regime that allows for national decisions concerning products that contain substances under evaluation.[258] The two Directives might merge in a proposed Regulation concerning the placing on the market of plant protection products, which will introduce a streamlined mutual recognition procedure.[259]

5.1 The Community procedure

The Plant protection products Directive provides a uniform set of risk assessment principles and decision-making criteria that Member States must use. Instead of the Commission, the Council further elaborates these criteria. It adopts the uniform principles by qualified majority, acting on a proposal from the Commission.[260] By contrast, the Commission is responsible for the listing of substances on the Annex to the Directive in accordance with the regulatory procedure. When Directive 91/414 was adopted, no substances had been listed in the Annexes to the Regulation. Therefore, the Commission started to review the active substances used in plant protection products.

Although the Commission expected to finish its review process in 2003, it had to extend this period to 2008.[261] The delay was caused by the need to create trust among the Member States, as agreement had to be reached on the safety standards. When they finally agreed, the safety standards for active substances were so strict that the industry needed more time than expected to file extensive

[258] Art. 8 Directive 91/414 EC.

[259] Explanatory Memorandum to the Amended Proposal for a Regulation of the European Parliament and of the Council concerning the placing of plant protection products on the market, COM (2006) 388, p. 3.

[260] Art. 18 Directive 91/414 and Council Directive 97/57/EC.

[261] Report from the Commission to the European Parliament and the Council, 'Evaluation of the active substances of plant protection products' (submitted in accordance with Art. 8 (3) of Council Directive 91/4141/EEC on the placing of plant protection products on the market) ('Report 2001'), COM (2001) 444 final, p. 2.

dossiers.[262] Consequently, it took the Member States more time than expected to assess the applications, which may also be considered as caused by a lack of resources. At the Community level, the establishment of the European Food Safety Authority ('EFSA') partly addressed this lack of resources.[263] Finally, ambitions were high, as the assessment was not going be limited to new substances. All uses of all existing substances have to be assessed.[264]

In the Community review process, the applicant – mostly producers acting as individual companies or collectively[265] – has to prove that an active substance can be used safely with respect to human and animal health and the environment, which boils down to establishing safe use.[266] The holders of a marketing authorization for a plant protection product are not obliged to apply for inclusion of the active substance in Annex I as long as someone applied for a listing decision, because otherwise the Member States have to withdraw previously issued marketing authorizations.[267] Either the Member State that received the application for the inclusion of an active substance in Annex I, or the Member State designated by the Commission carries out the evaluation of the dossier (the 'Member State rapporteur').[268] The Commission may replace a Member State rapporteur by another if an imbalance becomes apparent in the responsibilities borne by the Member States as rapporteurs.[269]

Once the Member State rapporteur finishes its assessment, it sends the application and the dossier to the Commission. The Member States have adopted one working language for this purpose.[270] In order to reduce the differences between the assessments by the various Member States, the Commission has adopted guidance documents to supplement the uniform principles.[271] The Commission refers the application and the report to the Scientific Committee on Plant Health and to the Standing Committee on the Food Chain and Animal Health.[272] The Commission then takes a draft decision, which it will refer to the Standing Committee. It may ask the applicant to submit his remarks to it, particularly

---

[262] The average dossier has 50,000 pages and takes four and a half years to prepare. See: Report 2001, p. 3.

[263] Report 2001, p. 9.

[264] Report 2001, p. 3.

[265] Report 2001, p. 4.

[266] See Art. 5 Directive 91/414.

[267] Art. 6 and 8 Directive 91/414. See: C-361/06 *Feinchemie Schwebda and Bayer Crop Science* v *College voor de toelating van bestrijdingsmiddelen* [2008] ECR I-0000.

[268] Art. 6 (2) Directive 91/414.

[269] Art. 5 (6) Commission Regulation 450/2000 laying down the detailed rules for the implementation of the second and third stages of the work programme referred to in Art. 8 (2) of Council Directive 91/414/EEC.

[270] Report 2001, p. 4. It does not indicate which language.

[271] Report 2001, p. 5.

[272] Artt. 6 and 21 Directive 91/414.

whenever an unfavourable decision is envisaged.[273] By contrast, the proposed Regulation prescribes that the applicant be heard.[274] Within three to six months after referral to the Standing Committee, a Member State may request the Commission, assisted by the Standing Committee, to decide (in accordance with the regulatory committee procedure) whether the dossier complies with the requirements of Annex II and III, which is a prerequisite for the issuance of provisional national authorizations.[275] The Directive does not grant this right to the applicant.

When the Commission issues its decision, the form depends on whether the active substance will be listed in Annex I to Directive 91/414 or not.[276] A positive decision is issued as a daughter directive to Directive 91/414, because it adds an active substance to Annex I. Then the Member States have to transpose the amendment of the Annex into national legislation. A negative decision is issued in the form of a Community decision.[277] Under the proposed Regulation, both a positive and a negative decision will be issued in the form of a Commission (or Council) Regulation. It is remarkable that the Directive does not require that the daughter directive or decision and the accompanying assessment report be made publicly available. It only provides that the Commission must not disclose confidential information, listing among the exceptions the summary of the assessment report.[278] By contrast, the proposed Regulation prescribes public access to the report in accordance with Directive 2003/4/EC, with the exception of certain confidential elements, and allows the public to comment on the draft decision, while imposing the duty that the statement of reasons, which accompanies the Community decision, should reflect their comments.[279]

5.2 The national procedure

It is prohibited for Member States to authorize a plant protection product unless its active substances are listed in Annex I to the Directive and the Directive's conditions for authorization are met.[280] However, not all plant protection products are covered by a national authorization issued in accordance

[273] Art. 6 (4) Directive 91/414.

[274] Art. 7 and 13 Amended Proposal for a Regulation.

[275] Art. 6 (3) Directive 91/414.

[276] Artt. 5, 6 and 19 Directive 91/414. The review takes place in accordance with Commission Regulation 3600/92 of 11 December 1992 laying down the detailed rules for the implementation of the first stage of the programme of work referred to in Art. 8 (3) of Directive 91/414, p. 10. The regulatory Comitology procedure is followed because Artt. 5 and 6, 19 and 20 Council Directive 91/414/EC refer to Artt. 5 and 7 Council Decision 1999/468.

[277] Art. 8 Directive 91/414; Report 2001, p. 6.

[278] Art. 14 Directive 91/414.

[279] Art. 60 and 12 Proposal to a Regulation.

[280] Art. 3 Directive 91/414.

with a Community listing decision. Since the Directive came into effect without any active substances listed in Annex I, a transition period allowed the Member States to maintain national authorizations of plant protection products containing active substances already on the market for two years after the notification of the Directive, until these active substances have been evaluated at Community level.[281] This means that two types of national decisions occur, depending on whether it contains an active substance that has already been approved by a Community decision or not.

It was an open question whether the transition regime meant that national decisions issued or renewed after the coming into force of Directive 91/414 had to be based on the Directive's conditions for authorization. The ECJ seemed to answer this question in the negative, as it held in *Monsanto* and *ZHM I* that the transition provisions allow the Member States to continue to apply the national authorization conditions (and not those of the Directive) to products containing an active substance not listed in the Annex.[282] However, the ECJ held in *ZHM II* that it follows from Article 10 EC in conjunction with Article 249 and from the Directive itself that not only during the implementation phase,[283] but also during the transition period the Member States must refrain from taking any measures that are seriously likely to compromise the result prescribed by the Directive.[284] Therefore, Member States must not amend the applicable legislation in such a manner as to allow themselves to authorize a plant protection product during the transition phase without taking due account of the effects which that product may have on human and animal health and on the environment.[285]

As the evaluations of active substances proceed, the authorizations issued in accordance with the dual authorization procedure of the Directive 91/414 are gradually replacing the previously issued national authorizations.[286] A decision to include an active substance in Annex I means that the Member States may maintain national authorizations issued for plant protection products containing that particular active substance, although perhaps a variation is required[287] and

[281] According to Artt. 8 (2) and (3) Directive 91/414/EC, the transition period was supposed to end 12 years after notification of the Directive. It appears from case law that the Court has accepted the extension of this period, e.g. C-443/02 *Schreiber* [2004] ECR I-7275. See for a critical review of Dutch practice: Rutteman (2002), pp. 312-317.

[282] C-306/98 *The Queen* v *Minister of Agriculture, Fisheries and Food and Secretary of State for the Environment ex parte Monsanto* [2001] ECR I-3279 and C-316/04 *Stichting Zuid-Hollandse Milieufederatie* v *College voor de toelating van bestrijdingsmiddelen (ZHM I)* [2005] ECR I-9759.

[283] As it held in: C-129/96 *Inter-Environnement Wallonie* [1997] ECR I-7411.

[284] C-138/05 *Stichting Zuidhollandse Milieufederatie* v *College voor de toelating van bestrijdingsmiddelen (ZHM II)* [2006] ECR I-8339.

[285] C-138/05 *Stichting Zuidhollandse Milieufederatie* v *College voor de toelating van bestrijdingsmiddelen (ZHM II)* [2006] ECR I-8339.

[286] Report 2001, p. 4.

[287] Art. 8 (2) Directive 91/414.

they may issue authorizations in accordance with the Directive.[288] This means that a plant protection product should only be authorized if the active substance it contains is listed in the Annex and – when properly applied for the purpose intended – if it is sufficiently effective and has no unacceptable effects on plants or plant products, no unacceptable influence on the environment in general and, in particular, no harmful effect on human or animal health or on groundwater.[289] The Directive does not prescribe that the applicant is heard before a decision is taken.[290] The Member States may disclose a summary of the assessment report, as this does not form part of the confidential information, either on request or on their own initiative.[291]

The consequence of a decision not to include an active substance in Annex I is that the Member States have to ban the substance from plant protection products and thus withdraw national authorizations.[292] The Directive allows the Member States to grant a period of grace for the disposal, storage, placing on the market and use of existing stocks, if they withdraw an authorization. It does not state how long the period of grace may be. However, if a period of grace is granted, its duration must be in accordance with the withdrawal.[293] The proposed Regulation has changed this formulation and states that it must be such that it will not interfere with the normal conditions of use.[294] Both provisions should be interpreted as an indication that the duration of a period of grace must be short, in view of the purpose of the proposed Regulation to ensure a high level of protection of animal and human health and the environment.[295] When the time limit set for the review process expires, which has been extended to 2008, the Member States will have to withdraw all national authorizations that were not issued in accordance with the procedure of Directive 91/414.[296]

5.3 Fragmented implementation

The Plant protection products Directive allows the Commission or Council that a decision not to include an active substance in Annex I can stipulate that the national authorities in their decision to withdraw the authorization may grant a period (established in the Community decision) in which

---

[288] Art. 4 Directive 91/414. A number of other conditions must be met as well.

[289] See the Preamble to Directive 91/414 and Art. 4 Directive 91/414.

[290] Art. 9 Directive 91/414.

[291] Art. 14 Directive 91/414.

[292] Art. 8 (1) Directive 91/414. An exception can be made in case of an emergency, see Art. 8(4) Directive 91/414/EC. Art. 50 Proposal for a Regulation contains the same rule.

[293] Art. 4 (6) Directive 91/414.

[294] Art. 45 Proposal for a Regulation.

[295] Rec. 8 Preamble to Proposal for a Regulation.

[296] Art. 8 (2) Directive 91/414 and Rec. 15 Preamble to Regulation 450/2000.

only 'essential use' is permitted.[297] Essential use means that a product does not have to disappear completely from the market before expiry of a period of grace despite the ban on a substance it contains, because there is no alternative for certain, limited uses in certain Member States.[298] It enables the Member States to protect the interests of farmers that would otherwise be confronted with the disappearance of products for which no alternative exists.[299] The ECJ held in the *Aldicarb* case that the Directive gives the Community institutions sufficient discretionary room to allow for essential use during a reasonable period.[300]

In the *Aldicarb* case, environmental organisations protested in vain against the period granted for essential use lasting until 2007 (while other previously authorized uses had to expire in 2004). The ECJ ranked the objectives of Directive 91/414: the first one is to remove barriers to intra-Community trade in plant products and the second to protect human and animal health and the environment. It considered that the preamble to the Decision clearly shows that the information before the Council was not sufficient to demonstrate that under the proposed conditions of use, plant protection products containing aldicarb satisfy the requirements of Article 5 of the Directive, but that it appeared necessary to allow further essential uses of those products for a limited period and under strict conditions aimed at minimising risk in the absence of efficient alternatives to certain limited uses in certain Member States. The ECJ concluded that the Council had carried out a global assessment of the advantages and drawbacks of the system to be established and that this system was not from any perspective manifestly inappropriate in the light of the objectives pursued.

It is possible that an essential use period expires before any alternatives have been placed on the market.[301] It may therefore not come as a surprise that it appears from the proposal for a Regulation that essential use will continue to be allowed albeit under another name, as it provides for specific rules for plant protection products containing a candidate for substitution. A substance becomes a candidate for substitution if an assessment (for this substance or for another substance) reveals that other active substances are significantly less toxic for consumers or operators or present significantly fewer risks to the environment.[302] The Member States should not issue an authorization for a plant protection product containing a candidate for substitution if a comparative assessment with an authorized plant protection product or a non-chemical control or prevention method that already exists reveals that the alternative is significantly safer

---

[297] Artt. 4 (6) and 8 (1) or 8 (2) Directive 91/414.

[298] Cf. Rec. 10 and Art. 3 Council Decision concerning the non-inclusion of aldicarb in Annex I to Council Directive 91/414/EEC and the withdrawal of authorizations for plant protection products containing this active substance, OJ 2003 L 75/21.

[299] Cf. Rutteman (2002), p. 312-317.

[300] C-316/04 *Stichting Zuid-Hollandse Milieufederatie* v *College voor de toelating van bestrijdingsmiddelen (ZHM II)* [2006] ECR I-8339.

[301] Report 2001, p. 8.

[302] Art. 24 and Rec. 15 Preamble to Proposal for a Regulation.

for human or animal health or the environment and does not present significant economic or practical disadvantages.[303] Moreover, the Member States do not have to recognize authorizations for plant protection products containing a candidate for substitution.[304] This means that the market for plant protection products will remain fragmented.

5.4 Towards a mutual recognition procedure

Both national decisions issued before or during the transition period and national decisions issued in accordance with the dual authorization procedure of the Plant protection products Directive may be subject to mutual recognition. The Directive facilitates mutual recognition, because it prescribes that a Member State should recognize tests and analyses carried out in another Member State and refrain from requiring their repetition, to the extent that other tests may be required due to agricultural, plant health and environmental (including climatic) conditions relevant to the use of the product that are not comparable in the regions concerned.[305] This rule applies not only to national decisions, but also to authorizations issued in accordance with the dual procedure established by Directive 91/414. If the applicant requests mutual recognition in other Member States,[306] they may refuse recognition on the same grounds as for the non-recognition of tests and analyses.[307] Moreover, each Member State may decide whether it needs an essential use exception, thus further preventing the streamlining of mutual recognition.

Despite the possibility of mutual recognition, the Member States can still take national decisions regarding the authorization of plant protection products. First of all, this is due to the possibility to refuse mutual recognition if both the Member State and the Commission decide that the conditions relevant to the use of the product are not comparable. Secondly, this is because authorizations may present variations in the conditions for use. The Directive provides that an authorization may be subject to conditions resulting from the implementation of other measures in accordance with Community law, relating to the conditions for distribution and use of plant protection products. Yet, subject to compliance with the Treaty, an authorization may be accompanied by restrictions on use, arising from differences in dietary patterns. The restrictions must be necessary in order to avoid exposure of consumers of treated products to the risks of dietary contamination in excess of the acceptable daily intake of the residues

[303] Art. 48 Proposal for a Regulation, elaborated in Annex IV Proposal for a Regulation. Note that it also constitutes a ground for withdrawal of an authorization.

[304] Art. 39 (2) Proposal for a Regulation.

[305] Artt. 4 (3) and 10 Directive 91/414. Joined Cases C-260/06 and C-261/06 *Criminal proceedings against Daniel Escalier and Jean Bonnarel* [2007] ECR I-9717. Cf. C-400/96 *Criminal proceedings against Jean Harpegnies* [1998] ECR I-5121.

[306] Art. 10 Directive 91/414/EC.

[307] Art. 10 (1) Directive 91/414.

concerned. Moreover, an authorization may be subject – with the agreement of the applicant – to changes in the conditions of use in order to render, in the regions concerned, any non-comparable agricultural, plant health or environmental (including) climatic conditions irrelevant for the purpose of comparability.[308]

The proposal for a Plant protection products Regulation creates a compulsory mutual recognition procedure. It divides the Member States into three authorization zones (North, Centre and South),[309] within which mutual recognition of the decision of the reference Member State of the same zone will be compulsory. The applicant can choose the reference Member State for each zone, but on request of the reference Member State, the Member States within a zone can cooperate in order to ensure a fair workload. Therefore, it is possible that another Member State agrees to examine the application.[310] The Regulation provides that the Member State rapporteur has to give the other Member State in the same zone the opportunity to submit comments.[311] The holder of an authorization can apply for authorization for the same plant protection product and for the same use in other Member States.[312] The Member State to which the application for mutual recognition is submitted must authorize the plant protection product concerned under the same conditions as the reference Member State of the same zone, but it may impose additional conditions with respect to its use unless the candidate for substitution exception analyzed above applies.[313]

5.5 The dispute settlement procedure

While non-recognition is possible under the Directive, the Member States cannot take a final decision in this regard because the Commission reviews their decision. They have to inform the Commission of cases where they have required repetition of tests and of cases where they have refused to recognize the authorization of a plant protection product issued by another Member State, with respect to which the applicant had claimed comparability, including the grounds on which these decisions were based.[314] The procedure is not framed as a dispute settlement procedure, but it is similar because the Commission decides whether or not comparability exists in accordance with the regulatory procedure.[315] If the Community decision is negative, it will specify the conditions of use under which the non-comparability may be deemed irrelevant. The Member State concerned will then have to accept the tests and analyses or

308 Art. 10 (1) Directive 91/414.

309 Annex I to Proposal for a Regulation.

310 Artt. 33 and 34 Proposal for a Regulation.

311 Art. 34 Proposal for a Regulation.

312 Art. 39 Proposal for a Regulation.

313 Artt. 39 and 40 Proposal for a Regulation.

314 Art. 10 (2) Directive 91/414.

315 Artt. 10 (3) and 19 Directive 91/414/EC.

authorize the product, possibly subject to additional conditions of use, as stipulated by the Community decision. The Commission also reviews (in accordance with the regulatory procedure) the necessity of restricting or prohibiting use and/or sale of a plant protection product.[316] This procedure does not contain any procedural guarantees for the applicant.

Apparently, the proposal for a Plant protection products Regulation does not expect that Member States in the same zone will disagree about authorizations, because it does not prescribe the use of the dispute settlement procedure in case of a refusal of recognition within the same zone. This means that disputes over authorizations can only be settled by consultation or in a committee meeting[317] and may perhaps be resolved by the imposition of different conditions for use. It is also possible that Member States will invoke the safeguard clause of the proposed Regulation in case of disputes.[318] The dispute settlement procedure is foreseen to serve only to settle disputes over applications filed under the simplified procedure in case the Member States dispute that the plant protection product has comparable effects to a plant protection product for which the applicant has obtained access to protected assessment reports, either because the data protection period has expired or because the applicant has been given access to the data by the marketing authorization holder.[319]

5.6 Free movement of authorized plant protection products

The Plant protection products Directive does not provide for a simplified authorization procedure for parallel import of a plant protection product from another Member State. This means that the legality of national measures restricting parallel imports must be examined in the light of Article 28 EC.[320] It follows from the *British Agrochemicals Association* case that the Member States have to facilitate parallel import of plant protection products by authorizing them through a simplified procedure. This rule applies when a plant protection product, which is imported from another Member State where it is covered by a marketing authorization, is nearly identical to a product already authorized in the Member State of importation (the reference product). That is the case if it shares a common origin, is manufactured using the same active ingredient and has the same effects.[321]

[316] Artt. 11 and 19 Directive 91/414.

[317] See above: section 2.4.

[318] Artt. 66-68 Proposal for a Regulation. See above: section 3.2.

[319] Artt. 33-37 and 56-59 Proposal for a Regulation. National courts should settle disputes between the authorization holder and (prospective) authorization holders about the mandatory sharing of the costs of research on vertebrates prior to the end of the data protection period.

[320] This also applies to import from a State belonging to the EEA. Joined Cases C-260/06 and C-261/06 *Criminal proceedings against Daniel Escalier and Jean Bonnarel* [2007] ECR I-9717. See also: section 4.6 of this chapter.

[321] C-100/96 *The Queen* v *Ministry of Agriculture, Fisheries and Food, ex parte: British Agrochemicals Association* [1999] ECR I-1499.

The ECJ extended the application of the rules developed in the medicines cases *Ferring* and *Paranova* to the parallel import of plant protection products when it held in *Commission* v *Germany* that Germany was not allowed to withdraw authorizations for parallel trade after the authorization holder of the reference product had withdrawn their authorization.[322] If the parallel imported plant protection product is not nearly identical to the reference product, the parallel importer has to apply for a normal authorization in the Member State concerned. It could be assumed that the ECJ would also extend its ruling in the medicines case *Kohlpharma* to the parallel import of plant protection products. Instead, the ECJ stuck to its ruling in the *British Agrochemicals Association* case, with the result that the condition of common origin is not contrary to Article 28 EC.[323] The *Kohlpharma* ruling did not supersede the *British Agrochemicals Association* ruling, because the Plant protection products Directive does not contain a similar procedure as the medicines legislation does for the comparison of a generic with a reference product. The Proposed Regulation may end the uncertainty as it contains a specific authorization procedure for parallel trade.[324]

5.7 Conclusions

The prevailing decisions in the area of plant protection products are Community decisions and national decisions, despite the introduction of a mutual recognition procedure. Due to the optional character of mutual recognition, the decisions taken by national authorities will often remain national decisions, as a Member State may refuse recognition of tests or of an authorization when the Commission agrees with it that the conditions of use are not comparable and therefore require additional tests or a different authorization decision. A centralisation trend might develop at the level of the Member States if the proposed Plant Protection Regulation enters into force, as it introduces compulsory mutual recognition within zones. Since non-recognition does not seem an option in the absence of a dispute settlement procedure, these mutual recognition decisions might be best characterized as single licences, but they are not for two reasons. First, it seems naïve to suppose that the Member States will recognize each other's decisions without any disputes arising and second, the Member States will still be able to rely on exceptions to refuse recognition. Therefore, it remains to be seen whether the proposed compulsory mutual recognition will prove successful.

At first sight, it appears that the Plant protection products Directive provides for uniformity, as Community decisions list active substances in the Annex to the Directive, while national authorities may only authorize products containing active substances listed in the Annex. Nevertheless, the regulation of plant protection products is also characterized by fragmentation, for two reasons.

322 C-114/04 *Commission* v *Germany* [2005] ECR I-0000. See also: Section 4.6 of this chapter.

323 C-201/06 *Commission* v *France* [2008] ECR I-0000. See also: Section 4.6 of this chapter.

324 Art. 49a Proposal for a Regulation.

First, many national decisions are not based on Community legislation due to the transition period, which applies until a Community listing decision has been taken. However, the discretionary room of the Member States is limited by the Court's rule that they have to take the criteria of the Directive into account when they take national decisions during the transition period. Second, even when a substance is listed in the Annex to the Directive, 27 different national decisions can be taken on authorization or refusal of a plant protection product containing this active substance because the Directive gives the Member States leeway to pursue their own policy. They may maintain authorizations for products that contain forbidden substances for essential use and refuse recognition of decisions from other national authorities when the conditions relevant to the use of the product are not comparable, although here their discretionary room is limited by the required Commission approval.

The proposed Plant protection products Regulation will change the situation with regard both to mutual recognition and to procedural guarantees. It aims to enhance uniformity by creating three zones in which compulsory mutual recognition decisions will apply, but it remains possible for the Member States to take a national decision by adding specific conditions on use in mutual recognition decisions, by using the candidate for substitution exception or by invoking the safeguard clause. Regarding procedural guarantees, the situation could not but improve as the Directive contains hardly any. For instance, while the Directive states that the Commission may ask the applicant to submit his remarks to a draft decision, the proposed Regulation prescribes that the applicant be heard. By contrast, neither the Directive nor the amended Proposal for a Regulation prescribes that the applicant be heard before a national decision is taken. For the general public, the entry into force of Directive 2003/4/EC improved their access to information, with the exception of confidential elements as mentioned in the current and future plant protection legislation. In addition, the proposed Regulation prescribes that the public be given the opportunity to comment on the draft decision and that their comments be reflected in the statement of reasons.

6 Conclusions

The European Union regulates products through Community decisions and through national decisions, single licences and mutual recognition decisions taken by national authorities. The Commission (or the Council) takes Community decisions in accordance with the regulatory Comitology procedure. These decisions have EU-wide effect if they are addressed to the applicant or to all Member States, but their effect may also be limited to the Member States to which they are addressed. They can be distinguished into Community listing decisions and Community marketing authorizations. Listing decisions occur for instance in the areas of CITES and plant protection products, where they create a common register of approved species and substances, which reduces the discretionary room for the Member States when they take decisions about specimens of these species or products containing these substances in accordance with a so-called dual authorization procedure. Listing decisions that are positive take the form of daughter directives and regulations that amend the Annex to the basic Act, while negative listing decisions take the form of decisions not to amend the Annex. Both are called decisions here, because they both implement the relevant secondary legislation in a concrete case, resulting in a decision to amend the Annex or not.

In general, the Member States issue marketing authorizations, in the form of a national decision, a single licence, or a mutual recognition decision, but the Commission (or the Council) can also issue marketing authorizations – e.g. in the area of medicines and of GMOs. A national decision, e.g. one that authorizes the placing on the market of a plant protection product, has effect in the Member State where it was issued. By contrast, a single licence, such as a CITES import document or a GMO marketing authorization for a GMO flower, is issued in a single Member State but has effect in all the Member States. A mutual recognition decision, e.g. a marketing authorization of a medicine, can be placed between these extremities, because it has effect in the Member State that issued the decision and in each Member State that takes a recognition decision. In theory, mutual recognition allows for non-recognition, but Community legislation can reduce the room for non-recognition by restricting the grounds for non-recognition and by requiring Commission approval, as occurs in the area of plant protection products, or by enabling the Commission to settle disputes between the Member States with a binding decision, as occurs in the area of medicines. Consequently, the Commission (or the Council) also issues marketing authorizations in accordance with the regulatory Comitology procedure. It appears from the reference areas of medicines and GMOs that frequent disputes – even if they are only potential – lead to the abandonment of the 'national' procedure in favour of the Community authorization procedure.

When Community legislation provides for a division of competences between the Member States, disputes between the Member States may arise. The Commission can solve disputes through a binding dispute settlement procedure, in accordance with the regulatory Comitology procedure, if secondary legislation provides for a dispute settlement provision. In the absence of such a provision, the Commission and the Council lack the competence to settle disputes through a binding Community decision. In that case, the Member States have to consult each other to solve a dispute or submit the dispute to the regulatory committee established by the applicable secondary legislation. If they still do not agree, they might consider allowing their national authorities to bring proceedings in another Member State or submitting their dispute to the ECJ under the procedure of Article 227 EC or 239 EC. They may not resort to arbitration to solve a dispute on the application or interpretation of Community law. Perhaps the easiest option is to persuade the Commission to become involved and, if necessary, start the infringement procedure of Article 228 EC.

It is possible to establish for each type of decision its advantages and disadvantages in the decision-making stage from the point of view of their effectiveness in that stage in ensuring free movement and a high level of protection of the environment or public health. It is taken into account that the reference areas demonstrated that the distinction between the various types of European administrative decisions has become a bit blurred, especially as regards decisions taken by national authorities. Therefore, it is noted below where Community legislation may succeed in reducing certain disadvantages.

Community decisions appear advantageous from the point of view of effectiveness, but they also have a disadvantage:

- Community decisions can restore uniformity if non-recognition or disputes that arise for other reasons are settled by a binding Community (authorization) decision that has effect in all the Member States or in all the Member States concerned.
- A Community listing decision can ensure that even if secondary legislation leaves the Member States sufficient discretionary room to take national decisions, these national decisions come close to achieving EU-wide effect.
- Community decisions allow for coordination between the Member States, as the States cooperate with each other and the Commission in the Community procedure and decide by qualified majority.
- In general, a Community decision has EU-wide effect, but a Member State overruled by qualified majority voting can prevent that a Community decision has effect on its territory by invocation of the safeguard clause in the Treaty or in the secondary legislation, as was the case with regard to Community authorized GMOs for food and feed use. This measure is subject to Commission approval in accordance with the regulatory Comitology procedure.

National decisions do not appear to be advantageous from the point of view of effectiveness:

- Each Member State has to take a decision, without any division of competence or coordination to reduce bureaucracy.
- National decisions apply only in the Member State that issued them.
- National decisions may differ from Member State to Member State. This can also be considered an advantage, because it gives the Member States discretionary room concerning the level of protection of public health or the environment, but it is a disadvantage when it results in barriers to free movement of products authorized in other Member States. If national decisions are taken in accordance with harmonized conditions or under a dual authorization procedure, which means that they implement a Community listing decision, they may be sufficiently similar to avoid being an obstacle to free movement.

Single licence decisions appear at first sight advantageous from the point of view of effectiveness, but they also present serious disadvantages:

- A single licence has EU-wide effect, as it applies in all the Member States without any implementing measures being necessary, which means less bureaucracy.[325]
- Non-recognition is virtually impossible in case of a single licence, but in the absence of Community legislation, Member States can impose a permit for use as an additional requirement, as occurs in the area of CITES, which can amount to a de facto non-recognition.
- A single licence decision does not stipulate different conditions of use in each Member State, unless Community legislation allows for coordination between the Member States and the imposition of specific conditions applicable only in certain Member States. Nevertheless, as stated above, Member States may impose specific rules for use or a permit for use as an additional requirement in the absence of Community legislation.
- A single licence decision gives the applicant the choice as to the reference Member State which will assess their application. In a single licence system without coordination, such as CITES, this may lead to a race for the bottom as regards the quality of the decision, because the applicant may choose the Member State where it is easiest to obtain an authorization. Although a single licence system will not necessarily lead the Member States to race for 'minimal results', it may induce applicants to search for the Member State offering such a minimum. However, Community legislation can stipulate that a draft single licence must be circulated to other Member States for approval or for comments in combination with a dispute settlement procedure, as occurs under the GMO Directive.

Mutual recognition decisions may appear slightly less advantageous than single licences from the point of view of effectiveness, but their advantages may well outweigh their disadvantages:

- The EU-wide effect of a mutual recognition decision is only potential, because it only applies in the Member States that took the decision or recognized it. This is a drawback because it allows for fragmentation of the internal market.
- A mutual recognition system allows for the imposition of different conditions of use, because it requires implementation of the foreign, original decision into a recognition decision before gaining effect in another Member State. As long as this does not hinder the free movement of authorized products, it is not a disadvantage.
- The Member States cooperate in a mutual recognition decision system when they review each other's decisions. Mutual recognition implies that a decision does not have EU-wide effect, if a Member State opted for non-

[325] Sydow (2004), pp. 150-151.

recognition, or the applicant did not request recognition in all the Member States, which fragments the market. However, non-recognition is not a final decision if Commission approval is required or if secondary legislation provides for a dispute settlement procedure that leads to a binding Community decision that applies in all the Member States concerned.

- A mutual recognition decision-making system offers applicants the choice of which reference Member State will assess their application. The promise of mutual recognition can create a race to the top, because it provides an incentive to choose a Member State whose authorities deliver correct and quick assessments that other Member States quickly recognize, as the area of medicines demonstrates.[326] This effect may be due to the combination of non-recognition and a binding dispute settlement procedure and in that case it is unlikely that the same effect will occur when mutual recognition is made compulsory, as might be demonstrated when the proposed Plant protection products Regulation enters into effect.

It will be seen in the next chapter to what extent enforcement influences the effectiveness of European administrative decisions.

Concerning procedural guarantees, the right to be heard should be guaranteed in the decision-making stage irrespective of the choice for a specific type of decision. The basic procedural rules governing decision-making can be found in the secondary legislation specific to the sector, which are supplemented by the regulatory procedure of the Comitology Decision when the Commission takes a decision and by national procedural rules when the Member States take a decision. As might be expected, differences will occur regarding the respect for the right to be heard. While sectoral legislation generally provides that the applicant is heard during the authorization procedure, other interested parties are usually forgotten. For instance, the GMO legislation provides that the applicant is heard and provides that the public may comment on draft decisions, but it does not state that their comments should be taken into account. The medicines legislation provides that the applicant or marketing authorization holder be heard, even during the dispute settlement procedure, but the public needs only to be informed that a decision is issued. A real gap occurs in the area of CITES, as the CITES Regulation does not contain any provision on the right to be heard. The Plant protection products Directive allows the Member States to opt for hearing the applicant, while the proposed Regulation will improve this by making it mandatory and by granting the public the right to comment on draft decisions and see their comments reflected in the statement of reasons that accompanies the final decision.

While it can be concluded that the right to be heard is generally respected concerning the applicant, it is alarming that it appears from the reference area of GMOs that this right is not respected at all during the safeguard procedure.

[326] See Cameron Mc Kenna and Andersen Consulting, Cameron-Mc Kenna-Anderson Report 2000 and the EFPIA Survey on the Mutual Recognition Procedure, both available at: http://pharmacos.eudra.org.

Since the Comitology decision does not include any provision on the right to be heard, it depends completely on sector specific secondary legislation, which limits the right to be heard to the authorization procedures. Since the right to be heard may also be guaranteed subsequently, for instance in case of safeguard or emergency measures, it is unfortunate that there is no provision to that effect to be found. It is also remarkable that secondary legislation hardly assigns other individuals any rights apart from the duty to make the decision and the summary of the assessment report public and occasionally the opportunity to comment on draft decisions, although these comments do not have to be reflected at all in the final decision. In the absence of a legal basis in secondary legislation, one depends on procedural guarantees established in national law or in the case law of the Community courts. It will be seen in the next chapter to what extent the legislation provides for procedural guarantees in the enforcement stage, while the chapters on judicial review will reveal what the impact is of a lack of procedural guarantees in the decision-making stage on judicial protection and to what extent the judicial review provisions of the Aarhus Convention may improve this in the area of environmental law.

CHAPTER 3

Enforcement

As the Commission put it in its White Paper on Good Governance, ultimately the impact of European Union rules depends on the willingness and capacity of Member State authorities to ensure that the rules are transposed and enforced effectively, fully and on time. The Commission suspects that in general, the Member States do not dedicate enough resources to ensure effective implementation of Community law. It has the impression that the feeling persists in the Member States that Community rules are 'foreign law'.[1] The effectiveness of European law is impaired if enforcement is indeed the Achilles' heel of European law.[2] If an enforcement deficit regarding EC product regulation occurs in one Member State, it can have Community-wide and even global effects due to the open borders of the internal market. On the basis of Article 10 EC, which obliges the Member States to take all appropriate measures to ensure fulfilment of the obligations arising from the Treaty or resulting from action taken by the institutions of the Community, it cannot be excluded that an enforcement deficit occurs, because it leaves the Member States ample discretion regarding their enforcement efforts. This may result in divergent enforcement of Community law,[3] as the considerable differences in the extent to which Member States comply with their Treaty obligations suggest.[4]

The question is whether the rules that govern the enforcement of European administrative decisions enable effective enforcement of EC product regulation while also complying with procedural guarantees.[5] In order to answer this question, in this chapter the enforcement of European administrative decisions will be analyzed in the context of the reference areas, following the enforcement sequence of control, emergency measures and (reparatory) sanctions.[6] Since the focus of this book is on the European legislation governing the regulatory activities of the administrative authorities, the rules that enable the imposition of punitive sanctions on the offender will hardly be considered.[7] Instead, this chapter will analyse in particular which authority monitors compliance and imposes reparatory sanctions, including the withdrawal of decisions, how administrative enforcement actions and decisions can gain EU-wide effect and which procedural guarantees apply. On the basis of these characteristics, various types of public enforcement can be distinguished, which each have their advantages and disadvantages, as will be seen in the reference areas. Finally, conclusions will be drawn about the qualities and gaps of the enforcement of European administrative decisions as they occur in the reference areas process concerning both the effectiveness and the procedural guarantees offered.

---

1 White Paper on Good Governance, Brussels 25.7.2001, COM (2001) 428 final, p. 25.

2 Cf. Somsen (1996), p. x.

3 Harding (1997), pp. 19-21.

4 E.g. 21 Annual Report on Monitoring the Application of Community Law (2003), COM (2004) 839 final.

5 Harding (1997), pp. 19-24.

6 The enforcement risks are assessed using the 'Table of Eleven', A versatile tool, available at: www.justitie.nl/images/English%20version%20versatile%20%tool%20act2006_tcm34-9098.pdf

7 See *inter alia*: Luchtman (2007), Jansen and Langbroek (2007), Vervaele (1999 C), Berg (1999), Veldkamp (1998).

1 Types of public administrative enforcement

Administrative enforcement action serves to force parties to comply with Community product legislation, respectively national law transposing Community product legislation.[8] This consists of compliance control and – in case of non-compliance – the imposition of reparatory or punitive sanctions.[9] The difference between reparatory and punitive sanctions is that the former aim at ending an illegal situation and – if possible – restoring the legal situation, while the latter aim to punish the offender.[10] In order to protect the rights of those faced with administrative enforcement action, the authorities should comply with procedural rules. Other procedural rules establish a division of competence between the administrative authorities of the Member States and the Community institutions or bodies. It will be seen below that administrative enforcement action – compliance control, emergency measures and sanctions – can be grouped into a typology.

1.1 Classification

Although the classical distinction between direct and indirect enforcement suggests that Community law can be enforced in two different ways, it is possible to distinguish four types of public administrative enforcement control. Similarly to the creation of European administrative decisions, their enforcement can be distinguished on the basis of the Community authority or national authority that acts and on the basis of the division of competences between the Member States. It will be seen in the reference areas to what extent there is a relation between a choice for a particular type of decision and for a particular type of enforcement. Self-enforcement, which refers to enforcement actions taken by private individuals, is excluded from this typology because it does not belong to public administrative enforcement.[11] However, it will be seen in the reference areas that self-enforcement can complement public enforcement as market participants – in particular the authorization holders – are in the best position to guarantee that their products are in compliance and should notify the competent authorities if anything is wrong.

Direct control means that the Commission (or a Community body acting on its behalf) takes enforcement action against individual parties (if this is directed against a Member State, it is called supervision). Indirect control means that national authorities take enforcement action. Instead of two types of control, public administrative enforcement can be further distinguished into Community control (or direct control), national control, home state control and network control. National control means that each administrative authority takes enforce-

---

8 Curtin and Mortelmans (1994), p. 428.

9 Vervaele (1999), p. 60.

10 Jans *et al.* (2007), p. 231.

11 E.g. Somsen (2000), pp. 311-360 and Widdershoven (1999), pp. 235-243.

ment action on its own territory. This can easily clash with the free movement rules, but it can be well suited to areas of Community law that do not include a market integration element.[12] If a product moves through the EU, it may be the subject of checks in the Member State of origin ('home state') and in the Member State of destination ('host state'). Both checks may be legitimate, but they double the burden on products that move through the EU. Therefore, home state control assigns the home state the responsibility for the control of the goods.[13] It should be noted that home state control requires mutual assistance between Member States when the object of control is located outside the home state.[14] Network control aims to ensure joint action and therefore relies on a flexible division of competence between the Member States coupled with enforcement cooperation between them, with the Commission or a Community agency acting as focal point of the network.[15]

Figure 3.1 The relationship between the four types of public administrative control

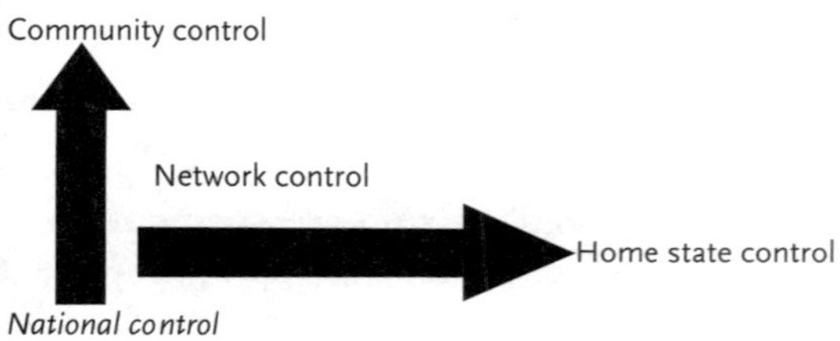

Seen from the angle of national control, Community control (or direct control) and home state control are examples of centralisation, the former vertically, the latter horizontally. At the horizontal – Member State – level, network control is placed as an intermediary between national control and home state control. This is because network control functions with the help of Community institutions and bodies and is based on a flexible division of competence between the national authorities, which inform and assist each other. This offers the advantage of allowing for variable participation between Member States. As will be seen in the reference areas, each type of control can occur in combination with another type of control or become similar to another type of control.

The question is whether a similar classification can also be made for administrative sanction decisions and emergency measures. It is expected that a relation exists with the choice for a type of European administrative decision or for a type of administrative control system. Instead, there is an asymmetry, as the imposition of administrative law sanctions is not extensively harmonized in the area of product regulation.[16] Community law only harmonized the with-

[12] National control in an area of Community law with market integration is also called host state control.

[13] Vervaele (1999 A), p. 136; Weatherill and Beaumont (1999), pp. 608-609.

[14] See section 1.3 below.

[15] It is called a joint action model by Harding (1996), pp. 35-38. See also: Swart (1999), p. 321; Vervaele (1999 A), p. 136 and Klip (1999), pp. 95-107.

[16] Cf. Adriaanse (2008), p. 336.

drawal of an authorization and thus created a European administrative sanction decision. However, these sanction decisions do not cover the whole spectrum of European administrative decisions. The withdrawal of an authorization is either a Community decision or a national decision, which is in accordance with the classical distinction between direct and indirect administration of Community law. As regards other sanctions, such as an administrative fine or a penalty payment, these are also either Community sanctions or national sanctions. The same is true for emergency measures, which are either Community measures or (temporary) national measures.

Figure 3.2 The relationship between the two types of sanction decisions and emergency measures

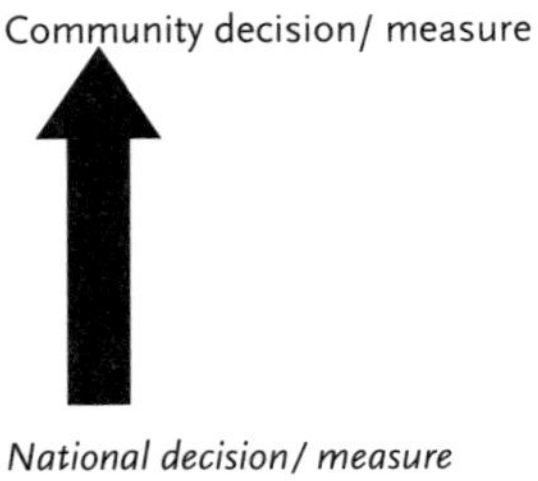

Seen from the angle of national sanction decision/ measure, the Community sanction decision or measure is an example of centralisation. A rare example of centralisation, in so far as Community sanction decisions about regulated products are concerned – the withdrawal of authorizations being the main exception to this rule –, while Community emergency measures are common. At the Member State level it is remarkable that only the national decision or measure is present. This is because the Member States can only effectuate sanctions or emergency measures within their own territory in the absence of Community legislation that enables the mutual recognition of decisions or their cross-border effectuation. Community legislation that applies to regulated products does not provide for a division of competence or mutual recognition of administrative sanction decisions or emergency measures. This means that administrative sanction decisions or emergency measures concerning regulated products can only be recognized and effectuated by another Member State on the basis of a bilateral agreement to that effect.

1.2 Enforcement action by national authorities

The enforcement of EC product regulation is primarily in the hands of the Member States, despite its Community dimension.[17] In a system of national control, each Member State enforces Community law on its own territory.[18] It follows from the case law of the ECJ that each Member State has to enforce Community law in order to ensure its effectiveness and has to proceed

[17] Jans *et al.* (2007), p. 200.

[18] The IPPC Directive is enforced in this manner, for instance. See: Blomberg and Michiels, (2005) pp. 181-208.

with the same diligence as when they enforce national law.[19] The realization of the internal market requires for that purpose that the Member States overcome territorial boundaries instead of remaining legal islands.[20] In order to extend the effect of enforcement beyond the territorial borders that confine the powers of the national authorities, the national legal systems – set up for enforcement within the national territory – had to be adapted to allow for enforcement on the internal market.[21] This adaptation led to the development of home state control and network control, which both constitute examples of integrated enforcement.[22]

In a system of home state control, the state where a product is produced or imported into the EU is responsible for its control.[23] The strong point of home state control is that one national administration enforces EC law on behalf of all Community citizens, not only its own.[24] Since a systematic second inspection is unlawful, the host Member States must trust the home state.[25] The weak point of home state control is that this trust may be misplaced. Why would national authorities enforce rules that potentially damage their own companies or traders to the benefit of out-of-state consumers?[26] The risk of an enforcement deficit is real, as the national authorities may be induced to deliberate lax enforcement, as that can be justified by pointing towards lax enforcement elsewhere.[27] A means to achieve a level playing field of enforcement is to establish a common framework, but that may not suffice to remove the differences between Member States.[28]

If a host state does not trust the home state, it may not unilaterally, on its own authority, adopt corrective or defensive measures designed to obviate a perceived enforcement deficit in another Member State.[29] The Member States must act within the context of the procedures and legal remedies laid down to that effect by the Treaty, which are starting a safeguard procedure or an infringement procedure against a defecting Member State. The alternative is that a Member State complains to the Commission in the hope that the Commission will start an infringement procedure or that citizens bring proceedings against the national authorities of the defecting Member State. Yet

---

[19] C-68/88 *Commission* v *Greece (Greek maize)* [1989] ECR 2965.

[20] Vervaele (1999), p. 361.

[21] Vervaele (1999 C), p. 361.

[22] Integrated enforcement should be distinguished from an integrated approach to enforcement, which means that there must be a direct relationship between the norm setting, the application and the enforcement, as the enforceability of norms must be taken into account in all stages. See: Vervaele (1999 C), p. 366.

[23] C-132/05 *Parmigiano Reggiano* [2008] ECR I-0000.

[24] Weatherill (2002), pp. 68-69.

[25] C-251/78 *Denkavit* [1979] ECR 3369 and subsequent case law. See: Craig and De Burca (2007), p. 703.

[26] Weatherill (2002), pp. 68-69; Vervaele (1992), pp. 14-15.

[27] Weatherill (2002), pp. 68-69; Vervaele (1992), pp. 14-15.

[28] Shapiro (1999), pp. 28-29; Harding (1997), pp. 5-24.

[29] E.g. C-5/94 *Hedley Lomas* [1996] ECR I-2553 and C-111/03 *Commission* v *Sweden* [2005] ECR I-8789.

these actions have in common that they take place after an infringement has occurred and cannot be used preventively.[30]

Administrative cooperation is expected to improve the enforcement efforts of the Member States.[31] This consists first and foremost of information exchange. If a Member State discovers an irregularity, it informs the Commission or the relevant Community agency, which on its turn informs the other Member States. The operation of rapid alert networks, such as RAPEX[32] and CIS,[33] facilitate the rapid exchange of information between the Member States. The Commission or a Community agency acts as a focal point to manage the flow of information in these databases.[34]

Figure 3.3 Information exchange in a system of network control[35]

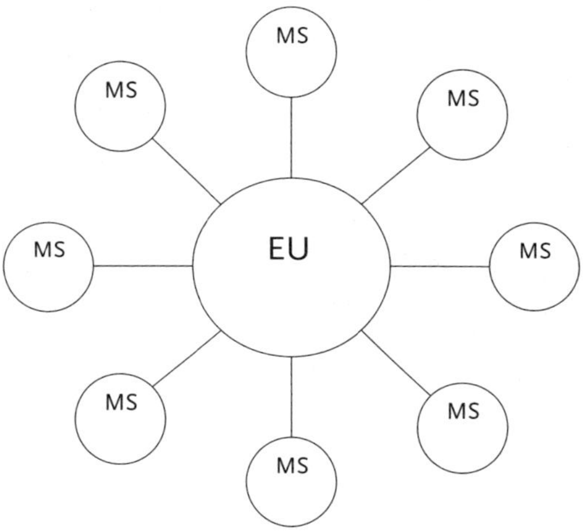

In a system of network control, a single Member State can take enforcement action for all other Member States, but the exchange of information may also trigger joint action. Administrative cooperation in a network control system thus extends the effect of control in one Member State to the other Member States (and beyond the EU if necessary). Network control can therefore be expected to improve enforcement where the object of regulation has a transbound-

30 Cf. Weatherill (2002), p. 68.

31 E.g. Communication from the Commission to the Council, the European Parliament, the European Economic and Social Committee and the Committee of the Regions, A Single Market for Citizens, Interim Report to the 2007 Spring European Council, COM (2007) 60 final and Report from the Commission to the Council and the European Parliament on Cooperation between administrations for the enforcement of internal market law, COM (1996) 20 final.

32 RAPEX was set up by Council Decision 84/133/EEC and incorporated in Directive 2001/95EC on general product safety. For the rapid alert systems in other areas, see the sections on GMOs and medicines in this chapter. For the medical device rapid alert system see: Frank (2003).

33 CIS was established by Council Regulation 515/97 on mutual assistance between the administrative authorities of the Member States and cooperation between the latter and the Commission to ensure the correct application of the law on customs and agricultural matters.

34 The programme IDABC, established by Decision 2004/387/EC, stimulates the exchange of electronic data between public administrations, businesses and citizens.

35 Sommer (2003), p. 6.

ary character, is of Community interest[36] and joint action is required. It is the sharing of information and the flexible division of competences between the Member States that makes network control less vulnerable to an enforcement deficit in one of the Member States. For example, in more than half of the cases in 2005 and 2006, the information exchange about dangerous products started with notifications from the five most active Member States: Germany, Hungary, Greece, the UK and Spain.[37] Unfortunately, network control systems operate independently and therefore do not necessarily connect the competent administrative authorities in one area with the other administrative authorities, let alone with the judicial authorities.[38]

Procedural rules

In the area of EC product regulation, secondary legislation does not necessarily elaborate compliance control and sanctions in detail, the most notable exception being the withdrawal of European administrative decisions. Although the Community legislator may not provide for detailed enforcement provisions, secondary legislation may oblige the Member States to ensure that the competent authorities have specific enforcement powers[39] and to sanction breaches of Community law with specific administrative law sanctions.[40] For the time being, the procedural rules that govern the enforcement of Community law in the area of product legislation are mostly national. These national procedural rules should comply with the common standards and cooperation obligations regarding the enforcement of Community law developed in the case law of the Community courts on the basis of Article 10 EC.[41]

As regards procedural guarantees, it is settled case law that the enforcement of Community law by the Member States should be in compliance with fundamental rights,[42] the general principles of Community law (in particular the rights of defence)[43] and the four freedoms.[44] The administrative authori-

36 Veldkamp (1999), p. 250. Van Rijn (1993), p. 159.

37 See: 'Keeping European Consumers Safe', 2006 Annual Report on the Operation of the Rapid Alert System for non-food consumer products RAPEX, Luxembourg: Office for Official Publications, 2007, p. 14.

38 See: Commission Staff Working Document Report from the Commission Mid-term evaluation of the Customs 2007 programme, SEC (2006) 35, p. 7; See for the cooperation between the administrative authorities and the judicial authorities Luchtman (2007), pp. 639-702 in particular.

39 See: Adriaanse (2008), pp. 328, 329.

40 E.g. C-240/90 *Germany* v *Commission (Mutton)* [1992] ECR I-5383. See about The competence of the Community to prescribe criminal sanctions: C-176/03 *Commission* v *Council* [2005] ECR I-7879 and C-440/05 *Commission* v *Council* [2007] ECR I-9097. See also: Ortlep and Widdershoven (2005), pp. 159-176.

41 See: Jans *et al.* (2007), pp. 187-238.

42 E.g. C-112/00 *Schmidtberger* [2003] ECR I-5659 and C-94/00 *Roquette Freres* [2002] ECR I-9011.

43 E.g. C-29/95 *Pastoors and Trans-Cap* [1997] ECR I-285, C-274/96 *Bickel* [1998] ECR I-7637 and C-210/00 *Käserei Champignon Hofmeister* [2002] ECR I-6453. See: Jansen and Langbroek (2007), pp. 27-50.

44 E.g. C-378/97 *Wijsenbeek* [1999] ECR I-6207 and C-348/96 *Calfa* [1999] ECR I-11.

ties should take the guarantees of the ECHR into account when they enforce Community law.[45] These guarantees apply in particular when their enforcement action is aimed to enable the imposition of a punitive sanction such as an administrative fine, because punitive sanctions constitute a criminal charge in the sense of Article 6 EHCR. In addition, the ECJ has established that if the administrative authorities react to an infringement by taking an individual measure adversely affecting a person, they have to respect the right to be heard, the right to be informed, the duty to act impartially and the duty to state reasons.[46] And sanctions imposed on breaches of primary or secondary Community law must at least be equivalent and in any event be effective, dissuasive and proportionate.[47]

In order to enable a transfer of the case (and the evidence) from administrative to criminal enforcement, the administrative authorities have to respect the rights of defence during the period of inspection.[48] Indeed, a transfer of the case should not endanger the individual rights of the offender, in particular his right to the presumption of innocence and the privilege against self-incrimination.[49] Sufficient respect for the ECHR standards requires convergence of the administrative rights of defence with the criminal rights of defence.[50] Convergence is also necessary if the administrative authorities want to impose an administrative fine, because an administrative fine qualifies as a punitive sanction and therefore falls within the definition of a criminal charge in the sense of Article 6 ECHR.[51] In the absence of harmonization, differences between Member States regarding the rights of defence can hinder punitive enforcement in cross-border cases.[52] It can lead to excess enforcement when an accumulation of sanctions occurs,[53] but also to a shortage of enforcement when punitive sanctions cannot be imposed due to insufficient respect for the rights of defence by the Member State that collected the evidence on request of the Member State that wanted to impose a punitive sanction.[54]

45 Sherlock (1996), pp . 48-52 and 55-57.

46 See: J. Schwarze (2004), pp. 85-105, pp. 91- 94 in particular. See also: Jansen and Langbroek (2007), pp. 27-38.

47 C-68/88 *Commission* v *Greece (Greek maize)* [1989] ECR 2965; C-240/90 *Germany* v *Commission (Mutton)* [1992] ECR I-5383; C-265/95 *Commission* v *France (Spanish strawberries)* [1998] ECR I-963. See also: C-304/02 *Commission* v *France* [2005] ECR I-6263.

48 E.g. ECtHR 17 December 1996 *Saunders* v *UK* Series A No 43/1994/490/572. See: Jansen and Langbroek (2007), pp. 63 and 66.

49 Swart (1999), p. 328.

50 Cf. Opinion Advocate General Colomer in C-387/97 *Greece* v *Commission* [2000] ECR I-5047. See: Jans *et al.* (2007), pp. 190-193.

51 E.g. ECtHR 21 February 1984 *Oztürk* v *Germany* Series A 73 No 9/1982/55/84. See: Sherlock (1996), pp. 48-52.

52 Widdershoven (1999 A); Luchtman (2007), pp. 639-702.

53 Dirkzwager (1999), pp. 277-279.

54 See: Vervaele (1995), pp. 14-16.

1.3 The Mutual Assistance Regulation

The Mutual Assistance Regulation establishes far-reaching cooperation duties between the customs authorities, which go beyond mere information exchange as they also enable operational cooperation.[55] It is based on Articles 43 and 235 EC and its scope is limited to the protection of the financial interests of the Community in the enforcement of customs and agricultural legislation. That raises the question whether this Regulation can play a role in the enforcement of product regulation. That seems likely in view of the Commission's new policy challenge that customs authorities should facilitate legitimate trade while protecting the Community from unfair and illegal trade by combating counterfeiting and piracy and securing the safety of the supply chain through common risk management and information exchange.[56] Surprisingly, the Proposal for a new Mutual Assistance Regulation does not take stock of this new challenge despite taking Article 135 EC as a legal basis, which provides a legal basis for customs cooperation in general and could therefore be used for customs cooperation to protect various Community interests. Nevertheless, the Mutual Assistance Regulation can facilitate customs control of EC product regulation when secondary legislation declares it applicable. This has occurred with regard to foodstuffs, toys, medicines for human use and veterinary medicines, in order to check conformity with the rules on product safety,[57] and with regard to counterfeit products in general.[58]

The Mutual Assistance Regulation establishes that the customs authorities can exchange information through the customs information system ('CIS'), where they can track, store and share records of traders with the aim to prevent, investigate and prosecute operations which are in breach of the applicable legislation.[59] In addition, the Mutual Assistance Regulation provides for inspections on request.[60] The customs authorities of a Member State or of the Commission can request the customs authorities in another Member State to keep special watch on persons, goods, storage places, movement of goods or means of transport and report any offences to the requesting customs authority or to the Commission. They can also request an administrative investigation, which can be executed by multinational teams, although the foreign customs authorities and the Commission officials cannot exercise independent enforcement

55 Jans *et al.* (2007), p. 220.

56 Communication from the Commission to the Council and the European Parliament, Community Programmes Customs 2013 and Fiscalis 2013, COM (2005) 111 final, p. 3.

57 Art. 8 Council Regulation 339/93 on checks for conformity with the rules on product safety in the case of products imported from third countries and Commission Decision 93/583/EC establishing the list of products provided for in Art. 8 of Regulation 339/93 OJ 1993 L279/39.

58 Regulation 1383/2003.

59 Artt. 23 to 42 Regulation 515/97/EC. See: Klip and Vervaele (2001),p p. 10, 11.

60 Artt. 4 to 16 and 18 Regulation 515/97.

powers.[61] The only limitation is that the information exchange through CIS and the operational cooperation requests remain prerogatives of the customs authorities.[62] They only share information with the competent authorities in these policy areas when a shipment may be, or is, in breach of Community legislation.[63] In other words, the customs authorities operate as one, but they do not operate as one with other administrative authorities.

Procedural guarantees

Information exchange under the Mutual Assistance Regulation is subject to constraints and procedural guarantees in order to ensure that evidence obtained through information exchange or mutual assistance can be invoked as evidence by the competent authorities that receive the information.[64] The collection and processing of personal data must be carried out fairly and lawfully, data must be collected for the purpose of preventing, investigating and prosecuting operations that are in breach of customs or agricultural legislation and must not be processed in a manner incompatible with these purposes. Personal data is included only for the purpose of sighting and reporting, discreet surveillance or specific checks. It may be included only if, especially on the basis of prior illegal activities, there is evidence to suggest that the person concerned has committed, is committing or will commit actions in breach of customs or agricultural legislation, which are of particular relevance at Community level. Moreover, the data must be adequate, relevant and not excessive in relation to the purposes for which they are processed, be accurate and kept up to date and in a form that permits identification of data subjects for no longer than is necessary for the envisaged purposes. National legislation or internal rules applicable to the Commission should guarantee adequate personal data protection[65] and each Member State has to designate a national supervisory authority responsible for personal data protection to carry out independent supervision of data included in CIS.[66]

It is alarming that it is not clear how a person may become aware of the inclusion of his personal data in CIS, nor whether the collection and exchange of data about him occurred 'fairly and lawfully', which in themselves are vague concepts that would benefit from further definition.[67] The Regulation only provides that if a person requests access to his personal data, a Member State must grant access, unless communication would be likely to prejudice

61 Artt. 13 to 16 and 9 to 12 Regulation 515/97. See: 'Communication on the role of customs in the management of external borders', COM (2003) 452 final.

62 Communication from the Commission to the Council and the European Parliament, Community Programmes Customs 2013 and Fiscalis 2013, COM (2005) 111 final, p. 7.

63 Art. 8 (3) Regulation 515/97.

64 Artt. 12, 16, 23, 24 to 27 and 35 Regulation 515/97.

65 Art. 34 Regulation 515/97.

66 Art. 37 Regulation 515/97.

67 See: Verheij (1995), pp. 90-96.

the prevention, investigation or prosecution of operations which are in breach of customs or agricultural legislation, or where refusal constitutes a measure necessary to safeguard national security, defence, public safety and the rights and freedoms of others. Of course, the Member States will refuse access during periods in which action is being taken for the purposes of sighting and reporting or discreet surveillance. Since the Commission is not directly involved in enforcement action, it can only refuse access where such refusal constitutes a measure necessary to safeguard the rights and freedoms of others. It is possible that a person requests access to personal data that has been supplied by another CIS partner. Then, the decision to give him access can be taken only after the supplying partner has been given the opportunity to state its position. If access reveals that personal data are factually inaccurate or were included or stored in CIS contrary to the aim of CIS or the principles for data inclusion and storage, any person is entitled to have his personal data corrected or deleted by each CIS partner.[68]

1.4 Enforcement action by Community institutions and bodies

Direct enforcement, in the sense that the Commission monitors and sanctions citizens,[69] rarely occurs in the field of EC product regulation. The example of medicines reveals that this assertion may not hold true for much longer, as the Commission has the power to impose financial sanctions on holders of Community marketing authorizations for medicines (to be further elaborated in the medicines section of this chapter).[70] When the Commission imposes a sanction, the Court's rule that these sanctions be effective, dissuasive and proportionate applies as well, even if it is not explicitly mentioned in the text of the legislation.[71] Usually, the Commission is involved in the enforcement of EC product regulation in order to facilitate the coordination of enforcement action and the withdrawal of European administrative decisions, as the obligation of loyal cooperation applies as well to enforcement.[72] The Commission can also contribute to the quality of enforcement by training, information and transparency campaigns, the creation of twinning arrangements between national administrations of old and new Member States, the publication of a scoreboard and by placing implementation issues on the agenda of committees, which can result in new guidelines being issued.[73]

68 Art. 36 Regulation 515/97.

69 Direct enforcement is based on Art. 211 EC and occurs, for instance, in the field of competition. See: Dannecker and Jansen (2004).

70 Regulation 726/2004 and Commission Regulation 658/2007.

71 E.g. C-210/00 *Kaserei Champignon Hofmeister* [2002] ECR I-6453.

72 E.g. C-2/88 *Zwartveld* [1990] ECR I-3365. See: Jans *et al.* (2007), p. 230 and David (2003), pp. 264-266.

73 Commission Communication: Better Monitoring of the Application of Community Law, COM (2002) 725 final, pp. 5-6.

The Commission's main enforcement role is to supervise the implementation efforts of the Member States.[74] Whereas the Commission systematically enforces non-transposition cases, the same is not true concerning infringement proceedings against weak enforcement.[75] The extreme character that weak enforcement cases often display,[76] may be explained by the fact that the burden of proof lays with the Commission, which has a limited capacity for the monitoring of the application and enforcement of EC law and therefore depends on complaints and national reports about implementation.[77] The introduction of the Article 228 EC procedure, which enables the Commission to request the imposition of sanctions on Member States that do not comply with an infringement ruling, improved the effectiveness of the infringement procedure, as this procedure seems to encourage the Commission to pursue more often infringement cases relating to the application and enforcement of EC law.[78] It seems that the Commission no longer waits and sees in cases where a Member State is unwilling to comply with a request to end an infringement.

Nevertheless, it remains uncertain to what extent Community supervision can contribute to the creation of a level playing field in implementation efforts. The Commission reports reveal that most infringement cases do not proceed any further than informal warnings. Only a small number of them are referred to the ECJ. On the one hand, this can be interpreted as a demonstration of the importance of the administrative stage as an instrument of cooperation between the Member States and the Commission in the monitoring of the application and enforcement of Community law.[79] This seems all the more so, since the Commission reports also reveal that when the Commission decides to bring a case before the ECJ, it usually wins.[80] Therefore, despite its slow pace, the infringement procedure is arguably not without success for the implementation of Community law.[81] On the other hand, this can also be seen as a confirmation of the hypothesis that – having to bear the burden of proving the infringement – the Commission only proceeds when the infringement is manifest.[82]

---

74 Art. 211 EC.

75 See: Communication from the Commission to the Council, the European Parliament, the European Economic and Social Committee and the Committee of the Regions, Internal Market Strategy, Priorities 2003-2006, COM 2003 (238) final, p. 29. E.g. C-364/03 *Commission* v *Greece*, [2005] ECR I-0000.

76 E.g. C-68/88 *Commission* v *Greece (Greek maize)* [1989] ECR 2965.

77 Hatje (1998), p. 139, Gil Ibanez (1999), p. 287.

78 E.g. C-361/05 *Commission* v *Spain* [2007] ECR I-71, C-423/05 *Commission* v *France* [2007] I-47, C-255/05 *Commission* v *Italy* [2007] ECR I-5767.

79 Commission Communication: Better Monitoring of the Application of Community Law, COM (2002) 725 final, p. 5.

80 E.g. Annex to the 23rd Annual Report on Monitoring the Application of Community Law (2005), COM (2006) 416 final. This includes cases in which a Member State ceases the infringement while the action is pending before the ECJ, because they do not lead to the Commission losing the case or hearing the case declared inadmissible.

81 Van Rijn (1993), p. 147.

82 Woldendorp (2002), p. 130-136. E.g. C-287/03 *Commission* v *Belgium* [2005] ECR I-3761.

Procedural rules

In general, the Commission does not have a clear mandate to assess the functioning of national authorities in the absence of alleged infringements.[83] In that case, the Commission takes action when complaints, reports or inspections reveal that a Member State may not be meeting its Community obligations. Secondary legislation increasingly allows the Commission to pursue a proactive supervision strategy instead of acting on complaints.[84] This is possible when secondary legislation includes reporting obligations that go beyond transposition. The Member States may 'put the rope around their own necks' when filling in the forms to report on their implementation efforts, which may even be based on their Commission approved national enforcement plans. Of course, national reports can state that enforcement information is not available, but then the Commission can take action on the basis that a Member State has failed to meet its reporting obligations. Another option is that secondary legislation provides the Commission with its own inspectors, which occurred for instance in the area of food safety, where the Food Veterinary Office ('FVO') may conduct inspections in order to effectively supervise the enforcement efforts of the Member States (to be further elaborated in the GMO section of this chapter).[85]

The Commission generally follows the following procedure: first, the Commission registers a possible infringement and proceeds to examine the case. It sends a letter of formal notice to the Member State concerned and – if it receives an unsatisfactory answer – a reasoned opinion, to which the Member State can respond.[86] This response may again be unsatisfactory. In that case, after this administrative stage, the Commission can bring infringement proceedings before the ECJ[87] and, if necessary, bring a proceeding before the ECJ to obtain interim relief measures.[88] In the first infringement procedure, the Commission cannot ask the ECJ to impose a fine on a Member State to punish it for its breach of Community law or a penalty payment to end the infringement.[89] If a Member State does not improve despite the infringement condemnation, the Commission can bring a second infringement procedure under Article 228 (2) EC, which allows the Commission to ask the Court to impose a penalty payment or a fine (or both) on a Member State that fails to comply with the ECJ judgment in the infringement case (after a written exchange of opinions with the allegedly defecting Member State).[90]

---

83 Allio and Fandel (2006), p. 21.

84 Veldkamp (1999), p. 251.

85 Another notable exception is OLAF. See: Vervaele (1999), Vervaele (1999 B), pp. 331-346 and Hetzer (2004), pp. 1571-8174.

86 Art. 226 EC. See: Van Rijn (1993), p. 145.

87 Commission Communication: Better Monitoring of the Application of Community Law, COM (2002) 725 final, p. 4.

88 E.g. C-76/08 R *Commission* v *Malta* [2008] ECR I-0000.

89 Arnull (2006), p. 48.

90 E.g. C-304/02 *Commission* v *France* [2005] ECR I-6263. See: 'Memorandum on Applying Article 171 [now 228] of the EC Treaty' OJ 1996 C 242/6.

2 Genetically modified organisms

The enforcement of the GMO legislation differs depending on whether the GMOs are intended for food or feed use or for other uses. The enforcement of the rules concerning GMOs for other uses, which are placed on the market in accordance with single licences or Community authorizations, is largely left to the discretion of the Member States. They cooperate in the context of the rapid alert system RAPEX to share information about GMO consumer goods and in the context of the pharmacovigilance rapid alert system to share information about biotechnological medicines.[91] By contrast, the Member States have to enforce the rules governing GMOs for food and feed use in accordance with a European framework. The competent authorities use RASFF, the rapid alert system for food and feed, while the customs authorities use CIS to mutually exchange information and they offer each other mutual assistance. Finally, Community supervision of the enforcement of national authorities of the rules on GMOs for food and feed use improved due to the inspections by the Food and Veterinary Office ('FVO'). Apart from these differences, the enforcement of both types of GMO has in common the dependency on self-enforcement.

The example of Bt10 maize illustrates the difficulties encountered in the enforcement of GMO legislation. In 2005, Syngenta (a GMO producer) reported to the American and European authorities that Bt10 maize had contaminated Bt11 maize. Bt11 maize is authorized in the EU for feed and food use and identical to Bt10 except for its antibiotics resistance, which was the reason why Bt10 maize is not authorized in the EU. An estimated 1,000 tonnes of Bt10 were shipped to the EU between 2001 and 2004. The illegal strain was never identified, since no detection method was available for that purpose. The infringement only came to light after Syngenta had notified the authorities of the contamination. The Commission reacted by requesting Syngenta to develop a detection method to identify Bt10, while adopting an emergency measure, which blocked all US exports of maize animal feed, unless a certificate from an approved laboratory could prove the absence of Bt10.[92] This measure induced the Irish customs authorities to reject a possibly contaminated shipment of Bt11 maize, which was to be unloaded in an Irish port.

2.1 Between home state control and network control

The GMO legislation does not make a clear distinction between enforcement at the EU borders and on the internal market, nor does it seem to ensure a clear division of competence between the Member States. Perhaps this can be explained by the fact that most GMOs in the EU are authorized by the Commission (or the Council) and imported from third countries. This means that the customs authorities of the Member State of entry play an important role

[91] See section 4.3 below.

[92] Commission Decision 2005/317/EC, repealed by Commission Decision 2007/157/EC.

in the control of the GMOs.[93] The authorities that have to enforce GMO legislation rely on self-enforcement because they cannot easily distinguish GMOs from regular products. Therefore, operators that handle GMOs should comply with specific labelling and traceability requirements in order to create an artificial distinction. In addition, the authorization holder has to monitor environment and health effects. The Member States are responsible for compliance control regarding these obligations.

Labelling and traceability

Since GMOs are hard to distinguish from ordinary products, the labelling and traceability requirements were created to facilitate post-marketing monitoring and targeted withdrawal of GMOs as products or in products and of GMOs for food or feed use.[94] The enforcement of the labelling and traceability requirements primarily relies on the operators. Each operator is obliged to inform its customers that the product contains or consists of GMOs and has a unique identifier (a code),[95] while operators of non-GMOs must be able to show the competent national authorities the evidence of the appropriate steps that they have taken to avoid the presence of GMOs.[96] In order to enable consumer choice, operators should ensure that the label or the display states that the product is or contains a GMO (above the threshold of 0,9%), e.g. flowers with genetically modified carnation, genetically modified canned maize or bread with a genetically modified ingredient.[97] The threshold applies indiscriminately, as the ECJ has ruled that not even the labels of baby foods need to indicate the adventitious presence of GMOs as long as the presence of GMOs remains below the threshold.[98] Nevertheless, it enables consumer choice only to some extent, because the meat of animals fed with GMOs does not require any labelling.

The Member States are responsible for ensuring compliance with the labelling and traceability requirements, but they depend on the statements of the traders as to the contents of a shipment, because it is not only hard to distinguish a GMO from an ordinary product, but also from another GMO. The limited traceability of GMOs makes it near to impossible for the authorities to detect illegal strains of GMO without the assistance of the operator. Nevertheless, the Labelling and Traceability Regulation orders the Member States to ensure that national authorities carry out inspections and other control measures, including sample checks and testing, without creating a division of competence.[99] In addition, the GMO Regulation provides that the Commission

---

93 See section 3.1 and 5.1 below.

94 Regulation 1830/2003.

95 Artt. 3 (4), 4 and 8 Regulation 1830/2003.

96 Art. 12 (3) Regulation 1829/2003.

97 Art. 4 (6) Regulation 1830/2003 and Artt. 12 (2) and 24 (2) Regulation 1829/2003.

98 C-132/03 *Ministero della Salute* v *Coordinamento delle asscociazioni per la difesa dell'ambiente e dei diritti degli utenti e dei consumatori (Codacons)* [2005] ECR I-4167.

99 Art. 9 Regulation 1830/2003 and Commission Regulation 65/2004.

contributes to the national enforcement efforts through the establishment of technical guidelines and a central register, which contains all available sequencing information and reference material for authorized GMOs and relevant information, where available, on GMOs not authorized within the EU. This register is only accessible to the competent authorities.[100] It depends on close cooperation between the competent authorities and the customs authorities whether this can contribute to the effectiveness of customs control, which can use CIS to mutually exchange information about GMOs for food and feed use.

Common framework for GMOs for food and feed use

The GMO Directive hardly mentions enforcement and it neither provides for an information exchange system nor for mutual assistance obligations. It only obliges the Member States to organize inspections and other control measures as appropriate and in case it discovers unauthorized GMOs, to take remedial action and inform the Commission and the other Member States, which points to network control.[101] By contrast, the GMO Regulation is enforced in accordance with Regulation 882/2004, which provides for a common framework for official controls on compliance with food (and feed) law and therefore also applies to GMOs for food and feed use.[102] It obliges the Member States to ensure that official controls are carried out regularly, on a risk basis and with appropriate frequency.[103] It reminds them that products intended for another Member State should be monitored with the same care.[104] Since GMOs for food and feed use, usually originate from a third country, the GMO Regulation adds to this the obligation that the Member States inspect operators[105] and monitor shipments from third countries.[106] It does not prescribe exactly how controls should occur, as this is elaborated in multi-annual national plans to be approved by the Commission. Progress is monitored by the Member States through national audits.[107] Regulation 882/2004 also contains the obligation that customs authorities and other competent authorities cooperate closely, without further elaborating this.[108]

The controls of GMOs may require mutual assistance.[109] This is only elaborated for GMOs for food or feed use. Regulation 882/2004 prescribes that if the outcome of official controls requires action in more than one Member State, the competent authorities of the Member States concerned have to provide each

[100] Art. 9 Regulation 1830/2003.

[101] Art. 4 (5) Directive 2001/18.

[102] Regulation 882/2004.

[103] Art. 3 Regulation 882/2004.

[104] Art. 3 Regulation 882/2004.

[105] Artt. 3 to 12 Regulation 882/2004.

[106] Artt. 14 to 24 Regulation 882/2004.

[107] Artt. 41 to 44 Regulation 882/2004.

[108] Art. 24 Regulation 882/2004.

[109] See section 3.1 below.

other administrative assistance. This may be spontaneous or on request. Spontaneous assistance is limited to information exchange, on the basis of which the authorities of the informed Member States can take enforcement action.[110] If the competent authorities receive a request for assistance from the competent authorities of another Member State, they have to provide them with all the information and documents necessary to enable them to verify compliance with food law in their jurisdiction. This may also include participation in on-the-spot controls carried out by the officials of another Member State.[111] If officials from the requesting Member State participate in inspections, they are not allowed to exercise the powers conferred on the officials of the requested authority on their own initiative. They only have access to the same premises and documents as the latter and, when asked, must be able to show an identity document and a document of their capacity as administrative authorities.[112]

It is possible that inspections in a Member State may reveal that the GMOs for food or feed coming from another Member State – where they passed customs control or were produced – are not in compliance with Community legislation or create a risk to human or animal health. Regulation 882/2004 elaborates that in that case the host state first has to contact the home state without delay. Then the competent authorities of the home state have to investigate the matter, take all necessary measures and report their enforcement action to the competent authority of the host state. If the competent authority of the host state is not satisfied with the enforcement action taken by the home state, the operational cooperation will go even further. First, the competent authorities have to discuss the issue and find a means of solving their dispute. The Regulation proposes that in this case they could carry out a joint on-the-spot inspection in accordance with the rules on mutual assistance on request. If the competent authorities fail to solve their dispute, they have to inform the Commission.[113] The Regulation does not state what the Commission should do after being so informed, but it seems likely that it will send in representatives of the FVO to solve the dispute.[114]

2.2 Vigilance

Not only the presence of GMOs is monitored, but their effects on human health or the environment may also require monitoring, as risks may emerge after authorization. This is the task of the holder of the authorization, to be executed in accordance with the monitoring plan of the authorization.[115] An authorization of a GMO for food and/or feed use can also include a post-market-

110 Art. 37 Regulation 882/2004.

111 Art. 34 Regulation 882/2004.

112 Art. 36 Regulation 882/2004.

113 Art. 38 Regulation 882/2004.

114 See section 3.5 below.

115 Art. 13 (2) (e) Directive 2001/18 and Art. 5 (5) (b) Regulation 1829/2003.

ing monitoring plan of the food or feed use.[116] If the authorization contains the duty to monitor the effects of the GMO, the authorization holder has to ensure that it is carried out and submit reports to the competent authorities and to the Commission in case of GMOs for other uses (the authority that issued the consent), or only to the Commission in case of GMOs for food or feed use.[117] In addition, authorization holders are obliged to inform the competent authority, respectively the Commission, of any new scientific or technical information that might pose a risk to human health or the environment or influence safety aspects in the use of the food or feed.[118] In particular, they must immediately inform the Commission if the competent authority of a third country restricts or prohibits the placing on the market of the GMO food or feed.[119] The competent authority shares information about GMOs for other uses with the Commission and the other Member States, while the Commission shares information about GMOs for food and feed use with the competent authorities of the Member States.[120]

2.3 Emergency measures

The GMO Directive does not define emergency, but it allows for invocation of the safeguard clause when a Member State has detailed reasons to assume that a particular GMO presents a risk to human health or the environment.[121] It may then provisionally restrict or prohibit the use and/or sale of the GMO on its territory. Moreover, in the event of a serious risk (in other words, an emergency), the Directive prescribes that the Member State must ensure that emergency measures are taken, such as suspension or termination of the placing on the market. The Member State must immediately inform the Commission and the other Member States and state reasons for its decision to take safeguard or emergency measures.[122] The Directive has not established a rapid alert system to that effect, but if the GMO in question is a consumer product, e.g. flowers with a genetically modified carnation, it is possible to use RAPEX to exchange the information.[123] Otherwise, information about GMOs for other uses is exchanged without an official rapid alert system or database. The Commission takes the final decision on the legitimacy of the safeguard or emergency measures in accordance with the regulatory Comitology procedure.[124]

---

116 Artt. 5 (3) (k) and 17 (3) (k) Regulation 1829/2003.

117 Art. 9 (1) Regulation 1829/2003; Art. 20 Directive 2001/18.

118 Art. 20 Directive 2001/18 and Art. 9 (3) and 21 (3) Regulation 1829/2003, respectively.

119 Artt. 9 (3) and 21 (3) Regulation 1829/2003.

120 Artt. 9 (4) and 21 (4) Regulation 1829/2003.

121 Art. 23 Directive 2001/18.

122 Art. 23 Directive 2001/18.

123 Artt. 2 and 11 to 13 Directive 2001/95/EC.

124 Artt. 23 and 30 (2) Directive 2001/18.

The GMO Regulation establishes that a certain situation constitutes an emergency when it is evident that food or feed originating in the EU or imported from a third country is likely to constitute a serious risk to human health, animal health or the environment[125] or when the EFSA concludes in an opinion that an authorization no longer meets the conditions set by the regulation.[126] In case of an emergency that requires immediate action, a Member State has to issue an alert notification through RASFF (the rapid alert system for food and feed) to the Commission, which will transmit it to the other Member States, so that they can take emergency measures as well.[127] If the GMO has been dispatched to a third country, the Commission will give that country appropriate information.[128] The GMO Regulation allows a Member State to adopt temporary emergency measures, provided that it has officially informed the Commission of the need to take emergency measures and the Commission has not yet acted in accordance with the emergency procedure.[129] The Commission will then put the matter before the Standing Committee on the Food Chain and Animal Health to discuss the extension, amendment or abrogation of the national provisional emergency measures.[130] A Member State may maintain its emergency measures until Community measures have been adopted,[131] i.e. until the Commission (or the Council) has extended the measures to other Member States or has amended or revoked them.

The GMO Regulation gives the Commission the power to take emergency measures at the request of a Member State or on its own initiative.[132] The latter category also comprises measures taken after the Commission has received a complaint or a request from a third country. Each authority should operate in accordance with an emergency plan.[133] As a rule, the placing on the market and the use of the food or feed in question will be suspended, but it is also possible that an emergency leads to suspension, modification or withdrawal of the authorization.[134] In emergencies concerning food or feed of EU origin, the Commission may provisionally adopt emergency measures after consulting the

---

125 Art. 53 (1) Regulation 178/2002.

126 The opinion is issued under Art. 10 or Art. 22 Regulation 1829/2003, which refers to Art. 34 Regulation 1829/2003.

127 Art. 50 Regulation 178/2002.

128 Art. 50 Regulation 178/2002. Third countries can participate in RASFF on the basis of agreements with the EU. RASFF can also be used when a competent authority rejects a shipment at the external border of the EU.

129 Artt. 53 and 54 Regulation 178/2002.

130 This is in accordance with the Committee procedure established in Art. 58 Regulation 178/2002, which refers to Art. 5, 7 and 8 Decision 1999/468/EC. The period provided for in Art. 5(6) Decision 1999/468 is 3 months.

131 Art. 54 Regulation 178/2002.

132 Art. 53 (1) Regulation 178/2002.

133 Art. 55 Regulation 178/2002 and Art. 13 Regulation 882/2004.

134 Art. 34 Regulation 1829/2003, referring to Art. 53 and 54 Regulation 178/2002.

Member State(s) concerned and informing the other Member States.[135] If the food or feed originates from outside the EU, no consultation obligation exists. As soon as possible, and no later than 10 working days after the event, the measures must be confirmed, amended, revoked or extended, in cooperation with the Standing Committee on the Food Chain and Animal Health.[136] The Commission decision[137] and the reasons for it must be made public without delay (confidential information excluded).[138]

2.4 Sanctions

If traders report the adventitious presence of an unauthorized GMO in a shipment, they will be confronted with sanctions, such as a Community import ban. Even reporting the presence of authorized GMOs can have negative consequences, because the value of organic or conventional food or feed is higher in the EU than the value of GMO food or feed. This may undermine the willingness of operators to comply with the notification duty.[139] Non-compliance with the labelling and traceability requirements should lead to the imposition of an effective, proportionate and dissuasive sanction.[140] The GMO Directive allows the Member States similar discretion as regards other infringements, as it prescribes that the Member States impose adequate, proportionate and dissuasive sanctions.[141] The GMO regulation does not even contain this reference, but the same rules apply, since the phrase about sanctions merely repeats ECJ case law.[142] Both do not contain any cooperation rules to allow for the cross-border imposition of sanctions, but only elaborate the withdrawal of an authorization.

Both the GMO Directive and the GMO Regulation provide that a marketing authorization can be amended or withdrawn if new scientific or technical information influences the risk assessment.[143] The GMO Directive leaves it to the reference Member State, which takes these decisions in accordance with the same procedure as the authorization procedure. This means that the other Member States are consulted and that if a conflict arises, the Commission (or the Council) will take the final decision.[144] The GMO Regulation provides that the Commission can suspend, modify or revoke an authorization in accordance

135 Art. 53 (2) Regulation 178/2002.

136 In accordance with the Committee procedure established in art. 58 Regulation 178/2002, referring to Art. 5 of Decision 1999/468/EC, in compliance with Art. 7 and 8 thereof. The period provided for in Art. 5(6) is 3 months.

137 Art. 10 Regulation 178/2002.

138 Art. 53 (2) and 52 Regulation 178/2002.

139 Cf. Van der Meulen and Freriks (2006), p. 174.

140 Art. 9 Regulation 1830/2003 and Commission Regulation 65/2004.

141 Art. 33 Directive 2001/18.

142 See section 2.4 of this chapter.

143 Art. 20 Directive 2001/18 and Art. 10 Regulation 1829/2003.

144 Art. 20 Directive 2001/18. See the chapter on decision-making for the authorization procedures.

with the same procedure as the authorization procedure.[145] Since the regular authorization procedure applies, the Commission cannot take a decision without an opinion from the EFSA, which may also issue an opinion on its own initiative or at the request of a Member State.[146] In view of changed circumstances, the authorization holder may also request a modification of the terms of the authorization.[147]

2.5 Community supervision

The Commission's supervision task regarding the GMO Directive is facilitated by the reporting obligations it contains. It prescribes that the Commission is informed through reports with monitoring data from the authorization holder[148] and through reports about the implementation of the GMO Directive from the Member States, which they should submit every three years. The Commission has to publish a summary of the reports from the Member States.[149] In addition, the Commission and the Member States have to meet regularly to exchange information on the experience acquired with regard to the prevention of risks related to the placing on the market of GMOs and other issues, such as the environmental assessment and the consultation and information of the public.[150]

The Commission supervises the Member States' implementation of the GMO Regulation through the general framework for supervision of food and feed law, whose pillars are reporting obligations, Community guidance and Community inspections. The Member States have to submit long-term national plans for approval to the Commission and also report to the Commission the progress as measured in national audits in their annual report on the implementation of the plan.[151] The Commission is also informed through reports with monitoring data from the authorization holder, which the Commission makes available to the Member States and to the public (excluding confidential information).[152] In addition, the Regulation provides a legal basis for the Commission (with the help of the FVO), to prepare rules and guidance to ensure uniform implementation, insofar as necessary.[153] The Commission can monitor whether the Member States effectively apply and enforce food and feed law, including the GMO Regulation, through the inspections by the FVO inspectors.

---

145 Art. 10 Regulation 1829/2003.

146 Art. 10 Regulation 1829/2003.

147 Art. 9 (2) and Art. 21 (2) Regulation1829/2003.

148 Art. 20 Directive 2001/18.

149 Art. 31 Directive 2001/18.

150 Art. 31 Directive 2001/18.

151 Artt. 41 to 44 Regulation 882/2004.

152 Artt. 9 and 29 Regulation 1829/2003.

153 Art. 25 Regulation 882/2004. E.g. Commission Decision 2006/677/EC OJ 2006 L278/15.

The FVO is a directorate of the DG for Health and Consumer Protection,[154] which was created to enforce food safety rules in the wake of various food scares.[155] Its legal basis is Articles 45 and 46 Regulation 882/2004. The FVO does not enforce food law vis-à-vis individuals, which means that it does not impose sanctions on individuals, although it is possible that the national authorities impose sanctions after its inspections have revealed irregularities. It only supervises the enforcement by the Member States (and third countries).[156] Its officials carry out inspections in the Member States (and in third countries) both at the offices of national authorities and at facilities, in order to verify whether the Member States have a sufficient level of food safety enforcement in place.[157] These inspections can be triggered by RASFF notifications.[158] The FVO prepares an annual Programme of Inspections, which allows for flexibility in case of emergencies, and reports its results in an Annual Report, to be published on the website of the DG for Health and Consumer Protection.

The FVO's audits and on-the-spot checks are organized in cooperation with the Member States' competent authorities. The Member States have to offer all necessary assistance and provide all documentation and other technical support that the FVO may request, to enable them to carry out their controls efficiently and effectively. Moreover, they have to ensure that the FVO officials have access to all premises or parts of premises and to all information, including computing systems, relevant to the execution of their duties.[159] After the FVO finishes its inspection, it will publish a report of its mission on the Internet. Prior to the publication of such a report, the FVO officials discuss their findings and recommendations with the national authorities and an action plan is agreed on, which includes a reporting obligation.[160] The Member States are obliged to take appropriate follow-up action in the light of the recommendations of the report.[161] The Commission can also take action on the basis of the FVO report, which can vary from taking emergency measures to the withdrawal of authorizations or starting an infringement procedure.

---

[154] Established by the General Food Law Regulation 178/2002.

[155] See: Van der Meulen and Freriks (2006), and Lugt (1999).

[156] The FVO is similar to the Euro-inspectors in other areas of Community law, of which fisheries was the first. See: Berg (1999).

[157] Art. 45 Regulation 882/2004.

[158] FVO Annual Report 2006, p. 19.

[159] Art. 45 Regulation 882/2004.

[160] E.g. Final report of a Mission carried out in Spain from 24/02/03 to 28/02/03 in order to evaluate the official control systems on foods consisting of or produced from genetically modified organisms (GMO), DG (SANCO)/9103/2003 B MR Final.

[161] Art. 45 Regulation 882/2004.

2.6 Conclusions

In line with the idea of network control, both the GMO Directive and the GMO Regulation do not provide for a strict division of competence between the Member States. This is because the Commission (or the Council) usually authorizes GMOs, at any rate those for food and feed use. If authorized under the single licence procedure, the reference Member State is the home state. If authorized under the Community procedure, the Commission is responsible for vigilance, while either the Member State of entry into the EU should assume the function of home state for controls of imported GMOs or the Member State where the GMOs were produced. The enforcement of GMOs for food and feed use and of GMOs for other uses are each other's opposites as regards the intensity of Community involvement in enforcement. A shared characteristic, apart from their reliance on self-enforcement, is that the applicable Community legislation does not contain many procedural guarantees with regard to the authorization holder or third parties. This deficiency means that individuals have to rely on the general rules established in the case law of the Community and national courts when they challenge a sanction imposed on them by the national authorities of their Member State or – in case their authorization is withdrawn – by the Commission.

On the one hand, the enforcement of the GMO Directive is almost completely left to the discretion of the Member States, which do not exchange information through a system set up specifically for GMOs for other uses, but through the rapid alert systems for GMO consumer goods or biotechnological medicines. In line with the home state control system, the reference Member State functions as the home state, but due to the feature of information exchange, the system resembles a network control system. On the other hand, the enforcement of the GMO Regulation is geared towards achieving a level playing field between the Member States and facilitating administrative cooperation. Firstly, it is enforced under a common framework for enforcement, which provides for information exchange between the Commission (responsible for vigilance) and the competent authorities through the rapid alert system for food and feed. Secondly, the Mutual Assistance Regulation applies and thus provides for information exchange and mutual assistance between customs authorities.[162] Thirdly, the Commission's supervision of the implementation of the GMO Regulation is facilitated by the obligation to submit enforcement plans and implementation reports, and by Community legislation allowing the Commission to deploy its own inspectors on the ground, based on FVO arrangements. It is problematic that due to Commission authorization it is not clear which Member State will function as the home state concerning controls, but since the control system is best characterized as network control, it is perhaps without severe consequences that the legislation does not explicitly mention that the Member State of entry or of production functions as the home state.

[162] See the section on the Mutual Assistance Regulation and the section on medicines in this chapter.

3 Medicines

The enforcement of medicines legislation consists of controls to prevent the import or production of substandard or counterfeit[163] medicines and to monitor the safety of authorized medicines, which is called pharmacovigilance. The thalidomide tragedy described below demonstrated that unexpected, serious adverse reactions may occur despite the quality, safety and efficacy of a medicine having been assessed prior to its authorization. Thalidomide was sold during the late 1950s and 1960s as a sleeping aid and as a medicine to combat morning sickness and other symptoms suffered by pregnant women. It was available in around fifty countries, but not in the United States. It became clear in 1961 that thalidomide seriously damaged the development of unborn children, after thousands of babies had been born without arms or legs and with other severe malformations.

This example is a reminder of the axiom that once many people use a medicine, any uncertainties about adverse reactions become certainties. Therefore, the authorities have to monitor the occurrence of adverse effects.[164] Since this is a shared interest of all competent national authorities, the Member States and the Commission have established a common system of pharmacovigilance. It relies on self-enforcement, as the marketing authorization holder should monitor and timely notify the authorities of any adverse effects or the lack of therapeutical effect of a medicine, but it can also be triggered by notifications from Member States, on the basis of their collection of adverse reactions as received from medical professionals. Labelling does not really play a role, as the packaging of the medicine and the leaflet inside merely serve to inform the consumer.

3.1 Between home state and network control at the EU borders

The enforcement of the medicines legislation at the external borders of the EU consists of controls on the quality of batches of medicines to detect substandard medicines, i.e. medicines that are not in conformity with the European quality standards.[165] A specific category of substandard medicines are counterfeit medicines, which the World Health Organization defines as medicines which are deliberately and fraudulently mislabelled with respect to identity and/or source. Counterfeiting can apply to both branded and generic products and counterfeit products may include products with the correct ingredients or with the wrong ingredients, without active ingredients, with insufficient active

[163] Council Regulation 1383/2003 declares Council Regulation 515/97 applicable.

[164] The thalidomide scandal strongly influenced pharmacovigilance, but also regulation prior to authorization. See: Abraham and Lewis (2000), pp. 76-77.

[165] See Artt. 18-20 Regulation 726/2004 and Art. 8 Directive 2001/83. The Community customs legislation is described in this chapter in the context of customs control of CITES shipments.

ingredients or with fake packaging.[166] The specific attention for counterfeit medicines is justified, because the recent increase in the number of seized counterfeit medicines suggests that counterfeit medicinal products are on the rise.[167] This can be explained by the possibility to sell counterfeit medicines through internet pharmacies which, contrary to normal pharmacies, do not necessarily include a secure supply chain.[168]

The customs authorities of the Member State of first entry into the EU are responsible for customs controls of imported medicines, which will then acquire the same status as goods produced in the Community.[169] They can exchange information through the customs information system ('CIS') about shipments of substandard or counterfeit medicines and persons that seem to be involved. They can also request operational cooperation from other customs authorities.[170] If customs authorities suspect that medicines are substandard, they can suspend the product's release and notify the national authority responsible for monitoring the marketing of the product.[171] If the customs authorities suspect that the medicines are counterfeit, they can also follow the procedure of Regulation 1383/2003 and only notify the right holder.[172] The authorization holders or the right holders can contribute to uncovering infringements, if they inform the customs authorities of their trademarks, patent rights and genuine products to increase awareness.[173] When the competent national authority is informed, it has to take appropriate action,[174] which either leads to a prohibition against placing the product on the market[175] or to free circulation, if inspection reveals that the product is compliant or if the competent authorities fail to react within three days.[176] If the procedure for counterfeit medicines is followed, the customs authorities take such action at the request and on the basis of the information from the right holder.[177] It is not clear why legislation does not require both procedures to be followed at the same time.

---

166 WHO fact sheet 275 (last revised on 14 November 2006), available at: http://www.who.int/mediacentre/factsheets/fs275/en/.

167 EMEA inspections: Counterfeit medicines, available at: http: //www.emea.europa.eu/Inspections/Counterfeits.html and Hill (2007).

168 European Generic Medicines Association, EGA position paper on Anti-counterfeiting Policy, 2007, available at: http://www.egagenerics.com/doc/ega_anticounterfeitpolicy_position.pdf

169 See section 5.1 below.

170 Art. 8 Regulation 339/93 and Commission Decision 93/583/EC and Council Regulation 1383/2003.

171 Art. 2 Council Regulation 339/93.

172 Art. 4 Council Regulation 1383/2003.

173 http://www.customs-law.com/pdfs/SSGK%20LLP%20WCO%20Alert%2011-15-07%20(00176474).PDF.

174 Art. 5 Council Regulation 339/93.

175 Art. 6 Council Regulation 339/93.

176 Art. 5 Council Regulation 339/93.

177 Regulation 1383/2003.

3.2 Home state control on the internal market

The national authorities have two responsibilities as regards compliance control with the medicines legislation. First of all, they have to take action in order to ensure that only medicinal products with respect to which a marketing authorization has been granted are distributed on their territory.[178] In that regard, internet pharmacies should be an important enforcement target because they can be used to distribute counterfeit, substandard or unauthorized medicines and medicines that require prescription without providing appropriate medical advice. The most frequently sold illegal and possibly fake medicines are lifestyle medicines, growth hormones for bodybuilding and sleeping pills.[179] Secondly, the national authorities have to control the quality of the production of medicines at the premises of manufacturers of medicines on their territory to whom they have granted a manufacturing authorization (irrespective of whether the medicine is authorized by them or by another Member State or by the Commission).[180]

It is a condition of the manufacturing authorization that the manufacturer allows the agents of the competent authority of the Member State concerned access to their premises at any and all time.[181] For medicines imported from third countries, the Member State that granted the manufacturing authorization to the importer is responsible for the quality controls carried out by the importer.[182] The importer is exempted from this duty if quality control occurs in a third country at the premises of the manufacturer, but this is only possible on the basis of an agreement between the Community and the exporting country.[183] A Member State may request assistance from another Member State or from EMEA for the inspections.[184] The Commission can also become involved, if it is informed that two Member States have different opinions on whether the marketing authorization holder, the manufacturer or the importer satisfies the requirements of respectively pharmacovigilance, manufacturing control or quality control. In such a case, the Commission can request an inspector from the Member State concerned to conduct a new inspection accompanied by two inspectors from Member States that are not party to the dispute or by two experts nominated by the Committee for Medicinal Products for Human Use.[185]

---

[178] Art. 76 Directive 2001/83.

[179] Press Release: 'Commission warns about fake drugs on the internet', Brussels 27 March 2006, IP/06/375.

[180] Title IV Directive 2001/83 and Artt. 18 to 20 Regulation 726/2004.

[181] Art. 46 (d) Directive 2001/83.

[182] Art. 51 Directive 2001/83 and Art. 18 Regulation 726/2004.

[183] Art. 51 Directive 2001/83 and Art. 18 (2) Regulation 726/2004. The opposite situation is also possible if this is a precondition for export from an EU Member State to a third country.

[184] Art. 18 Regulation 726/2004. See: Vervaele (1999 A), pp. 143-144.

[185] Art. 19 Regulation 726/2004.

3.3 Pharmacovigilance

Pharmocovigilance is important to ensure the safety of authorized medicines. The legislation obliges the authorization holder to inform the authorities if (serious) adverse effects occur. The national authorities share this information with each other and with EMEA and the Commission via the rapid alert system for pharmacovigilance, which boils down to sharing information through a database.[186] The medicines legislation defines an adverse reaction as a response to a medicinal product which is noxious and unintended and which occurs at doses normally used in man for a medical treatment. An adverse reaction is considered serious when it results in death, is life threatening, requires in-patient hospitalization or prolongation of existing hospitalization, results in persistent or significant disability or incapacity, or is a congenital anomaly or birth defect. It is considered unexpected if its nature, severity or outcome is not consistent with the summary of product characteristics.[187]

The medicines legislation provides for a minimal division of competence and a coordinating role for EMEA. The holder of a mutual recognition authorization submits a periodic safety update to the reference Member State,[188] whereas the holder of a Community authorization sends it to EMEA.[189] If a suspected or unexpected serious adverse effect occurs, the holder of the authorization should immediately report it to the competent authorities of the Member State on whose territory the incident occurred, which will then report it to EMEA.[190] If it concerns a Community authorization, however, the authorization holder will report it both to the Member State on whose territory it occurred and to EMEA, which is also informed by the Member State concerned.[191] If a suspect adverse reaction occurs in a third country, the holder should communicate this as well to the competent authority. The Member States and EMEA share pharmacovigilance information through a database, which is coordinated by EMEA.[192]

The Directive does not state to which Member State holders should report suspect adverse reactions which occurred in a third country. That means that they should either report this to all Member States or only to the reference Member State, since that Member State is responsible for the analysis, control and sharing of adverse reactions.[193] The first option is more likely though, because the Regulation provides that when a serious adverse reaction occurs in a third country, the holder should report it to EMEA and to all Member States.

[186] Artt. 102 and 105 Directive 2001/83. Art. 57 (1) (b) Regulation726/2004 provides the legal basis for the establishment of the database.

[187] Art. 1 (11), (12) and (13) Directive 2001/83.

[188] Art. 104 (6) Directive 2001/83.

[189] Art. 24 (3) Regulation 276/2004.

[190] Artt. 103-104 Directive 2001/83.

[191] Art. 24 Regulation 726/2004.

[192] Art. 22 Regulation 726/2004.

[193] Art. 104 Directive 2001/83.

Pharmacovigilance does not completely depend on self-enforcement. Both the national authorities and the holders of authorizations are responsible for the collection of data on adverse reactions.[194] For information, both depend on doctors and other healthcare professionals.[195] If someone reports an adverse reaction only to a Member State, this Member State should also report the information about the incident to the holder of the authorization.[196] Vice versa, based on the authorization, the holder of the authorization is obliged to register all adverse reactions and report them to the national authorities in accordance with the reporting guidelines.[197] Although the double collection of information gives the authorities the opportunity to assess information on adverse reactions independently, the holders of the authorization remain primarily responsible, because they are in a better position to value the information.

Enforcement of pharmacovigilance duties is required because it is not necessarily in the interests of the marketing authorization holder to report adverse reactions as long as it is not completely clear that they are serious and justify a modification of the authorization or withdrawal. This possible reluctance is mitigated by the reputation damage and the pecuniary damage a company will suffer if its medicines prove to be unsafe and also by the public enforcement of their pharmacovigilance duties under the medicines legislation.[198] Enforcement is primarily the responsibility of the Member States,[199] but with regard to Community authorized medicines, the competent authorities are obliged to cooperate with EMEA and the Commission to enable them to carry out their duties.[200] This is because the Commission can impose sanctions on a Community marketing authorization holder in case of a violation of the pharmacovigilance requirements.[201] The investigations that may lead to the imposition of such a sanction can start with a request for information from EMEA to the authorization holder,[202] but also with inspections by the competent authorities of the Member States at EMEA's request.[203]

3.4 Emergency measures

The emergency measures are virtually the same for medicines, irrespective of whether they are authorized under the Directive or under the Regulation. If the evaluation of the pharmacovigilance data leads a Member

---

194 Art. 101 et seq. Directive 2001/83, rec. 58 Preamble to Directive 2001/83.

195 Art. 101 Directive 2001/83.

196 Art. 105 Directive 2001/83. This requirement was introduced by Directive 2004/27.

197 Artt. 104 and 106 (2) Directive 2001/83.

198 Art. 104 Directive 2001/83 and Artt. 25 and 84 Regulation 726/2004.

199 Art. 104 Directive 2001/83 and Art. 19 Regulation 726/2004.

200 Artt. 6 and 3 Commission Regulation 658/2007.

201 See below section 4.5.

202 Art. 8 Commission Regulation 658/2007.

203 Art. 8 Commission Regulation 658/2007.

State to consider that urgent action is required to protect public health, it may immediately suspend the marketing authorization.[204] The rapid alert system for pharmacovigilance must be used by the Member State that takes this measure to inform EMEA, the Commission and the other Member States no later than the following working day. EMEA will then request the CHMP to prepare an opinion.[205] On the basis of this opinion, the Commission may request all Member States concerned to take temporary emergency measures. The final measures will be adopted in accordance with the regulatory Comitology procedure.[206] In case of a medicine authorized by the Commission, immediate suspension may also occur at the Commission's request.[207] Moreover, the Regulation prescribes that a Member State that takes emergency measures should rapidly inform health-care professionals of its action and the reasons for the action.[208] Of course, public intervention is not required if the marketing authorization holder voluntarily takes the necessary emergency measures, which is usually the case.[209]

3.5 Sanctions

While the Medicines Directive prescribes that the Member States should impose adequate, proportionate and dissuasive sanctions on the holder of the authorization in case of non-compliance with the pharmacovigilance requirements,[210] the Medicines Regulation states that not only the Member States but also the Commission can impose sanctions.[211] In the event that holders of Community marketing authorizations fail to meet their obligations under the Regulation, the Commission can impose a financial sanction on the basis of the report and investigations of EMEA, if one out of three conditions are met. Either the infringement may have significant public health implications in the Community or it has a Community dimension, by taking place or having its effects in more than one Member State, or – the third possibility – the interests of the Community are involved.[212]

---

204 Art. 107 Directive 2001/83 and Art. 20 (4) Regulation 726/2004.

205 Art. 107 Directive 2001/83. In case of variations, the Member State may also request the CHMP to prepare an opinion.

206 Artt. 107 and 36 (2) Directive 2001/83.

207 Art. 20 (4) Regulation 726/2004.

208 Art. 20 Regulation 726/2004.

209 Lisman (2006), p. 34.

210 Art. 104 Directive 2001/83 and Art. 25 and 84 Regulation 726/2004, which provides the legal basis for Commission Regulation 658/2007 concerning financial penalties for infringement of certain obligations in connection with marketing authorizations granted under Regulation 726/2004 of the European Parliament and of the Council.

211 Art. 84 Regulation 726/2004.

212 Artt. 1 and 5 to 10 Commission Regulation 658/2007.

The Community sanction procedure offers procedural guarantees to the authorization holder. He is invited to state his views before EMEA adopts its report and before the Commission adopts its decision.[213] In addition, without going so far as to preclude double jeopardy or ne bis in idem, the Regulation prescribes that EMEA and the Commission take into account any infringement procedure by a Member State against the same marketing authorization holder and based on the same legal grounds and the same facts.[214] The Commission has the power to impose a fine and a penalty payment for infringement of the pharmacovigilance duties and for non-cooperation with the administrative authorities.[215] It publishes the names of the offenders, the amount of the sanction and the reasons for imposition.[216]

The modification or withdrawal of an authorization may occur at the request of the holder of the authorization or on the initiative of a Member State or the Commission.[217] Usually, the authorization holder is prepared to cooperate with the authorities and to take the necessary measures if pharmacovigilance data indicate that a medicine presents safety risks.[218] Except in cases of emergency, it is prohibited for Member States to act unilaterally if they want to suspend, modify – e.g. by introducing a warning for a certain side effect – or revoke the authorization. The suspension, modification or withdrawal of an authorization occurs by Commission decision, or by Council decision. A Member State that wants the Commission to act has to notify EMEA, the other Member States concerned and the holder of the authorization.[219] In order to ensure uniformity, the arbitration procedure of the Directive is always used.[220] This procedure gives the authorization holder the right to be heard before the Commission takes its decision.[221] The medicines legislation provides for grounds for suspension, modification or revocation of an authorization. These grounds are the opposites of the grounds for authorization, i.e. where the product proves to be harmful under normal conditions of use or where its therapeutic efficacy is lacking or where its qualitative and quantitative composition is not as declared in the application for authorization.[222]

---

[213] Artt. 9 and 11 to 13 Commission Regulation 658/2007.

[214] Art. 2 Commission Regulation 658/2007.

[215] Artt. 16 and 19 Commission Regulation 658/2007.

[216] Art. 84 Regulation 726/2004.

[217] Artt. 16 and 20 Regulation 726/2004.

[218] Lisman (2006), p. 34.

[219] Art. 107 Directive 2001/83.

[220] Art. 36 Directive 2001/83.

[221] Art. 36 Directive 2001/83 and Art. 81 Regulation 726/2004.

[222] Art. 116 Directive 2001/83 and Art. 81 Regulation 726/2004.

The CFI reviewed the grounds for withdrawal of a marketing authorization in the *Artegodan* case.[223] It found that the revocation of a marketing authorization is only justified where a new potential risk or the lack of efficacy is substantiated by new, objective, scientific and/or medical data or information, leaving aside the exceptional situation that the competent authorities admit that they have assessed a medicine incorrectly.[224] According to the CFI, this is compatible with the aim to achieve the highest level of protection of public health, since the applicant has to prove that the medicine fulfils the admission criteria in order to obtain an authorization and the authorities can re-evaluate an initial authorization after five years. In those circumstances, the system of prior authorization allows for the assumption that in absence of solid, new evidence to the contrary, the medicinal product fulfils the requirements to be placed on the market during the first five years.[225] The CFI decided that the grounds for revocation are limitative, rejecting the ground that medicines with a better benefit/risk balance have become available as a new ground for revocation during the first five years of authorization.

3.6 Community supervision

Under the Medicines Regulation, the Commission is required to publish, at least once every ten years, a general report on the experience acquired with the implementation of the Regulation.[226] Since the Member States fulfil an important role in the enforcement of the Medicines Regulation, one would assume that national reports serve as a basis for this report, but the Regulation does not contain a reporting obligation directed towards the Member States. The Medicines Directive only prescribes a reporting obligation about transposition. The absence of reporting obligations does not exclude that the Member States may cooperate voluntarily in the drafting of the Commission report. The medicines legislation does not include a duty for EMEA to send inspectors to the Member States for the purpose of supervision. Due to the close cooperation with the Member States, it is likely that EMEA can nevertheless inform the Commission when one of the Member States fails to meet its Community obligations.

---

[223] T-74/00, T-76/00, T-83/00 to T-85/00, T-132/00, T-137/00 and T-141/00 *Artegodan* [2002] ECR II-4945, appealed: C-39/03P *Artegodan* [2003] ECR I-7885. In the appeal, the ECJ only discussed the competence of the Commission. Since legislation has been changed to accommodate the criticisms of the ECJ, this aspect will not be discussed here.

[224] The exception made for mistakes should apply to corruption and fraud cases as well.

[225] T-74/00, T-76/00, T-83/00 to T-85/00, T-132/00, T-137/00 and T-141/00 *Artegodan* [2002] ECR II-4945.

[226] Art. 85 Regulation 724/2004.

3.7 Conclusions

What is striking about the Community legislation that applies to medicines is that it has integrated enforcement to such a great extent. It obliges the customs authorities to cooperate in their fight against the import of substandard or counterfeit medicines at the external borders, thus ensuring that their system of home state control has incorporated the characteristics of information exchange and mutual assistance that belong to a system of network control. Their control is supplemented by national control of internet sales and by home state control of EU manufacturers and of importers, unless they import from manufacturers outside the EU that are already controlled by their home country in accordance with an agreement between the EU and their country.

An important aspect of the control of the quality, safety and efficacy of medicines is pharmocovigilance, which depends to a large extent on the willingness of the authorization holder to report to the competent authorities of the reference Member State or to EMEA in case of Community authorized medicines. However, the Member States also collect reports from health care professionals, thus reducing their dependency. Pharmacovigilance is organized as home state control concerning medicines authorized by the Member States, while it is organized as Community control concerning medicines authorized by the Commission (or the Council). However, the enforcement does not really differ, because in both cases the original system has incorporated the features of network control in order to enable joint action when a Member State or EMEA issues an alert notification. Moreover, irrespective of whether medicines were authorized by the Commission or by the Member States, a Community decision is required to withdraw an authorization. This decision is taken after the authorization holder has been heard, but third parties, who may have requested this decision or want it to be reconsidered because they benefit from the use of the medicine, are not granted any rights, which means that the minimum amount of procedural guarantees cannot be considered to be met.

Yet perhaps the most remarkable aspect of the enforcement of the medicines legislation is that the Medicines Regulation gives the Commission the power to take over the enforcement role from the Member States if an infringement of the Medicines Regulation has a Community dimension. This led to the adoption of a Commission Regulation governing the exercise of this power and containing procedural guarantees, including the right to be heard before a decision is taken, for those subject to it. In a sense, the Commission's power is limited to issuing sanctions, as the EMEA officials depend on the Member States for inspections of the Community authorization holders. Yet EMEA can orchestrate these inspections, because it has the power to request the Member States to conduct inspections and have its own inspectors accompany the national officials on their inspections. Strangely enough, this direct involvement does not seem to be supplemented by strong supervision powers. Indeed, it is remarkable that neither the Medicines Regulation nor the Medicines Directive prescribes a reporting obligation for Member States vis-à-vis the Commission about the implementation. Only the Commission is supposed to report on the implementation, at least once every ten years. Perhaps the close cooperation between the Member States, EMEA and the Commission makes up for the absence of national reports.

4 CITES

Due to the single licence system, the Member State that issued a CITES document is responsible for the correctness of its assessment. When a shipment from a third country arrives at the borders of a Member State that did not issue the documents, administrative cooperation is required in order to prevent that the shipment escapes compliance control. The enforcement of CITES is complicated because only specialists can detect infringements. This task is easier when animals are chipped or birds have a closed ring on their leg to demonstrate their status as born and bred in captivity, although even then it remains possible to commit fraud.[227] The control at the external borders can be complemented by enforcement action within the territories of the Member States, because the possession of CITES-listed fauna and flora requires CITES documents.

Inevitably, enforcement of the European wildlife trade regulations in the Member States varies.[228] The risk of variation is that weak enforcement efforts in one Member State may shift trade patterns, possibly illegal, to that particular state. Once trade patterns shift to that state, enforcement of wildlife trade regulation in the entire EU is as strong as its weakest link, as trade patterns easily shift to the Member State providing the easiest point of entry into the Community.[229] Italy's past performance is a case in point. During the eighties and early nineties of the twentieth century, Italy attracted wildlife trade destined for the European Union due to its low enforcement efforts.[230] The old Regulation did not provide for non-recognition of CITES documents. As a result, Member States even accepted manifestly incorrect CITES documents issued by other Member States.[231] The Commission did not bring an infringement procedure against Italy. Instead, the CITES secretariat first issued several warnings to Italy and then a recommendation to all parties to suspend trade with Italy. It was recommended not to issue any CITES documents for specimens consigned to Italy nor to accept any CITES documents issued by Italy.[232]

[227] See: Van Kreveld (2007).

[228] See: Berkhoudt (2003).

[229] Reeves (2002), pp. 117-119.

[230] See for a more detailed account of the situation: Reeves (2002), pp. 120-123.

[231] Reeves (2002), p. 113.

[232] Notification to the Parties No 675 'Italy: Recommendations of the Standing Committee', 30 June 1992, based on Res. Conf. 7.5 and on Art. XIV CITES, which allows for more stringent national measures.

Although the CITES Convention does not provide for any reaction if a state does not implement it effectively, a way of dealing with non-compliance by states that are party to it has evolved in practice. If a state does not send reports to the Secretariat or if the Secretariat is informed that a State has major problems with implementing the Convention, the Secretariat first tries to help the state to solve the problem, offering advice or technical assistance. Only if the state does not cooperate and does not improve its level of compliance, the Secretariat brings the matter before the Standing Committee. The Standing Committee may recommend to suspend all CITES trade with the non-compliant state on the basis of Article XIII, on international measures and Article XIV, which allows states to adopt stricter domestic measures.[233] Due to international pressure, Italy dramatically improved its enforcement efforts, which resulted in a withdrawal of the recommendation in 1995. The Community itself could not have intervened in this manner, because it is contrary to the Community spirit to take trade measures. It will become clear below that the Community has improved the effectiveness of enforcement as regards the control and withdrawal of CITES documents.

4.1 From home state control to network control at the EU borders

The customs authorities are responsible for compliance control of products imported from third countries.[234] The European customs control of CITES shipments is different from the international regime, as the latter prescribes checks and prior presentation of documents at the border of each State.[235] Instead, import into an EU Member State only requires customs control at the external borders of the EU, since a CITES import permit is valid throughout the EU.[236] Customs control serves to avoid the smuggling of protected wildlife into or out of the EU.[237] In legal terms, customs control serves to assign the goods a customs approved treatment or use.[238] That includes their entry into a warehouse, re-exportation, destruction or placement under another customs procedure, e.g. release into free circulation, transit, temporary admission and exportation.[239] Once non-Community goods have been cleared for customs, i.e. import formalities have been completed and any customs duties or charges having equivalent effect have been levied in the State of entry, they are released

[233] Res. Conf. 11.3 Compliance and Enforcement.

[234] Regulation 339/93.

[235] Artt. 3, 4, 5 Regulation 338/97.

[236] Artt. 3, 4 and 5 Regulation 338/97.

[237] Art. 4 Regulation 338/97.

[238] Artt. 3 (15) and 3 (16) and 42 Regulation 2913/92, as further elaborated by Commission Regulation 2454/93.

[239] Art. 59 Regulation 2913/92.

for free circulation.[240] The goods have then obtained the status of Community goods.[241]

The question is whether customs controls should respect the division of competence established by the Regulation, under which the Member State of destination issues an import permit even if the shipment arrives at another Member State ('the Member State of arrival'). It could be assumed that the Member State of arrival cannot take enforcement action because it cannot refuse recognition of a single licence.[242] However, the division of competence as regards decision-making does not mean that a Member State should not take enforcement action when a shipment is subject to their customs control in order to be imported into the Community. The Member State of arrival should check the import authorization issued by the Member State of destination because otherwise a shipment can escape control.[243] The introduction of the possibility to declare CITES documents void made it clear that customs control should take place at the borders of the Member State of arrival.

The CITES Regulation and the Community Customs Code provide for a procedure for customs clearance of CITES-listed species into the Community. As soon as a shipment arrives, the party who imported the goods into the Community, or the party who assumes responsibility for the transport of the goods within the Community, should notify the customs authorities of the arrival of the goods at the customs office.[244] They should present the shipment to the customs authorities and provide them with all the requisite documents and information (including confidential information) and assist them if so requested.[245] The goods presented to customs must be accompanied by a summarised declaration in order to identify the goods.[246] In case of a CITES shipment, the CITES documents serve to identify the goods.[247] The customs authorities check the CITES documents and if they consider it necessary, they may also examine the goods or take samples.[248] They may request additional

---

[240] Art. 24 EC and Art. 79 Regulation 2913/92.

[241] C-199/84 *Procuratore della Repubblica* v *Migliorini* [1985] ECR 3317. See: Lasok (1998), p. 49.

[242] See the CITES section in the chapter on decision-making.

[243] A Dutch example is: CBB 17 januari 1992 *Italrille tegen de minister van LNV* MenR 1993/2, p. 134. See: Van Rijswick (1996), pp. 110-112.

[244] Art. 12 Regulation 338/97 and Artt. 3 (19) and 37- 40 Regulation 2913/92. According to Art. 39 of Regulation 2913/92, if, for some unforeseeable reason or force majeure, the goods cannot be conveyed to the appropriate place, the party liable to do so or anyone acting on their behalf should inform the customs authorities without delay. They should indicate their precise location, unless the goods suffered complete loss. See for the list of designated customs offices: http://ec.europa.eu/environment/cites/pdf/points_entry.pdf.

[245] Artt. 14 and 15 Regulation 2913/92.

[246] Art. 43 Regulation 2913/92.

[247] Art. 44 Regulation 2913/92.

[248] Art. 13 Regulation 2913/92.

proof to ensure that the indication of origin complies with the rules laid down in the CITES Regulation.[249]

The enforcement activities of the customs authorities benefit from the administrative cooperation rules established under the Community Customs Code. The legal basis for customs cooperation is Article 135 EC, which states that the Council will take measures to strengthen customs cooperation between the Member States and between the latter and the Commission within the scope of the EC Treaty. This is also stated specifically in Article 250 Community Customs Code, which states that where a customs procedure is used in several Member States:

- the decisions, identification measures taken or agreed on, and the document issued by the customs authorities of one Member State have the same legal effects in other Member States as such decisions, measures taken and documents issued by the customs authorities of each of those Member States;
- the findings of checks carried out by the customs authorities of a Member State have the same conclusive force in the other Member States as the findings of the customs authorities of each of those Member States.

Consequently, CITES notifications issued by customs authorities are valid in all Member States and evidence of irregularities discovered by the Member State of arrival can be used to withdraw the CITES documents.

If the customs authorities find that goods have been brought into the customs territory of the Community without authorization or have been withheld from customs surveillance, they may take any measures they consider necessary (see the section on sanctions).[250] The CITES regulation adds a few infringements which customs controls may reveal and that warrant enforcement action. For instance, it is an infringement if the state of export has not issued the prescribed documents before export or re-export, and the correct document is not submitted retrospectively in compliance with the conditions specified by the Commission. Other infringements include sending a shipment covered by a false, falsified or invalid permit or covered by a 'recycled' permit, which refers to the situation that the specimen for which it was issued is not the one in the shipment.[251]

One may expect that the customs authorities and the CITES authorities share information on offenders in order to impose stricter controls on traders with a track record of non-compliance and to prevent that offenders can start again in another Member State. Unfortunately, the Mutual Assistance Regulation does not apply to CITES, because it is based on Article 43 and Article 308 EC (and, explicitly, not on Article 95 EC) and it is designed to ensure the correct application of the law on customs and agricultural matters, with the aim of

---

[249] Art. 26 Regulation 2913/92.

[250] Artt. 56 and 57 Regulation 2913/92 and Art. 8 (6) Regulation 338/97.

[251] Art. 16 (1) Regulation 338/97.

combating fraud and irregularities in order to protect the financial interests of the Community.[252] No secondary legislation has been put in place to extend its use to CITES.[253] Nevertheless, the instruments of the Mutual Assistance Regulation can be used on a voluntary basis. However, even if it were used for CITES and relevant information could be stored in CIS,[254] its contribution to the enforcement of CITES would be reduced because the information in CIS is not available to other authorities than the customs authorities.[255] The CITES Regulation does not fill this gap. This means that administrative cooperation in order to enforce the CITES Regulation can only take place when the customs or CITES authorities cooperate with each other on a voluntary basis. It will become clear below that such voluntary cooperation exists and is facilitated by the EU-TWIX database.

4.2 From national control to network control on the internal market

The Member States have to complement the compliance controls at the external borders with compliance controls on their own territory. The CITES Regulation provides for a number of offences that require internal control.[256] The national enforcement authorities should particularly check whether the holder of listed fauna and flora is able to present CITES documents. They should also check whether the holder treats the specimen properly and does not use it for commercial purposes in violation of the rules or the import permit conditions.[257] If, at any time, the competent authorities have reason to believe that the CITES Regulation is being infringed, they should take the appropriate steps to ensure compliance or to institute legal action.[258] They should monitor legal traders, such as importers, pet shops and breeders. In addition, they should control internet sales, because that seems to be an important vehicle for illegal trade.[259] Finally, national enforcement of the Habitat and Birds Directives complements the enforcement of the CITES Regulation.[260] These directives not

[252] C-209/97 *Commission* v *Council* [1999] ECR I-8067. See in particular Artt. 1 and 2, and the first two recitals of Regulation 515/97.

[253] Art. 6 (3) Regulation 339/93 extends the application of the Mutual Assistance Regulation to dangerous products and Commission Decision 93/583/EC OJ 1993 L 279/39 extends it to toys, medicines and foodstuffs.

[254] As Klip and Vervaele (2001), p. 15 suggested.

[255] Artt. 1 and 23 Regulation 515/97. See: Study on the Enforcement of the EU Wildlife Trade Regulations in the EU 25, study contract no 07-07010406/2005/411826/MAR/E.2, p. 6.

[256] Art. 16 Regulation 338/97.

[257] ANP news 24-04-2006.

[258] Art. 14 Regulation 338/97.

[259] Study on the Enforcement of the EU Wildlife Trade Regulations in the EU 25, study contract no 07-07010406/2005/411826/MAR/E.2, Final Report, pp. 4-5.

[260] Directive 92/43 and Directive 79/409, respectively.

only protect the wild fauna and flora living in the European Union against loss of habitat, but also against exploitation.[261] The connection between the Birds Directive and the CITES Directive became especially clear when ECJ allowed the Netherlands to prohibit Van der Feesten to breed with Cuban flamingos – despite CITES documents issued by Cuba and accepted by Danmark – to protect European flamingos against artificial alterations.[262]

The CITES Regulation does not establish an information exchange system. It only states that the Member States should communicate to one another and to the Commission the information necessary for the implementation of CITES[263] and that they can discuss enforcement matters in the enforcement group, which consists of Member States representatives and is chaired by a Commission representative.[264] This enables the Member States to coordinate enforcement.[265] That was the situation until 2005, when the database EU-TWIX (Trade in Wildlife Information Exchange) was set up by TRAFFIC (a CITES research office, established by WWF and others) in cooperation with various European and national institutions.[266] In the absence of a legal basis, it allows for voluntary administrative cooperation between all designated officials who apply or enforce CITES. Each service/agency/authority assigns a contact point, a so-called focal point, which can enter information into the database.

The fact that EU-TWIX enables cooperation between various types of enforcement officials makes it particularly interesting. The Croatian reptile seizure provides a good example of the functioning of EU-TWIX. When the Croatian CITES management authority seized reptiles from Madagascar in 2007, it requested assistance for their identification and got help from the German CITES management authority, the Belgian Police and a UK health inspector. Moreover, through the exchange of information about the Croatian reptiles seizure, the Dutch General Inspection Service (AID) learned that Dutch traders were involved. They requested information from the Belgian police and were offered assistance to help them monitor trade.[267]

4.3 Emergency measures

The Commission may stipulate general trade restrictions, or restrictions relating to a certain country of origin, on the introduction into

[261] Art. 5 Directive 92/43 and Art. 12 Directive 79/409. E.g. C-10/96 *Ligue royale belge pour la protection des oiseaux and Société d'études ornithologiques* v *Région Wallonne* [1996] ECR I- 6775.

[262] C-202/94 *Criminal proceedings against Godefridus van der Feesten* [1996] ECR I-355.

[263] Art. 15 Regulation 338/97.

[264] Art. 14 Regulation 338/97.

[265] European Commission, '1997-2002: Five years of new wildlife trade regulations. The European Union's contribution to sustainable trade and species conservation', Luxembourg: Office for Official Publications of the European Communities, 2002, p. 5.

[266] See: http://www.traffic.org/eu-wildlife-trade.

[267] See: http://www.traffic.org/eu-wildlife-trade.

the Community.[268] The Regulation establishes the grounds for restriction and requires that the Commission should consult the countries of origin concerned and take any opinion of the Scientific Review Group into account. The Commission may adopt the measure in accordance with the regulatory Comitology procedure.[269] If the Commission takes such a measure, a Member State may impose restrictions on the holding of specimens to which the Commission measure applies.[270] National emergency measures are not allowed, not even temporarily. Only the Commission is competent to order changes in the trading regime concerning third countries or species. This should not appear strange, since species are also listed on the Annexes to the Regulation in accordance with a Community procedure.[271] Although secondary legislation has not established a rapid alert system for CITES, the Commission can act swiftly by issuing a recommendation prior to or instead of taking a decision in accordance with the Comitology decision.[272] The Member States have to implement the Community measure when issuing CITES documents and monitoring compliance.

4.4 Sanctions

When the customs authorities discover a shipment of CITES-listed fauna or flora without CITES documents, they should take enforcement measures.[273] Both administrative and criminal sanctions may be imposed on those who violate the CITES Regulation. The CITES Regulation leaves it to the Member States to punish the offenders, as long as the sanctions for infringements are equivalent and appropriate to the nature and gravity of the infringement. This may not be the case in all Member States, as there is huge variation in penalties imposed by the various Member States.[274] A Commission Recommendation has tried to address this issue, as it recommends that the Member States ensure that penalties act as a deterrent, in particular by taking market value, conservation value and the costs incurred into account in the determination of the sanction.[275]

The CITES Regulation prescribes seizure and confiscation as reparatory sanctions.[276] If a shipment arrives at the external border without correct CITES

---

[268] Art. 4 (6) Regulation 338/97.

[269] Artt. 4 (6) and 18 Regulation 338/97.

[270] Art. 9 (6) Regulation 338/97.

[271] See the Chapter on Decision-making.

[272] C-182/89 *Commission* v *France (Bolivian wildcat skins)* [1990] ECR I-04337. See: Krämer (1993), pp. 206-215.

[273] Art. 14 Regulation 338/97.

[274] See: Garstecki (2006).

[275] Commission Recommendation 2007/425 identifying a set of actions for the enforcement of Council Regulation 338/97 on the protection of species of wild fauna and flora by regulating trade therein OJ 2007 L 159/45.

[276] Art. 16 Regulation 338/97.

documents, it can either be seized[277] or be rejected. The authorities can then order the carrier to return the shipment to its place of departure.[278] If a shipment is seized, the CITES management authority has to assume responsibility for it and decide whether it can be legalized or whether it is illegal. It first has to consider whether the shipment can be returned to the state of export, at the expense of the convicted party.[279] If it is impossible to return the shipment to the state of origin, the management authority should consult the scientific authority and then place the specimen under conditions it deems to be appropriate and consistent with the purposes and provisions of the Convention and the Regulation, or destroy the specimen.[280] The shipment may go to a zoo, but confiscated specimens of species listed in the Annexes B to D may also be sold, provided that they are not thus returned to the party from whom they were confiscated or who was party to the offence.[281]

Void CITES documents

The CITES Regulation does not specify whether invalid CITES documents must be revoked by the Member State that issued them. Since a CITES permit is issued prior to the arrival of the shipment, it may occur that customs authorities discover that a shipment is covered by a flawed permit issued by the CITES authorities from another Member State. This raises the question whether revocation or seizure are legitimate in these cases as well.[282] The *Bolivian wildcat skins* case is a good example to illustrate the difficulties that arise when a mistake requires correction.[283] The Commission had brought an infringement procedure against France, because the French authorities had issued an import permit for 6,000 wildcat skins from Bolivia despite a Commission recommendation not to trade with Bolivia. Advocate General Mischo argued that a decision should only be issued – and remain valid – if the material criteria of the CITES Regulation are met. The ECJ did not discuss this point, nor whether the German authorities had legitimately seized the skins in the absence of any legal basis in the CITES Regulation. Advocate General Mischo argued that Community loyalty compelled the French authorities to withdraw the invalid CITES documents despite the fact that their administrative law did not provide for this possibility.

In response to this problem, the renewed CITES Regulation stipulated that the authorities may deem a decision void if it establishes that it was issued on the false premise that the conditions for its issuance were met, after consultation

[277] Art. 16 (2) Regulation 338/97. Note that national legislation should provide enforcement authorities with the necessary competences, powers and instruments.

[278] Art. 16 (4) Regulation 338/97.

[279] Art. 16 Regulation 338/97.

[280] Art. 16 (3) Regulation 338/97.

[281] Art. 8 (6) Regulation 338/97.

[282] See: Van Rijswick (1996).

[283] C-182/89 *Commission* v *France (Bolivian wildcat skins)* [1990] ECR I-04337.

with the authorities that issued it.[284] The CITES Regulation does not prescribe that the authorization holder be heard. When the competent authorities have declared the CITES documents void, they can seize the shipment, because it is no longer covered by CITES documents.[285] It seems that they can act irrespective of the outcome of the consultation procedure. It is possible that consultation between the Member States reveals fundamental differences of opinion and that the competent authorities fail to reach agreement on the course of action to be taken. In order to solve such a dispute, they can discuss the issue in the enforcement group, consisting of enforcement officials from each Member State, chaired by a Commission official, which was set up to examine technical questions relating to enforcement.[286]

4.5 Community supervision

In general, the Commission and the Member States give each other the information necessary for the implementation of CITES.[287] The Commission can influence the Member States when they discuss enforcement matters in the enforcement group, which can be brought forward by a Member State, the Commission or by the CITES committee.[288] In addition, the Commission is informed of serious infringements, as the CITES Regulation obliges the Member States to report to the Commission how they enforced the CITES Regulation with regard to significant infringements, including seizures and confiscations. If this happens with regard to species that are listed on the Appendixes to the CITES Convention, the Member States should also inform the CITES Secretariat. This rule also applies if the Commission draws the attention of the competent authorities of the Member States to matters that require investigation.[289] In addition, the Commission sends an annual report to the Secretariat about the implementation of the CITES Convention in the EU, on the basis of the annual reports sent to it by the CITES authorities of the Member States.[290]

4.6 Conclusions

The CITES legislation established a home state control system on the basis of the division of competence between the Member States under its single licence system. However, the example of Italy and the *Bolivian wildcat*

---

[284] Art. 11 Regulation 338/97. E.g. Rechtbank Roermond 26 mei 2004 *Holland International Bird Trading, Van der Feesten's Zoo and Breeding Farm for Birds and Mammals tegen Staatssecretaris van Landbouw, Natuur en Voedselkwaliteit* 03/718 and 03/719 Wet K1.

[285] Art. 11 Regulation 338/97.

[286] Art. 14 Regulation 338/97.

[287] Art. 15 Regulation 338/97.

[288] Art. 14 Regulation 338/97.

[289] Art. 14 Regulation 338/97.

[290] Art. 15 Regulation 338/97.

skins case clearly demonstrated the limitations of this system. Consequently, the division of competences between the Member State of destination and the Member State of arrival changed, as the Member State of arrival became the home state for the control of the shipment upon arrival into the EU and may declare the documents issued by the Member State of destination void in case of manifest invalidity, after consultation with the Member State of destination that issued these documents. This only partially reduced the risk of a race for the bottom, because traders can still pick a Member State of arrival that least controls compliance with the CITES Regulation. As regards procedural guarantees, it is a serious shortcoming that the CITES Regulation does not prescribe that the authorization holder is heard before his documents are declared void.

Although these developments are definitely improvements, they do not guarantee the absence of an enforcement deficit caused by a shift in trade to the Member State whose enforcement of the CITES Regulation is the weakest. Community legislation did not reduce these risks through a system for information exchange or mutual assistance duties. Due to its limited resources, the Commission can only partially compensate for arising enforcement deficits. It monitors the enforcement efforts of the Member States through their reports of serious infringements (like the CITES Secretariat). The Commission becomes involved in enforcement if these reports or the CITES secretariat indicate that enforcement action is required as regards a species or trade with a certain country. The Commission will then alert the Member States that they have to take action.[291] The administrative cooperation has improved since 2005, when TRAFFIC Europe and other European and national institutions set up the EU-TWIX database to enable designated CITES enforcement authorities to exchange information on a voluntary basis, due to the absence of a legal basis. It is a great step forward, as this allows for true network control because different networks – customs, CITES authorities, police and other inspection services – can cooperate through a single information exchange system.

5 Plant protection products

Directive 91/414 aims to prevent risks at the source. It provides for a risk assessment of active substances and plant protection products before they can be placed on the market. Customs control at the border should ensure that illegal or counterfeit plant protection products are not imported. Unfortunately, the Mutual Assistance Regulation only applies to the control of counterfeit plant protection products.[292] Directive 91/414 does not address enforcement of its rules during the actual use phase, which means that it does not address the use of illegal plant protection products or illegal use of authorized plant protection products. This is partly compensated for by other Commu-

[291] Art. 14 Regulation 338/97.

[292] Regulation 1383/2003.

nity legislation, which sets maximum residue levels of active substances in food and feed.[293] The monitoring of pesticide residues in food and feed contributes to ensure that farmers comply with the plant protection product regulation,[294] which is reinforced by the supervision of the Commission's inspectors (the FVO). In addition, the customs authorities monitor pesticide residues in food and feed and also monitor counterfeit plant protection products. Nevertheless, undesirable amounts of pesticides can be found in the environment and residues above the regulatory limits can be detected in around 5% of agricultural products.[295]

5.1 National control

The Plant protection products Directive states somewhat cryptically that the Member States have to make the necessary arrangements for plant protection products that have been placed on the market and for their use to be officially checked. The purpose of the check is to see whether they comply with the requirements of the Directive and particularly with the requirements of the authorization and information appearing on the label.[296] The label and the packaging of plant protection products are harmonized by Directive 1999/45 because differences can create barriers to trade and because essential safety information on the label and the package protects the general public, users and the environment.[297] Directive 91/414 neither contains any specific requirements nor any reference to sanctions. It thus leaves the Member States broad discretionary room as to their enforcement efforts. New legislation may provoke a change in this regard.

New legislation may change this situation. The proposal for a new Regulation slightly rephrases the Directive, as it states that the Member States have to carry out official controls in order to enforce compliance with the Regulation.[298] A more important change is that it gives the Commission the competence to adopt an implementing Regulation (in accordance with the regulatory Comitology procedure) that will provide specific requirements for these controls.[299] In addition, in line with the Sixth Environmental Action Plan, the Commission has proposed a Directive that aims to achieve a more sustainable use of pesticides,

---

293 Regulation 396/2005.

294 Explanatory Memorandum to Proposal for a Directive of the European Parliament and of the Council establishing a framework for Community action to achieve a sustainable use of pesticides, COM (2006) 373 final, p. 5.

295 Explanatory Memorandum to Proposal for a Directive of the European Parliament and of the Council establishing a framework for Community action to achieve a sustainable use of pesticides, COM (2006) 373 final, pp. 2, 3.

296 Art. 17 Directive 91/414.

297 Directive 1999/45.

298 Art. 65 Proposal for a Regulation.

299 Art. 65 Proposal for a Regulation.

in particular plant protection products, which will also contain enforcement provisions.[300] It aims to improve controls on the use and distribution of pesticides and to create a transparent system for planning, reporting and monitoring the progress made towards sustainable use of pesticides through national action plans.[301]

5.2 Vigilance

Despite the risk assessment made prior to the authorization of a plant protection product, unforeseen negative effects may occur when it is used. The holder of the authorization or a user might discover that the product has negative effects. The Plant protection products Directive prescribes that the Member States should include a provision in the authorization that obliges holders of the authorization that they must immediately notify the competent authority of all new information concerning the potentially dangerous effects of any plant protection product, of residues of an active substance on human or animal or on groundwater, or their potentially dangerous effects on the environment. The same provision should be included if an extension of the field of application is granted to an official or scientific body involved in agricultural activities, professional agricultural organizations or professional users.[302]

This means that the holder of such an extension of the authorization for a minor use becomes responsible for the reporting of negative effects. Since the Directive does not prescribe that authorizations or extensions contain monitoring obligations, the authorization holder is not obliged to collect information and therefore, the reporting obligation in the authorization may not have any effect. If the holder of the authorization or of the extension reports new information on potentially dangerous effects, the (reference) Member State must ensure that the holder passes on this information to the other Member States and to the Commission.[303] This is a strange feature in the Directive, which reveals the disadvantage of the absence of a rapid alert system for information exchange between the Member States and the Commission. If the Commission receives information, it will refer the information to the Standing Committee on the Food Chain and Animal Health for discussion about the measures to be taken.[304]

---

[300] Proposal for a Directive of the European Parliament and of the Council establishing a framework for Community action to achieve a sustainable use of pesticides, COM (2006) 373 final.

[301] Explanatory Memorandum to Proposal for a Directive of the European Parliament and of the Council establishing a framework for Community action to achieve a sustainable use of pesticides, COM (2006) 373 final, pp. 3, 4.

[302] In accordance with Art. 9 (1) Directive 91/414.

[303] Art. 7 Directive 91/414.

[304] Artt. 7 and 19 Directive 91/414.

5.3 Emergency measures

The Directive does not state what constitutes an emergency, but the safeguard procedure applies if a Member State believes that there are valid reasons to find that a product which it has authorized, or which it is bound to authorize in accordance with the mutual recognition procedure, constitutes a risk to human or animal health or the environment (possibly on the basis of information received from the authorization holder). The relevant Member State may then provisionally restrict or prohibit the use and/or sale of that product on its territory. It should immediately inform the Commission and the other Member States of such actions and give reasons for its decision.[305] Strangely enough, it is not obliged to inform the authorization holder. This procedure was used, for instance, when Germany notified the Commission and the other Member States that tolylfluanide presented a risk for public health when present in water used for drinking water after purification by ozone treatment. Other Member States provisionally withdrew the authorization for products containing tolylfluanide as well in anticipation of the final Commission decision on the matter, which was to be taken within three months in accordance with the regulatory Comitology procedure.[306]

5.4 Sanctions

The Directive (and the proposal for a Regulation) does not say more about sanctions than that the Member States should provide for effective, proportionate and dissuasive penalties,[307] with the exception of review and withdrawal of listings and authorizations. They are connected as the review of the listing in the Annex can lead to withdrawal or modification of the listing of a certain substance and consequently compel the Member States to modify or withdraw authorizations for products containing that substance. The Commission reviews active substances ten years after their inclusion in order to assess whether they still meet the conditions for inclusion. The renewal procedure is the same as the authorization procedure. Where necessary, the Member States may renew a product authorization for the time it takes to complete the review, provided that an application for renewal has been made.[308] The Commission is not bound by the rule that a substance is initially included for ten years. It may review an active substance at any time if there are indications that the conditions for its inclusion are no longer met.[309] Moreover, a renewal does not lead to permanent inclusion of the substance in the Annex. The Proposal for a Regulation

305 Art. 11 Directive 91/414.

306 Artt. 11 and 19 Directive 91/414 and Artt. 5 and 7 Comitology Decision. The regulatory Comitology procedure is described in the chapter on decision-making.

307 Art. 69 Proposal for a Regulation.

308 Art. 5 (5) Directive 91/414.

309 Art. 5 Directive 91/414.

will change this, as it provides that after review an initially included substance can acquire a permanent listing.[310] However, the Commission may still review an active substance at any time.[311]

The Directive ensures that authorizations are regularly reviewed.[312] An authorization granted in accordance with the Directive must be withdrawn if it is established that: (a) the requirements for obtaining the authorization are not or are no longer satisfied or (b) the authorization was granted on the basis of false or misleading information.[313] A Member State may modify an authorization if it is established on the basis of developments in scientific and technical knowledge that the manner of use and amounts used can be modified.[314] It has to inform the authorization holder of this and may request information from him.[315] Authorization holders may also request the cancellation or modification of the authorization.[316] It is important to note that a withdrawal does not mean that a product will immediately disappear from the market. The Member States may grant a grace period for the disposal, storage, placing on the market and use of existing stocks and they may authorize essential use for a limited period.

The Directive does not provide for a division of competence. It does not state which Member State reviews the authorization, so each Member State that has issued an authorization should review it. According to the Directive, the rules on withdrawal and modification apply without prejudice to the mutual recognition of authorizations by other Member States.[317] However, in the absence of prescribed consultation or coordination and in view of the broad discretionary room that the Member States have in the recognition phase, it seems likely that Member States may decide for themselves about withdrawal or modification. It is likely that the results of a review will be shared if the outcome of the review reveals that the conditions for authorization are no longer met, because then the safeguard procedure will apply. The Directive does not provide for a reporting obligation if the results of the review indicate that the conditions of use should be adapted, but of course a Member State is free to notify the Commission or inform other Member States and discuss the issue in a committee meeting. The other Member States will then be free to decide whether to amend the authorization or extension they have issued, as long as no Commission decision has been taken about the listing of the active substance of the authorized product.

By contrast, the Proposal for a Regulation provides for a division of competence. The reference Member State will be responsible for the review. On the basis of its assessment, the other Member States will decide on the renewal

310 Art. 14 (2) Proposal for a Regulation.

311 Art. 21 Proposal for a Regulation.

312 Art. 4 (4) Directive 91/414.

313 Art. 6 Directive 91/414.

314 Art. 6 Directive 91/414.

315 Art. 4 (6) Directive 91/414.

316 Art. 6 Directive 91/414.

317 Art. 6 Directive 91/414.

of the authorization when the initial authorization is due to expire.[318] Yet the Member States may still review an authorization at any time. If a Member State decides to withdraw or amend an authorization, it must immediately inform the holder of the authorization, the other Member States and the Commission. The other Member States belonging to the same zone must withdraw or amend the authorization accordingly.[319] However, each Member State may grant a period of grace.[320] Thus, the Proposal for a Regulation streamlines renewal, withdrawal and amendment, while leaving discretion to the Member States concerning the period of grace to be granted.

5.5 Community supervision

The Commission supervision of the Member States' enforcement efforts regarding plant protection products is facilitated through the reporting obligation as stipulated in the Directive.[321] The Member States are obliged to submit annual reports on the results of the inspection measures taken in the previous year to the other Member States and the Commission.[322] Data on enforcement are not readily available from the website of DG Sanco, which can be explained by the absence of an obligation for the Commission to draw up a combined report and publish it. The Proposal for a Regulation may facilitate Commission supervision on plant protection products, as it provides that Commission experts may carry out general and specific audits in the Member States for purposes of verifying the official controls carried out by the Member States.[323] A drawback is that the reporting obligation of Directive 414/91 does not apply to plant protection products that have been authorized by the Member States according to their own standards and not yet under the Directive (or the future Regulation). The Commission cannot influence enforcement activities regarding these products, as the separate reporting obligation that applies to national authorizations does not oblige the Member States to report the results of inspection measures. It only obliges them to report which products they have authorized and which authorizations they have withdrawn, including the reasons for withdrawal.[324]

---

318 Art. 42 Directive 91/414.

319 Art. 43 Proposal for a Regulation.

320 Art. 45 Proposal for a Regulation.

321 Art. 17 Directive 91/414.

322 E.g. the Dutch Annual Report 2006, available at: http://www.ctb.agro.nl/pls/portal/docs/page/website_ctb/organisatie/04jaarverslag/070503_jaarverslag_2006_tekst520web.pdf.

323 Art. 65 Proposal for a Regulation.

324 Art. 12 Directive 91/414.

5.6 Conclusions

Compliance control of the plant protection product legislation is the responsibility of the individual Member States. Despite European harmonization of the regulation of plant protection products, enforcement has hardly been harmonized by Directive 91/414 and may therefore differ between the Member States. They take enforcement action on their own territory on the basis of their own procedural rules without a clear division of competence, not even with regard to the withdrawal of authorizations. Enforcement depends on information reported to the Member States and the Commission by the authorization holder and by other authorities that monitor the maximum level of residues in food and feed and water quality, which offer indications of illegal or irresponsible use of plant protection products. In the absence of a rapid alert system, information exchange takes place informally and in committee meetings.

Although the Member States have to report to the Commission regarding the implementation of Directive 91/414, it is not clear how they apply and enforce Directive 91/414 in the absence of a combined report published by the Commission. It may therefore not come as a surprise that the Commission has proposed a new Directive on sustainable use and a Regulation to improve the enforcement of the regulation of plant protection products. As regards procedural guarantees in the enforcement phase, the legislation does not mention any, thus assuming that the procedural guarantees developed in the case law of the Community courts and the national courts will be respected, without offering any explicit guarantees – in particular the right to be heard in case of withdrawal of an authorization – to the authorization holder or to third parties, such as users of the product or environmental organizations.

6 Conclusions

Due to the open borders, a flawed, illegal or dangerous product can be anywhere on the internal market. While customs control should prevent the import of illegal products, internal control should prevent the movement of illegal products within the EU. It appears from the reference areas that self-enforcement is established to facilitate public enforcement, as the manufacturer, importer or authorization holder are best aware of the quality of their products and should therefore cooperate with the authorities. Their reports about situations of non-compliance should trigger enforcement action by the public authorities. Self-enforcement can therefore improve the effectiveness of public enforcement, but it may be too weak to ensure effective enforcement in bad times and therefore compliance control of the self-enforcement obligations and the imposition of sanctions in case of an infringement remain important.[325]

[325] Widdershoven (1999), pp. 240-241.

Public enforcement by administrative authorities of Community legislation starts with compliance control, which can take the form of national control, home state control, network control or Community control. National control refers to control by national authorities, whose powers are limited to their own territory. Home state control refers to control by the authorities of the reference Member State or the Member State of entry into the EU, whose powers are limited to their own territory, while the host states should not systematically control compliance in order to prevent double controls. Network control refers to control by the authorities of a Member State, which may achieve EU-wide effect through information exchange or mutual assistance, with the Commission or a Community body acting as a focal point, in order to achieve joint action. When compliance control reveals an infringement, it may be followed by the imposition of emergency measures or sanctions, which take the form of either a Community decision or a national decision. Community control refers to control by Community officials of Community legislation. Community control of individuals hardly exists. Instead, the final stage of the enforcement of Community law is Community supervision of the enforcement efforts of the Member States.

Both home state control and network control can provide enforcement with EU-wide effect. In a system of home state control, it is crucial to achieve a level playing field in enforcement, as trade patterns can shift to the Member State with the weakest enforcement level. This is known to occur in the enforcement of CITES, but it may affect all imported products, since a single Member State is responsible for customs control of imported products at the external borders of the EU and assigns them their status of Community goods, while smuggled products escape customs control altogether. The common rules in the Community Customs Code contribute towards achieving a level playing field, but it depends on the implementation of these rules whether a level playing field can actually be achieved. In the EU 27, achieving a level playing field will most likely be unrealistic, since even harmonized control requirements coupled with preventive measures, such as training and twinning, cannot prevent that divergent enforcement between Member States will occur. In that case a Member State may not take unilateral measures, but has to make use of Community procedures, such as the safeguard procedure, or request the Commission to take action.[326]

In order to establish a level playing field of enforcement efforts, the Commission can police the enforcement efforts of the Member States. Yet infringement proceedings are not a panacea against weak enforcement efforts for many reasons. First of all, infringement proceedings take many years, especially since financial penalties can only be imposed on a Member State in the second procedure against the same infringement. Perhaps the interim relief procedure can be used to speed up the time needed to achieve compliance, as it is possible to request a financial penalty in a 228 EC procedure if a Member State fails to comply with the interim relief procedure. In the second place, the infringement

[326] See Chapter 2, section 2.4.

procedure may not be adequate for small or incidental infringements. In the third place, the Commission's limited resources coupled with the rule that the Commission has the burden of proof make it near to impossible for its supervision to guarantee a level playing field at a sufficiently high level. This remains true despite the improvement of the Commission's information position through the increasingly common reporting obligations in secondary legislation and through the establishment of its own inspection agencies on the ground such as the FVO, which is unfortunately less common.

Network control is established because administrative cooperation is expected to provide a counterweight to variations in enforcement level between Member States and it can provide enforcement EU-wide effects. The basic feature is information exchange, facilitated by a Community database, while the feature of operational assistance is less common. Administrative cooperation in a network enables the competent authorities to continue to exercise their powers within their national territory while at the same time providing their enforcement efforts with Community-wide effects. In other words, it enables them to act as one. That is a huge step forward from national control, but also from home state control, where enforcement also has EU-wide effects, but requires faith in the enforcement efforts of the home state. Administrative cooperation in a network is less dependent on the efforts of each individual Member State because it does not matter which Member State finds a flawed, illegal or dangerous product, but only that this finding is communicated to the Commission and the other Member States through a rapid alert system in order to enable joint action. It also involves the Commission to a greater extent, as its task is not limited to supervision, but it or a Community agency facilitates the administrative cooperation between the Member States.

On the basis of the above, it is possible to rank the four types of enforcement control of European administrative decisions from the point of view of their effectiveness in ensuring free movement and a high level of protection of the environment or public health:

- Community control should not be included in this ranking because it is hardly exercised due to a lack of Community competence in the area of EC product regulation (as in most other areas of Community law). Indeed, the present Community inspection services in the area of EC product regulation are mostly used for supervision of the Member States.
- National control ranks last because it cannot be effective on the internal market due to the absence of a division of competence, which leads to double controls. Nevertheless, national control can be effective for the protection of public health and the environment in so far as it controls the use of the authorized product. However, even though this aspect is generally not regulated by Community legislation, the Proposal for a Sustainable use Directive in the area of plant protection products demonstrates that the complementary function of national control is finally acknowledged at the European level.

- Home state control seems the most effective control system because only a single Member State controls a product. However, this type of control only ranks second, because it is vulnerable to variations in enforcement levels due to the fixed division of competences it prescribes.
- Network control deserves the first place, because it overcomes the legal boundaries between the Member States as it is geared towards the exchange of information and joint action in order to enable enforcement on the internal market. Since this type of control does not prescribe a fixed division of competences between the Member States, it can be used as a superstructure to enable Community control or to improve home state control or national control. It is therefore not surprising that the reference areas reveal a trend towards network control.

What is remarkable is the lack of a uniform framework for administrative cooperation in enforcement matters. Huge differences exist between the reference areas. For instance, the information exchange and operational assistance between the customs authorities in accordance with the Mutual Assistance Regulation does not systematically apply to the protection of other Community interests related to product regulation, since it only applies to toys, medicines, food and feed (including GMOs for food and feed use) and counterfeit products. It is also problematic that each category of authority seems to have its own system for information exchange. A separate information exchange system may enable the customs authorities or the medicines authorities to operate as one, but it does not enable the Community administration to operate as one. This is achieved only in the context of CITES, even though the CITES Regulation did not provide for a rapid alert system. In order to remedy this, TRAFFIC Europe and several European and national institutions established the voluntary information exchange system EU-TWIX, which enables all designated CITES enforcement officials to exchange information. In the area of plant protection products an information exchange system is absent, which means that information exchange can only occur informally through consultations and committee meetings.

A similar remarkable lack of Community harmonization occurs regarding the administrative sanctions to be imposed when an infringement is found, such as a penalty payment, administrative coercion or a fine. Usually, there is nothing more than the general rule developed in the Community courts' case law that the national authorities have to impose equivalent, effective, dissuasive and proportionate sanctions. The exception is the Regulation about Community sanctions in the area of medicines with a Community authorization, which provides that the Commission should take into account whether national authorities have also started a procedure or imposed a sanction. At least this points towards coordination. Yet it is remarkable that such a provision is absent regarding the sanctions imposed by national authorities in other areas, including medicines authorized under the mutual recognition procedure. This means that coordination between Member States is not ensured and that huge differences regarding the severity of sanctions can occur between the Member States.

It appears from the reference areas that the withdrawal of products, a form of administrative coercion, is usually not elaborated on in regulation, with the provisions in the CITES Regulation about seizure and forfeiture forming a notable exception. However, as a rule, the Commission is empowered to decide about emergency measures, which the Member States have to implement, as they may only take temporary safeguard measures. Therefore, it may be expected that the Commission emergency decision will include provisions that ensure that products are withdrawn in all the Member States. The lack of rules or recommendations in the reference areas can perhaps be explained by the reliance on self-enforcement in this regard. The authorization holder will withdraw a defective product because of reputation damage and liability claims, in the area of medicines, plant protection products and GMOs. However, this is only possible if the authorization holder can be held responsible. For unaccompanied shipments of illegal products, e.g. CITES protected animals without valid CITES documents or counterfeit medicines, the state will have to take action in order to withdraw the product and cost recovery will be impossible until the responsible party or company can be identified.

This can be contrasted with the Commission's involvement in the withdrawal of authorizations. Of course, the Commission withdraws Community authorizations, but it can also withdraw mutual recognition decisions – for instance those that authorize the placing on the market of medicines – and it can withdraw single-licence marketing authorizations which occurs with regard to GMOs for other uses when the Member States are unable to agree about withdrawal. The Commission is not involved in the withdrawal of the single licence CITES decisions. In that area, the reference Member State can withdraw these decisions, but it is also possible that another Member State takes a decision with this effect after consultation with the reference Member State, if it has detected an infringement that justifies a void declaration of the CITES documents. Where it concerns the withdrawal of authorizations for plant protection products, Member States withdraw their own authorizations, but these decisions must comply with the Commission's listing decisions.

Concerning the procedural guarantees, the right to be heard should be guaranteed during the enforcement phase, independent from the choice for a specific type of control, measure or sanction. In the absence of a general European Administrative Law Code, the right to be heard ought to be elaborated in sectoral legislation in order to ensure that those who are adversely affected by a decision are heard. Unfortunately, it follows from the area of CITES that it is possible that authorization holders are confronted with enforcement action without being granted the right to be heard. Even in the absence of a provision to that effect, the national authorities should hear the authorization holder before declaring his CITES documents void. This is because this declaration constitutes de facto a sanction and the Community courts acknowledge that the right to be heard should be observed when the administration takes a sanction decision. It is also a shortcoming that the rights of third parties are generally ignored in the enforcement stage. In none of the reference areas third parties are granted the right to be heard, even though they may have requested enforcement action to be taken or want a withdrawal to be reconsidered, for instance because they benefited from the use of a withdrawn product. In the absence of an explicit provision on the right to be heard in secondary legislation, the authorities may not take the interests of those affected by their enforcement action into account. Another consequence is that the right to be heard may not be equally respected in all the Member States. It must be concluded that EC product legislation pays insufficient attention to the right to be heard during the enforcement stage.

CHAPTER 4

Direct Actions Before the Community Courts

One might assume that the Community courts offer judicial protection in all cases regarding Community decisions, be they listing decisions or marketing authorizations. After all, judicial review of administrative acts of the Community institutions serves to ensure that the Commission and the Council act within their powers and exercise their discretion properly.[1] Moreover, it corresponds with the idea that the European Community is a Community based on the rule of law, acting on the basis of conferred powers, whose administration is subject to judicial review of the compatibility of their acts with the Treaty and with the general principles of law, including fundamental rights.[2] Nevertheless, Article 220 EC attributes the task to ensure that the law is observed in the interpretation and application of the Treaty to the Community courts, without promising that the Community courts offer judicial protection to anyone whose Community rights are infringed or whose interests are affected by a Community act.[3] Consequently, not all applicants, be they the holders or the prospective holders of an authorization, competitors or organizations championing environmental protection, consumer rights or patient rights may be able to realise their rights to effective judicial protection before the Community courts.

This chapter will answer the questions when individual parties can bring a direct action before the Community courts to challenge a Community act and which remedies are available to them. These two aspects of judicial protection are essential in transnational cases, because direct access to the Community courts offers individual parties a uniform remedy, which can remove the need to bring proceedings in up to 27 Member States. Therefore, both the available remedies and the conditions that govern access to the Community courts will be analyzed. In the context of the reference areas, attention will be paid to circumstances that enable or hinder individuals who need to comply with the standing requirements in order to challenge a Community marketing authorization or a Community listing decision. Finally, a conclusion will be drawn on whether the available remedies and rules on direct access to the Community courts offer effective judicial protection to authorization holders, prospective authorization holders and third parties.

1 The remedies

The Treaty offers four types of remedies. Provided that applicants meet the standing requirements, they can request the annulment of a Community act under Article 230 EC or a declaration of failure to act by the Community institutions under Article 232 EC and, as a connected remedy,

---

1 Arnull (2001), p. 23. See also: Somsen (2000), pp. 311-360; Curtin (1992), p. 34. De Sadeleer, Roller and Dross (2005), p. 177; Betlem (1999), pp. 391-418 and Van Hoek (2006), pp. 313-337.

2 Art. 5 EC; C-294/83 *Les Verts* v *European Parliament* [1986] ECR 1339 and C-50/00 P *Union de Pequenos Agricultores* v *Council (UPA)* [2002] ECR I-6677.

3 Schmidt-A mann (2004), p. 395; Borowski (2004), p. 880.

request for interim relief under Articles 242 and 243 EC. By contrast, an individual party may institute proceedings to obtain compensation for damages under Articles 235 and 288 (2) EC without any *locus standi* conditions imposed. Due to the integrated administration of Community law, it is important to know when a Community Court or a national court is competent to settle a dispute and offer a remedy. The remedies will be analyzed here, while the next section will analyze the standing conditions under which they are available.

Action for annulment

Individual parties can bring a direct action for annulment to contest the legality of a Community act. This action can also be used to challenge a fine issued by the Commission. Provided applicants meet the standing requirements, they must start the proceedings within two months of the publication of the act.[4] Those who have brought an admissible action against a Community act which implements another Community act, can also challenge the validity of the underlying act on the grounds of Article 230 EC.[5] These grounds are: lack of competence, infringement of an essential procedural requirement, infringement of the Treaty or of any rule of law relating to its application, or misuse of powers. The grounds for annulment particularly reflect the obligation of Article 5 EC that the Community must act within the limits of its powers and have a legal basis within the Treaties for every legal act it adopts.[6] If an action for annulment is well founded, the Community Court declares the act void *ab initio*. However, it may impose limits on the temporal effects of its ruling.[7] The institution is obliged to comply with the Court's judgment.[8]

The Community courts do not restrict their review capacities to compatibility with the Treaty, as they interpret 'any rule of law' in the sense that infringement of a general principle of Community law, including fundamental rights, constitutes a ground for annulment as well.[9] Their review includes the duty established by Article 253 EC to state the reasons on which the act is based. This is an essential procedural requirement, because it enables the parties concerned to determine whether the act is well founded or invalidated by an error.[10] In their

---

4 See Art. 230 (5) EC for exceptions.

5 C-92/78 *Simmenthal* v *Commission* [1979] ECR 777; C-33/80 *Albini* v *Council* [1981] ECR 2141, T-154/94 *Comité des Salines de France* v *Commission* [1996] ECR II-1377. See: Jaeger (1999), in the translated version: p. 6.

6 See: Van Ooik (1999).

7 Art. 231 EC only mentions Regulations, but in C-295/90 *European Parliament* v *Council* [1992] ECR I-4193 and C-22/96 *European Parliament* v *Council* [1998] ECR I-3231, the Court extended this rule to Directives and Decisions.

8 Art. 233 EC.

9 Case 11/70 *Internationale Handelsgesellschaft* v *Einfuhr und Vorratstelle für Getreide und Futtermittel* [1970] ECR 1125.

10 E.g. C-269/90 *Hauptzollamt München Mitte* v *Technische Universität München* [1991] ECR I-5469, C-199/99 P *Corus UK* v *Commission* [2003] ECR I-11177, T-228/02 *Organisation des Modjahedines du people*

review, the Community courts take into account whether the institutions have a significant degree of discretionary room. If that is the case, judicial review is limited to verifying that the authorities exercised the room for discretion by taking all relevant factors and circumstances into account and that the measure in question is not invalidated by any manifest error or misuse of powers, and that the authority concerned has not manifestly exceeded the limits of its discretion.[11] Examples where the limits of discretion were exceeded included a complex decision taken without requesting scientific advice and a decision that disregarded the requested scientific opinion because the representatives of a Member State discerned potential risks, without substantiating this with other scientific advice.[12]

Failure to act

An individual party may also challenge a failure to act if a Community institution, in violation of the Treaty, has failed to communicate to a party any act other than a recommendation or an opinion[13] or has not acted within a prescribed time limit. Provided the standing requirements are met, the action for failure to act is only admissible if the institution concerned has first been called upon to act. If, within two months, the institution has not defined its position, the action may be brought within a further period of two months. A letter emanating from an institution, stating that examination of the questions raised is in progress, does not constitute the definition of a position which brings a failure to act to an end.[14] Where a definition of position is presented after an action for failure to act is instituted, this terminates the Commission's failure to act and deprives the action of its subject matter.[15] If the Court declares that the Community institution has failed to act, it neither issues a positive or negative fictitious decision, nor any directions to the institution concerned. Instead, it is for the institution concerned to act in order to comply with the order of the Court, as follows from Article 233 EC.[16] The Court does not have the competence to impose a penalty payment on the institution in case of failure to comply with its judgment. This may explain why this procedure is rarely followed.

---

d'Iran v *Council* [2006] ECR II-4665.

11 C-120/99 *Italy* v *Council* [2001] ECR I-7997, C-189/01 *Jippes* [2001] ECR I-5689 and C-310/04 *Spain* v *Council* [2006] ECR I-7285.

12 C-212/91 *Angelopharm* v *Freie Hansestadt Hamburg* [1994] ECR I-171; T-31/07 R *Du Pont de Nemours et al.* v *Commission* [2007] ECR II-2767 and T-229/04 *Sweden* v *Commission* [2007] ECR II-2437.

13 T-395/04 *Air One* v *Commission* [2006] ECR II-1343.

14 Joined Cases 42 and 49/59 *SNUPAT* v *High Authority* [1961] ECR 53, C-13/83 *Parliament* v *Council* [1985] ECR 1513, T-95/96 *Gestevisión Telecinco* v *Commission* [1998] ECR II-3407 and Case T-212/99 *Intervet* v *Commission* [2002] ECR II-1445.

15 C-282/95 P *Guérin automobiles* v *Commission* [1997] ECR I-1503, and T-28/90 *Asia Motor France and Others* v *Commission* [1992] ECR II-2285.

16 T-74/92 *Ladbroke* v *Commission* [1995] ECR II-115 and T-127/98 *UPS Europe* v *Commission* [1999] ECR II-2633.

Interim relief

Challenging a Community act does not have suspensory effect. However, suspension of the operation of a Community act may be necessary to safeguard effective judicial protection. Therefore, Article 242 EC provides that the President of the CFI or the ECJ may order that application of the contested act be suspended if circumstances so require. This action is only admissible if the applicant is challenging the act before one of the Community courts.[17] The President considers the interests of the applicant, which includes (1) whether they have a prima facie case, i.e. whether the action is prima facie admissible and the applicant's argument is serious and not clearly untenable, (2) the urgency, i.e. the imminence of serious and irreparable damage, and (3) the preservative nature of the requested measures.

The President has to balance the interests of the applicant against the interests of the Community.[18] The President grants interim relief if it seems justified and necessary to adopt measures that take effect before a decision on the substance of a case is given in order to avoid serious and irreparable damage to the party seeking interim relief.[19] In addition, Article 243 EC provides that the President may prescribe any necessary interim measures in any cases before it. This means that other measures than the mere suspension of an act are possible as well and that interim relief is also available to applicants following other procedures, e.g. in case of a failure to act. Of course, the applicant has to specify which measures the President of the Court should prescribe in the order.[20] It can be deduced from the handful of successful cases that it requires a strong case to be granted interim relief.[21]

Damages

An individual party can seek compensation for damages caused by a Community act, or absence thereof, insofar as the damage is caused by the Community institutions or servants in the performance of their duties. Three cumulative conditions must be met in order to obtain compensation for damages.[22] The first two conditions are that the unlawful act or conduct must constitute a sufficiently serious breach of a superior rule of law conferring rights on individual parties. If a Community institution has exercised discretionary power, the decisive test is whether it manifestly and gravely disregarded the limits of its discretion. If the Community institution concerned had little or no discretionary room, the mere infringement of Community law may constitute a

17 As follows from Art. 104 of the Rules of Procedure of the CFI. E.g. Order of the President of the Court in C-380/04 *Bactria* v *Commission* [2004] ECR I-0000.

18 E.g. T-31/07 *Du Pont de Nemours et al.* v *Commission* [2007] ECR II-2767.

19 Cf. Joined Cases C-143/88 and C-92/90 *Zuckerfabrik Süderditmarschen* [1991] ECR 415.

20 Order of the President of the Court in C-380/04 *Bactria* v *Commission* [2004] ECR I-0000.

21 Castillo de la Torre (2007), p. 352.

22 C-5/71 *Schöppenstedt* v *Council* [1971] ECR 975 and C-352/98 P *Bergaderm and Goupil* v *Commission* [2000] ECR I-5291.

sufficiently serious breach.[23] The third condition is the reality of the damage and the presence of a causal link between the breach of the obligation falling on the institution and the damage complained about.[24]

The action for damages is an autonomous remedy, but it can be combined with the action for annulment. Prior exhaustion of remedies is required, provided that those remedies give effective judicial protection to the individual parties concerned and can result in compensation for the asserted damage.[25] In particular, an action for annulment before the Community courts is required when financial decisions (including fines) are concerned,[26] because otherwise the applicant could circumvent the time limit of Article 230 EC.[27] The time limit for a claim for damages, which is five years from the time that all requirements governing an obligation to provide compensation for damage are satisfied and, in particular, the damage to be compensated materialised,[28] is longer for those who institute annulment proceedings, which a party may do in order to limit the damage (but is not obliged to). In that case, the period of limitation starts at the time that the measure is declared void for those who institute annulment proceedings.[29] The scope of this exception is only extended to those who are directly affected by the annulled act.[30]

An action for damages does not present an equivalent course of action, compared with the action for annulment or for failure to act, since a successful claim only results in compensation of damage, not in the annulment of the act or in a declaration that the institutions failed to act.[31] Moreover, the intensity of judicial review differs, because the Community courts only review whether an unlawful act constitutes a sufficiently serious breach of a rule that is intended to confer rights on individual parties.[32] Therefore, it depends on the discretionary

---

23 C-358/98 P *Bergaderm and Goupil* v *Commission* [2000] ECR I-5291, C-312/00 P *Commission* v *Camar and Tico* [2002] ECR I-11355.

24 C-5/71 *Aktien-Zuckerfabrik Schöppenstedt* v *Council* [1971] ECR 975.

25 C-81/86 *De Boer Buizen* v *Council and Commission* [1987] ECR 3677; T-138/03 *E.R. and Others* v *Council and Commission* [2006] ECR II-4923.

26 C-5/71 *Schöppenstedt* v *Council* [1971] ECR 975 and T-199/96 *Bergaderm and Goupil* v *Commission* [1998] ECR II-2805, upheld in appeal: C-352/98 P *Bergaderm and Goupil* v *Commission* [2000] ECR I-5291.

27 C-543/79 *Birke* v *Commission and Council* [1981] ECR 2669 and C-310/97 P *Commission* v *AssiDomän Kraft et al.* [1999] ECR I-5363.

28 C-282/05 P *Holcim* v *Commission* [2007] ECR I-6441. See: Ward (2000), p. 291.

29 T-52/99 *T. Port* v *Commission* [2001] ECR II-981, upheld in appeal in C-213/01 P *T. Port* v *Commission* [2003] ECR I-0000 and T-174/00 *Biret International* v *Council* [2002] ECR II-17, upheld in appeal in C-93/02 P *Biret* v *Council* [2003] ECR I-10497.

30 See C-310/97 P *Commission* v *AssiDomän Kraft et al.* [1999] ECR I-5363. Other cases might also be resolved by a duty of the administration to re-examine unlawful decisions, see: Joined Cases C-42 and 49/59 *Snupat* v *High Authority* [1961] ECR 53 and Joined Cases C-97, 99, 193 and 215/86 *Asteris and Others* v *Commission* [1988] ECR 2181.

31 C-63/89 *Assicurance du Crédit* [1991] ECR I-1799.

32 E.g. Opinion of Advocate General Geelhoed in C-491/01 *The Queen* v *Secretary for Health, ex parte British American Tobacco (Investments) and Imperial Tobacco* [2002] ECR I-11453 and Opinion of Advocate

room left to the institutions how difficult it will be to establish a sufficiently serious breach.[33] As a consequence, the Court may declare a Community act invalid, but dismiss the ensuing action for liability because the breach is not sufficiently serious or no causal link is established.[34]

2 Access to court

While privileged parties, such as a Member State, the Commission or the Council, can bring a direct action against Community acts intended to produce legal effects vis-à-vis third parties, an individual party is in a different position. Only the action for damages is available to parties without *locus standi* limitations,[35] except for the requirement that the applicant has a legal interest in bringing proceedings.[36] Any natural or legal person who wants to bring an action for annulment, failure to act[37] or interim relief proceedings before the CFI and in appeal before the ECJ has to meet the conditions of Article 230 (4) EC, which are that they can bring an action against decisions, provided that the decision is addressed to them or that the decision – taken either in the form of a regulation or in the form of a decision addressed to another party – is of direct and individual concern to them. A legal person – including legal persons governed by public law, such as regions and devolved authorities – needs to have legal personality under national law.[38] First the general standing conditions, then two exceptions that facilitate access to court and often apply in the area of product regulation, and finally the division of competence between the Community courts and the national courts will be analyzed.

General Tesauro in C-63/89 *Assicurance du Crédit* [1991] ECR I-1799. See also: Ward (2000), p. 291.

33 C-5/94 Hedley Lomas [1996] ECR I-2553; T-480 and 483 *Antillean Rice Mills* v *Commission* [1995] ECR II-2305, C-390/95 P *Antillean Rice Mills* v *Commission* [1999] ECR I-769; C-352/98 P *Laboratoires Parmaceutiqus Bergaderm and Goupil* v *Commission* [2000] ECR I-5291; Opinion AG Poiares Maduro and the ECJ judgment in C-243/05 P *Agraz, SA and Others* v *Commission* [2006] ECR I-10833. See: Ward (2000), pp. 313-318 and pp. 338-340.

34 E.g. T-226/01 *CAS Succhi di Frutta* v *Commission* [2006] ECR II-2763. See: Meij (1997), p. 276 and Jans *et al.* (2007), p. 258.

35 Cf. the Opinion of Advocate General Jacobs in C-50/00 P *Union de Pequenos Agricultores* v *Council (UPA)* [2002] ECR I-6677.

36 T-304/01 *Julia Abad Pérez and Others against Council and Commission* [2006] ECR II-4857.

37 C-68/95 *Port* v *Bundesanstalt für Landwirtschaft un Ernährung* [1996] ECR I-6065; T-395/04 *Air One* v *Commission* [2006] ECR II-1343.

38 E.g. Order in C-95/97 *Région Wallone* v *Commission* [1997] ECR I-5245 and Order in C-180/97 *Regione Toscana* v *Commission* [1997] ECR I-8973; C-288/97 *Regione Autonoma Friuli-Venezia Giulia* v *Commission* [1999] ECR II-2575; C142/00 P *Commission* v *Nederlandse Antillen* [2003] ECR I-3483; C-417/04 P *Regione Siciliana* v *Commission* [2006] ECR I-3881. See: Lenaerts *et al.* (2006), p. 273.

2.1 The general standing conditions

The standing conditions require first of all that the act against which proceedings are brought be a reviewable act. Decisions are reviewable acts if they constitute 'a measure the legal effects of which are binding on and capable of affecting the interests of the applicant by bringing about a distinct change in their legal position'.[39] It does not matter whether the decision is addressed to an individual party or to a Member State.[40] This means that both a marketing authorization and a decision not to include a certain substance in the Annex to a Regulation can be challenged. A committee opinion cannot be challenged directly, even though the form of the measure is not decisive,[41] because it does not have a final character. It is an intermediate measure, whose purpose it is to prepare for the final Commission or Council decision.[42] However, as it constitutes an integral part of the statement of reasons, it can be challenged in the course of the action for annulment against the Community decision taken on the basis of the committee opinion. The Court can then be asked, first, to review the legality of the underlying committee opinion and second, to review the Commission's exercise of discretion in deciding whether or not to accept that opinion.[43]

It is the question whether individuals can challenge a Commission Regulation or Directive that lists a certain substance in its Annex. Article 230 EC includes the possibility that a decision is taken in the form of a regulation. In order to determine whether a regulation is susceptible to judicial review by private applicants, the ECJ does not make a distinction between acts adopted through a legislative procedure involving the Council and the European Parliament and acts adopted through the Comitology procedure.[44] This means that legislative acts are placed in the same category as acts implementing secondary legislation. The main criterion for distinguishing between a regulation and a

---

39 C-8-11/66 *Cimenteries Cementbedrijven et al.* v *Commission* [1967] ECR 75; C-60/81 *IBM* v *Commission* [1981] ECR 2639. See also: Joined Cases T-377/00, T-379/00, T-390/00, T-260/01 and T-272/01 *Philip Morris International and Others* v *Commission* [2003] ECR 2639, upheld in appeal C-131/03 P *Reynolds and Others* v *Commission* [2006] ECR I-7795 and C-547/03 P *Asian Institute of Technology (AIT)* v *Commission* [2006] ECR I-845.

40 C-25/62 *Plaumann* [1963] ECR 95.

41 C-60/81 *IBM* v *Commission* [1981] ECR 2639. Cf. C-22/70 *Commission* v *Council (ERTA)* [1971] ECR 263. See: Arnull (2006), p. 56 et seq.

42 C-60/81 *IBM* v *Commission* [1981] ECR 2639.

43 T-326/99 *Nancy Fern Olivieri* v *Commission* [2003] ECR II-6053 and Joined Cases T-74/00, T-76/00, T-83/00 to T-85/00, T-132/00, T-137/00 and T-141/00 *Artegodan and Others* v *Commission* [2002] ECR II-4945. The latter judgment was upheld on appeal in C-39/03 P *Commission* v *Artegodan* [2003] ECR I-7885, but the ECJ did not consider this issue. See: Craig (2006), p. 186.

44 Kapteyn and VerLoren van Themaat (2003), pp. 1181- 1182; Prechal (2005), pp. 486-489. This distinction is introduced in the Constitutional Treaty, see: Liisberg (2006).

decision is the general or individual application of the measure in question.[45] This is determined via the abstract terminology test.[46] A 'true' regulation applies to objectively determined situations and produces legal effects with regard to categories of persons envisaged in a generalized and abstract manner.[47] This applies to the amendment of an Annex that concerns an active substance and applies to economic operators who hold marketing authorizations that are referred to in a general and abstract manner.[48]

Since the ECJ cancelled the rule that individuals cannot challenge true regulations,[49] individual parties may also challenge a Regulation that amends the Annex to a Regulation, provided that they can establish direct and individual concern.[50] The ECJ confirmed this approach in the *Jégo Quéré* case, based on the argument that even a measure of general application such as a Regulation can be of direct and individual concern to some individual parties and thus has the nature of a decision in their regard.[51] This means that the distinction between decisions and acts of general application has become somewhat blurred in European case law.[52] However, the judgments in *Codorniu* and *Jégo Quéré* did not end the debate about the question of whether a decision can also be taken in the form of a Directive or whether a Directive as such can be challenged in a direct action. Even though both the ECJ and the CFI have accepted, in principle, that individual parties can challenge Directives,[53] the characteristics of the Directive as a legal instrument make it unlikely for individual parties to be able to challenge a Directive amending the Annex to a Directive in practice.[54] Nevertheless, in the absence of discretion it might be possible to challenge such a directive.

Direct and individual concern

The applicant to whom the decision is addressed can institute proceedings without any *locus standi* limitations, but other individual parties, the so-called third parties, need to establish both direct and individual concern in order to

45 C-307/81 *Alusuisse* v *Council and Commission* [1982] ECR 3463.

46 E.g. C-789 and 790/79 *Calpak SpA and Societá Emiliana Lavorazione Frutta SpA* v *Commission* [1980] ECR 1949. See: Craig and De Burca (2007), pp. 493-495.

47 E.g. C-263/02 P *Jégo Queré* v *Commission* [2004] ECR I-3425.

48 T-475/07 R *Dow AgroSciences and Others* v *Commission* [2008] II-0000.

49 C-309/89 *Codorniu* v *Council* [1994] ECR I-1853, preceded by a string of anti-dumping cases, e.g. C-191/82 *Fediol* v *Commission* [1983] ECR ECR 2913.

50 E.g.T-37/04 *Regiao autonoma dos Acores* v *Council* [2008] ECR II-0000.

51 C-263/02 P *Jégo Queré* v *Commission* [2004] ECR I-3425. Advocate General Jacobs calls this the hybridity theory in his Opinion in C-358/89 *Extramet Industrie* v *Council* [1991] ECR I-2501.

52 See: Arnull (2006), pp. 70-74.

53 T-99/94 *Asociación Espanalo de Empresas de la Carne (ASOCARNE)* v *Council* [1994] ECR II-71; upheld in appeal, C-10/95 P [1995] ECRI-4149; T-135/96 *UEAPME* v *Council* [1998] ECR II-2335; T-172, 175 and 177/98 *Salamander* v *Parliament and Council* [2000] ECR II-2487; T-94/04 *EEB and Others* v *Commission* [2005] ECR II-4919.

54 See: Craig and De Burca (2007), p. 488 and Lenaerts *et al.* (2006), p. 253.

gain access to court.[55] The same applies when the institutions failed to take a decision that would be addressed to the applicant or of direct and individual concern to him.[56] In addition, all applicants need to establish a legal interest in bringing proceedings,[57] but not an infringement of their public law rights.[58]

Individual parties, including associations, can establish direct concern if a Community act constitutes a complete set of rules which in themselves would be sufficient, not requiring implementing measures.[59] If an act is directed to the Member States, it should directly affect the individual party's legal situation and leave no discretionary room to the addressees of that measure who are entrusted with the task of implementing it, such implementation being purely automatic and resulting from Community rules without the application of other intermediate rules.[60] Regarding Directives, the CFI ruled in the *Salamander* case that the applicant failed to establish direct concern in relation to a Directive, because a Directive cannot of itself impose obligations on individual parties and leaves the Member States the power of assessment.[61] This makes it near to impossible for individual parties to challenge Directives.[62] Perhaps this is different when Directives leave no room for discretion, as is the case with Directives that amend the Annex to a Directive.

The main hurdle to take for individual parties, including associations,[63] is that they need to establish individual concern. There has been little development since the ECJ established in the *Plaumann* case that parties are individually concerned if a decision affects them by reason of certain attributes which are specific to them or by reason of circumstances in which they are differentiated from all other parties and, by virtue of these factors, distinguishes them individually as if it concerned the party addressed.[64] This means that parties are not individually concerned by a decision if it affects them by reason of a commercial activity which may at any time be practised by anyone.[65] In the case *Piraiki-Patraiki* v *Commission*,[66] the ECJ demonstrated that even in the face of a

---

55 Craig (2006), p. 319.

56 C-68/95 *T. Port and Co* [1996] ECR I-6065.

57 Arnull (2006), pp. 80-81. E.g. Joined Cases T-480 and 483/93 *Antillean Rice Mills and Others* v *Commission* [1995] ECR II-2305; Joined Cases T-125/96 and T-152/96 *Boehringer* v *Council and Commission* [1999] ECR II-3427, T-141/03 *Sniace SA* v *Commission* [2005] ECR II-1197.

58 See: Borowski (2004), p. 889.

59 C-294/83 *Les Verts* v *Parliament* [1986] ECR 1339.

60 C-354/87 *Weddel* v *Commission* [1990] ECR I-3847; C-404/96 P *Glencore Grain* v *Commission* [1998] ECR I-2435; C-386/96 P *Dreyfus* v *Commission* [1998] ECR I-2309; T-69/99 *DSTV* v *Commission* [2000] ECR II-4309.

61 T-172, 175 and 177/98 *Salamander* v *Parliament and Council* [2000] ECR II-2487.

62 Craig and De Burca 2007, p. 488.

63 See: T-122/96 *Federolio* v *Commission* [1997] ECR II-1559.

64 C-25/62 *Plaumann and Co* v *Commission* [1963] ECR p. 95. See: Jacobs (2004), p. 314.

65 C-25/62 *Plaumann and Co* v *Commission* [1963] ECR p. 95.

66 C-11/82 *Piraiki Patraiki* v *Commission* [1985] ECR 207.

plausible explanation that no new companies could enter the market during the three months in which the decision applied, it would still rule that a commercial activity may at any time be practised by anyone.[67] Similarly, associations established to protect a general interest, such as protection of the environment, cannot establish individual concern when they want to defend a general or collective concern.[68]

2.2 The procedural guarantees exception

Individual parties can rely on the so-called procedural guarantees exception to establish direct and individual concern.[69] This exception is often relied on in actions regarding Community marketing authorizations or Community listing decisions as it may allow those involved in the decision-making procedure that resulted in the relevant act to challenge it when the decision is not addressed to them. The ECJ only accepts a right to be heard and hence standing on procedural grounds, where their participation in the decision-making procedure is based on Community legislation laying down specific procedural guarantees that apply to the applicant.[70] The same applies to associations.[71] Participation in the decision-making procedure is not sufficient in itself. The Court does not seem inclined to accept the argument that a party who has sent comments to the Commission during the preparation of a decision is different from other members of the public.[72]

If Community law provides for procedural guarantees, it does not necessarily grant them to other individuals than the applicant, which means that third parties may be unable to challenge a Community marketing authorization or a Community listing decision.[73] This raises the question whether Community legislation that provides for Community decisions on the authorization of products or the composition of an Annex should allocate procedural rights to interested parties. Advocate General Geelhoed answered this question in the

---

67 Craig and de Burca 2007, pp. 492-493.

68 T-585/93 *Greenpeace* [1995] ECR II-2205, upheld in appeal, C-321/95 P *Greenpeace* [1998] ECR I-1651 and Joined Cases T-236/04 and T-241/04 *European Environmental Bureau, Stichting Natuur en Milieu*, v *Commission* [2005] ECR II-4919. See: Sands (1996), pp. 23-35.

69 See for other circumstances: Lenaerts *et al.* (2006), pp. 251-260.

70 T-135/96 *UEAPME* v *Council* [1998] ECR II-421; Joined Cases T-125/96 and T-152/96 *Boehringer* v *Council and Commission* [1999] ECR II-3427; T-13/99 *Pfizer Animal Health SA* v *Council* [2002] ECR II-3305, C-258/02 P *Bactria* v *Commission* [2003] ECR I-15105; T-475/07R *Dow AgroSciences and Others* v *Commission* [2008] ECR II-0000. See: Craig (2006), pp. 263 and 314-318.

71 E.g. C-72/74 *Union syndicale-Service public européen and Others* v *Council of the European Communities* [1975] ECR 401; C-191/82 *Fediol* v *Commission* [1983] ECR 2913; T-481 and 484/93 *Exporteurs in Levende Varkens and Others* v *Commission* [1995] ECR II-2653.

72 See C-321/95 *P Stichting Greenpeace Council (Greenpeace International) and Others* v *Commission* [1998] ECR I-1651.

73 E.g. T-350/07 R *FMC Chemical SPRL, Arysta Lifesciece, Belchim Crop Protection, FandN Agro Slovenkso, FandN Agro Ceska republika, FandN Agro Polska and FMC Corp* v *Commission* [2007] ECR II-0000.

affirmative with regard to Community listing decisions in his Opinion in the *Alliance for Natural Health* case.[74] He considered that even though these decisions are of general application and have effect *erga omnes*, they may affect the vital interests of individuals. Their interests can only be taken into account in the decision-making process in a manner which is open to judicial review if the basic legislative act provides for minimal procedural guarantees, which can be a hearing, but also a duty to inform applicants of any gaps in their dossier and allowing them to provide the necessary information.[75] Unfortunately, the Community courts did not prescribe the inclusion of procedural guarantees in Community legislation with regard to interested parties, not even regarding the applicant.[76]

2.3 The environmental disputes exception

Without an exception for environmental disputes, the strict standing requirements would prevent environmental organizations from bringing a direct action against Community acts that have a negative impact on the environment, because the environment is a collective and not an individual interest.[77] The Aarhus Regulation, which implements the Aarhus Convention with regard to the European institutions and bodies, establishes standing requirements for an administrative review procedure on completion of which qualified environmental organizations may gain access to court. Essentially, an environmental organization qualifies if it is an independent non-profit legal person, whose primary objective has been to promote environmental protection for more than two years.[78]

Environmental organizations may challenge administrative 'acts' and 'omissions' taken by Community institutions and bodies contravening 'environmental law'.[79] A measure qualifies as an administrative act in the sense of the Aarhus Regulation, if it is a measure of individual scope under environmental law, taken by a Community institution or body, having legally binding and external effects.[80] An omission refers to the failure of a Community institution

---

74 Joined Cases C-154/04 and C-155/04 *The Queen on the application of Alliance for Natural Health and Nutrilink* v *Secretary of State for Health and the Queen, on the application of National Association of Health Stores and Health Food Manufacturers* v *Secretary of State for Health and National Assembly for Wales* [2005] ECR I-6451.

75 E.g. T-392/02 *Solvay Pharmaceuticals* v *Council* [2003] ECR II-4555.

76 E.g. C-258/02 P *Bactria* v *Commission* [2003] ECR I-1505 and T-70/99 *Alpharma* v *Council* [2002] ECR II-3495.

77 T-585/93 *Greenpeace and Others* v *Commission* [1995] ECR II-2205, upheld in appeal: C-321/95 *Greenpeace and Others* v *Commission* [1998] ECR I-1651.

78 Art. 11 Regulation 1367/2006 and rec. 20 Preamble Regulation 1367/2006.

79 Art. 9 Aarhus Convention. See the Explanatory Memorandum to the Proposal for the Aarhus Regulation, COM (2003) 622 final.

80 Art. 2 (g) Regulation 1367/2006.

or body to adopt an administrative act, where it is legally required to do so.[81] A measure falls within the ambit of environmental law in the sense of the Aarhus Regulation irrespective of its legal basis, if it contributes to the pursuit of the objectives of Community policy on the environment as set out in the Treaty, which are preserving, protecting and improving the quality of the environment, protecting human health, the prudent and rational utilisation of natural resources, and promoting measures at the international level to deal with regional or worldwide environmental problems.[82] Yet the scope of the Aarhus Regulation may be narrow despite its broad definition of environmental law, if the ECJ interprets measure of individual scope in a strict sense.

Reading Aarhus into the Treaty

The provisions of the Aarhus Regulation that offer qualified environmental organizations access to the Community courts do not seem in accordance with the Treaty.[83] Indeed, despite the EU ratification of the Aarhus Convention, the CFI refused to grant standing to environmental organizations in an action against a decision taken in the area of plant protection product regulation, even though the organizations met the conditions of the proposed Aarhus Regulation.[84] It argued that secondary legislation cannot broaden the scope of primary legislation. However, one should not conclude that this means that the Aarhus regulation cannot offer environmental organizations access to court in environmental disputes. The trick of the Aarhus Regulation is that it offers access to court after an administrative review procedure.[85]

The Aarhus Regulation prescribes that an environmental organization must first file a request for review with the authorities that issued the act.[86] This procedural novelty is designed to give the Community institutions the opportunity to reconsider their decision or act[87] and creates a review decision addressed to the applicant of administrative review. If the authorities do not issue a review decision (in time), the Aarhus Regulation will allow for access to court to protest against failure to act.[88] This means that the Aarhus Regulation does not change the Treaty requirements of direct and individual concern, but simply avoids them through the operation of its administrative review procedure with its

81 Artt. 1 (h) and 10 (1) Regulation 1367/2006. Cf. The Explanatory Memorandum to the Proposal for the Aarhus Regulation, COM (2003) 622 final, p. 10.

82 Art. 2 (f) Regulation 1367/2006.

83 Jans (2006), pp. 419-423.

84 Cf. Joined Cases T-236/04 and T-241/04 *European Environmental Bureau, Stichting Natuur en Milieu* [2005] ECR II-4945, see: Keessen (2007), pp. 26-36.

85 Widdershoven (2004), p. 532. Administrative review should not be confused with public participation. Public participation takes place during the decision-making process, while administrative review takes place on request after a decision has been issued. Note that administrative review is called internal review in Regulation 1367/2006.

86 Artt. 10 to 12 Regulation 1367/2006.

87 Rec. 18 Preamble to Regulation 1367/2006.

88 Art. 12 (2) Regulation 1367/2006.

own conditions for access, as the CFI suggested in the case R*egiao autonoma dos Acores* v *Council*.[89] Since this procedure creates a review decision addressed to the applicant, the applicant is entitled to judicial review in his capacity of 'addressee' of a Community act without having to establish direct and individual concern.[90] Nevertheless, trying to obtain standing on the basis of the Aarhus Regulation could be a sobering experience for environmental organizations if the ECJ does not interpret the standing conditions of the Aarhus Regulation broadly.[91]

2.4 The vertical division of competence

Due to the shared administration of Community law, conflicts of jurisdiction can arise. The Community courts have developed rules for annulment proceedings, which also apply in case of failure to act and to interim relief, while there are separate rules that apply to damages cases. The conflict rules that determine whether the Community courts or a national court is competent should avoid both parallel jurisdiction and a denial of jurisdiction. The Community courts determine the conflict rules departing from the *locus standi* conditions as established by the EC Treaty in the assumption that national courts can always assert jurisdiction. Therefore, it should not come as a surprise if some gaps can be discerned in the system of remedies, although the system is said to be complete. Perhaps these gaps will be filled in the future by a change of interpretation or by a change of the Treaty.

Division of jurisdiction

It is possible that the Community and the national authorities take a decision together. If a Community decision is taken on the basis of a national decision, it follows from the *Oleifici Borelli* case that an individual party cannot challenge such a Commission decision without having first challenged the national, preparatory decision.[92] The opposite situation occurs when a Community decision has to be implemented into a national decision. It is possible that an individual party has the option of bringing a direct action against a Community decision, but prefers to bring proceedings before a national court against the national implementing decision and rely on the preliminary ruling procedure for an assessment of the validity of the Community decision.[93] The wording of Article 230 EC does not exclude this choice.[94]

---

89 T-37/04 *Regiao autonoma dos Acores* v *Council* [2008] ECR II-0000.

90 Widdershoven (2004), p. 532.

91 See also: Jans (2006), pp. 483-484.

92 C-97/91 *Oleificio Borelli* [1992] ECR I-6313.

93 See Jans *et al.* (2007), pp. 254-256. See Chapter 5 section 2 about access to a national court and the preliminary ruling procedure.

94 Nowak (2000), p. 278.

If one can still rely on the *Universität Hamburg* case, an individual party may choose not to bring proceedings at the Community level.[95] The Court found in that case that the national enforcement act was the only measure directly addressed to the applicant of which they had necessarily been informed in good time and which they might challenge in the courts without having to prove their direct and individual concern. However, the ECJ established in the *TWD* case that a party who would have passed the direct and individual concern test could not choose to challenge the Community decision in proceedings before a national court because that would in fact enable the party concerned to defeat the definitive nature which the decision assumes against that party after expiry of the time limit for bringing an action.[96] In that situation, the national court is bound to assume the validity of the Community decision.[97] The ECJ ended the uncertainty when it confirmed that the scope of *TWD* is limited to situations where an individual party is undoubtedly directly and individually concerned, and therefore did not preclude that Roquette Freres challenged a Regulation through proceedings against the French implementing measure.[98]

The division of jurisdiction in damages cases depends on the underlying cause. The Community courts will decide the case without imposing any *locus standi* limitations if Community institutions or their servants are said to have caused the damage. If the damage is caused both by Community institutions and by the Member State, an individual party may need to bring actions for damages both before a national court and before the CFI.[99] The Community courts will not declare such parallel actions inadmissible. It will only affect the amount of compensation that can be granted if the claim is well founded. The Community courts will decide in these cases after the national court has ruled in the case.[100] By contrast, an individual party will only need to bring an action for damages before the Community courts if the damage was caused by a Community act which was implemented by a national authority, provided that the national authority was obliged to limit itself to automatic implementation.[101] The Community bears the risk of incurring liability in these circumstances.

95 Joined Cases 133 to 136/85 *Rau* v *BALM* [1987] ECR 228; Case 216/82 *Universität Hamburg* v *Hauptzollamt Hamburg-Kehrwieder* [1983] ECR 2771.

96 C-188/92 *Textilwerke Deggendor* v *Deutschland* [1994] ECR I-833, confirmed in C-178/95 *Wiljo* [1997] ECR 585.

97 See: Widdershoven (2002), p. 291.

98 C-408/95 *Eurotunnel and Others* v *Sea-France* [1997] ECR I-6315 and C-441/05 *Roquette Freres* v *Ministre de l'Agriculture, de l'Alimentation, de la Peche et de la Ruralité* [2007] ECR I-1993. See: Jans *et al.* (2007), pp. 254-256.

99 T-304/01 *Julia Abad Perez and Others, Confederacion de Organizaciones de Agricultores y Ganaderos and Unió de Pagesos* v *Council and Commission* [2006] ECR II-4857 and T-138/03 *E.R. and Others* v *Council and Commission* [2006] ECR II-4923.

100 E.g. T-138/03 *E.R. and Others* v *Council and Commission* [2006] ECR II-4923.

101 C-165/84 *Krohn* [1986] ECR 768, Joined Cases 106-120/87 *Asteris II* [1988] ECR 5538, Joined Cases C-104/89 and C-37/90 *Mulder II* [1992] ECR I-3061. See: Meij (1997), p. 282.

because the Member States are obliged to apply and enforce Community acts until the Community courts have declared them invalid.[102]

Parallel proceedings

It is possible that some individual parties affected by a Community act can bring a direct action before the Community courts, while others have to wait for national implementing measures before they can challenge the underlying Community act before a national court and perhaps through the preliminary ruling procedure obtain a ruling from the Community courts. In this event, the strict *locus standi* conditions may lead to parallel proceedings. This results in procedural inequality in two respects. First, one individual party has direct access to the Community courts, while the other depends on a referral by the national courts.[103] Second, a party with *locus standi* before a Community court may be allowed to intervene in the national proceedings, while a party without *locus standi* is not allowed to intervene in the proceedings before the Community court. It is also possible that parallel proceedings occur before the Community courts, because the CFI decides direct actions in first instance, while the ECJ decides a preliminary reference from a national court and direct actions in appeal.[104]

Those who cannot bring a direct action may face two more disadvantages of challenging the implementing acts of a Community act before a national court.[105] One disadvantage, as the applicants in the *EEB* case fruitlessly argued, is that an unchallengeable Community act can trigger a myriad of complex, lengthy and costly procedures in those Member States where authorizations for plant protection products containing that substance were extended on the basis of the Community act.[106] Unfortunately, it is possible that not even the Aarhus Regulation will change this situation, as this depends on the interpretation of its conditions for standing, as analyzed above. Another disadvantage of the narrow standing criteria is that a Community act can be challenged via implementing measures long after expiry of the limitation period of Article 230 EC.[107] This is to the detriment of legal certainty, particularly for those who are affected by the Community act and want to challenge it. This is particularly the case if, as argued in vain in the Asocarne case, proceedings before the national court last

[102] Joined Cases T-344 and 345 /00 *CEVA and Others* v *Commission* [2003] ECR II-229; the issue was not brought up in appeal: C-198/03 P *Commission* v *CEVA and Pfizer* [2005] ECR I-6357.

[103] See Chapter 5.

[104] See: Tridimas (2003), pp. 20, 21, Vesterdorf (2003), pp. 311-315, 321 and 322.

[105] Koch (2005), p. 515.

[106] Joined Cases T-236/04 and T-241/04 *European Environmental Bureau, Stichting Natuur en Milieu* v *Commission* [2005] ECR II-4945.

[107] See the Opinions of AG Jacobs in C-358/89 *Extramet Industrie* v *Council* [1991] ECR I-2501, C-50/00 P *Union de Pequenos Agricultores* v *Council* [2002] ECR I-6677 and C-263/02 *P Jégo Queré* v *Commission* [2004] ECR I-3425.

excruciatingly long.[108] Yet these problems may be considered luxury problems compared to the possibility of denial of jurisdiction.

Denial of jurisdiction

Complaints of denial of jurisdiction regard the situation where an individual fails to pass the standing test in relation to a self-executing Community act (i.e. an act which does not require implementation by the Member States).[109] If the Community act in question does not require any national implementing measures, national courts may declare that they lack jurisdiction as well. Nevertheless, Advocate General Jacobs and the ECJ did not propose to make standing before the Community courts conditional on the question whether an individual could bring proceedings before a national court, because they considered that this would entail examination of national procedural rules on a case-by-case basis which would go beyond their jurisdiction.[110] Moreover, it should be taken into account that those unable to establish direct and individual concern are denied bringing an action for annulment, but that they can still resort to the alternative of bringing an action for damages before the Community courts.[111]

Nevertheless, it seems that the CFI is willing to circumvent the problem of denial of jurisdiction by ruling on the merits before examining the issues of admissibility. The first case in which the CFI took this approach was *Boehringer* v *Commission and Council*.[112] It dismissed the case on the merits without ruling on its admissibility in the interest of the proper administration of justice. The Council was satisfied with the substantive part of the ruling, but filed an appeal to the ECJ to set aside the judgment to the extent that the Court had declared that there was no need to rule on the objection of inadmissibility.[113] The ECJ refused to rule solely on this procedural issue because it did not appear from the contested judgment that the CFI intended to rule by way of decision on the admissibility of the action. It found that it was up to the CFI to assess whether in the circumstances of this case the proper administration of justice justified the dismissal of the action on the merits without ruling on the objection of inadmissibility raised by the Council. The ECJ declared the action inadmissible because this course of action cannot be regarded as adversely affecting that institution and therefore the Council lacked a legal interest in bringing proceedings. These arguments limit this approach to cases where the action is dismissed on the merits.

[108] T-99/94 *Asociacion Espanalo de Empresas de la Carne (ASOCARNE)* v *Council* [1994] ECR II-71; upheld in appeal, C-10/95 P *Asociacion Espanalo de Empresas de la Carne (ASOCARNE)* v *Council* [1995] ECRI-4149.

[109] Koch (2005), p. 515.

[110] C-50/00 P *Unión de Pequeños Agricultores* v *Council* [2002] ECR I-6677.

[111] Cf. Borowski (2004), p. 902.

[112] Joined Cases T-125/96 and T-152/96 *Boehringer* v *Commission and Council* [1999] ECR II-3427. See also: T-216/05 *Mebrom* v *Commission* [2007] ECR II-1507.

[113] C-23/00 P *Council* v *Boehringer* [2002] ECR I-1873.

Changing the rules

Being aware of a possible gap in the system of remedies, Advocate General Jacobs proposed to interpret individual concern in a different sense.[114] He criticized the *Plaumann* formula in his Opinion in the UPA case, because it means that the larger the number of persons affected by an act, the less likely it is that they can challenge it. By contrast, the fact that an act causes widespread harm instead of limited harm should be a good reason to accept a challenge by those it affects.[115] Inspired by this Opinion, the CFI proposed in the *Jégo Quéré* case that individual parties are individually concerned by a Community measure of general application which affects their legal position, in a manner which is both definite and immediate, by restricting their rights or by imposing obligations on them.[116] The Commission appealed to the ECJ in both cases. The ECJ then made it clear that it did not wish to change its interpretation of the term 'individual concern' because the asserted absence of a national remedy should not lead to the meaning of individual concern being stretched.[117] The ECJ considered that the Treaty provided for a complete system of legal remedies, which enables the Court to review the legality of Community acts.

Only a change in the Treaty could alter the wording of Article 230 EC, according to the ECJ. The momentum for reform may have passed, in particular since the ECtHR has not criticized the Community's judicial protection system in its *Bosphorus* ruling.[118] Yet, the Lisbon Treaty has adopted a slight change (in italics) to the present wording of Article 230 (4) EC.[119] It states that any natural or legal person may institute proceedings against an act addressed to that person or which is of direct and individual concern to him or her, *and against a regulatory act which is of direct concern to him or her and does not entail implementing measures.*[120] Presumably, this undefined regulatory act can be defined as an act adopted to implement secondary legislation, i.e. acts adopted following a Comitology procedure, be they Decisions, Regulations or Directives.[121] This might enable third parties to challenge Community marketing authorizations, but it is uncertain whether it will also enable them to challenge Community listing decisions, because the issuance of marketing authorizations by national authori-

[114] See the Opinions of AG Jacobs in C-358/89 *Extramet Industrie* v *Council* [1991] ECR I-2501, C-50/00 P *Union de Pequenos Agricultores* v *Council* [2002] ECR I-6677 and C-263/02 P *Jégo Queré* v *Commission* [2004] ECR I-3425. See: Brown and Morijn (2004), pp. 1650-1652.

[115] Opinion of AG Jacobs in case C-50/00 P *Union de Pequenos Agricultores* v *Council* [2002] ECR I-6677.

[116] T-177/01 *Jégo Queré* v *Commission* [2003] ECR II-2365.

[117] C-50/00 P *Union de Pequenos Agricultores* v *Council* [2002] ECR I-6677 and C-263/02 P *Jégo Queré* v *Commission* [2004] ECR I-3425.

[118] ECtHR *Bosphorus Airlines* v *Ireland* (2006) 42 EHRR 1.

[119] The entry into effect of the Lisbon Treaty is uncertain until all Member States have ratified it.

[120] Art. 263 Lisbon Treaty (Art. III-365 Constitution). See: Barents (2004), pp. 130-134 and Barents, (2005), p. 16.

[121] Cf. Usher (2003), p. 598; Brown and Morijn (2004), p. 1655. Contrary, i.e. including decisions: Barents (2004), p. 134 and Koch (2005), p. 523.

ties on the basis of Community listing decisions might qualify as implementing measures.

3 Genetically modified organisms

Whether individual parties can bring a direct action against a Community decision regarding a GMO differs, depending on whether it is a GMO for other uses or a GMO for food and feed use. In the first case, the applicant obtains a national decision, which is based on a Community decision if the various Member States were unable to agree about the authorization. That raises the question whether the applicant or other third parties will be able to challenge the Community decision before the Community courts. In the second case, the authorization holder – or prospective authorization holder – will receive a Commission decision addressed to them. Since the addressee can always challenge a decision, this only leaves the question whether third parties, such as environmental organizations, can challenge this decision as well.

3.1 National decision implementing a Community decision

In order to determine whether individual parties can bring a direct action against a decision regarding a GMO for other uses, it is necessary to distinguish between GMOs authorized with or without making use of the dispute settlement procedure. In the latter case, the national authority of the reference Member State issues a decision, which cannot be challenged directly before a Community court. In the former case, the national decision is based on a Community decision to solve the dispute between the Member States. This decision is addressed to the reference Member State and not to the applicant.[122] Therefore, the applicant needs to establish direct and individual concern.

The applicant can challenge the decision before the Community courts because the Community decision is of direct concern to them, since it does not leave the national authority of the reference Member State significant room for discretion in the implementation into a national decision and because it is of individual concern to them, since the decision determines whether he is granted or denied a marketing authorization. Therefore, the applicant does not have to rely on the procedural guarantees exception, which would not have been possible anyway, because the GMO Directive does not confer any procedural guarantees on the applicant. It follows from the *TWD* and *Roquette Freres* cases that the applicant has no choice but to bring proceedings against this 'preparatory' Community decision before the Community courts. It is not expected that third

[122] E.g. Decision 2006/47/EC concerning the placing on the market, in accordance with Directive 2001/18/EC of the European Parliament and of the Council, of a maize product (Zea mays L., hybrid MON 863 x MON 810) genetically modified for resistance to corn rootworm and certain lepidopteran pests of maize (notified under document number C(2005) 5980), OJ 2006 L 26/17.

parties will be able to establish direct and individual concern and therefore they cannot bring proceedings before the Community courts, unless they can rely on the environmental disputes exception.[123]

3.2 Community decision

Marketing authorizations for GMOs for food and feed use issued under Regulation 1829/2003 are addressed to the applicant, who therefore can bring a direct action without any *locus standi* conditions being imposed on him.[124] Perhaps he is obliged to first file a request for administrative review, since Regulation 1829/2003 provides for administrative review of the EFSA Opinion.[125] The administrative review procedure gives the Commission the power to review any decision taken under, or failure to exercise the powers vested in the EFSA by, Regulation 1829/2003. It can act on its own initiative or in response to a request from a Member State or from any person directly and individually concerned. This naturally includes the applicant. A request for administrative review must be submitted to the Commission within two months from the day on which the party concerned became aware of the act or omission in question. Then the Commission will take a decision, requiring, if appropriate, the EFSA to withdraw its decision or to remedy its failure to act. This allows the Commission to exercise control over the operations of the EFSA.

The administrative review procedure is available to privileged parties, the authorization holder, prospective authorization holder and others who can establish direct and individual concern relating to the relevant act or omission. The question is whether it is mandatory to follow this procedure prior to bringing proceedings before the Community courts. Regulation 1829/2003 does not refer to the consequences of skipping administrative review. Therefore, the Court might consider this an option and not sanction an applicant seeking judicial review of a Commission decision based on an EFSA opinion against which they failed to file a request for administrative review. On the other hand, the Court may also decide not to review any complaints about acts or omissions of the EFSA if no previous administrative review procedure has taken place.

Third parties will generally not be able to gain access to court. The administrative review procedure is not intended to widen access to the Community courts. Since the same standing conditions apply as before the Community courts, the administrative review procedure is not expected to have a widening effect. Third parties will not be able to rely on the procedural guarantees

---

[123] C-6/99 *Association Greenpeace France and Others* v *Ministere de l'Agriculture et de la Peche and Others* [2000] ECR I-1651. See section 3.3 below.

[124] E.g. Commission Decision authorizing the placing on the market of products containing, consisting of, or produced from genetically modified maize NK603xMON810 pursuant to Regulation 1929/2003 of the European Parliament and the Council OJ 2007 L 285/37.

[125] Art. 36 Regulation 1829/2003/EC. Note that the marketing of GMOs for other uses, e.g. genetically modified flowers, is authorized under the procedure established by Part C of Directive 2001/18/EC.

exception because the GMO legislation does not confer procedural guarantees to others than the applicant for a marketing authorization. Even when competitors or other interested individual parties send comments to the Commission, they cannot rely on the procedural guarantees exception, as that requires a firm legal basis in secondary legislation. Those who cannot establish direct and individual concern cannot bring a direct action and have to rely on the national rules on access to court of the reference Member State, unless they can rely on the environmental disputes exception.

3.3 The environmental disputes exception

The provisions on judicial review in the Aarhus Regulation apply to decisions about the cultivation of GMOs as both the Aarhus Convention and the Aarhus Regulation specifically include GMOs in their definition of environmental law.[126] It is however not certain that these provisions apply as well to their marketing. On the one hand, the legal basis of Directive 2001/18 and Regulation 1829/2003 place the regulation on the marketing of GMOs squarely in the ambit of agricultural law and internal market law. On the other hand, the website of the Commission places the regulation of GMOs entirely in the ambit of environmental law. The other condition, that the decision is of individual scope, is definitely met concerning marketing authorizations. That means that environmental organizations that are qualified, such as Greenpeace, might challenge Community authorizations for the marketing of GMOs in a direct action. In addition, if the public participation provisions will apply to the marketing of GMOs after the implementation of the GMO amendment into the Aarhus Regulation, members of the public that submitted comments may also be able to challenge the Community GMO authorizations.

3.4 Conclusions

Although GMOs are regulated under various authorization procedures, depending on whether the GMO in question is destined for other uses or for food or feed use, some individuals can bring proceedings before the Community courts. This is illustrated by the table below.

[126] See Art. 2 (3) Aarhus Convention and Art. 2 (1) (d) (i) Regulation 1367/2006.

Table 4.1 Standing of individuals in GMO cases before the Community courts

Community decision	Applicant	Third party	Qualified environmental organization
Marketing authorization GMO for other uses – addressed to MS	+	-	?
Marketing authorization GMO for food/ feed use – addressed to applicant	+	-	?

If the authorization holder, or prospective authorization holder, of a GMO for other uses receives a national decision that is not based on a Community decision, he has to bring proceedings before a national court of the reference Member State. If he receives a national decision that is based on a Community decision – because the Member States were unable to agree on the decision to be taken – he has to bring a direct action against the Community decision, even though that decision is addressed to the reference Member State and not to him, because the decision is of direct and individual concern to him. The GMO Regulation is more straightforward, since it results in a Community decision addressed to the applicant, who can therefore bring a direct action. Third parties will generally be unable to establish direct and individual concern and therefore cannot bring proceedings before the Community courts. Unfortunately, it is not to be expected that this will change after the change of the general standing conditions by the Lisbon Treaty, unless the Community courts interpret regulatory act so broadly that decisions are included. Perhaps the Aarhus Regulation will improve the position of environmental organizations, provided that they meet its standing conditions and that the marketing authorizations for GMOs, which are decisions of individual scope, fall indeed within the broad definition of environmental law.

4 Medicines

The Medicines Regulation provides for a Community authorization, while the Medicines Directive provides for a mutual recognition authorization of a medicinal product. However, a Community decision may also be taken if initially the mutual recognition authorization procedure was followed and a dispute arises between Member States or if a mutual recognition decision must be amended or withdrawn. The first type of Community decisions is addressed to the applicant or authorization holder, while the second type of Community decision is addressed to the Member States. The question is whether the authorization holder, or prospective authorization holder, can bring a direct action and whether third parties, such as competitors or patient associations can bring proceedings as well. The ECJ has shed light on the latter issue in a case brought against a Community marketing authorization by a researcher, who feared that the EU had authorized a medicine without taking into account the weaknesses of the underlying research.[127]

4.1 Community decision

The holder, or prospective holder, of a Community authorization can bring a direct action against the Community decision and can also bring an admissible action, because the authorization, rejection or revocation will be addressed to him and does not require implementation by the Member States. The holder of a mutual recognition authorization can be confronted with a Community decision as well, because the settlement of disputes about mutual recognition decisions and their amendment or revocation occurs by a Commission decision addressed to the Member States, who have to implement these Community decisions into their mutual recognition decisions.[128] These Community decisions are only reported for information to the holder of the original mutual recognition authorization. He can bring proceedings against these Community decisions before the Community courts because he can establish individual concern on the basis of his participation rights.[129] He can establish direct concern because the Community decision does not leave the national authority of the reference Member State any room for discretion in the implementation into a mutual recognition decision.[130]

4.2 The procedural guarantees exception

Competitors are only able to bring proceedings before the Community courts if the decision-making procedure provides them with procedural guarantees, thus enabling them to establish individual concern. The holder of an authorization for the marketing of a medicine, in particular, may want to bring proceedings against authorizations granted for the marketing of a similar medicine. In the absence of legislation that gives them procedural guarantees during the Community procedure, they may not be able to challenge the decision. The ruling of the ECJ in the *Nancy Fern Olivieri* case sheds some light on the rights of third parties to bring a direct action against a marketing authorization.[131]

---

[127] T-326/99 *Nancy Fern Olivieri* v *Commission and EMEA* [2003] ECR II-6053.

[128] Art. 34 Directive 2001/83/EC.

[129] Art. 32 Directive 2001/83/EC.

[130] See section 3.1 of this chapter.

[131] T-326/99 *Nancy Fern Olivieri* v *Commission and EMEA* [2003] ECR II-6053.

The ECJ held that Ms Olivieri (who had led the first clinical trials and concluded that the medicine lacked efficacy) was not entitled to participate in the authorization procedure or to participate as interlocutor of the CPMP and of the Commission in regard to the assessment of the scientific data relating to the medicine deferiprone. Yet Olivieri was entitled to make sure that the CPMP and the Commission examined the information which she had sent directly to the CPMP in order to contribute to the scientific assessment of deferiprone and to ensure the authenticity of the results obtained in the course of trial LA-01. This right ceased when the information had been examined and taken into account in the course of this particular assessment procedure. After that moment, Olivieri no longer had an interest in bringing proceedings to contest the legality of the contested decision and obtain judicial review of the examination of the correctness and completeness of the scientific information relating to deferiprone.

According to the ECJ, the authorization procedure established by Regulation 2309/93 is purely bilateral. It is a procedure between the applicant for a marketing authorization and the administration, during which the administration must take into account the applicant's interest in obtaining a marketing authorization procedure and the public interest in the protection of human health. Nevertheless, it may be deduced from the *Nancy Fern Olivieri* case that if the comments of relevant third parties are not taken into account in the decision, they may be able to challenge the decision in a direct action on that ground. This does not offer much hope for patient organizations. The only associations that may bring proceedings are environmental organizations, if they pass the conditions of the Aarhus Regulation. They are not expected to bring proceedings against medicines authorizations, especially since it is not the authorizations but the subsequent use that may have a significant impact on the environment. Nevertheless, they might use the environmental disputes exception, if authorization contravenes environmental law, if only to place environmental concerns about biodegradability of medicines higher on the agenda.

4.3 Conclusions

The possibilities of the holder, or prospective holder, of the authorization and of third parties to bring proceedings before the Community courts are illustrated in the table below.

Table 4.2 Standing of individuals in medicines cases before the Community courts

Community decision	Applicant	Third party	Qualified environmental organization
Community medicines authorization – addressed to applicants.	+	-/+	?
Mutual recognition authorization: Community decision – addressed to MS	+	-/+	?

The holder, or prospective holder, of a Community authorization does not have to meet any *locus standi* conditions, because the decision is addressed to them. If holders of a mutual recognition authorization are faced with a Community decision, for instance about the amendment or withdrawal of their mutual recognition decision, it is sent to them for information but addressed to the Member States, who should implement it into their mutual recognition decision. Yet they can – and should – bring a direct action, because the decision is of direct and individual concern to them. Others, be they competitors or patient associations, will not so easily pass the direct and individual concern test, due to the purely bilateral character of the authorization procedure, in which only the interest of the applicant is weighed against the public interest in protecting human health. Their position will not be improved by amendment to the general standing conditions by the Lisbon Treaty, unless the Community courts interpret regulatory act so broadly that decisions are included. Instead, it can be deduced from the *Nancy Fern Olivieri* case that without being granted procedural guarantees in the medicines legislation an interested third party can nevertheless bring an admissible direct action if their comments – in the public interest of protecting human health – are not taken into account in the decision-making stage. This might be a first step towards granting broader standing to third parties.

5 CITES

The CITES Regulation provides for Community decisions, in order to amend the Annexes to the CITES Regulation. However, these listing decisions are not based on a dossier filed by an applicant, even if the listing of a species is important for big traders because it determines the legality of their trade in that species. Instead, these decisions implement the decisions taken at the Conference of the Parties and – insofar as they differ from the international listing decisions – reflect the position of the EU and its Member States. This means that such decisions are taken in the public interest, but may not sufficiently take other interests into account, such as the interests of traders or of tourism organizations. In view of the stringent standing criteria, it may not come as a surprise that individual parties have never challenged these Community decisions in a direct action so far. Below, the current hurdles and the opportunities introduced by the implementation of the Aarhus Convention will be analyzed to determine whether individual parties can challenge CITES listing decisions.

5.1 Community decision

If the amendment of an Annex to the CITES Regulation results in a ban on trade in a certain species instead of regulation of trade, the Member States can no longer issue import authorizations for that species. This means that traders are forced out of business, be it legal business or otherwise, and are thus directly concerned – due to the absence of discretionary room for the Member States. Yet their pursuit of economic trade means that they are never individually concerned and they cannot rely on the procedural guarantees exception because they are not involved in the decision-making process. They are thus prevented from challenging a listing decision before the Community courts. The Aarhus Regulation does not offer them any new options, since it only offers administrative and judicial review to qualified environmental organizations. Consequently, traders can only invoke the invalidity of a listing decision of a species if they challenge the rejected application for an import authorization or a seizure of an illegal shipment before a national court.

5.2 The environmental disputes exception

Environmental organizations may be able to challenge a Community decision that amends the Annexes to the CITES Regulation (or the failure to take one), provided they meet the criteria of the Aarhus Regulation and can gain access to administrative review. This requires that they are qualified environmental organizations and that the listing decision constitutes a measure of individual scope under environmental law, taken by a Community institution or body, having legally binding and external effects. Assuming that organizations such as WWF can qualify, the main hurdle is that the amendment of the Annex to the CITES Regulation may not constitute a reviewable act under the Aarhus Regulation for two reasons. First, it could be argued that a Regulation to amend the Annexes to the CITES Regulation does not fall within the scope of environmental law in the sense of the Aarhus Regulation. Second, the listing decision may not be considered as a measure of individual scope, because it is a measure of general application with effect *erga omnes*, even though it implements the CITES Regulation with regard to a specific species.

It is unlikely that a Community act implementing the CITES Regulation does not constitute environmental law in the sense of the Aarhus Regulation. First, the CITES trade regime has a legal basis which is of an environmental nature. Second, even though it protects endangered species on a global scale, exclusion on that ground is unlikely, since the Aarhus Regulation refers to the definition of environmental law in the Treaty and that definition does not contain any geographical limitations.[132] The second objection is not so easy to rebut. If the ECJ were to qualify an amendment of an Annex to a Regulation as a measure of general application, which is likely in view of its case law,[133] environmental organizations might be unable to challenge amendments to the Annexes of the CITES Regulation.[134] Since they cannot establish direct and individual concern either, it is likely that it remains impossible for them to challenge CITES listing decisions before the Community courts despite the environmental disputes exception.

5.3 Conclusions

It is unlikely that the Community listing decisions taken in the area of CITES can be challenged by an individual party before a Community court. This is illustrated by the table below.

Table 4.3 Standing of individuals in CITES cases before the Community courts

Community decision	Applicant	Third party	Qualified environmental organization
CITES listing decision	*	-	?

* *There is no applicant.*

The impossibility for individuals to challenge Community listing decisions before a Community court arises because the Annexes to the CITES Regulation are amended on the basis of the decisions of the Conference of the Parties to the CITES Convention or – insofar as they diverge from these international decisions – on the basis of the position of the EU and its Member States regarding these international decisions. The CITES Regulation does not involve individual parties in the decision-making procedure. Since traders cannot rely on the procedural guarantees exception, they will lack individual concern and hence they will be denied standing. It is unlikely that the change of the general standing conditions by the Lisbon Treaty will enable individuals to bring proceed-

[132] Art. 2 (f) Regulation 1367/2006. Cf. C-293/02 *Jersey Produce Marketing Organisation* v *States of Jersey and Jersey Potato Export Marketing Board (Jersey Potatoes)* [2005] ECR I-9543.

[133] Cf. T-213/02 *SNFSA Commission* [2004] ECR II-3047; C-482/04 P *SNFSA* v *Commission*, OJ 2006 C143/20; T-475/07 R *Dow AgroSciences and Others* v *Commission* [2008] ECR II-0000.

[134] Keessen (2007), p. 35.

ings before the Community courts against CITES listing decisions, because the CITES documents could well be interpreted as implementing measures of the listing decision. The only ones who might be able to bring proceedings – after having obtained an administrative review decision – are environmental organizations, provided that they meet the conditions of the Aarhus Regulation. It seems likely that organizations such as WWF will qualify and that an implementing act of the CITES constitutes a measure under environmental law, but a listing decision may not qualify as an act of individual scope, but rather of general scope, and therefore the Aarhus criteria may not be met.

6 Plant protection products

Plant protection products may only be authorized if their active substances appear on the Annex to Directive 91/414, unless they fall under the transition regime. Since these decisions either take the form of Directives that amend the Annex or of decisions that reject the amendment, but allow for exceptions for essential use or a period of grace, they are usually controversial. Parties who file a dossier may want to challenge an unfavourable decision, but as the Pfizer and SNFSA judgments demonstrate, this is not always easy. Environmental organizations take an interest as well and are eagerly waiting for the Aarhus legislation to take effect. There have even been some Member States that took the step to challenge a Community decision, which, interestingly enough, was also challenged – in vain – by environmental organizations.

6.1 Community decisions

Companies that have filed a dossier to the application for the inclusion of an active substance used in plant protection products in Annex I to Directive 91/414/EC ('notifiers') stand good chances to gain access to court in order to challenge a listing decision, in particular when inclusion is refused.[135] Since a negative listing decision is taken in the form of a decision addressed to the Member States, notifiers have to establish direct and individual concern. This is possible because the decision is of direct concern to them due to the limited room for discretion in the implementation and they can rely on the procedural guarantees exception to establish individual concern.[136] It is not certain that notifiers can also challenge a positive listing decision because of its unfavourable conditions, despite being able to establish individual concern due to the procedural guarantees exception. This is because positive listing decisions take the form of directives, which may render it impossible to establish direct concern, even though the Member States have little room for discretion in the

[135] C-326/05 P *Industrias Chimicas del Valles* v *Commission* [2007] ECR I-6557, C-236/07 P (R) *Sumitomo Chemical Agro Europe* v *Commission* [2008] ECR I-0000.

[136] T-31/07 R *Du Pont de Nemours and Others* v *Commission* [2007] ECR II-2767.

implementation. By contrast, the holders of a marketing authorization that failed to file a dossier will be unable to bring proceedings against a positive or negative listing decision, even if it causes the withdrawal of their authorization, because they lack individual concern.[137]

Member State action

Due to qualified majority voting, Member States can be outvoted in the decision-making process concerning the listing of an active substance for plant protection products. This can result in the listing of an active substance that they consider unsafe. Since the Member States have the right to defend the general interest and are not hindered by any *locus standi* limitations, Sweden (supported by Denmark, Austria and Finland) could bring proceedings against the Community listing decision of Paraquat, which was taken in the form of a Commission Directive. Sweden won, because it was able to show that substantial scientific evidence of the risks involved with the use of plant protection products containing the active substance had not sufficiently been taken into account in the decision-making process.[138] Interestingly enough, environmental organizations challenged the Paraquat decision as well, but they were not granted standing, despite their status as advisors to the Commission, because they lacked individual concern.[139]

6.2 The procedural guarantees exception

The *Pfizer* case and the *SNFSA* case provide an illustration of possible haphazard results following from the application of the procedural guarantees exception.[140] These cases are in the area of food or feed additives and cosmetics, respectively, but they are discussed here because similar disputes could have arisen in the area of plant protection products. Pfizer challenged a Regulation that resulted in the withdrawal of the authorization of an additive in foodstuffs, a Regulation that was enacted in response to a Spanish safeguard measure. The Regulation was of direct concern to Pfizer insofar as it withdrew the authorization of virginiamycin as an additive in foodstuffs. It could also be of individual concern to Pfizer because prior to the start of the safeguard procedure, Pfizer had submitted a scientific dossier in order to obtain a new authorization, which required a re-evaluation of virginiamycin. Following the adoption of the Regulation, the Commission notified Pfizer that, as a consequence of the Regulation, virginiamycin was no longer subject to the authorization procedure.

---

137 This should become clear when the CFI issues its judgment in T-31/07 *Du Pont de Nemours and Others* v *Commission*.

138 T-229/04 *Sweden* v *Commission* [2007] ECR II-0000.

139 T-94/04 *European Environmental Bureau (EEB) and Others* v *Commission* [2005] ECR II-4919.

140 T-13/99 *Pfizer Animal Health SA* v *Council* [2002] ECR II-3305; T-213/02 *SNFSA Commission* [2004] ECR II-3047; C-482/04 P *SNFSA* v *Commission* OJ 2006 C143/20.

In the *Pfizer* case, the simultaneous application of the authorization and safeguard procedures created an exceptional situation, because the authorization procedure offered the applicant procedural guarantees, while the safeguard procedure did not. As a consequence of their procedural rights under the authorization procedure, the Community courts held that the Regulation was of individual concern to Pfizer and declared their action admissible.[141] A less positive consequence of the *Pfizer* judgment could be that if it were not for the pending application for a new authorization, the applicant would not have been able to challenge the withdrawal of the authorization in a direct action, because the safeguard procedure itself does not offer any procedural guarantees to the holder of the authorization. This indeed seems to be the case, considering the outcome of the *SNFSA* case, upheld in appeal.[142]

In the *SNFSA* case, a producer of polyacrylamides tried to challenge restrictions on the use of polyacrylamides in the composition of cosmetic products. A directive amending an Annex of the Cosmetics Directive imposed these restrictions. The fact that the contested measure was a directive did not lead to inadmissibility. The producer argued that they had standing, because Article 13 Cosmetics directive required that if individual measures placing a restriction or ban on the marketing of cosmetic products are taken, precise reasons must be given for those measures, and that the measures must be notified to the party concerned with particulars of the remedies available under the laws of the Member States. However, the contested measure did not restrict or ban a product, but a substance. Therefore, the Community courts considered that the contested measure did not constitute an individual measure but a general measure. It amended an Annex, and was therefore correctly based on Article 8 (2) Cosmetics Directive, which did not confer any procedural rights on individual parties. Consequently, the producer could not rely on the procedural guarantee exception.

Thus, the holder of an authorization that is withdrawn because of a Community safeguard measure cannot challenge the safeguard measure in a direct action, unless the applicable secondary legislation provides for procedural guarantees for the marketing authorization holder when the safeguard procedure is used. In the absence of procedural guarantees, judicial review at Community level is not available against the adoption of a Community safeguard measure.

6.3 The environmental disputes exception

The Aarhus Regulation was still only a proposal when some environmental organizations, including the European Environmental Bureau ('EEB'), first relied on it to gain access to the CFI in order to challenge two Commission decisions regarding the non-inclusion in Annex I of atrazine and

[141] Note that the Community courts do not apply a *Schutznorm*.

[142] T-213/02 *SNFSA* v *Commission* [2004] ECR II-3047; C-482/04 P *SNFSA* v *Commission* OJ 2006 C143/20.

simazine, two active substances used to make plant protection products.[143] They were not entitled to challenge these decisions for lack of individual concern, as their aim to protect the environment from these substances by shortening the period of grace conferred by the Commission is a collective and not an individual concern. They unsuccessfully argued that the CFI should grant them standing because they met the requirements of the proposal for the Aarhus Regulation for environmental organizations. The CFI responded that the hierarchy of norms precludes secondary legislation from conferring standing on individual parties who fail to meet the standing requirements of Article 230 EC, which applies a fortiori to proposals for secondary legislation. They had not put forward any reason why this status would lead to the conclusion that they were individually concerned.[144]

Yet, the *EEB* judgment may not mean that environmental organizations can never challenge a Community listing decision in the area of plant protection products. If they are admitted to the administrative review procedure, they will obtain a decision directed to them, which should allow them to bring a direct action at the same level as the addressee or parties who can establish direct and individual concern with regard to the original Community decision. Nevertheless, some hurdles need to be overcome in order to be admitted to the administrative review procedure, and thus to the judicial review procedure. While it is obvious that a listing decision constitutes an environmental measure in the sense of the Aarhus Regulation, it is not certain whether it constitutes a measure of individual scope as it might qualify as a measure of general application. That makes it unlikely that environmental organizations will be able to challenge Community listing decisions.

[143] Joined Cases T-236/04 and T-241/04 *EEB and Others* v *Commission* [2005] ECR II-4945; T-94/04 *EEB and Others* v *Commission* [2005] ECR II-4919.

[144] See also: T-37/04 *Regiao autonoma dos Acores* v *Council* [2008] ECR II-0000.

6.4 Conclusions

It is possible for certain individual parties to challenge Community listing decisions before the Community courts, as the table below illustrates.

Table 4.5 Standing of individuals in plant protection products cases before the Community courts

Community decision	Applicant	Third party	Qualified environmental organization
Community PPP listing decision – addressed to MS	+/-	-	?
Comm. PPP listing decision refusal – addressed to MS	+	-	?

Notifiers can challenge a refusal to list an active substance in Annex I, even though this Commission or Council decision is addressed to the Member States. This is because they can establish individual concern, due to the procedural guarantees exception, and direct concern, due to the limited room for discretion this decision leaves to the Member States. A related uncertainty is whether notifiers can also challenge a positive listing decision (with unfavourable conditions attached) because this decision is taken in the form of a Directive amending the Annex to the basic Directive. The interim relief order in the Du Pont de Nemours case suggests that this is the case, but it remains to be seen in the judgment of the CFI – and, if one of the parties appeals, of the ECJ – whether it is true that an individual party can even challenge a directive. Moreover, the *Pfizer* and *SNFSA* cases demonstrate that if a listing decision takes the form of a safeguard measure, it may be impossible to challenge it, due to the absence of procedural guarantees in the safeguard procedure, unless an applicant has already filed a dossier under the listing procedure.

Third parties will generally be unable to challenge Community listing decisions, be they positive or negative. This will not change under the future Plant protection products Regulation. Parties that failed to file a dossier may not be able to bring a direct action, even if the refusal obliges the Member States to withdraw their authorizations for lack of individual concern, as follows from the order of the President of the CFI in the *Du Pont de Nemours* case. Perhaps they will benefit from the change of the general standing conditions by the Lisbon Treaty and be able to bring proceedings before the Community courts against listing decisions. However the marketing authorizations for plant protection products could well be interpreted as implementing measures of the listing decision and thus prevent the use of the amendment to be granted standing. Environmental organizations are unable to challenge Community listing decisions as well, unless the Aarhus Regulation changes this situation. Unfortunately it is unlikely that those who qualify as environmental organization may challenge Community listing decisions regarding plant protection products, since these decisions could well qualify as measures of general application and the Aarhus Regulation explicitly states that only measures of individual scope can be challenged.

7 Conclusions

Even though in *Les Verts* v *Parliament*, the ECJ recognized that the Community is based on the rule of law – meaning that the acts of the Community institutions are subject to judicial control – it does not grant individual parties extensive standing rights to bring an action against a Community act before the Community courts, not even if it concerns an implementing act such as a listing decision or a marketing authorization. This also affects these parties' options to request interim relief, because that remedy is only available in connection with an action for annulment or for failure to act. Only the action for damages is available without *locus standi* conditions. It can lead to compensation for damage resulting from a measure or from unlawful conduct, attributable to a Community institution or body.[145] However, a claim can only lead to compensation in case of a serious infringement and it cannot lead to the annulment of the act.[146] Thus, only obtaining the annulment of a Community act can correct an unlawful situation. Therefore, parties that are unable to establish direct and individual concern can only hope that the national courts provide a safety net, as the Community courts expect the national courts to, in order to ensure the completeness of the Community system of remedies.

Both privileged applicants, such as the Member States, and parties to whom a Community decision is addressed can bring a direct action without having to meet *locus standi* conditions. Individual parties to whom a decision is not addressed have to establish direct and individual concern in order to challenge a Community decision. The figure below shows the position of applicants and third parties with regard to Community marketing authorizations and listing decisions.

---

[145] C-118/93 *CMC* v *Commission* [1985] ECR 2325; C-308/87 *Grifoni* v *Commission* [1990] ECR I1203; C-146/91 *KYDEP* v *Council and Commission* [1994] ECR I4199.

[146] C-63/89 *Assicurance du Crédit* [1991] ECR I-1799. See: Ward (2000), p. 291.

Table 4.6 Standing of individuals in Community product regulation cases before the Community courts

Community decision	Applicant	Third party	Qualified environmental organization in environmental dispute
Marketing authorization	+	-/+	+
Listing decision	+/-	-	?

Applicants of a Community marketing authorization – for instance for medicines or a GMO – have access to a court, whether the decision is addressed to them or to the Member State. In the latter case, they will pass the direct and individual concern test, because the Member States do not retain significant room for discretion and because it is their application that is being decided and secondary legislation therefore grants them procedural guarantees. Applicants of a Community listing decision – for instance for a substance to be used in plant protection products – can challenge a refusal, but it is not certain whether they can challenge a positive listing decision as well if it contains unfavourable conditions. This is because a positive decision is taken in the form of a Regulation or a Directive amending the Annex to the basic Act, which is not directed to them but to the Member States and therefore they need to establish direct and individual concern. While the procedural guarantees exception will enable them to establish individual concern, it is not certain whether they can also establish direct concern due to the characteristics of a Directive. In the area of CITES, individuals do not have a role in the decision-making about amendments of the Annexes to the CITES Regulation and will therefore be unable to rely on the procedural guarantees exception in order to pass the general standing conditions.

Third parties that are market participants, particularly competitors, have to pass the test of direct and individual concern if they want to challenge another party's marketing authorization. Many fail, since pursuing a commercial activity does not distinguish an applicant individually. In the area of medicines, it is unlikely that competitors will be able to bring proceedings, since the Commission (or the Council) only issues authorizations for innovative medicines and therefore does not have to involve competitors in the decision-making procedure. In the area of plant protection products, it is possible that parties whose marketing authorization will be withdrawn as a consequence of a negative decision – but who have not filed an application for inclusion of a substance in an Annex – may be unable to bring proceedings for lack of individual concern irrespective of whether the listing decision is taken in the form of a decision or a directive.

This remains the same when the Proposal for a Plant protection products Regulation will enter into effect and the listing decision will be taken in the form of a regulation.

The general standing conditions make it impossible for associations, such as patient organizations, to bring actions against Community marketing authorizations or listing decisions before the Community courts in order to defend a collective interest. The Aarhus Regulation will provide a 'testing ground' for granting environmental organizations easier access to the Community courts to defend the environment without amending the *locus standi* conditions of the action for annulment. It allows qualified environmental organizations to challenge Community acts of individual scope that contravene environmental law before the Community courts, after an administrative review procedure established by the Aarhus Regulation. Since the criteria of direct and individual concern only apply in relation to non-addressees, it seems impossible for the Community courts to refuse standing to environmental organizations that obtained a review decision addressed to them, provided that they were entitled to and made use of the administrative review procedure. The importance of the Aarhus Regulation will depend on the interpretation given to its key concepts, in particular to individual scope, as that will certainly include Community marketing decisions but might exclude Community listing decisions, which means that also environmental organizations may have to continue to rely on the judicial protection offered by the national courts.

Regarding the judicial protection offered against Community decisions, the standing conditions of the Community courts create a division of competence between them and the national courts. This division of competence does not sufficiently take the administrative role of the Commission into account. It is possible that Community decisions negatively affect others than those to whom they are addressed, but that these third parties are unable to bring a direct action for lack of direct or individual concern and therefore depend on the national courts. This means that parallel proceedings may occur, which are in themselves undesirable because of the procedural inequalities they create. They are also disadvantageous because not all the interests involved are considered in a single judicial review procedure. Moreover, those who have to bring proceedings before a national court are not bound by the time limit of Article 230 EC, but by the time limit that applies to the national implementing decision. This means that the validity of the Community decision remains uncertain for a long time, which infringes the principle of legal certainty. Finally, it is not certain that the national courts will be able to provide judicial protection against Community decisions. It will be seen in the next chapter whether the assumption that the national courts can offer supplementary judicial protection is true. For this reason, it is not possible to conclude yet whether the Community courts offer sufficient judicial protection.

CHAPTER 5

Actions Before the National Courts

The national courts act as ordinary Community courts as they provide for judicial control over the application and enforcement of Community law by the Member States in administrative law, civil law and criminal law proceedings.[1] The ECJ already recognized the importance of individuals controlling the Community administration in its *Van Gend and Loos* judgment, as it held that 'the vigilance of individuals concerned to protect their rights amounts to an effective supervision in addition to the supervision entrusted by Articles 169 and 170 EEC [now 226 and 227 EC] to the diligence of the Commission and of the Member States.[2] The ECJ cooperates with the national courts through the preliminary ruling procedure in order to ensure the uniform interpretation and application of Community law.[3] In the absence of a Community Code of Administrative Law, the ECJ has occasionally harmonized national procedural rules on remedies or access and issued guidelines relating to the use of the preliminary ruling procedure to achieve these results.[4] Yet the attempts of the ECJ to measure national procedural law against its standards of equivalence and effectiveness still leave doubts as to what is exactly required to make judicial protection effective.[5]

This chapter will answer the questions whether the national courts offer effective judicial protection against European administrative decisions and what their impact is on the uniformity to be achieved. One can think of individuals contesting decisions concerning marketing authorizations issued by national authorities, be they prospective holders of the authorization, prospective holders of an authorization, competitors or organizations championing environmental protection, consumers' or patients' rights. However, in view of the strict standing conditions that govern access to the Community courts, the national courts should also offer judicial protection against decisions issued by the Community institutions. Therefore, after a general introduction to the available remedies and access to a national court, it will be seen whether the so-called complete system of judicial protection guarantees access to a national court or presents gaps with regard to Community decisions. Then judicial protection in the reference areas will be analyzed in order to understand the similarities and the differences in relation to the various types of European administrative decisions as regards the attainment of uniformity and the protection offered to individuals.

1 The remedies

The Community courts have influenced national procedural rules on remedies through their case law on the principle of effective judicial

1 Curtin (1992), pp. 34, 35.

2 C-26/62 *Van Gend en Loos* [1963] ECR 1.

3 Information note on references from national courts for a preliminary ruling OJ 2005 C 143/01.

4 Cf. Dougan (2002), p. 153 and Van Gerven (2000), p. 525.

5 Caranta (1995), p. 705.

protection. The ECJ even influenced national remedies to the extent that it created a few Community law remedies.[6] Whether the conditions of the remedies available in Community law cases are harmonized to a greater or lesser extent seems to depend on the object of the dispute. The ECJ seems to be keen on ensuring uniformity when a Community act is the underlying object of the dispute. When a national act is the object of the dispute, a remedy only needs to meet the equivalence and effectiveness standards of the ECJ.[7] The main remedies are the actions for annulment, failure to act, interim relief and damages. It will be seen below to what extent these remedies against European administrative decisions are harmonized, while the standing conditions under which these remedies are available will be analyzed in section 2.

Annulment

An individual may challenge the compatibility of a national decision with Community law before a national court. Since all national courts must be competent to set aside national measures which conflict with EC law,[8] incompatibility with Community law constitutes a ground for the annulment of national acts. The other grounds for the annulment of a national act have to include non-compliance with the Community rights of defence. The annulment of a national act does not have effect in other Member States, which is problematic in case of mutual recognition decisions.[9] If a national decision is challenged because of the alleged invalidity of the Community act which it implements, the national court cannot annul the national decision on this ground, because it lacks the competence to declare a Community act invalid. Instead, it has to refer validity questions to the ECJ.[10] This rule also applies where a national court doubts the validity of a Community decision because it deems the underlying (preparatory) national decision to be invalid.[11]

When the ECJ decides on the validity of a Community act by a preliminary ruling, the grounds for annulment are those under the Treaty and are therefore the same irrespective of the Member State where the applicant had access to a court. The effects of the annulment of a Community act by a preliminary ruling are also the same as under an Article 230 EC ruling.[12] The only difference is that

6 Van Gerven (2000), p. 503.

7 C-33/76 *Rewe* [1976] ECR 1989, C-45/76 *Comet* [1976] ECR 2043, C-199/82 *Amministrazione delle Finanze dello Stato* v *San Giorgio* [1983] ECR 3595. This is referred to as national procedural autonomy or national procedural competence. See *inter alia*: Kakouris (1997), p. 1389-1412, Prechal, (1998), p. 681-706, Van Gerven (2000), p. 501, 502; Delicostopoulos (2003), p. 603. My views on this subject can be found in: Keessen (2006), pp. 55-64.

8 C-106/77 *Simmenthal* [1978] ECR 629.

9 See section 2.2 and 4.1 below.

10 C-314/85 *Foto Frost* [1987] ECR 4199.

11 C-6/99 *Association Greenpeace France and Others* v *Ministere de l'Agriculture et de la Peche and Others* [2000] ECR I-1651.

12 I.e. *ex tunc* and *erga omnes*. See: C-66/80 *International Chemical Corporation* [1981] ECR 1191.

the time-limit of Article 230 EC does not apply to actions before the national courts.[13] Hence, those who cannot directly challenge a Community act may do so many years after it came into force when they challenge a national implementing act, as they are only bound by the time-limit imposed by national law.[14]

Failure to act

Individuals can challenge a failure to act before the national courts when Community law prescribes action by the national authorities, in particular after a set time-limit has elapsed. The conditions of this remedy are not harmonized. Therefore, the national courts will judge these actions according to their own procedural rules, provided that they meet the conditions of effectiveness and equivalence.[15] In this regard, the ECJ has not ruled against a national rule prescribing a fictitious refusal or fictitious permission. Instead, in the case *Merck, Sharp and Dohme* it ruled that, in the absence of a Community law provision, national law governs the consequences of a failure to act within a prescribed time-limit.[16] The Community courts ensure uniformity regarding a failure to act by the Community institutions or bodies, because national courts are not competent to decide on disputes about a failure to act by the Community institutions or bodies, since Article 234 EC does not include this option.[17] Perhaps the ECJ will also accept preliminary questions in cases brought before national courts by individuals who have failed to meet the standing conditions of the Community courts in order to ensure a complete system of judicial protection.[18]

Interim relief

Where individuals challenge a national act or a failure to act or claim damages because national law is allegedly incompatible with Community law, the national courts must be competent to grant interim relief.[19] This remedy should be available, because effective legal protection implies immediate legal protection.[20] This rule also applies to an application for interim relief made in connection with an action for damages, if the dispute concerns the compatibility of a national rule with Community law.[21] The ECJ has not harmonized the conditions for granting interim relief when the compatibility of national

---

13 Opinion of AG Jacobs in case C-50/00 P *Union de Pequenos Agricultores* v *Council* [2002] ECR I-6677.

14 E.g. C-336/00 *Austria* v *Martin Humber* [2002] ECR I-7699.

15 Unfortunately, the Dutch Supreme Court did not refer questions in the *Waterpakt* case as to whether it was obliged to set aside a national constitutional rule according to which a court cannot order the Dutch Parliament to implement EC law by adopting legislation. See: Besselink (2004), p. 1429-1455, in particular pp. 1439 and 1440.

16 C-245/03 *Merck, Sharp and Dohme* v *Belgium* [2005] ECR I-237.

17 C-68/95 *T. Port and Co* [1996] ECR I-6065 and T-395/04 *Air One* v *Commission* [2006] ECR II-1343.

18 See section 3.5 below.

19 C-213/89 *Factortame* [1990] ECR I-2433 and C-432/05 *Unibet* v *Justitiekanslern* [2007] ECR I-2271.

20 Widdershoven (2004 A), p. 318.

21 C-432/05 *Unibet* v *Justitiekanslern* [2007] ECR I-2271.

law with Community law is disputed.[22] By contrast, the ECJ has harmonized the conditions for granting interim relief when the suspension of the enforcement of a national act based on a Community act is requested, even though the national courts lack jurisdiction to declare the Community act invalid. The urgency of interim relief justifies a temporary exception to this rule.

When a national court refers validity questions to the ECJ, it may suspend the operation of the Community act provided that the necessary conditions are met which must be satisfied for the ECJ to allow an application for interim measures.[23] This means that the applicant must establish that he has a *prima facie* case, that it is urgent and that the requested measures have a preservative nature. The national court has to weigh this against the interest of the Community and take ECJ and CFI rulings into account. If either Court decides on the subject after the national court has granted interim relief, the national court may have to revoke the interim measures. Despite the harmonized conditions for interim relief, the suspension of a Community act granted by a national court has no effect in other Member States. The national authorities in other Member States may not decide to suspend the application on the basis of its order until someone has obtained a court order in their Member State.[24] The suspension of a national act does not have effect in other Member States either. The lack of coordination places an additional burden on those who challenge (the implementation of) a Community act before a national court in more than one Member State, but the ECJ has not created cooperation obligations between national courts in interim relief proceedings in order to prevent different outcomes.[25]

Damages

Individuals who suffered damage because a Member State has breached its obligations under Community law can bring proceedings before a national court. The ECJ has harmonized the conditions governing Member State liability along the lines of the conditions governing Community liability.[26] This means that the rule of law infringed must be intended to confer rights on individu-

---

22 C-432/05 *Unibet* v *Justitiekanslern* [2007] ECR I-2271. In contrast, considering that the Zuckerfabrik criteria (should) also apply to Factortame-like cases: Bebr (1994), p. 320.

23 Joined Cases C-143/88 and C-92/90 *Zuckerfabrik Süderditmarschen* [1991] ECR 415, as further developed in C-465/93 *Atalanta Fruchthandelsgesellschaft and Others* v *Bundesamt für Ernährung und Forstwirtschaft* [1995] ECR I-3761 and C-68/95 *T. Port and Co* v *Bundesanstalt für Landwirtschaft und Ernährung* [1996] ECR I-6065.

24 Joined Cases C-453/03, C-11/04, C-12/04 and C-194/04 *ABNA and Others* [2005] ECR I-10423.

25 Opinion of Advocate General Jacobs in C-358/89 *Extramet* v *Council* [1991] ECR I-2501. E.g. Joined Cases C-453/03, C-11, 12 and 194/04 *ABNA and Others* [2005] ECR I-10423. See Jans *et al.*. (2007), p. 282, 283; Van Ooik and Vandamme (2005), pp. 60-69; Widdershoven (1996), pp. 175-178.

26 C-6 and 9/90 *Francovich and Bonifaci* v *Italy* [1991] ECR I-5357 and Joined Cases C-46 and 48/93 *Brasserie du Pecheur* v *Germany, R* v *Secretary of State ex parte Factortame* [1996] ECR I-1029.

als, the breach must be sufficiently serious[27] and there must be a direct causal link between the breach and the damage. These harmonized conditions form a deviation from the standard practice of the ECJ regarding remedies. However, the Community conditions governing State liability for breaches of Community law only constitute a minimum standard. The harmonized minimum standard ensures that individuals can obtain compensation if they have suffered damage from the wrongful application of Community legislation or from the wrongful exercise of the discretion left to the Member States by a Community act,[28] and that if a Member State has more generous rules, that those rules apply to State liability claims for breach of Community law.[29]

The question is whether not issuing an authorization may render a Member State liable in damages. While it is for the national courts to determine this, the ECJ has given some guidance in the *Synthon* case.[30] The facts of the case were as follows. Synthon had obtained a Danish authorization to place Varox on the (Danish) market in accordance with the simplified procedure, using Seroxat as a reference medicine.[31] It then applied for mutual recognition of its marketing authorization in Great Britain. The British competent authority questioned the Danish assessment of essential similarity between Varox and Seroxat and therefore refused to recognize the Danish authorization because that was against its own policy. It did not start the dispute settlement procedure. Synthon requested and obtained its British authorization only after the ECJ had held in another dispute that a medicine that contains another salt than the reference medicine may nevertheless be essentially similar.[32]

The ECJ held that the non-recognition of the Danish authorization constituted a sufficiently serious breach of Community law because Great Britain had neither justified non-recognition on the basis of a risk to public health, nor used the dispute settlement procedure after it refused recognition. The British national court did not ask – and the ECJ did not answer – the question whether the other conditions for liability were met. Yet it can be safely assumed that the other two conditions were met, since there is a direct causal link between the non-recognition and the damage suffered by the delay and the mutual recognition provision conferred the right on the applicant that the Danish authorization be recognized unless that would present a serious potential risk for public health. Thus, this judgment encourages the authorization holder or the prospec-

---

27 See section 4.1 of this chapter for an analysis of C-452/06 *The Queen, on the application of Synthon* v *Licensing Authority of the Department of Health* [2008] ECR I-0000.

28 Meij (1997), p. 282.

29 C-6 and 9/90 *Francovich and Bonifaci* v *Italy* [1991] ECR I-5357 and Joined Cases C-46 and 48/93 *Brasserie du Pecheur* v *Germany*, *R* v *Secretary of State ex parte Factortame* [1996] ECR I-1029. See *inter alia*: Dougan (2002), p. 171; Van Gerven (1996), pp. 520-542.

30 C-452/06 *The Queen, on the application of Synthon* v *Licensing Authority of the Department of Health* [2008] ECR I-0000.

31 See chapter 2, section 3 in particular section 3.3.

32 C-74/03 *Smith Kline Beecham* [2005] ECR I-595.

tive authorization holder to claim damages when the national authorities do not act in compliance with the authorization procedures as established under Community product legislation.

While ECJ case law and the Directive on liability for defective products ensure that individuals can claim damages from the manufacturer or the importer, it is not certain whether consumers can claim damages from the Member State that authorized the placing on the market of a product when it should not have done so.[33] In this regard, it is a complicating factor that the ECJ has limited Member State liability to a sufficiently serious breach of a rule of law intended to confer rights on individuals.[34] It is not certain that product legislation – even though it strives to protect the environment, public health or consumers – creates rights for individuals and can hence be relied upon in a damages case brought against a Member State.[35] This uncertainty can be resolved by Community legislation, as the Mutual Assistance Regulation demonstrates. It states that each CIS partner that has included data is responsible for the accuracy, currency and lawfulness of that data and can be held liable for any injury caused to a person through the use of the CIS in the Member State concerned or at the Commission.[36] Indeed, any person may bring an action or a complaint before the national court or authority designed for that purpose.[37]

Another uncertainty is whether a lack of supervision by national authorities constitutes a breach for which Member States are liable.[38] In *Peter Paul*, a case concerning failed banking supervision, the ECJ held in a liability context that the concept of Community rights does not include the right to (effective) supervisory measures and hence it excluded a finding of liability under German law.[39] It is uncertain whether Peter Paul applies outside the ambit of banking supervision and what its consequences may be for liability in other areas of Community law.[40] Yet it makes it at least questionable whether a right exists that national authorities protect consumers from defective products from a manufacturer or distributor in breach of Community legislation and whether a failure should lead to liability.[41] The CFI did not answer this question when it established in the *Julia Abad Perez* case that the Community institutions could not be held liable

33 Directive 85/374/EEC. See on ECJ case law on this subject *inter alia*: Arnull (2006), pp. 326-329 and Eilmansberger (2004), pp. 1199-1246.

34 See: Prechal (2008), esp. pp. 159-161 and p. 165-170.; Jans *et al.* (2007), pp. 336-344.

35 Joined Cases C-178/94, C-179/94, C-188/94, C-189/94 and C-190/94 *Dillenkofer* [1996] ECR I-4845. E.g. the Air Quality Directive seems to confer rights on everyone, as follows from C-361/88 *TA Luft* [1991] ECR I-2567 and C-237/07 *Janecek* [2008] ECR I-0000. See: Prechal (2008), pp. 155-182, Ruffert (1997), pp. 324-325.

36 Art. 40 Regulation 515/97.

37 Art. 36 Regulation 515/97.

38 See also: section 3.4 in this chapter on the judicial protection of rights.

39 C-222/02 *Peter Paul* [2004] ECR I-9425.

40 Prechal (2008), pp. 166-167.

41 Cf. Van der Meulen (2007), p. 22.

for failed supervision in the Member States, because the national authorities are responsible for supervision.[42]

2 Access to court

The Member States apply their own standing conditions concerning individuals in administrative Community law cases. While the Community standing conditions determine the vertical division of jurisdiction, the national standing conditions determine the horizontal division of jurisdiction, i.e. the division of jurisdiction between the Member States. Environmental disputes are an exception to the rule that the Member States may apply their own standing conditions, as the Aarhus Convention has harmonized the standing conditions in these cases to a certain extent. Access to a national court in Community law cases is important for those who are unable to bring a direct action. While the ECJ has established that, in the absence of Community rules, national procedural rules must comply with Community requirements of equivalence and effectiveness in order to ensure effective judicial protection in Community law cases,[43] it only stressed the duty of national courts under Article 10 EC to interpret and apply national procedural rules on standing – as far as possible – in a way that enables natural and legal persons to bring proceedings in order to enforce the rights they derive from Community law.[44] That raises the question whether this is sufficient to prevent any gaps in the system of judicial protection against European administrative decisions.

2.1 National standing conditions

National administrative law generally requires that a national administrative act must be a starting point for bringing proceedings. However, the precise standing conditions for bringing an action for annulment vary from one Member State to another. Yet this diversity only remains within a certain radius. It appears that national standing rules either require that an applicant establishes a sufficient interest in bringing administrative law proceedings or that he maintains that his rights are impaired.[45] A glance at the applicable rules in France, the United Kingdom, the Netherlands and Germany provides an illustration of the variation within these two sets of rules. In the absence of Community harmonization, the vague Community standards of equivalence

---

[42] T-304/01 *Julia Abad Perez and Others* v *Council and Commission* [2006] ECR II-4857. See also: T-138/03 *E.R. and Others* v *Council and Commission* [2006] ECR II-4857.

[43] Lenaerts *et al.* (2006), p. 85. Jans *et al.* (2007), pp. 286-288.

[44] C-263/02 P *Jégo Queré* v *Commission* [2004] ECR I-3425. See: Brown and Morijn (2004), p. 1646.

[45] Cf. Art. 9 Aarhus Convention. See: Jans *et al.* (2007), pp. 288-293.

and effectiveness leave it open to debate whether all Member States comply with the European principle of effective judicial protection.[46]

Both France and the United Kingdom have liberal standing conditions. French administrative law requires that an individual should establish a sufficient interest in order to challenge an administrative act with the nature of a decision. This threshold is easily met, since the Conseil d'État defines this concept broadly, looking at factual concerns. Consequently, in general not only the addressees of an administrative act but also third parties, including organizations like Greenpeace, can bring proceedings.[47] The United Kingdom provides access to the courts to those who assert that their public law rights are infringed by a public body and are able to establish a sufficient interest in bringing proceedings.[48] The broad interpretation of 'public law right' and a 'sufficient interest' by the national courts ensures wide-scale access. Moreover, administrative decisions can often be challenged before a tribunal, as is the case with product legislation.

Like French and English law, Dutch administrative law provides for broad access to the courts. It grants standing before an administrative court to a person whose personal interests are directly affected by an administrative act, provided that he has first submitted the decision to an administrative review.[49] Access to a court (and to prior administrative review) is also available to associations who defend collective or general interests.[50] In the latter case, their interest should be evident from their statutes and activities.[51] The Constitution ensures that the Dutch civil courts provide for judicial review in case an individual cannot bring proceedings before an administrative court.[52] The civil courts only require a 'sufficient interest' in bringing proceedings.[53] Moreover, the Dutch civil courts have jurisdiction if proceedings outside the Netherlands turn out to be impossible.[54]

By contrast, German administrative law imposes strict standing conditions. Whereas access to an administrative court is guaranteed for addressees of an administrative act, a non-addressee must establish that his substantive public law rights are affected by the administrative act he wishes to challenge.[55] In order to meet this threshold, the so-called *Schutznorm*, the applicant has to establish that the legislator did not create the rule in the general interest but

---

46 See section 2 above.

47 Auby (2002), p. 77-83 and Willemsen (2005), pp. 62-77.

48 Jones and Thompson (2002), p. 223-232.

49 Arts 8:1 and 7:1 Algemene wet bestuursrecht.

50 Seerden and Stroink (2002), pp. 181, 182.

51 Art. 3:2 Algemene wet bestuursrecht.

52 Art. 112 Grondwet.

53 Widdershoven in his annotation of C-263/02 P *Jégo Queré* v *Commission*, AB 204/210.

54 Art. 1:9 (b) Wetboek van Rechtsvordering.

55 Art. 19 IV Grundgesetz; Schröder (2002), pp. 1333, 1334.

intended to protect individual interests, which include its interests.[56] It often suffices to establish that constitutional rights are at stake, but that may be easier for an authorization holder who can invoke the right to property than for a third party. The German interpretation of Community rights limits third parties' access to a court and their right to rely on directly effective Community law before a national court.[57] After the ECJ condemned Germany for implementing Community law in provisions that cannot be enforced by individuals before a national court,[58] the German courts are under pressure to apply their standing conditions less stringently to Community law cases.[59]

2.2 Horizontal division of jurisdiction

As a rule, the jurisdiction of a national court is limited by the territoriality principle. Since administrative decisions are also limited by the territoriality principle, parallel jurisdiction between national administrative courts is unexpected and collision norms need not to be made.[60] However, where a national decision can have Europe-wide effect, as occurs with single licence or mutual recognition decisions, it is necessary to determine which administrative court should settle disputes.[61] Unfortunately, there are no European rules, which can create confusion. Yet confusion is unnecessary, since any division of competence departs from the rule that the national courts can only control the national authorities of their own Member State.[62]

For products regulated by European legislation, the division of the national courts' jurisdiction should closely follow the competence given to national authorities by the material norms laid down in Community legislation.[63] Consequently, the national court of a Member State that issued the single licence or the first mutual recognition decision would have exclusive jurisdiction to settle disputes concerning this decision.[64] In the case of subsequent mutual recognition decisions, the national court of the Member State that recognized the first decision would also have jurisdiction, but only to rule on the recognition.

---

56 Ruffert (1997), pp. 310-312.

57 Jans *et al.* (2007), pp. 292, 293; Willemsen (2005), pp. 41-48; Ruffert (1997), p. 327.

58 E.g. C-131/88 *Commission* v *Germany* [1991] ECR I-825, C-351/88 *Commission* v *Germany* [1991] ECR I-2567, C-59/89 *Commission* v *Germany* [1991] ECR I-2607 and C-298/95 *Commission* v *Germany* [1996] ECR I-6747.

59 See *inter alia*: Schmidt-Aßmann (2004), p. 74 et seq.; Hofmann (2004) p. 359; Ruffert (1997), pp. 307-336; Dingemans and Widdershoven (2005), pp. 327-337.

60 Meng (1994), pp. 186, 187.

61 See: Hofmann (2004).

62 Cf. Meng (1994), p. 744.

63 In the absence of European harmonisation, mutual recognition entails a duty for the national courts to apply the national law of the Member State which issued the original authorization, according to Meng (1994), pp. 204-210.

64 Neßler (1995), pp. 865-866.

This division of competence coupled with the preliminary ruling procedure should ensure the uniformity of the application of Community law. This can be further enhanced by informal cooperation between the national courts,[65] which occurs for instance in the context of the Association of the Councils of State and Supreme Administrative Jurisdictions of the European Union and the European Network for Councils of the Judiciary ('ENCJ').[66]

2.3 The environmental disputes exception

The Member States have to implement the Convention provisions on access to court into national law, because they are all Parties to the Aarhus Convention.[67] The implementation of the Aarhus Convention by the Member States should harmonize their standing conditions for individuals and environmental organisations in environmental disputes,[68] which include actions brought against acts or omissions of national authorities.[69] The Aarhus Directive about judicial review is still a proposal, but it contains a useful definition of Community environmental law. This is defined as Community legislation and legislation adopted to implement Community legislation which have as their objective the protection or the improvement of the environment, including human health and the protection or the rational use of natural resources.[70] It repeats the Convention as it states that individuals and environmental organizations should have access to the courts in order to challenge the procedural and substantive legality of administrative acts and omissions where (a) they have a sufficient interest or (b) they maintain the impairment of a right, where administrative procedural law requires this as a precondition.[71]

The Member States may determine what constitutes a sufficient interest or the impairment of a right and hence can still deny individuals from having access to a court but they have to take the privileged position of environmental organisations into account.[72] Under the Aarhus Convention, environmental

---

65 European Parliament, Report on the role of the national judge in the European judicial system, 2007/2027 (INI).

66 Prechal (2005), pp. 22-23. See: www.juradmin.eu and www.encj.eu.

67 Proposal for a Directive of the European Parliament and of the Council on access to justice in environmental matters, COM (2003) 624 final.

68 De Sadeleer, Roller and Dross (2005), p. 178 et seq.

69 Art. 4 Proposal for a Directive of the European Parliament and the Council on access to justice in environmental matters, COM (2003) 624 final.

70 Art. 1 (g) Proposal for a Directive of the European Parliament and the Council on access to justice in environmental matters, COM (2003) 624 final. In addition this provision offers a (non-exhaustive) list of various areas, including chemicals and nature conservation and biological diversity.

71 Art. 4 proposed Aarhus Directive on access to justice in environmental matters. Cf. Art. 9 (2) and (3) Aarhus Convention.

72 Articles 3 to 5 proposed Aarhus Directive on access to justice in environmental matters. See the Explanatory Memorandum to the Proposal for a Directive of the European Parliament and the Council on access

organizations which promote environmental protection and meet any requirements under national law, must be deemed to have an interest.[73] The proposed Aarhus Directive elaborated this by requiring that environmental organisations are entitled to access to the courts without having to prove a sufficient interest or maintaining the impairment of a right, provided that they bring an action against a matter that is specifically covered by their statutory activities and falls within their specific geographical area of activities.[74] The Aarhus Convention and the proposed Aarhus Directive thus increase the possibility that environmental organizations and, to a lesser extent, individuals can gain access to a national court in environmental disputes, although differences may continue to exist between the Member States. It is unfortunate that the Convention Secretariat cannot impose a sanction in case of non-compliance with the Convention.[75] However, it could well follow from the Court's case law that the Commission can bring an infringement case against a Member State for non-compliance with the judicial review provisions of the Aarhus Convention, provided that these provisions have become part of Community law even though they are not yet implemented into a Directive.[76]

2.4 The preliminary ruling procedure

Individuals who have gained access to a national court can indirectly gain access to the Community courts through the preliminary ruling procedure.[77] However, the preliminary ruling procedure is not devised as a means of redress for individuals, but as a means for the national courts to obtain answers to questions of Community law. The Treaty established that any national court or tribunal may ask the Court of Justice for a preliminary ruling if a question arises about (a) the interpretation of the EC Treaty, (b) the validity and interpretation of acts of the institutions of the Community and (c) the interpretation of the statutes of bodies established by an act of the Council, where those statutes so provide.[78] The ECJ issues its rulings on the basis of the facts

to justice in environmental matters, COM (2003) 624 final, pp. 11-14.

73 Art. 9 and 2 (5) Aarhus Convention.

74 Art. 5 Proposal for a Directive of the European Parliament and the Council on access to justice in environmental matters, COM (2003) 624 final. Cf. Art. 2 (5) and 9 (2), (3) Aarhus Convention.

75 On the basis of a complaint from a Belgian environmental organisation, the Aarhus Convention Compliance Committee has warned Belgium that if the jurisprudence of the Council of State is not altered, Belgium will fail to comply with Art. 9, paragraphs 2 to 4, of the Convention by effectively blocking most, if not all, environmental organizations from access to justice with respect to town planning permits and area plans, as provided for in the Wallonian region. See: Communication ACCC/C/2005/11.

76 See: C-239/03 *Commission* v *France (Etang de Berre)* [2004] ECR I-9325; C-459/03 *Commission* v *Ireland (MOX Plant)* [2006] ECR I-8151; Opinion AG Colomer in C-431/05 *Merck Genericos-Produtos Farmaceuticos* v *Merck and Co and Merck, Sharp and Dohme* [2007] ECR I-0000.

77 See: Arnull (2006), pp. 159-252 and Craig and De Burca (2007), pp. 178-229.

78 Art. 234 EC.

and the questions that the national courts send to it in their reference decisions and therefore the procedure is objective and non-contradictory.[79] The effect of a ruling by the ECJ is to bind the referring court, which will apply it to the facts of the case.[80] Yet the effect extends beyond that court, as a judgment on the validity of a Community act has effect *erga omnes*, which is also arguably true for a judgment on the interpretation of a Community act due to its declaratory nature.[81]

Access

The ECJ does not apply strict admissibility conditions in the preliminary ruling procedure,[82] because it considers that this procedure is a means of cooperation between the ECJ and national courts.[83] However, the ECJ can only give preliminary rulings – and hence ensure the uniformity of Community legislation – if the national courts refer questions to it. Since individuals cannot request a preliminary ruling, the effectiveness of the procedure depends on the manner in which the national courts exercise their discretion as to whether a preliminary ruling should be asked and how it should be formulated.[84] In general, any court or tribunal of a Member State 'may' refer a question to the ECJ if it considers that a decision on the question is necessary to enable it to give judgment, while they must refer a question when no appeal against their judgment is possible. If they need an answer with exceptional urgency, they may request the ECJ to use the accelerated procedure of Article 104 (a) Rules of Procedure. The ECJ decides whether it will grant the request.[85]

The mere fact that a question of Community law arises does not mean that the national court is compelled to ask a question.[86] It follows from CILFIT that a court does not have to ask questions if the question concerns an acte clair or an acte éclairé, i.e. if the answer to the question is obvious or has been answered in a previous ruling.[87] The national courts can then interpret Community

79 Sydow (2004), p. 293.

80 Joined Cases C-28/62, 69/62 and 30/62 *Da Costa* v *Nederlandse Belastingadministratie* [1963] ECR 31.

81 See: Lenaerts *et al.* (2006), pp. 194-197.

82 See: Tridimas (2003), pp. 21-26.

83 Opinion of Advocate General Geelhoed in C-491/01 *British American Tobacco (Investments) and Imperial Tobacco* [2002] ECR I-11453. See also: Timmermans (2000), pp. 397-398.

84 Opinion of AG Jacobs in C-50/00 P *Union de Pequenos Agricultores* v *Council* [2002] ECR I-6677. See: Information Note on references from national courts for a preliminary ruling OJ 2005 C 143/01.

85 The first example is C-189/01 *Jippes and Others* [2001] ECR I-5689.

86 C-283/81 *CILFIT* [1982] ECR 3414. See also C-112/00 *Eugen Schmidberger* v *Austria* [2003] ECR I-05659 and C-495/03 *Intermodal* [2005] ECR I-8151.

87 C-283/81 *CILFIT* v *Ministro della Sanitá* [1982] ECR 3415, in which it refers for an early application of the acte éclairé rule to Joined Cases C-28 to 30/62 *Da Costa en Schaake* [1963] ECR 31. AG Jacobs is critical about the CILFIT criteria in his Opinion in C-338/95 *Wiener* [1997] ECR I-6495. According to Rasmussen (2000), pp. 1107-1110 the ECJ ought to reverse its judgment in CILFIT, because it has led to an all too abundant harvest of questions, diminishing the court's ability to deal with cases swiftly. See also: Wattel (2004), p. 177-190.

law themselves and apply it to the case at hand. The ECJ has given additional guidelines for validity questions in the *Foto Frost* case.[88] It restricted the discretion of the national courts by establishing that they do not have the competence to declare a Community act invalid. Only the Community courts can annul Community acts. If an individual brings proceedings against a marketing authorization because it contests the validity of the underlying Community listing decision, the national court should refer questions if it doubts the validity of the Community decision, either of its own motion or because it considers the arguments put forward by the parties well founded.[89] If the national court does not refer validity questions, it must decide the case on the basis of the assumption that the underlying Community decision is valid.[90] This approach prevents divergences between courts in the Member States as to the validity of Community acts, which would be liable to jeopardise the uniformity of the Community legal order.[91]

2.5 Judicial protection of rights

Due to the narrow standing conditions under Article 230 EC, the EC judicial system can only appear to offer effective judicial protection to individuals if the national courts always do their job.[92] This explains why the ECJ established in the cases *Johnston* and *Heylens* that the principle of effective judicial protection requires that individuals have access to a national court in order to enforce the rights they derive from Community law.[93] Consequently, a national court may even have to declare an action admissible that would otherwise not be admissible under national law by setting aside the national procedural rule in question.[94] Since the ECJ restricts the application of the principle of effective judicial protection to Community law creating rights for individuals, the question is whether Community product legislation is intended to create rights and for which individuals.[95] The answer to this question is relevant for those who bring an action for annulment and for those who bring an action for

---

88 C-314/85 *Foto Frost* [1987] ECR 4199.

89 Cf. C-344/04 *The Queen, on the application of International Air Transport Association and European Low Fares Airline Association* v *Department for Transport* [2006] ECR I-403.

90 E.g. C-6/99 *Greenpeace* v *Ministere de l'Agriculture et de la Peche and Others* [2000] ECR I-1651.

91 C-314/85 *Foto Frost* [1987] ECR 4199 and C-461/03 *Gaston Schul* [2005] ECR I-10513.

92 Cortés Martin (2004), p. 261.

93 C-222/84 *Johnston* [1986] ECR 1651 and C-222/86 *Heylens* [1987] ECR 4097. See also: C-340/89 *Vlassopoulou* [1991] ECR I-2357, C-97/91 *Oleifici Borelli* v *Commission* [1992] ECR I-6313, C-1/99 *Kofisa Italia* [2001] ECR I-207, C-226/99 *Siples* [2001] ECR I-277 and C-424/99 *Commission* v *Austria* [2001] ECR I-9285.

94 C-15/04 *Koppensteiner* v *Bundesimmobliliengesellschaft* [2005] ECR I-4855. See: Lenaerts *et al.* (2006), p. 87.

95 See: Prechal (2008).

damages. In addition, it is a factor that determines the availability of the preliminary ruling procedure.

The rights of third parties

While it is obvious that a marketing authorization creates the right to market a product for the applicant or holder of an authorization, who therefore has to be able to challenge decisions regarding his authorization, it is hard to say whether it can also create rights to the benefit of third parties, be they consumers, competitors or associations. For a long time, the ECJ equated direct effect with the creation of rights and considered the legal consequences of this qualification as a matter of national law within the limits of procedural autonomy.[96] Arguably, only Community law on which individuals can rely before the national courts can confer them with rights and hence standing.[97] That might limit the provisions of Community law that can grant individuals a right to the directly applicable provisions of Regulations and Decisions and to those provisions of Directives that have direct effect, because the subject-matter of the provision concerned is unconditional and sufficiently precise.[98]

For example, the ECJ established in the *Smith Nephews and Primecrown* case that the holder of an original marketing authorization may rely on the provisions of the medicines directive in proceedings before a national court in order to challenge the validity of an authorization issued by the competent national authority on the basis of that directive to one of its competitors for a proprietary medicinal product bearing the same name, because those provisions are sufficiently unconditional and precise for that purpose.[99] Yet this ruling does not say whether the national court should confer standing to the holder of the original marketing authorization, as that was not an issue in this case.

However, individuals in Member States with strict standing conditions can only rely on a certain provision after they have gained access to a court to enforce a Community right and therefore it matters who can rely on provisions of Community law. Who can derive rights from a provision of Community is determined on the basis of the substance and aims of the legislation.[100] For instance, it is the question whether product legislation, which aims to protect public health or the environment, can create rights for individuals other than the applicant or authorization holder. Perhaps all people who may be affected by authorizations for products that are unsafe or harm the environment have to be able to enforce their Community right to safe products, if the ECJ consid-

96 Prechal (2008), pp. 155 -156.

97 Van Gerven (2000), p. 503.

98 Opinion of Advocate General Kokott in C-127/02 *Landelijke Vereniging tot Behoud van de Waddenzee and Nederlandse Vereniging tot Bescherming van Vogels* v *Staatssecretaris van Landbouw, Natuurbeheer en Visserij* [2004] ECR I-7405.

99 C-201/94 *The Queen* v *The Medicines Control Agency, ex parte Smith and Nephew Pharmaceuticals and Primecrown* v *The Medicine Control Agency* [1996] ECR I-05819.

100 Jans *et al.* (2007), p. 290.

ers these rights to be comparable with the right to clean air.[101] It is difficult to deduce from the case law of the ECJ how big the group of people will be that can rely on certain provisions. As long as the ECJ has not pronounced on this issue, the fear that its line of reasoning could lead to a mandatory *actio popularis* in various fields of Community law might be unfounded.[102]

Indeed, the ECJ case law on access to the courts for third parties that do not meet the national standing conditions seems contradictory. On the one hand, the ECJ established in the *Verholen* case that the right to rely on a provision of Community law with direct effect is not confined to persons who fall within the scope of Community legislation. It broadened standing rights to persons who have a direct interest in ensuring that the principle of non-discrimination is respected as regards persons who are protected by the Directive.[103] On the other hand, it did not broadly interpret direct interest in the *Österreichischer Zuchtverband* case, as it established that a competitor does not necessarily have a direct interest.[104] Therefore, national procedural law could deny an existing association the right to demand the authorities to refuse recognition or approval of a new association and to challenge their decision in court proceedings because the relevant provision conferred broad discretionary powers on the national authorities.[105]

What can be concluded from the ECJ's case law is that a direct interest in the enforcement of the right is required. Consequently, the national courts may not have to confer standing on a broad group of individuals, especially since product legislation confers broad discretionary powers on the national authorities. However, competitors may also rely on the ruling of the ECJ in the *Streekgewest* case in order to gain access to the courts.[106] The ECJ held in that case that an individual may have an interest in relying on the direct effect of a provision in order to erase the negative effects of a distortion of competition. Since the competitor in this case already had access to a court in order to challenge a certain tax, which was an integral part of the aid measure he wanted to contest as well, the ECJ did not have to rule on the question whether access to court should be guaranteed. Nevertheless, it can be deduced from the *Streekgewest* case that the distortion of competition on the internal market can be a ground for being granted standing before a national court. Perhaps the ECJ would consider a distortion of the right to free movement a ground for being granted standing as well.

---

101 E.g. C-361/88 *TA Luft* [1991] ECR I-2567.

102 Eilmansberger (2004), pp. 1199-1246.

103 Joined Cases C-87/90 to C-89/90 *Verholen and Others* [1991] ECR I-3757.

104 C-216/02 *Österreichischer Zuchtverband für Ponys, Kleinpferde und Spezialrassen* [2004] ECR I-10683.

105 C-120/97 *Upjohn* v *The Licencing Authority established by the Medicines Act* [1968] ECR I-223 presents the altogether different situation that a third party complains about the intensity of a national court's review of discretionary powers exercised by the national authorities. Cf. C-72/95 *Kraaijeveld* [1996] ECR I-5403, C-435/97 *WWF* [1999] ECR I-5613 and C-287/98 *Linster* [2000] ECR I-6917.

106 C-174/02 *Streekgewest Westelijk Noord-Brabant* [2005] ECR I-85.

2.6 Mind the gap

The ECJ expects the national courts to offer complementary judicial review in order to ensure a complete system of judicial protection that offers equivalent protection of human rights when compared with the system of the European Convention on Human Rights.[107] They should ensure in particular that individuals can challenge the legality of any national decision or other measure relative to the application to them of a Community act of general application.[108] That may not be possible when the national authorities do not have to take implementing measures and national procedural law does not provide for a free standing action. However, it is never impossible for an individual to challenge (the implementation of) a Community act before a national court, provided that he is willing to breach the law, as that offers the opportunity to raise the invalidity of the Community act as a defence in enforcement proceedings before a national court. The question is whether that constitutes effective judicial protection. It is easy to agree with Advocate General Jacobs that having to breach the law to secure judicial review does not constitute effective judicial protection, because the risks involved in violating the law may prevent people from seeking a judicial review.[109]

Contrary to the position taken by the CFI and Advocate General Jacobs, the ECJ did not consider that it had to grant standing in the *Jégo Quéré* case for this reason.[110] In the same vein, the ECJ held in the *Safalero* case that the principle of effective judicial protection of the rights Community law confers on individuals is to be construed as not precluding national legislation under which an importer cannot bring court proceedings to challenge a measure adopted by the public authorities under which goods sold to a retailer are seized, where there is available to him – because the said authorities also fined him – a legal remedy which ensures respect for the rights conferred on him by Community law.[111] Perhaps the ECJ departed from this position in the *Unibet* case, as it held that having access to a national court solely after breaking the law could not secure effective judicial protection in the absence of other remedies, which are: first, that a person can apply for an authorization and can then challenge a rejection or, second, that a person can obtain judicial control of the compatibility of national law with Community law in the course of damages proceedings.[112] This could mean that the ECJ has finally adhered to the judgment of the ECtHR in

---

[107] See *inter alia*: Costello (2006).

[108] C-50/00 P *Unión de Pequeños Agricultores* v *Council* [2002] ECR I-6677.

[109] Opinion of AG Jacobs in C-263/02 P *Jégo Queré* v *Commission* [2004] ECR I-3425.

[110] T-177/01 *Jégo Quéré* v *Commission* [2002] ECR II-2365 and C-263/02 P *Commission* v *Jégo Quéré* [2004] ECR I-3425. See: Arnull (2007), pp. 1775, 1776.

[111] C-13/01 *Safalero* v *Prefetto di Genova* [2003] ECR I-8679.

[112] C-432/05 *Unibet* v *Justitiekanslern* [2007] ECR I-0000.

Posti and Rahko v *Finland* that no one can be required to breach the law so as to be able to have a 'civil right' determined.[113]

The ECJ established in the *Unibet* case that if neither a free standing action nor other remedies enable the applicant to obtain an examination of the compatibility of national provisions with Community law, a national court has to examine the compatibility with EC law irrespective of the assessment of the merits of the case with regard to the requirements for damage and a causal link in the claim for damages.[114] This gives the action for damages at the national level the same complementary status compared to the action for annulment as the action for damages at the Community level. Yet it is debatable whether this is really the case. When a court establishes State liability, the Member State must adequately compensate the damage caused by the breach of Community law.[115] However, there is no guarantee that a Member State will change the law on the basis of a damages claim.[116]

The action for a failure to act may present an even bigger risk of a gap in the so-called complete system of remedies than the action for annulment, since the ECJ has held that national courts are not competent to decide these cases.[117] They lack competence because the cooperation mechanism of Article 234 EC does not include this option.[118] That means that individuals who would not be the addressees of the decision which the institution has failed to adopt or which would be of direct and individual concern to them cannot rely on the national courts for a supplementary judicial review. Instead, they can only complain to the European Ombudsman about this failure to act. Perhaps the ECJ will change its case law, as it adhered to its rulings in *UPA* and *Ten Kate* when it held that the national courts are required, as far as possible, to interpret and apply national procedural rules about standing in a way that enables individuals to challenge before a national court the legality of any decision or other national measure relative to the application to them of a Community act of general application, by pleading the failure to take a decision, which it considers to be contrary to Community law.[119] In the absence of an explicit departure from earlier case law, it can only be presumed that the ECJ will allow the national court to ask preliminary questions concerning an alleged failure to act by the Community institutions or bodies.[120]

---

[113] Lenaerts *et al.* (2006), pp. 91 and 92. See: ECtHR 24 Sept. 2002 *Posti and Rahko* v *Finland* Case 27824/95.

[114] C-432/05 *Unibet* v *Justitiekanslern* [2007] ECR I-2271.

[115] C-6 and 9/90 *Francovich and Bonifaci* [1991] ECR I-5357.

[116] Arnull (2007), p. 1175.

[117] C-68/95 *T. Port and Co* [1996] ECR I-6065.

[118] T-395/04 *Air One* v *Commission* [2006] ECR II-1343.

[119] C-511/03 *Ten Kate Holding Musselkanaal and Others* [2006] ECR I-8979.

[120] Lenaerts (2007), pp. 1634, 1635.

Creative solutions

The ECJ has proposed how the national courts can ensure a complete system. It held that it is possible for national law to permit an individual directly concerned by a general legislative measure of national law which cannot be contested before a court to seek from the national authorities under that legislation a measure which may itself be contested before the national courts so that the individual may challenge the legislation indirectly. It is likewise possible that under national law an operator directly concerned by a regulation may seek from the national authorities a measure under that regulation which may be contested before the national courts, thereby enabling the operator to challenge the regulation indirectly.[121] This reasoning may ensure access to a national court to challenge a Community act of general or individual application, but it is regrettable that the ECJ remained so vague. Of course it is possible that this option exists under national law and thus prevents a gap, but it is equally possible that this option does not exist. In order to substantiate its claim that the Community legal order provides for a complete system of remedies, the ECJ had better prescribe that this option should be available under national law[122] instead of condoning the absence of a mandatory declaratory remedy, provided that the national courts ensure effective judicial protection by other means.[123]

Yet one can point to two cases as examples that solutions can be created at the national level.[124] In the *BAT* case the implementation of an allegedly invalid Directive was challenged before the expiry of the transposition period by requesting a declaration that the United Kingdom would keep its promise in the Act of Accession that it would not implement invalid Directives. Advocate General Geelhoed recommended that the ECJ accommodate this solution and therefore does not close off the preliminary reference avenue, as that would create a legal vacuum.[125] Indeed, the ECJ accepted the reference in this case. As the English courts interpret both right and sufficient interest very broadly, individuals can bring actions against Community acts in England and Wales involving national authorities which have not taken any national implementing measures.[126] The *ABNA* case reveals that similar actions can also be brought in the Netherlands and in Italy.[127] It remains to be seen whether similar actions are possible in all the Member States.

---

[121] C-263/02 P *Jégo Queré* v *Commission* [2004] ECR I-3425.

[122] Widdershoven, in his case note on C-263/02 P *Jégo Queré* v *Commission* [2004] ECR I-3425 in AB 2004/210.

[123] C-432/05 *Unibet* v *Justitiekanzlern* [2007] ECR I-2271. See: Lenaerts (2007), p. 1646.

[124] C-491/01 *British American Tobacco (Investments) and Imperial Tobacco* [2002] ECR I-11453.

[125] Opinion of AG Geelhoed in C-491/01 *British American Tobacco (Investments) and Imperial Tobacco* [2002] ECR I-11453.

[126] Opinion of AG Geelhoed in C-344/04 *The Queen, on the application of International Air Transport Association and European Low Fares Airline Association* v *Department for Transport* [2006] ECR I-403.

[127] Joined Cases C-453/03, C-11/04, C-12/04 and C-194/04 *ABNA and Others* [2005] ECR I-10423.

3 Genetically modified organisms

The national courts may have a limited role for individuals who want to challenge a GMO decision due to the fact that most GMO decisions are Community decisions.[128] Prospective authorization holders or authorization holders cannot challenge a Community GMO authorization before the national courts, because they can bring a direct action before the Community courts. Therefore, they can only challenge single licence GMO authorizations, national enforcement decisions and national safeguard measures before the national courts. By contrast, third parties who are unable to establish a direct and individual concern can only challenge GMO decisions – including Community authorizations – before the national courts. However, it is not certain that third parties will meet the national standing conditions. In particular the lack of a national decision could be an unsurmountable hurdle.

3.1 Single licence decision

Authorizations for the placing on the market of GMOs for other uses under Directive 2001/18 Part C have a single licence character. This also applies when objections from one or more Member States necessitate the use of the Community procedure. When a Community decision has ended the dispute, the national authority that received the application for an authorization (the reference Member State) has to implement the Community decision by issuing a written consent or rejection to the applicant. The applicant can then challenge this decision before the Community courts, while third parties who are unable to establish a direct and individual concern can challenge the validity of the written consent and the underlying Commission decision before the national court of the reference Member State, provided that they meet the applicable national standing conditions.[129] It is unlikely that competitors can invoke the right to free movement or the safety of GMOs in trade. This is because they would not be directly affected by an authorization issued to a competitor in the absence of a simplified procedure for the authorization of GMOs in which dossiers from competitors are used.[130] In general, individuals would lack a direct interest in the protection of the environment or their health and therefore they will not be able to challenge the authorization of a GMO.

Since disputes over GMO authorizations should be settled by the national court of the Member State where the consent or rejection is issued, the absence of the harmonization of standing conditions means that it matters for third parties which Member State acted as the reference Member State. Due to the single licence character of the national consent, which also applies when it

[128] See Chapter 2, section 3.

[129] Cf. C-6/99 *Association Greenpeace France and Others* v *Ministere de l'Agriculture et de la Peche* [2000] ECR I-1651, brought under (the from this point of view similar) Directive 90/220/EC.

[130] See section 4 .1 in this chapter for an example of a succesful claim on that basis.

implements a Community decision, access denied in the reference Member State means access denied in all the Member States. However, there is another option, which is to request the competent authorities to use the safeguard procedure, because a safeguard measure can suspend the application of the written consent.[131] However, a safeguard measure applies only on the territory of the Member State that issued it and is not intended to be used for this purpose. Nevertheless, theoretically, it is possible that in order to suspend the authorization in more than one Member State, third parties request in each Member State that the authorities apply the safeguard procedure and challenge a rejection before the national courts of that Member State. The authorization holder could then rely on the principle of judicial protection to intervene in the proceedings, as his right to free movement of the authorized GMO would be jeopardized by a safeguard measure.

3.2 Community decision

National courts may be unable to offer a complementary judicial review of Community marketing authorizations for GMOs. This is a difficult task because both under Directive 2001/18/EC (de facto) and Regulation 1829/2003/EC authorizations for the marketing of GMOs are issued following the Community procedure and therefore a national decision may lack. It is obvious that the applicant for an authorization for the placing on the market of GMOs for food or feed use under Regulation 1829/2003 does not need – and, indeed, is not allowed to either – to rely on the national courts, because as the addressee of this decision he can bring proceedings before the Community courts. He can only bring proceedings before a national court if the national authorities of the reference Member State authorize a GMO for other uses without having made use of the Community dispute settlement procedure or if the national authorities of a Member State take a decision that diverges from the relevant Community decision, which applies in particular when they take enforcement or safeguard measures.

Third parties who are unable to establish a direct and individual concern and hence are unable to challenge an authorization or a rejection before the Community courts need access to a national court to challenge Community authorizations that affect their interests. They depend on national standing provisions, unless they enforce a Community right established for their benefit, but that seems unlikely as seen above. The Community decision under the Directive will be implemented by the Member State that should have taken the decision and therefore third parties can challenge it indirectly in that Member State, provided that they meet the national standing conditions. By contrast, it might prove impossible for third parties to gain access to the courts to challenge a GMO food or feed marketing authorization issued under the GMO Regulation due to

[131] C-6/99 *Association Greenpeace France and Others* v *Ministere de l' Agriculture et de la Peche* [2000] ECR I-1651.

the absence of a national decision, as the GMO Regulation does not prescribe the implementation of the Community marketing authorization in a national marketing authorization. This will prove an obstacle in many Member States, but due to the prescribed uniform effect of the Community decision, meeting the standing conditions and thus gaining access before a national court of another Member State through a free standing declaratory action may compensate for access being denied in the other Member States.

3.3 The environmental disputes exception

Judicial review may be available against GMO marketing authorizations in various Member States for two reasons. First, access to court can be based on national legislation, as the Aarhus Directive allows the Parties to maintain or introduce more extensive public participation and wider access to justice.[132] Second, it may follow from the Aarhus Convention and the proposed Aarhus Directive on judicial review that its provisions apply to GMOs. The Directive's definition of environmental law refers to Community legislation and legislation adopted to implement Community legislation which have as their objective the protection or the improvement of the environment, including human health and the protection or the rational use of natural resources in areas such as biotechnology. Since the marketing of GMOs is regulated because of the potential risks for human health, it may fall within the definition. In view of this uncertainty, it will depend on the implementation of the Aarhus Convention and the GMO amendment in European and national legislation whether third parties may challenge a GMO marketing authorisation.

The implementation of the GMO amendment to the Aarhus Convention in European and national legislation may not close a possible 'gap' in the system of judicial protection.[133] A possible gap may persist because the GMO amendment provides that the regular public participation procedure – which provides for judicial review – will continue not to apply to public participation in decisions about the deliberate release into the environment and the marketing of GMOs.[134] Instead, it introduces a specific procedure for effective information on and public participation in decision-making about the deliberate release of GMOs into the environment and the marketing of GMOs that does not prescribe a judicial review. The Parties should only endeavour to ensure that when decisions are taken on whether to permit the deliberate release into the environment, including placing on the market, due account is taken of the outcome of the public participation procedure.[135] Unfortunately, it is not clear whether the omission of judicial review of GMO marketing authorizations was a deliberate choice or

---

[132] Art. 3 (5) Aarhus Convention.

[133] See: Council Decision 2006/957/EC.

[134] Art. 6 Aarhus Convention.

[135] The new Art. 6 bis and Annex I bis Aarhus Convention.

whether it is considered unproblematic because it is already ensured through other provisions of the Convention.

3.4 Conclusions

Since GMOs are regulated in a different manner, depending on whether the GMO in question is destined for other uses or for food or feed use, different situations exist as regards access to a national court. This is illustrated by the table below.

Table 5.1 Standing of individuals in GMO cases before the national courts

European administrative Decision	Applicant	Third party	Qualified environmental organization
Community dispute settlement authorization GMO for other uses – addressed to reference MS	-	+/-	+/-
Community authorization GMO for food/ feed use – addressed to applicant	-	-/+	-/+
Single licence authorization GMO for other uses issued by reference MS	+	+/-	+/-

While it does not make a difference for the position of the authorization holder or the prospective authorization holder whether the authorization of a GMO is for other uses or for food or feed use, it matters to third parties. The prospective authorization holder or the authorization holder can file an admissible action for annulment before the Community courts and is therefore unable to bring an admissible annulment action before the national court. He can only bring proceedings before a national court if the national authorities of the reference Member State authorize a GMO for other uses or if the national authorities of a Member State take a decision that diverges from the relevant Community decision, which applies in particular when they take enforcement or safeguard measures. It is to be expected that the authorization holder will be able to challenge these decisions before the national court of the Member State that issued them.

The possibility that third parties can bring proceedings before a national court against marketing authorizations is less certain. This is because they depend on the standing conditions of the reference Member State that issued the single licence decision or implemented the Community decision. This exclusivity ensures uniformity but it also means that those who neither meet the standing conditions of the Community courts nor of the reference Member State are denied access to a court. Their only option might be to request the use of the safeguard procedure in each Member State in order to be able to challenge a rejection before the national court of that Member State. By contrast, a Community authorization for a GMO for food and feed use does not require implementation, which can make it more difficult to challenge it in Member States where a free standing declaratory action does not exist, but perhaps that does not exclude that it can be challenged in other Member States. Member States that offer a freestanding declaratory action might be able to compensate for strict conditions in other Member States. The Aarhus Convention may facilitate access to court for individuals, assuming that marketing authorizations for GMOs fall within its definition of environmental law.

4 Medicines

The national courts can be confronted with individuals who want to challenge mutual recognition decisions or Community decisions regarding the authorization of medicines. The authorization holder can bring proceedings before the Community courts against Community decisions and before the national courts against mutual recognition decisions. While it can be safely assumed that the authorization holder has access to a court, it is not certain that third parties will be granted access to a court to challenge Community or mutual recognition decisions. Each type of decision presents its own challenges. Mutual recognition decisions are a challenge for the national courts because they have to determine whether and to what extent they have jurisdiction. The challenges that arise with regard to Community decisions are similar to those analyzed in the context of the Community authorizations for GMOs and will therefore not be analyzed again. The application of the environmental disputes exception will not be discussed here either because the environmental impact of medicines is not (yet) reflected in their authorization.

4.1 Mutual recognition decision

Who can bring proceedings before a national court against the authorization of a medicine depends on national procedural law, unless an individual enforces a Community right conferred for his benefit. Some third parties should be able to invoke the principle of effective judicial protection since the medicines legislation aims to facilitate the free movement of authorized medicines and requires that medicines are only authorized if the risk-benefit balance, quality, safety and efficacy requirements are met. Competitors, especially those whose dossier is used in the authorization procedure, can easily establish a direct interest in the enforcement of the authorization requirements. Since they were involved in the authorization procedure, it does not seem likely that access to the courts can be denied to them on the basis of the discretionary room that the authorities have. Other third parties, such as patients or patient organizations, may invoke the same right, but they will find it difficult to establish a direct interest in the enforcement of the authorization requirements and therefore they will depend on national procedural law.

In the absence of a duty of coordination between national courts, parallel proceedings before national courts in various Member States can occur. These proceedings can result in divergent decisions, because administrative law court rulings do not have to be recognized by the courts of other Member States. The question is how a system of mutual recognition of decisions counters the risk of divergent outcomes as a consequence of court proceedings. The medicines legislation does not provide for a solution to this situation. However, a solution can be found if its dispute settlement procedure is used. After all, the dispute settlement procedure applies to divergent decisions taken by national authorities regarding the authorization of medicines for human use at the request of a national authority, the applicant or the Commission. Therefore, one of them can also request that this procedure be used when decisions diverge due to court proceedings.

This may, for instance, occur when a Member State recognizes a mutual recognition authorization while an action for annulment is pending in the reference Member State. If the holder of an authorization ('A') wishes to challenge an authorization issued for parallel import or a generic issued to a competitor ('B') on the basis of his dossier, he should challenge B's authorization before the national courts of the reference Member State (i.e. the Member State whose authorities first issued the authorization).[136] It is possible that while A or another third party challenges B's authorization, another Member State will have already recognized it. If A wants to challenge the recognition as well, he has to take into account that the court of the recognizing Member State will assume that a decision from another Member State is valid. Therefore, he can challenge the recognition but in order to challenge the substance of the decision – and not the mere recognition – it suffices that he brings proceedings against B's authorization in the reference Member State.

It is possible that A is unable to gain access to the courts in the reference Member State, but can gain access to the courts of the recognizing Member State. That Member State should then refer him for a substantial review to the court of the reference Member State. Such a referral to another Member State is justified if it is possible to bring proceedings in that Member State. If that is not the case, a referral results in a gap in legal protection.[137] Of course, a referral should not be hindered by the nationality of those who seek a judicial review as the principle of non-discrimination forbids the national courts from denying access to a court to individuals on the ground that they are inhabitants of

[136] Sydow (2004), p. 280.

[137] Hofmann (2004), p. 77.

other Member States. However, that may not prevent inadmissibility on other grounds, in particular when the standing conditions are not met.

It is possible that B's authorization is suspended in the reference Member State by a court order. Since the legislation offers full harmonization regarding the grounds for rejection and includes neither pending court proceedings nor suspension, the other Member States may not refuse recognition solely on this ground.[138] Therefore, A, or other third parties, may need to bring (interim relief) proceedings in the recognizing Member States as well. The clarity of the medicines legislation would be improved if a clear-cut provision were introduced stating either when a decision may be mutually recognized or what the consequences are of starting a mutual recognition procedure before an administrative decision has become unassailable if it is annulled later on.[139] However, court proceedings can take a long time, especially if a national court decides to use the preliminary ruling procedure.[140] Therefore, the rationale of the absence of such a rule could well be that it would hinder the parallel import and marketing of generics if the national decision to authorize their marketing of the medicine should not be deemed valid until a court judgment proves otherwise.

Mutual recognition while court proceedings are pending impairs the effectiveness of the judicial protection sought by A, because it means that he cannot limit himself to requesting interim relief and bringing an action for annulment in the reference Member State. As the effect of interim relief measures is limited to the Member State where they have been granted, A will have to request interim relief in all the Member States concerned. Each court will decide the request for interim relief according to its own national procedural law. Those rules may well include the obligation of connectivity, i.e. that interim relief is only available to those who bring proceedings on the merits, which means that A also has to bring proceedings for annulment. Since neither the Court's case law nor the medicines legislation obliges the national courts to take a judgment from another Member State into account, interim relief may be granted in one Member State and denied in another. However, A does not need to bring an action for annulment in a Member State other than the reference Member State, since only the court of the reference Member State can exert judicial control over the decision to issue an authorisation.

Bringing annulment proceedings in the recognizing Member States is of less relevance to A, because in those Member States he can only challenge the decision to recognize the contested authorization. B does not have to bring proceedings in a Member State that refuses recognition, because the dispute settlement procedure prevents national authorities from taking such a decision unilaterally. If any of the proceedings brought by A result in a judgment declaring that the decision is invalid and therefore should neither have been

---

138 Cf. Opinion of AG Geelhoed in Joined Cases C-211/03, C-299/03 and C-316/03 to C-319/03 *HLH Warenvertriebs, Orthica v. Deutschland* [2005] ECR I-5141.

139 Van der Meulen (2003), pp. 114-117.

140 C-74/03 *SmithKline Beecham plc* v *Laegemiddelstyreisen* [2005] ECR I-595.

issued nor recognized, the dispute settlement procedure should apply, resulting in a Community decision that restores uniformity.[141] Even though A's dossier provides the basis for the authorization, it is not certain whether A is entitled to challenge the Community decision that settles the dispute before the Community courts on the same footing as B.[142] Other third parties will certainly not meet the Community standing conditions and thus be unable to challenge the Community decision, despite their involvement in national proceedings. Since the Community decision will be implemented in a national decision by the Member States concerned, A can challenge the implementing mutual recognition decision and hence the Community decision before the national courts of one of the concerned Member States. Finally, both A and B may bring an action for damages before a national court, e.g. because interim relief was granted or because it was not granted.

4.2 Conclusion

The tables below illustrate the positions of the applicant and the third parties that want to challenge a Community or a mutual recognition decision before a national court.

Table 5.2 Standing of individuals in medicines cases before the national courts

European administrative decision	Applicant	Third party	Qualified environmental organization
Community Medicines marketing authorization – addressed to the applicant	-	-/+	-
Community dispute settlement – addressed to the MS concerned	-	+/-	-
Mutual recognition decision: first medicines marketing authorization	+	+/-	-
Subsequent mutual recognition decisions of first medicine marketing authorization	+	+/-	-

The applicant cannot challenge a Community decision before a national court, because he can challenge this decision before a Community court in a

[141] See Chapter 2.

[142] See Chapter 4.

direct action. It is not certain whether third parties can challenge Community authorizations or Community authorizations that settle a dispute between the Member States before a national court if access to a Community court was denied to them. Similar to the situation regarding GMOs, it will depend on the national procedural rules of the Member States, with the exception of competitors who can establish a direct interest in the enforcement of the authorization requirements. While a Community authorization for medicines is not implemented by the Member States and therefore can only be challenged in a Member State that offers a free standing declaratory action, a Community decision that settles a dispute about a mutual recognition decision is implemented by the Member States concerned and can therefore be challenged before a national court by those third parties who meet the national standing conditions. Uniformity is not threatened by court proceedings, because when a Community decision is in dispute, the Community courts decide on its validity.

The applicant of a mutual recognition decision can challenge the decision before the national courts of the reference Member State and before the courts of the recognizing Member States. It depends on the national standing conditions whether a third party can also challenge a mutual recognition decision. If the standing conditions of the reference Member State are strict, a third party may be tempted to opt to challenge the decision in one of the recognizing Member States. But the court of a recognizing Member State can only review the recognition and not the original decision. It is problematic that in the absence of a duty of coordination, court proceedings in various Member States can have different outcomes, even as regards the suspension of the decision. Although the medicines legislation does not contain any reference to this issue, it is assumed that the dispute settlement procedure can be used as well when divergent decisions occur due to court proceedings. If that is the case, it is not certain whether the third parties that brought proceedings before the national courts will be able to challenge the Community decision that settles the dispute. However, they might resume the proceedings before the national courts against the revised mutual recognition decision. If the dispute settlement procedure is also used when court proceedings have different outcomes, the uniformity of the mutual recognition decision system is not threatened by court proceedings.

5 CITES

An authorization in a single licence system, such as the one established by the CITES Regulation, seems to present the straightforward situation that disputes should be settled by the national courts of the Member State where the import or export authorization is issued. While this rule also applies if an authorization is rejected, because rejections must be notified to the Commission and be recognized by the other Member States as well, a different rule may apply when a CITES document has to be changed or revoked, due to the possibility of the void declaration. Moreover, the CITES listing decisions present a situation that is different from usual due to the lack of involvement of individuals. That raises the question how individuals can challenge these decisions before national courts. Assuming that any third parties that want to challenge a CITES authorization or its underlying Community listing decision will do so on environmental grounds, their position and the challenging of Community listing decisions is analyzed only in the section on the environmental disputes exception.

5.1 Single licence decision

Disputes over an authorization in the single licence system established by the CITES Regulation should be settled by the national courts of the Member State where the import or export authorization is issued. This rule also applies if an authorization is rejected, because rejections must be notified to the Commission and be recognized by the other Member States as well. It is certain that the applicant of an authorization can challenge the authorization or the rejection before the national courts of the Member State that issued or refused the authorization. It is not certain whether third parties can challenge CITES documents, and the underlying Community listing decision, as it may be difficult to establish a direct interest in the enforcement of species protection for parties other than those who can rely on the environmental disputes exception. Since a CITES document is a single licence that applies to a single shipment, it is not possible to bring proceedings before the national court of another Member State.

The division of jurisdiction between the national courts along the lines of the division of jurisdiction between the national authorities may not endanger the uniformity of the Community legal order with regard to each decision viewed on its own, but uniformity may nevertheless be threatened when national authorities or national courts in various Member States take different decisions. Due to the margin of discretion that the Member States have in assessing applications, a trader may challenge a rejection on the ground that another Member State has recently authorized the import of a similar shipment. A Dutch administrative court responded to this argument that if the CITES Regulation is possibly not correctly applied in another Member State, that does not create a legally enforceable right for the applicant that the Dutch authorities convert to that policy.[143] In the absence of other coordinating mechanisms, only the preliminary ruling procedure can create more certainty as to the correct interpretation of the CITES Regulation.

Enforcement

Enforcement cases present an exception to the rule that CITES documents have to be challenged in the Member State that issued them due to their single

[143] Dutch Council of State 11-02-2004, LJN AO3387, available at www.rechtspraak.nl.

licence character. A CITES shipment for which no documents have been issued may be seized and then the national courts of the Member State where the shipment is seized are competent to review the seizure.[144] However, if CITES documents have been issued but do not match the shipment due to fraud,[145] a mistake in the application of the CITES Regulation or a difference in the interpretation of the CITES Regulation,[146] the Member State which controlled the shipment should consult the authorities of the issuing Member State before declaring the documents void and taking enforcement measures.[147] Since the CITES Regulation does not oblige the authorities of the issuing Member States to change the legal status of the CITES documents, the holder of the void CITES documents may not be able to seek judicial review in the issuing Member State. In general, the holder of the void CITES documents will depend for a judicial review on the national court of the Member State that seized the shipment. As the Regulation does not mention judicial review, it will depend on that Member State whether administrative judicial review is available against the decision to declare the CITES documents void. It is not certain that the declaration to declare the documents void will qualify as a decision against which a judicial review is open under the administrative law of each Member State, as such decisions arguably lack legal effect.

It is a serious complication that if the administrative law of a Member State does not foresee judicial review of the decision to declare the documents void and no replacement decision will be taken because of the seriousness of the offence, judicial review of the declaration that the CITES documents are void will only be available in the enforcement proceedings brought against the offender, be they administrative or criminal proceedings. In these proceedings he can raise as a defence that the documents are valid or that the shipment can be brought in compliance with the CITES Regulation. This approach used to be in line with the case law of the ECJ, but since the ECJ no longer considers that offering a judicial review as to the legality of a Community act in criminal proceedings is in itself not contrary to the principle of effective judicial protection, it may no longer condone this practice.[148] Another complication is that the Regulation does not provide for a substitution of the original decision with the declaration that the CITES documents are void, not even when this declaration is confirmed by a ruling of a national court that authorizes the confiscation of the shipment and of the CITES documents.[149] Nevertheless, both the void decla-

[144] Seizure is the temporary taking of a specimen suspected of being involved in an offence by law enforcement authorities as evidence or pending a final decision on confiscation. See: Garstecki (2006), p. 8.

[145] E.g. birds caught in the wild but ringed and accompanied by captive born and bred CITES documents. See: Van Kreveld (2007).

[146] C-182/89 *Commission* v *France (Bolivian Wildcat Skins)* [1990] ECR I-04337.

[147] Art. 11 Regulation 338/97.

[148] See section 2.6 above.

[149] Confiscation is the irreversible withdrawal of a specimen involved in an offence by law enforcement authorities, possibly following seizure, based on administrative procedures or court decisions. Forfei-

ration and the judgment have de facto EU-wide effect. Perhaps that will avoid procedural difficulties from arising as a consequence of the absence of a rule that the issuing Member State is obliged to withdraw the void authorization on the basis of a foreign decision or judgment.[150]

5.2 The environmental disputes exception

Environmental organizations may want to challenge CITES decisions, be they listing decisions or CITES documents for specific shipments. As stated in the previous chapter, CITES constitutes environmental law in the sense of the Aarhus Convention. Yet due to the general character of the amendments to Annexes, environmental organizations may be unable to challenge CITES listing decisions in a direct action.[151] That leaves them with the option of challenging a CITES document before the national courts and, in the course of those proceedings, challenging the underlying CITES listing decision.[152] They then depend on the willingness of the national court to ask preliminary questions. Under the rules of the proposed Aarhus Directive, which implements the Aarhus Convention, access to the national courts is not limited to qualified environmental organisations. It is open for all members of the public at the national level provided that they meet the standing conditions of the Directive and therefore this does not amount to an *actio popularis*. The implementation of the Aarhus Convention should therefore enable environmental organizations and perhaps also other third parties to bring proceedings before a national court against CITES decisions.

5.3 Conclusions

The figures below illustrate the positions of the applicant and the third parties that want to challenge a Community or a single licence decision before a national court.

---

ture is the loss of ownership of the object, whether seized or not, as a result of a court order in either civil or criminal proceedings. See: Garstecki (2006), p. 8.

150 As proposed by Advocate General Mischo in his Opinion in C-182/89 *Commission* v *France (Bolivian Wildcat Skins)* [1990] ECR I-04337.

151 See the previous chapter.

152 Respectively Art. 4 and Art. 3 Proposal for a Directive of the European Parliament and the Council on access to justice in environmental matters, COM (2003) 624 final.

Table 5.3 Standing of individuals in CITES cases before the national courts

European administrative decision	Applicant	Third party	Qualified environmental organization
Community CITES listing decision	+	-/+	+
Single licence CITES document	+	-/+	+

Since individuals are not involved in the coming into being of CITES listing decisions, they cannot challenge them before a Community court. Instead, a trader who has requested a CITES document before a national authority can challenge both the single licence decision and the underlying Community listing decision in proceedings brought before the national courts of the issuing Member State. Due to the single licence character of a CITES document issued by national authorities, it depends on the standing conditions of the issuing Member State whether third parties can also challenge these decisions – and the underlying Community listing decision – before a national court. The implementation of the Aarhus Convention by the Member States should alter this situation, at least for environmental organizations and perhaps also for other third parties. The only real gap in the system of judicial protection occurs with regard to enforcement, as it is not certain in which Member State the holder of CITES documents should bring proceedings when his documents are declared void, in the absence of any provisions on judicial review in the CITES Regulation. If the holder of the CITES documents cannot challenge the decision to declare the documents void and does not obtain new CITES documents, he can only challenge the void declaration in the course of criminal proceedings. It follows from the Court's case law that that does not constitute effective judicial protection.

6 Plant protection products

The judicial review of decisions taken in the area of plant protection products seems a complicated task due to the discretionary room that national authorities have when taking marketing authorizations, in particular when their decisions are not even based on listing decisions because no Community decision has yet been taken on the active substances in the product. This makes it uncertain whether it suffices to challenge a listing decision before the Community courts, either for those who can bring a direct action or for those who became involved in a preliminary ruling procedure before the Community courts after a national court asked preliminary questions. The national decision character of plant protection product authorizations may make it necessary to bring proceedings in all Member States where a product is authorized. In the absence of a streamlined mutual recognition process, the question is whether proceedings against national plant protection product authorizations before various national courts further reduce uniformity.

6.1 National decision implementing a Community decision

In the area of plant protection products regulation, the risk of divergent decisions is not countered by a mutual recognition procedure with a dispute settlement procedure. The risk of divergence is therefore already present when national authorities decide on authorizations of plant protection products and may further increase due to court proceedings. The Community legislation allows the Member States to recognize plant protection product authorizations or test results, but they have a broad discretion to refuse recognition and demand additional tests or to use an exception in order to grant authorization despite a rejection by another Member State.[153] Even where the Member States have only limited room for rejection, because the product contains a substance that the Commission did or did not list on Annex I to the Directive, the Member States may use temporary exceptions to avoid aligning their authorizations with these Commission decisions. In the absence of a dispute settlement procedure, proceedings before national courts can also result in divergence in so far as they concern aspects where a Member State can exercise discretion. This means that individuals may have to bring proceedings in every Member State.

6.2 Community decision

For third parties who are unable to establish a direct and individual concern, the only possible means to obtain a judicial review of the Community decision is to bring proceedings before the national courts against a marketing authorization that is based on it. The national courts can offer supplementary judicial protection to individuals who cannot bring proceedings before the Community courts against Community acts of general application in the field of product legislation, provided their standing conditions are met. This is easier once a Commission or Council listing decision – generally taken in the form of an implementing Directive or Regulation if it amends the Annex to the relevant Directive or Regulation and in the form of a Decision if it does not amend an Annex – is implemented by the national authorities in authorization decisions that can be challenged before the national courts.

The addressee of the national marketing authorization or of the rejection will certainly be able to bring proceedings against this decision and thus be able to challenge the underlying Community listing decision. If the addressee of the national marketing authorization is the same legal person as the applicant for the listing decision, he could have challenged the listing decision in a direct

[153] Preamble to Council Directive 91/414/EC.

action and is therefore not entitled to indirectly challenge the Community decision before a national court, but only the national decision in so far as it contains specific conditions that were set by the national authorities. By contrast, if the addressee of the national marketing authorization was not among the applicants for the listing decision, he can challenge both decisions before a national court. This is because the ECJ has held that being a marketing authorization holder does not distinguish a person sufficiently to be individually concerned by the listing decision.[154]

It will depend on the applicable national standing conditions whether third parties can bring proceedings against an authorization and thus challenge the underlying Community listing decision unless they benefit from a Community right conferred on them. They may invoke their right to safe plant protection products, but it will not be easy to establish a direct interest in the enforcement of this right. Perhaps competitors may be able to establish a direct interest on the basis of the right to safe plant protection products or to free movement. Those who invoke environmental concerns can rely on the environmental disputes exception. When third parties only want to bring actions against a national marketing authorization in order to challenge the underlying Community listing decision, denying access to the courts in one Member State can be compensated if they can gain access to the courts in another Member State. This offers no solution if they wish to challenge both the listing decision and the specific conditions in the national marketing authorization.

6.3 The environmental disputes exception

Environmental organizations are expected to gain access to the Community courts once the Aarhus Regulation enters into force in June 2007.[155] Yet they will only be able to challenge listing decisions if the Community courts will broadly interpret the conditions of the Aarhus Regulation. Moreover, due to the lack of uniformity in the implementation of the listing decisions in national authorizations, they may prefer to bring proceedings in each Member State where an authorization is granted or refused as well. The implementation of the Aarhus Convention by the Member States should ensure that they – and perhaps other third parties as well – be granted standing in environmental disputes before national courts, including disputes concerning the authorization of plant protection products.[156] Nevertheless, as the *Aldicarb* case demonstrates, environmental organizations have to confront various difficulties in challenging a national authorization because of the alleged invalidity of the underlying Community act, even after they have obtained standing.[157]

---

154 See Chapter 4, section 2.1 and 6.1.

155 See also the parts on the environmental disputes exception in the previous chapter.

156 See section 5.2 above.

157 CBb 19 April 2005: AWB 04/300 32010; C-174/05 *Stichting Zuid-Hollandse Milieufederatie, Stichting Natuur en Milieu* v *College voor de toelating van bestrijdingsmiddelen* [2006] ECR I-2443.

Two Dutch environmental organisations brought proceedings before a Dutch court against the decision by the Dutch competent authority to allow essential uses of plant protection products containing aldicarb, even though by Council Decision 2003/199 aldicarb would not be included in Annex I to Council Directive 91/414/EEC. The Council had ordered the withdrawal of national authorizations for plant protection products containing aldicarb in 2003, but it allowed limited uses considered as essential until 30 June 2007. The Dutch court asked validity questions about the period granted for essential use. The ECJ held that Article 8 (2) of the Directive does not establish the period within which Member States must ensure that those authorizations are withdrawn or varied, but refers to a prescribed period, i.e. a period to be fixed in an implementing measure, which is exactly what the Council did in its Decision. Article 2 (3) of the Decision set the time-limits for the withdrawal of plant protection products containing aldicarb. The ECJ held that is not inconsistent that a decision sets different time-limits, since the Directive does not contain a restriction in that regard. Regarding the proportionality of the time-limits in the Decision, it concluded that they were not manifestly inappropriate.

In the *Aldicarb* case, the national court granted third parties standing – because they were so entitled under Dutch administrative law – and was willing to refer questions to the ECJ. However, the time lapse between the issuance of the Aldicarb Decision in 2003 and the ECJ judgment in 2006 may diminish the relevance of the outcome of the judicial proceedings, as the period for essential use expired in 2007. If the ECJ had ruled that the period of grace in the Council Decision was invalid because it was not proportionate; this answer would have led the referring court to invalidate the national decision allowing for essential uses during the period of grace. Yet such an ECJ judgment would certainly have had an impact, because a national court confronted with disputes similar to the one where the ECJ reports that preliminary questions were asked, should either suspend the case pending the ruling or refer questions itself, which is mandatory if it grants interim relief. Therefore, a preliminary ruling can contribute to the same extent to the creation of uniform decisions as a ruling in a direct action.[158]

6.4 Conclusions

The figures below illustrate the positions of the applicant and the third parties that want to challenge a Community or a national decision before a national court.

[158] Craig (2003), p. 503-504 considers it a waste of resources for the ECJ to answer technical questions which do not involve any point of general importance for Community law.

Table 5.4 Standing of individuals in plant protection product cases before the national courts

European administrative decision	Applicant	Third party	Qualified environmental organization
Community PPP substance listing decision	-	+/-	?
National PPP marketing authorization	+	+/-	+

With regard to plant protection product authorizations, the absence of a streamlined authorization procedure with a dispute settlement procedure reduces the uniformity that can be achieved when a Community decision is challenged through indirect proceedings. Of course the preliminary ruling procedure enhances uniformity – provided that applicants meet the national standing conditions and national courts refer questions – and therefore a Member State with liberal standing conditions may be able to compensate for third parties that were denied access to the courts in another Member State. However, due to the possibilities for divergence, it may still be necessary to bring proceedings in each Member State as exceptions allow for different authorizations even when authorizations are based on a Community listing decision. That may not be possible for parties other than the marketing authorization holder, as standing conditions may differ between the Member States. The implementation of the Aarhus Convention by the Member States should facilitate access to the courts for environmental organizations and individuals that meet its standing conditions.

7 Conclusions

Despite the introduction of European administrative decisions that can have EU-wide effect, the Community system of judicial protection has remained unchanged. It still provides limited standing for individuals, to be compensated by vertical cooperation between the ECJ and the national courts through the preliminary ruling procedure. This causes procedural inequalities between those who can bring a direct action and those who cannot, in particular because the preliminary ruling procedure is not established to grant individuals access to the Community courts. Instead, it depends on the discretion of national courts whether this procedure is used. Moreover, it is not certain that third parties who were unable to challenge a Community decision before a Community court will be able to challenge this decision or an implementing decision before a national court in the absence of harmonized standing conditions (see below). That only leaves them the option to close the gap in judicial protection by bringing an action for damages, in which the national court is obliged to review the compatibility with Community law, possibly with the help of a preliminary ruling from the ECJ. Unfortunately, it is uncertain whether a successful claim will lead to annulment and therefore it remains questionable whether third parties are offered sufficient judicial protection against Community decisions in each Member State.

As regards European administrative decisions issued by national authorities, minimum harmonization characterizes both national remedies against national decisions and the national standing conditions. This is in line with the principles of procedural autonomy and effective judicial protection. The principle of effective judicial protection aims to ensure access to the courts to those enforcing their Community rights, but it is not always clear when provisions grant individuals certain rights and who can rely on them and thus ensure access to a national court. While it can be safely assumed that addressees of marketing authorizations issued by national authorities will be able to challenge this decision before a national court, it is not certain that third parties can also bring proceedings before national courts. Since the division of competence as established by Community legislation is mirrored by a division of jurisdiction between national courts along the same lines, they depend on whether a decision is taken by a Member State with narrow or broad standing conditions. Perhaps they can rely on their right to protection of the environment, human health or free movement of products or on the environmental dispute exception. After all, the implementation of the Aarhus Convention into national law should enable third parties who want to defend the environmental interest to bring proceedings against plant protection marketing authorizations, CITES documents and perhaps GMO marketing authorizations.

A gap in the judicial protection of individuals may also arise because the Community system of judicial protection does not provide for horizontal cooperation between national courts. As a consequence, the effect of a remedy offered by a national court in proceedings brought against a national decision is confined to that Member State. This is unproblematic as long as Community law is implemented through national decisions whose effect is limited to the national territory or through a single licence decision, which can only be challenged before a national court in the Member State where it was issued. However, it is problematic that the effect of a national court ruling on a mutual recognition decision is limited to the national territory of a single Member State. Consequently, if a court judgment suspends or annuls a mutual recognition decision in the reference Member State, the recognition decisions still have effect in recognizing Member States, thus compelling parties to bring proceedings in more than one Member State against the same decision.

Table 5.5 Standing of individuals in Community product regulation cases before the national courts

European administrative decision	Applicant	Third party	Qualified environmental organization
Community listing decision – addressed to MS	-	+/-	?
Community marketing authorization – addressed to applicant	-	+/-	-
Community dispute settlement decision (about marketing authorization) – addressed to the MS	-	+/-	-
National marketing authorization	+	+/-	+
Single licence marketing authorization	+	+/-	+
Mutual recognition decision	+	+/-	+

Regarding Community decisions, such as the Community marketing authorizations for medicines or GMOs or the listing decisions in the area of CITES and plant protection products, judicial protection is offered by the Community courts to the applicant and to qualified environmental organizations, provided that the conditions of the Aarhus Regulation are met. They are therefore not entitled to bring proceedings before a national court. Third parties will generally depend on the national courts, provided that they pass the national standing conditions. In the absence of harmonized provisions on access to a national court, which also applies to environmental disputes as long as the Aarhus judicial protection directive remains a proposal, gaps in the complete system of judicial protection may arise due to different standing conditions. In this regard the implementation of a Community decision in a national decision can be both a blessing and a curse. Implementation may facilitate access to a national court in Member States that require a national decision as a prerequisite for bringing proceedings. In case the Community decision is not implemented into a 'national' decision, it will only be possible to bring an action for annulment in Member States with broad standing conditions and a freestanding declaratory action. Perhaps that gives those who are unable to meet the standing conditions in their home Member State the opportunity to try to challenge a Community decision in another Member State.

When the national authorities issue decisions, the availability of judicial protection and the uniformity to be achieved depends on the type of decision and the position of the party. A national decision system requires bringing proceedings – and fulfilling the national standing conditions – in each Member State that takes a decision. This will not be a problem for applicants, but a gap in the system of judicial protection arises if a third party is unable to rely on the principle of effective judicial protection or the environmental disputes exception in a Member State with narrow standing conditions. If the Member States take national decisions in accordance with Community listing decisions, as occurs in the area of plant protection products, court proceedings against the national decision and the underlying Community decision can be brought in just one Member State, which may make it possible to choose a Member State with broad standing conditions. Then, proceedings only have to be brought in more than one Member State if they are directed against specific national conditions that are not regulated by the underlying Community decision and fall outside the scope of Community law.

In a single licence system, such as CITES, only the national court of the Member State where the decision is issued or declared void can offer judicial protection. This means that a gap in the system of judicial protection easily arises for others than the applicant, since access denied in that Member State is access denied overall. That is especially a cause for concern in case of a dual authorization procedure, such as CITES, where a third party unable to bring a direct action against the listing of a species depends on the standing conditions of a single Member State that issued CITES documents for a shipment of specimen of that species to challenge the underlying Community decision. It can also be considered an advantage that proceedings need to be brought in only one Member State, because this means that de facto, a national court ruling has EU-wide effect. It should be noted, however, that in the absence of information exchange on rulings between national courts, national courts do not know each other's judgments and therefore differences between the Member States in the interpretation of Community legislation may persist until an ECJ judgment becomes available.

Finally, in a mutual recognition system, it follows from the application of the territoriality principle that an individual has to contest the substantive aspects of the decision in the reference Member State, while he can only contest the recognition in the recognizing Member State. This means that third parties are confronted with a gap in the system of judicial protection if the national standing conditions in the reference Member State or the recognizing Member States are narrow. Another drawback is that the judgments in the reference Member

States or the recognizing Member States can have different outcomes in the absence of the mutual recognition of administrative judgments. That means that a mutual recognition decision suspended by court order in the reference Member State can still have effect in the Member States that recognized it. This issue may be solved in so far as secondary legislation gives the Commission the power to issue a Community decision in case of divergent decisions through the use of the Community procedure for the withdrawal of a mutual recognition decision or for dispute settlement between the Member States, provided that the Community procedure may be used in case of divergent court rulings. Unfortunately, the use of the Community procedure may have as a consequence that parallel proceedings will occur. This occurs when the marketing authorization holder and perhaps some others bring proceedings against the Community decision before the Community courts, while those who cannot bring a direct action bring proceedings against the Community decision before the involved national courts.

CHAPTER 6

Conclusions

This chapter gives an overall view of the outcome of this research and answers the central research question. As was set out in Chapter I, the research question was how Community product regulation that produces European administrative decisions with potentially EU-wide effect can be shaped effectively and offer sufficient procedural guarantees. The hypothesis was that the point of departure is implementation by the Member States with procedural autonomy, because Article 10 EC leaves the administration of Community law primarily in the hands of the Member States and a specific legal basis for the unification of procedural administrative law is lacking in the Treaty. It was assumed that the concern for the effectiveness of Community policies that produce European administrative decisions with (potentially) EU-wide effect, coupled with the rule of law requirement that sufficient procedural guarantees be offered to individuals, might lead to a new situation, where Community rules and actions increasingly govern and enable the coordination of European administrative decision-making, enforcement and judicial review. Since these procedural rules serve to facilitate implementation of the substantive rules of a policy, they can be based on the same legal basis as the substantive rules of the policy.

This was investigated in the area of Community product regulation, in the context of four reference areas: genetically modified organisms, medicines, endangered fauna and flora (CITES) and plant protection products, because they offer examples of various European administrative decisions used in Community regulation: Community decisions, national decisions, single licences and mutual recognition decisions. The selected reference areas share the substantive aim of achieving both the free movement of authorized products on the internal market and a high level of protection for the environment or public health. Most reference areas combine various types of European administrative decisions and means of enforcement to achieve these aims. In addition, respect for the right to be heard and judicial protection depends to a certain extent on sectoral secondary legislation. This chapter starts with some conclusions on the legal effectiveness of European administrative decisions with potential EU-wide effect in the decision-making and enforcement stage. It continues with conclusions on whether sufficient procedural guarantees are offered and where gaps may arise concerning the right to be heard and judicial protection. The chapter ends with general conclusions and recommendations.

1 Effectiveness

The effectiveness of Community product regulation depends on whether the aims of ensuring both the free movement of EC-regulated products and the protection of public health or the environment can be met at a sufficiently high level. Tension can still arise between these two aims, because different balances can be struck between free movement and the protection of public health or the environment. Although both are shared competences of the Community and the Member States, free movement of goods is a cornerstone of the internal market and requires a high degree of uniformity, while the protection of public health or the environment leaves the Member States some room for discretion. Nevertheless, if disagreement occurs as to which decision should be taken or how intensive enforcement efforts should be, the differences between the Member States should neither endanger the free movement of products nor result in the free movement of dangerous, flawed or illegal products.

1.1 Decision-making

In the field of Community product legislation, European administrative decisions are taken to authorize the placing of products such as medicines on the single market, to settle disputes between the Member States or to amend the Annex to a Regulation or a Directive. These decisions are binding decisions, which create rights and duties for individuals. They are either taken by a competent authority of a Member State or by a Community institution, in particular the Commission or the Council. Their legal basis is either a Regulation or a transposed Directive. Their effect can be EU-wide or limited to one Member State. Four types of European administrative decisions can be distinguished: Community decisions, national decisions, single licence decisions and mutual recognition decisions. Their advantages and disadvantages can be assessed from the point of view of their effectiveness in ensuring free movement and a high level of protection for the environment or public health, taking into account that Community legislation may succeed in mitigating the disadvantages:

- The advantage of the mutual recognition decision is that it does not force Member States to accept a decision that is below their standards. The disadvantage is that it cannot completely ensure free movement, because it does not apply in Member States that did not (have to) take a recognition decision and non-recognition can further fragment the internal market. Its effectiveness is increased if – as the example of medicines demonstrates – the option of non-recognition occurs in combination with a binding dispute settlement procedure. Then non-recognition does not fragment the internal market, but instead creates an incentive for a race to the top as it induces the applicant to seek a Member State that takes correct and quick decisions that are quickly recognized by other Member States.
- The advantage of the single licence decision is that it automatically gains EU-wide effect after being issued by a single Member State. The disadvantage is that the assessment of a single Member State may well be below the standards of other Member States that have to accept the decision. In an uncoordinated system such as CITES, this can provoke a race to the bottom, as it induces applicants to search for the Member State with the

lowest standards. This disadvantage can be mitigated by circulating the draft decision between the Member States for approval in combination with a dispute settlement procedure, as the example of GMOs for other uses demonstrates, but that may not be suitable for bulk decisions.

- The advantages of the Community decision, which is taken by the Commission or the Council, are that it can have EU-wide effect and involves the Member States in the decision-making through the regulatory Comitology procedure. The disadvantage is that this procedure is based on qualified majority voting and therefore the outcome may be below the standards of some Member States, which nevertheless have to comply with the decision. They can avoid compliance by invoking the safeguard clause to ban the product from their market. However, this might be an exceptional issue, as it only occurs in the area of GMOs and not in other areas.
- The national decision obliges each Member State to take a decision concerning the protection to be offered, which occurs in the area of plant protection products. This can be considered an advantage because it enables the Member States to choose the appropriate level of protection, but it also constitutes a disadvantage because the ensuing differences may hinder the free movement of authorized products.

Dispute settlement

The free movement of authorized products is hindered when the Member States disagree about a European administrative decision. They may not take unilateral action to solve their dispute. The Member States should first try to resolve the dispute informally. If consultation does not end their dispute, they may request the Commission to solve the dispute through a binding dispute settlement procedure, provided that the applicable secondary legislation contains a dispute settlement provision which gives the Commission the power to settle disputes in accordance with the regulatory Comitology procedure. When an area is prone to the frequent occurrence of disputes, secondary legislation may even skip a 'national' procedure in favour of the Community procedure, as occurred in the area of GMOs and medicines.

In the absence of a dispute settlement provision in secondary legislation, the Commission lacks the competence to settle disputes through a binding Community decision, which occurs in the area of CITES and – if the proposed Regulation enters into effect – in the area of plant protection products (the Directive prescribes Commission approval of non-recognition). This leaves the Member States with three options to solve disputes. The first option is to solve disputes informally by consulting each other or by discussing the issue in a meeting of the regulatory committee established by the applicable secondary legislation. The second option is to solve disputes through legal proceedings, either by allowing their national authorities to bring proceedings in another Member State or by submitting their dispute to the ECJ under the procedure of Article

227 EC or 239 EC. Arbitration is not an option, because the Member States may not resort to arbitration to solve a dispute on the application or interpretation of Community law. If a Member State does not want to bring an infringement procedure itself, its third option is to persuade the Commission to become involved and, if necessary, to start an infringement procedure against the allegedly defecting Member State.

These three options are obviously not as effective in solving disputes as a binding dispute settlement procedure, since the first option does not guarantee a positive outcome, while the second and the third option are generally considered as a last resort and may take too much time to be effective. Even though a binding Community decision seems the best option, it may not solve the dispute. Similar to other Community decisions taken under the regulatory Comitology procedure, the Member States decide by qualified majority on a draft dispute settlement decision. If they fail to achieve a qualified majority, the Commission can take the draft decision. In that case Member States that 'lost' the dispute may not want to comply with the Community decision, which occurred in the area of GMOs. Perhaps the Commission can reduce the controversial nature of such a Community decision by taking the concerns of each Member State into account during the decision-making stage. Another means is to allow for limited diversity. In the absence of Community rules on use, the Member States can retain control on the appearance of a product in their territory if operators need an authorization before they may use a product that benefits from an authorization with EU-wide effect, for instance as is the case in the area of CITES. Yet this option may not always be available. In the area of plant protection products, a Proposal for a Directive on Sustainable Use will reduce the discretionary room of the Member States concerning the use of products when it enters into effect.

1.2 Enforcement

Effective enforcement on the internal market of European administrative decisions with potentially EU-wide effect requires that the Member States overcome territorial boundaries instead of remaining legal islands. In order to extend the effect of enforcement beyond the territorial borders that confine the powers of the national authorities, the national legal systems – set up for enforcement within the national territory – have to be adapted. Administrative enforcement of Community product legislation consists of compliance control (of individuals), emergency measures, sanctions and Community supervision of the Member States. Similar to European administrative decisions, compliance control can be divided into Community control, national control, home state control and network control. By contrast, emergency measures and sanctions are either Community measures or national measures. This raises the question of which type of compliance control, emergency measures or sanctions is used for which type of European administrative decision and whether it is effective.

Although there are four types of compliance control, there is a weak relation between the type of European administrative decision and the type of compliance control. Therefore, their occurrence and their effectiveness will be considered separately for each type of compliance control:

- Community control does not really occur because Community competence is lacking in the area of Community product regulation. In areas where the Commission (or the Council) authorizes products, such as GMOs and medicines, this might be changing. For instance, EMEA, the inspection service in the area of medicines, may request assistance from national enforcement officers if it suspects an infringement by a holder of a Community authorized medicine. By contrast, the FVO, the inspection service in the area of GMOs for food and feed use, serves to supervise the enforcement efforts of the Member States. Community involvement is expected to increase the effectiveness of enforcement action by the Member States.
- National control exists in all the reference areas, even though exclusive reliance thereon seems to be ineffective, since the realization of the internal market has made the compliance control efforts of the Member States interdependent. Nevertheless, it occurs exclusively in the area of plant protection products, which may not surprise in view of the national authorizations issued for these products. What is more important, national control takes place and can be effective when it comes to controlling the legal use of products. This is virtually unregulated by Community law, as this is considered the responsibility of the Member States, but that might change, as the example of the proposal for a Directive on the sustainable use of plant protection products demonstrates.
- Home state control on the internal market occurs in the reference areas of CITES, medicines and GMOs and is effective because it prevents double controls of products that move on the internal market. The reference Member State is then the home state for the control of the authorization holder. Home state control takes place in each reference area with regard to imported products, because this is how customs control at the external borders of the EU functions. The division of competence between the home state and the host state makes the overall effectiveness of home state control particularly vulnerable to variations in enforcement efforts between the Member States.
- Network control appears in each reference area except plant protection products, where information exchange and mutual assistance can therefore only occur informally. The division of competence between the Member States in a system of network control is not fixed. This is because the aim of network control is that if one Member State discovers an infringement, all the Member States will take action in so far as this is necessary. The effectiveness of enforcement is increased because it enables the competent authorities to act as one and it enables active

> Member States to compensate for inactive Member States. This characteristic makes network control suitable to be used as a superstructure in relation to other types of control in order to improve their effectiveness.

Whether a Community or a national emergency measure is taken does not depend on the choice of a certain type of European administrative decision. In general, Community product legislation gives the Commission the competence to take emergency measures. The Member States have to implement these measures. They may only take temporary emergency measures on their own initiative in accordance with the safeguard clause procedure. This means that the Commission decides whether a temporary national emergency measure is justified and will therefore be replaced by a Community emergency measure. If a measure is not justified, the Member State is obliged to return to the normal state of affairs. Thus it does not matter by which type of European administrative decision a product is authorized. The choice of Community emergency measures, coupled with temporary national emergency measures, is effective because it provides for uniformity on the internal market and at the external borders of the EU, while enabling rapid action when it is impossible to wait for a Community emergency measure.

So far as sanctions are concerned, in general the Member States impose national sanctions in accordance with national procedural rules subject to the Community requirement that they are equivalent, effective, dissuasive and proportionate. In the absence of Community legislation, the Member States can only effectuate sanctions within their own territory, unless they have concluded bilateral agreements with other Member States. The absence of Community law thus reduces the effectiveness of enforcement if the offender is located in another Member State. There is an exception to this rule, as the Commission recently obtained the competence to impose financial sanctions on holders of Community authorized medicines. Another exception concerns the withdrawal of an authorization, which is harmonized to a great extent in sectoral secondary legislation. A certain type of European administrative decision can be withdrawn by the same type of European administrative decision. That is not always the case, as the example of medicines demonstrates, where Community decisions are taken to withdraw medicines authorized by mutual recognition decisions.

Enforcement deficit

It cannot be left entirely to the Member States to enforce Community product legislation on their own territory, because if an enforcement deficit occurs in one Member State, it can have EU-wide and even global effects due to the open borders of the internal market. In this regard, it is a shortcoming that Community legislation in general and Community product legislation in particular does not necessarily provide for specific enforcement provisions on compliance control. It is obvious that the focus of attention in each reference area is on the risk assessment *prior* to approval instead of on the enforcement of the rules. It also appears from the reference areas that self-enforcement is considered to facilitate public enforcement, as the manufacturer, importer or authorization holder are best aware of the quality of their products and should therefore cooperate with the authorities. Their reports on situations of non-compliance should trigger enforcement action by the public authorities. Self-enforcement can therefore improve the effectiveness of public enforcement, but it may be too weak to ensure effective enforcement in bad times. Therefore, compliance control of the self-enforcement obligations and the imposition of sanctions in the case of an infringement remain important. In view of the effect on the internal market of differences between the Member States in enforcement efforts, let alone in case of an enforcement deficit, it can be reasonably expected that the effectiveness of the enforcement by the Member States of Community product legislation would increase if it were harmonized to a greater extent.

As in other fields, the Commission has a supervision task regarding the enforcement efforts of the Member States and should therefore try to prevent an enforcement deficit through training, twinning, guidance and the like and react to an enforcement deficit, if necessary by means of an infringement procedure. The Commission is informed of deficits through complaints from individuals or Member States. The information position of the Commission is improved when secondary legislation contains reporting obligations and even provides for the establishment of a Community inspection agency on the ground, such as the annual enforcement plans and the establishment of a Community inspection service (the FVO) in the area of GMOs for food or feed use. However, infringement proceedings are not a panacea against weak enforcement efforts for many reasons. First of all, infringement proceedings take many years, especially since financial penalties can only be imposed on a Member State in the second procedure against the same infringement. In the second place, the infringement procedure may not be adequate for minor or incidental infringements. In the third place, the Commission's limited resources make it well nigh impossible to guarantee a level playing field at a sufficiently high level. Thus, the effectiveness of enforcement requires more than Commission supervision.

An additional means to counter an enforcement deficit is administrative cooperation between the Member States in a network structure, with the Commission or another Community body acting as a focal point. The basic feature is information exchange, facilitated by a Community database, while the feature of operational assistance is less common. Administrative cooperation in a network enables the competent authorities to continue to exercise their powers within their national territory while at the same time providing their enforcement efforts with Community-wide effects. In other words, it enables them to act as one, which means, for instance, that information about offenders can be shared with other Member States. Moreover, the effectiveness of network control is less dependent on the efforts of each individual Member State because it does not matter which Member State finds a flawed, illegal or dangerous product, but only that the finding is communicated to the Commission and the other Member States through a rapid alert system in order to enable joint action. Since network control does not depend on a fixed division of competence between the Member States, it is not surprising that the reference areas reveal a trend towards the full use of network control, because its features of information exchange and mutual assistance can make national control, home state control and Community control more effective.

The only limitation to network control is that it does not necessarily connect all authorities involved in enforcement. This is especially obvious with regard to the cooperation between the competent authorities in a given area and the customs authorities. While the former should protect the EU from dangerous products on the internal market, the latter should protect the EU from imports of illegal or dangerous products. Common risk management and information exchange would increase the effectiveness of their actions. However, the scope of application of the Mutual Assistance Regulation, which provides for information exchange and mutual assistance between the customs authorities, does not include all goods. In addition, the Mutual Assistance Regulation aims to allow the customs authorities to operate as one and is therefore not geared towards cooperation with the competent authorities. Sector-specific secondary legislation has the same limitation. Yet it is possible to connect all the authorities involved in enforcement, because the EU-TWIX database – developed in the area of CITES by TRAFFIC (an NGO) and several European and national institutions to compensate for the lack of a system of network control under the CITES Regulation – is used by the CITES authorities, the customs authorities and the judicial authorities.

2 Procedural guarantees

In a Community based on the rule of law, Community rules should ensure sufficient respect for procedural guarantees in the administration of Community law, which means that the administration should give consideration to the interests of persons affected by the administrative decisions they are taking and that they should be able to enforce compliance with the law before the courts. In the absence of a Community Administrative Code, these rights take the form of principles in the case law of the Community and national courts. It is problematic that their scope may be limited to the applicant or marketing authorization holder, to the detriment of third parties. This also applies where sectoral legislation in the reference areas expands these rights into provisions, which provide that the applicant or marketing authorization holder be heard before a decision is taken, as it does not contain a similar right for third parties, such as competitors or consumer organizations. Similarly, a judicial review of these decisions before a Community or a national court is to a great extent ensured for the applicant or marketing authorization holder, but hardly for third parties. Only environmental organizations should be in a better position, provided that the Aarhus Convention is correctly implemented.

2.1 The right to be heard

Although it is expected that the right to be heard is at least respected regarding the applicant for a marketing authorization or the marketing authorization holder before a decision is taken about his marketing authorization, this research revealed three instances where that is not the case. The first instance, found in all the reference areas, was that the authorization holder is not heard before emergency or safeguard measures are taken. In the absence of a provision on the right to be heard in the Comitology decision, sector-specific secondary legislation should include such a provision. Unfortunately, such a provision is lacking in all reference areas in so far as the emergency or safeguard procedure is concerned. Consequently, a (prospective) marketing authorization holder does not have to be heard before an emergency measure is taken concerning his products. It follows from Community case law that the administration may adopt safeguard or emergency measures without a hearing. However, that is only justified when interested parties are given the opportunity to contest the measures and make their views known in subsequent proceedings, for instance in an administrative review procedure.

The second instance was found in the area of plant protection products, where the Commission takes Community listing decisions on active substances of plant protection products without hearing all the affected marketing authorization holders, because the Commission only hears those who have filed an application for the listing decision and have submitted a dossier. Other affected marketing authorization holders are only heard when a national authority adapts or withdraws their marketing authorization on the basis of the Community listing decision. The third instance was found in the area of CITES, where the national authorities are not even obliged to hear the holder before declaring his CITES documents void, as the CITES Regulation does not contain any provision on the right to be heard. It is a serious shortcoming that an investigation of the reference areas revealed that the right to be heard is not guaranteed under all circumstances for authorization holders.

As might be expected in view of the case law of the Community courts, third parties fare worse. In the absence of any explicit provisions in Community product legislation, third parties whose interests might be affected by a marketing authorization issued to another individual or who have filed a request for enforcement or for the withdrawal of an authorization depend on national legislation and case law for respecting the right to be heard. There is no exception for environmental decisions, because the public participation provisions of the Aarhus Convention do not apply to listing decisions or marketing authorizations. Yet third parties are not necessarily forgotten. For instance, the GMO legislation provides that the public may comment on draft decisions, although it does not state that their comments should be taken into account and therefore their comments may not be considered seriously.

2.2 Judicial protection

The European system of judicial protection is not adapted to the existence of European administrative decisions with EU-wide effect. One consequence is that a gap in the judicial protection against European administrative decisions may arise. Another consequence is that judicial protection may be offered before more than one court. This occurs when the division of competence between the administrative authorities does not reflect the division of jurisdiction between the courts. That may lead to parallel proceedings either before both a Community court and a national court or before two or more national courts. It depends on the type of European administrative decision to what extent these problems occur:

- A Community decision system carries with it the risk of a denial of justice. Either the Community courts or the national courts, which may refer questions to the ECJ, should offer judicial protection. However, due to the strict standing conditions of the ECJ coupled with the minimum harmonization of national standing conditions it cannot be guaranteed that the Community system of judicial protection is complete. The implementation of a Community decision by a national decision may facilitate access in Member States where a national decision is a prerequisite for bringing proceedings before an administrative court. In the absence of implementation into a national decision, proceedings can only be brought in Member States with broad standing conditions or a freestanding declaratory action. It is also possible that parallel procedures occur, which result in procedural inequalities between those who can and those who cannot bring a direct action (see below).
- A national decision system may not be able to guarantee sufficient judicial protection, because those affected by the decision need to pass the national standing conditions. If the Member States take decisions in accordance with Community listing decisions and have little room for discretion, court proceedings against the national decision and the underlying Community decision can be brought in a Member State with broad standing conditions, provided that it is possible for a party to bring proceedings in that Member State. Proceedings may have to be brought in all Member States if they are directed against specific national conditions that are not regulated by the underlying Community decision and fall outside the scope of Community law.
- A single licence system does not guarantee sufficient judicial protection, because only the national court of the Member State where the decision is issued or declared void can offer judicial protection. This means that access denied in that Member State is access denied overall. That is

especially a cause for concern when a third party who is unable to bring a direct action depends on the standing conditions of a single Member State to challenge the single licence and the underlying Community decision.

- In a mutual recognition system, an individual has to contest the substantive aspects of the decision in the reference Member State, while he can only contest the recognition in the recognizing Member State. Sufficient judicial protection may not be guaranteed because it depends on national standing conditions whether a third party can gain access to a court. Moreover, national judgments can have different outcomes in the absence of the mutual recognition of administrative judgments (see below).

Denial of judicial protection

At the Community level, applicants or marketing authorization holders can bring proceedings against Community listing decisions and marketing authorizations in their capacity of addressees. Even if the Community decision is not addressed to them, they will be able to establish direct and individual concern, because secondary legislation gives them procedural guarantees and therefore distinguishes them from others. When secondary legislation does not contain procedural guarantees for the authorization holder, they cannot bring proceedings before the Community courts and therefore depend on the national courts. This is the case in the safeguard or emergency procedure and in the listing procedure of the Plant protection products Directive. This places them in the same position as other third parties, who are usually unable to pass the strict standing conditions of the Community courts. The amendment of Article 230 EC by the Treaty of Lisbon (if it enters into effect) is not expected to increase their possibilities to bring a direct action either. The amendment provides that only direct concern needs to be established when an individual wants to bring proceedings against a regulatory act which does not require implementation measures. It is unlikely that Community listing decisions taken in the form of a Directive or a Regulation amending the Annex to the basic Act will fall within this extension, because the national authorities take implementing measures when they issue marketing authorizations on the basis of the listing decisions, as is the case in the area of plant protection products. It is also unlikely that Community marketing authorizations will fall within this extension, because they are taken in the form of a Decision.

The implementation of the Aarhus Convention into the Aarhus Regulation is expected to ameliorate the position of certain third parties in the area of Community environmental law, which includes CITES, plant protection products and, probably, GMOs. It will introduce environmental organizations as interested parties in environmental disputes before the Community courts. This is possible without a Treaty amendment because those who meet the standing conditions of the Aarhus Regulation may file objections against the disputed Community decision in an administrative review procedure before the Commission and then become the addressees of a Community decision, which means that they no longer have to establish a direct and individual concern. However, it is not certain what the impact of the Aarhus Regulation will be until the Community courts have decided the first cases, as that will depend on their interpretation of environmental measures of individual scope that do not require implementation.

The ECJ presumes that the national courts are able to function as a safety net to ensure the completeness of the Community system of judicial review, but it is not certain that those whose rights or interests are affected by a Community decision can bring proceedings against it before a national court. Since each of the 27 Member States has different rules on access to the courts and available remedies, access to a national court is not certain either for those whose rights or interests are affected by a single licence decision, a mutual recognition decision or a national decision. This is not surprising in view of the Community court's case law on the principle of effective judicial protection, which aims to ensure access to the courts to those enforcing their Community rights. While it can be safely assumed that the addressee of a marketing authorization decision will be able to challenge it before a national court, it is far from clear whether third parties are entitled to bring proceedings before national courts as well.

Third parties that do not pass national standing conditions have various options to try to gain access to a national court. Their best option seems to rely on the environmental dispute exception. After all, the implementation of the Aarhus Convention in national law should enable those who want to defend the environmental interest to bring proceedings in environmental disputes, which includes plant protection marketing authorizations, CITES documents and probably also GMO marketing authorizations. Their second best option is to rely on the principle of effective judicial protection in order to enforce the rights they derive from Community law. Unfortunately, it is an open question whether the provisions of Community product regulation also create rights for third parties. Perhaps they may invoke their right to the protection of human health or the free movement of products. Whether these options suffice to gain access to a national court is not certain in view of the required willingness of national courts to ask the ECJ for guidance on this matter through the preliminary ruling procedure.

Parallel proceedings

Arguably, the division of competence in Community legislation should ensure that only one court is competent to settle disputes about a European administrative decision. That is not necessarily the case. Parallel proceedings before a Community court and a national court can take place with regard to Community decisions when some individuals pass the standing conditions of the Community courts, while others have to bring proceedings before a national court. This results in procedural inequalities between those who can and those who cannot bring a direct action:

- It fragments the interests taken into account by the court, as the interests

of those who cannot bring a direct action will not be considered in the direct action. This is not expected to be a problem at the national level, because those who can bring a direct action will usually also be able to join the proceedings before the national court.
- Those who want to challenge the validity of a Community decision but have to bring proceedings before a national court depend on the willingness of the national court to use the preliminary ruling procedure, since individuals do not have any right whatsoever to make such a reference.
- Those who have to bring proceedings before a national court against a Community decision are not bound by the time-limit of Article 230 EC, but by the time-limit that applies to the national, implementing decision.

Parallel proceedings before national courts of various Member States may occur due to the absence of a duty of judicial cooperation in administrative law cases. The need for judicial cooperation is unexpected, since the division of jurisdiction between the national courts mirrors the division of competence established by the sectoral secondary legislation concerning decision-making or enforcement. Consequently, judicial cooperation between national courts does not seem to be required, especially since national courts can ask the ECJ for guidance on the Community law aspects of the case through the preliminary ruling procedure. However, many Community law cases are decided without a reference being made and, in the absence of information exchange, national courts may not even be aware of judgments issued by other national courts on Community law issues of common concern. This is regrettable because it makes it possible that national courts issue different rulings on similar decisions.

For mutual recognition decisions it is even more problematic that judicial cooperation between national courts in administrative law cases is absent. Due to the absence of judicial cooperation, the effect of a national court ruling in which the suspension or annulment of a European administrative decision is ordered is limited to a single Member State. While a single licence decision will nevertheless be de facto suspended or annulled in the whole EU, this is not the case with a mutual recognition decision. If a mutual recognition decision is suspended or annulled in one Member State, it remains effective in other Member States. This makes it necessary to bring proceedings in all Member States that issued a mutual recognition decision instead of bringing them only in the reference Member State.

When proceedings are brought in more than one Member State diametrically opposed judgments on substantively the same decision are possible. It is assumed that the ensuing fragmentation of the internal market can be ended in so far as secondary legislation gives the Commission the power to issue a Community decision in order to restore unity, e.g. through the subsequent use of the regulatory Commitology procedure for the settlement of disputes between the Member States. However, that does not ensure that a national court decision is correctly implemented. This will in particular be the case when national court decisions have opposite outcomes. Another complication is that not all the parties to the disputes before the national courts may be able to file proceedings before the Community courts against the Commission or Council decision, which in its turn may give rise to parallel proceedings (see above).

3 General conclusions

The research question is how Community product regulation that produces European administrative decisions with potentially EU-wide effect can be shaped effectively and offer sufficient procedural guarantees. The answer to this question lies in the development of administrative cooperation between Member States, with the Commission or a Community body acting as a focal point to settle disputes, and to facilitate information exchange and mutual assistance between the Member States. Since this research reveals that the choice of a certain type of European administrative decision and its enforcement has consequences as to the effectiveness that can be achieved, it is also considered whether the choice of certain types of European administrative decisions or types of enforcement in the reference areas was a coincidence and whether there is a best choice to be made. As regards offering sufficient procedural guarantees, it is regrettable that the development of administrative cooperation is hardly matched by the development of Community procedural rules. Consequently, sufficient procedural guarantees – the right to be heard and judicial protection – are not necessarily available for third parties.

The reference areas illustrated that the Commission is strongly involved in decision-making, as it takes listing decisions in the area of CITES and plant protection products, issues marketing authorizations for GMOs and medicines and settles disputes about medicines and GMOs. Especially the introduction of Community authorizations for high-tech medicines and GMOs for food and feed use might indicate a centralisation trend. It is not certain that this trend will manifest itself also in other areas, because the Commission lacks the administrative capacity to become primarily responsible for the implementation of Community law. This is remedied to a certain extent by the involvement of the Member States in the regulatory Comitology procedure. Another aspect is that the increasing importance of the administrative role of the Commission may enhance the effectiveness of the administration of Community law, but is undesirable from the point of view of respect for procedural guarantees, especially when the position of the ECJ on the standing of individuals who are not addressees of a Community decision is taken into account.

The choice of a type of European administrative decisions in the reference areas may have been a coincidence, but a best choice can be made. At first sight, it seems that single licences are most suitable when the implementation does not leave much room for discretion, while mutual recognition decisions are more adequate when a case-by-case assessment needs to be made, with the added benefit of enabling the Member States to control each other's assessment. Community decisions are most suitable to settle disputes or prevent them when they occur too frequently. National decisions do not seem a good choice, because they do not allow for reaping the benefit of a division of competence. A closer look at the reference areas reveals, first of all, that combinations usually occur of Community decisions with decisions issued by national authorities, be they mutual recognition decisions, single licence decisions or national decisions and, secondly, that the distinctive features of each type of decision are melting away, which is most obvious when mutual recognition is combined with binding dispute settlement in the case of non-recognition and a draft single licence is circulated for approval. Thus, it may depend on the context which European administrative decision is the most appropriate, but it is possible to adopt adaptations developed to minimize the negative consequences of this initial choice.

The reference areas also illustrated that enforcement receives less attention than decision-making, which is true both for the instrumental and for the procedural guarantees side of enforcement. It seems that enforcement is only exceptionally as tightly regulated as in the area of GMOs for food and feed use, where it is part of the general framework for the enforcement of food law. In other areas, enforcement is mainly left to the discretion of the Member States. That may not be good enough to achieve effective enforcement, since the removal of borders in the internal market made the enforcement efforts of the Member States interdependent, which is reinforced by the division of competence between the Member States brought about by home state control. This can be remedied by the introduction of network control, which provides the enforcement efforts of the Member States with EU-wide effect and enables strong Member States to compensate for weak Member States by not prescribing a fixed division of competence. The Commission limits itself to supervising the Member States and facilitate network control, with the exception of its newly gained power to impose sanctions on holders of Community authorized medicines.

As regards enforcement, the reference areas demonstrate the predominance of the traditional division of competence between the Community and the Member States. The choice for a certain type of compliance control does not depend on the choice for a certain type of European administrative decision. Despite the existence of Community decisions, Community control hardly exists in the area of Community product legislation although it is being developed to control compliance by holders of Community authorized medicines. In general, the Community continues to leave enforcement in the hands of the Member States and only supervises their enforcement efforts. National control serves to control use, while home state control serves to prevent double controls on the internal market, but is vulnerable to divergencies in enforcement efforts. Network control serves to connect the competent authorities in order to enable joint action. It is less vulnerable to divergencies because it does not prescribe a fixed division of competence and therefore allows active Member

States to compensate for inactive Member States. Network control can be placed as a superstructure above other types of compliance control, be they based on Community, national or home state control, in order to improve their effectiveness.

Similarly, emergency measures and sanctions do not depend on the choice of a certain type of European administrative decision or compliance control. In order to provide for unity on the internal market, emergency measures are mostly Community measures, as the Member States may only take temporary emergency measures. By contrast, sanctions are national decisions in the absence of Community legislation that would enable mutual recognition or effectuation by other Member States, with two exceptions. The first exception is that Community financial sanctions can be imposed on the holders of Community authorized medicines. The second exception is that the withdrawal of European administrative decisions usually occurs with respect to the same type of European administrative decision. That is not always the case, as the example of medicines authorized by mutual recognition decisions and withdrawn by Community decisions demonstrates.

Respect for the right to be heard and the right to judicial protection should be guaranteed by the case law of the courts, national legislation and the applicable sectoral legislation. At the Community level, the right to be heard is in principle limited to those who are adversely affected by a decision, which means that only applicants and marketing authorization holders can rely thereon in the absence of an extension of this right in secondary legislation. Similarly, the possibility to bring a direct action at Community level is limited to applicants and marketing authorization holders. Even they may be unable to challenge certain Community decisions when they are not the addressees of a decision with a general character. In general, third parties do not have to be heard before (or after) a Community decision is taken and they are unable to pass the strict standing conditions of the Community courts. Therefore, they have to rely on the safety net of the national courts in order to obtain judicial protection. An interesting innovation in this respect is the administrative review procedure introduced by the Aarhus Regulation. It should enable environmental organizations to defend the environmental interest before the Community courts in their capacity of addressees of a review decision.

It is not certain that national procedural rules can compensate for the lack of judicial protection at the Community level, since national standing conditions are hardly harmonized by Community law. Moreover, national procedural rules are not necessarily drafted to meet the challenges posed by the EU-wide effect that European administrative decisions can have. For instance, it should not be expected that national rules can solve the problems caused by parallel proceedings against a Community decision or against a substantively similar mutual recognition decision. Vertical cooperation with the ECJ through the preliminary ruling procedure does not suffice to enable the national courts to take the same approach when settling disputes about European administrative decisions. Instead, the national courts would benefit from the development of horizontal judicial cooperation in administrative law cases, in particular from the introduction of the mutual recognition of judgments, but also from information exchange through a Community database of national court judgments or a voluntary database, as set up by the network of Councils of State.

4 Recommendations

Assuming that it is possible to generalize the outcomes of this research, a few points merit attention in the drafting of Community legislation which establishes European administrative decisions with potential or actual EU-wide effect. That would prevent the reinvention of the wheel every time effective implementation of Community legislation requires administrative cooperation between the Member States and the Community institutions and bodies. For this purpose, the reference areas were selected to represent the various combinations of European administrative decisions and should at least be representative for other regulated goods. As regards the other freedoms, it should be recalled that the principle of mutual recognition and the rule of reason originate in the sphere of the regulation of goods and are now applicable in all other freedoms and even in criminal law. It is assumed that the same can apply to administrative procedural rules concerning European administrative decisions with potential or actual EU-wide effect that have been developed in the area of regulated goods. Research in other fields of Community law will reveal whether this is really the case:

- The inclusion of a provision that allows the authorities to reject a manifestly invalid single license decision. See for a convincing example the area of CITES.
- The inclusion of a provision that limits the grounds for non-recognition of a mutual recognition decision. See for a convincing example the area of medicines.
- The inclusion of a binding dispute settlement provision in secondary legislation, which gives the Commission the power to settle disputes between the Member States with a binding Community decision, in accordance with the regulatory Comitology procedure. See for a convincing example the area of medicines. In the absence of such a provision, the Commission (or the Council) cannot solve disputes by binding decision, which means that disputes should either be solved informally or through legal proceedings. While the first option does not guarantee a positive outcome, the second option is generally considered as a last resort.
- The inclusion of a provision that allows for limited diversity in order to prevent or end disputes on non-essential aspects of the regulation. See for a convincing example the rules on use in the area of CITES.
- The inclusion of all established options to make enforcement on the inter-

nal market more effective, e.g. specific provisions on compliance control, reporting obligations concerning implementation plans and reports – in order to pin down the Member States on their planned and achieved application and enforcement efforts – and supervision of the Member States by Community inspectors. See for a convincing example the area of GMOs for food and feed use.
- The inclusion of provisions that enable network control – information exchange and mutual assistance – in order to increase the effectiveness of enforcement by national authorities on the internal market. Network control gives enforcement EU-wide effect and can be applied as a superstructure above national control, home state control and Community control. It should also be considered how all authorities involved can benefit from administrative cooperation. See for a convincing example the area of CITES.
- The elaboration of the right to be heard in secondary legislation. This may seem superfluous for individuals who can rely on the right to be heard, such as the applicant during the authorization procedure, but for them it is an advantage if secondary legislation clarifies when they should be heard. By contrast, it is not certain that third parties are able to rely on the right to be heard in the absence of a provision to that effect in secondary legislation and therefore their position merits consideration in the drafting of secondary legislation. This can take the form of:
  - o The right to be heard prior to the taking of a decision; or
  - o The introduction of an administrative review procedure.
- In order to ensure that judicial protection is offered both to the applicant or marketing authorization holder and to third parties, there are two options:
  - o The first option is that secondary legislation provides that third parties are entitled to judicial protection at the Community level. This prevents procedural inequalities from arising. In order to create this possibility without Treaty amendment and to manage the number of cases that might additionally come before the Community courts, an administrative review procedure could be introduced, similar to the administrative review procedure introduced by the Aarhus Regulation within the ambit of environmental law.
  - o If the first option is considered too far-fetched, it might be more feasible to provide at least that third parties have access to the national courts to challenge a Community decision.
- In order to ensure that the national courts not only offer judicial protection to those who may be adversely affected by a European administrative decision issued by a national authority, but also to third parties, secondary legislation should provide that national courts have to offer judicial protection to those who are directly involved and to third parties.
- In order to avoid different outcomes of national court rulings concern-

ing European administrative law decisions issued by national authorities, Community legislation should provide for judicial coordination in administrative law cases.

- o The first step is to set up a system for information exchange between national courts, such as the information exchange database of the Councils of State, in order to prevent different outcomes in disputes on similar European administrative decisions.
- o The second step is to provide the judgment of the national court of the reference Member State on the mutual recognition decision with EU-wide effect.
- o Note that the second step is not necessary for judgments on single licence decisions, because these judgments have de facto EU-wide effect. The second step is also not required for judgments on national decisions, in so far as these decisions already differ from each other.

Bibliography

ABRAHAM AND LEWIS (2000)
J. Abraham and G. Lewis, *'Regulating Medicines in Europe, competition, expertise and public health'*, London and New York 2000.
ADRIAANSE (2008)
P.C. Adriaanse, T. Barkhuysen, P. Boswijk, K. Habib, C. De Kruif, M.J.J.P. Luchtman, W. den Ouden, S. Prechal, B. Steunenberg, J.A.E. Vervaele, W.J.M. Voermans, S.A. de Vries, R.J.G.M. Widdershoven, *Implementatie van EU-handhavingsvoorschriften*, Den Haag 2008.
ALLIO AND FANDEL (2006)
L. Allio and M. Fandel, 'Making Europe work: improving the transposition, implementation and enforcement of EU legislation', *EPC Working Paper No. 25*, 2006.
ARMSTRONG (1999)
K. A. Armstrong, 'Mutual Recognition', in: C. Barnard and J. Scott, *The Law of the Single European Market. Unpacking the Premises*, Oxford and Portland, Oregon 1999, pp. 225-268.
ARNULL (2001)
A. Arnull, 'Private Applicants and the Action for Annulment since Codorniu', *CMLRev* 2001, pp. 7-52.
ARNULL (2006)
A. Arnull, *The European Union and its Court of Justice, 2nd edn*, Oxford 2006.
ARNULL (2007)
A. Arnull, 'Annotation of Unibet' in *CMLRev* 2007, pp. 1763-1780.
AUBY (2002)
Jean-Bernard Auby, 'Administrative Law in France', in: R. Seerden and F. Stroink (eds), *Administrative Law of the European Union, its Member States and the United States, A Comparative Analysis*, Antwerp 2002, pp. 77-83.
BAARDA AND DE GOEDE (2001)
D.P. Baarda en M.P.M. De Goede, *Methoden en Technieken van kwalitatief onderzoek*, Groningen 2001.
BACKES ET AL (2004)
Ch. Backes, A.B. Blomberg and M.P. Jongma, *Hoofdlijnen milieubestuursrecht*, Den Haag 2004.
BARENTS (2004)
R. Barents, 'The Court of Justice in the Draft Constitution', 11 *MJ* 2 (2004), pp. 121-140.
BARENTS (2005)
R. Barents, 'Een grondwet voor Europa (V): rechtspraak', *NTER* 2005, pp. 16-22.
BARNARD (2004)
C. Barnard, *The Substantive Law of the EU, The Four Freedoms*, Oxford 2004.

BEBR (1994)
G. Bebr, 'Court of Justice: Judicial Protection and the Rule of Law', in: D. Curtin and T. Heukels (eds), *Institutional Dynamics of European Integration.* Essays in Honour of Henry G. Schermer, Volume II, Dordrecht/Boston/London, 1994, pp. 303-334.

BERG (1999)
A. Berg, *The Implementation and the Enforcement of the Common Fisheries Policy in the Netherlands and in the United Kingdom*, Leiden/ Boston, 1999.

BERENDSCHOT AND DE WIT (2005)
H.G.M. Berendschot and T. de Wit, 'Parallel import in farmaceutische producten', (3) *JGR plus* 2005, pp. 13-23.

BERKHOUDT (2003)
K. Berkhoudt, 'Focus on EU Enlargement and Wildlife Trade: Review of CITES Implementation in Candidate Countries', *A TRAFFIC Europe Report*, 2003.

BESSELINK (2004)
L.F.M. Besselink, 'Supreme Court of the Netherlands (*Hoge Raad der Nederlanden*), 21 March 2003, Civil Chamber, No. C01/327HR, Stichting Waterpakt, Stichting Natuur en Milieu, Vereniging Consumentenbond and three others v State of the Netherlands', *CMLRev* 2004, pp. 1429-1455.

BETLEM (1999)
Gerrit Betlem, 'Cross-border Private Enforcement of Community Law', in: J.A.E. Vervaele (ed), *Compliance and Enforcement of Community Law*, Deventer 1999, pp. 391-418.

BIGNAMI (2004)
F. Bignami, 'Three Generations of Participation Rights before the European Commission', *Law and Contemporary Problems* 2004, pp. 61-84.

BLOMBERG AND MICHIELS (1997)
A.B.Blomberg and F.C.M.A. Michiels, *Handhaven met Effect*, Den Haag 1997.

BLOMBERG AND MICHIELS (2005)
A.B. Blomberg and F.C.M.A. Michiels, Between Enforcement and Toleration of Breaches of Environmental Law – Dutch Policy Explained, in: T.F.M. Etty and H. Somsen (ed), *Yearbook of European Environmental Law*, Oxford 2005, pp. 181-208.

BOROWSKI (2004)
M. Borowski, 'Die Nichtigheitsklage gem. Art. 230 Abs. 4 EGV', *EuR* 2004, pp. 879-909.

BROWN AND MORIJN (2004)
C. Brown and J. Morijn 'Case C-263/02 P Commission v Jégo Queré and Cie SA', *CMLRev* 2004, pp. 1639-1659.

CANOR (1998)
I. Canor, 'Can Two Walk Together, Except They Be Agreed? The Relationship Between International Law and European Law: The Incorporation of United Nations Sanctions Against Yugoslavia into European Community Law Through the Perspective of the European Court of Justice', *CMLRev* 1998, pp. 137-187.

CARANTA (1995)
Roberto Caranta, 'Judicial Protection Against Member States: A New Ius Commune Takes Shape', *CMLRev.* 1995, pp. 702-726.

CARSON (1962)
R. Carson, *Silent Spring*, Boston, New York, 1962.

CASTILLO DE LA TORRE (2007)
F. Castillo de la Torre, 'Interim Measures in Community courts: Recent Trends', *CMLRev* 2007 pp. 273-353.

CHITI (2000)
E. Chiti, 'The Emergence of a Community Administration: the Case of European Agencies', *CMLRev.* 2000, pp. 309-343.

CHITI (2004)
M.P. Chiti, 'Forms of European administrative action', *Law and Contemporary Problems*, 2004, pp. 37-60.

CIAVARINI AZZI (1999)
G. Ciavarini Azzi, 'Comitology and the European Commission', in: C. Joerges and E. Vos (eds), *EU Committees, Social Regulation, Law and Politics*, Oxford-Portland 1999, pp. 51-58.

CORTES MARTIN (2004)
J.M. Cortes Martin, 'Ubi ius, Ibi Remedium? – Locus Standi of Private Applicants under Article 230 (4) EC at a European Constitutional Crossroads', *MJ* 2004, pp. 233-259.

COSTELLO (2006)
C. Costello, The Bosphorus Ruling of the European Court of Human Rights: Fundamental Rights and Blurred Boundaries in Europe, *Human Rights Law Review* 2006, p. 87-130.

CRAIG (2003)
P. Craig, 'Standing, Rights, and the Structure of Legal Argument', *European Public Law* 2003, p. 493-508.

CRAIG (2006)
P. Craig, *EU Administrative Law*, Oxford 2006.

CRAIG (2006 A)
P. Craig, 'The Locus and Accountability of the Executive in the European Union', in P. Craig and A. Tomkins (eds), *The Executive and Public Law, Power and Accountability in Comparative perspective*, Oxford: Oxford University Press, 2006, pp. 315-345.

CRAIG AND DE BÚRCA (1999)
P. Craig and G. de Burca (eds), *The Evolution of EU Law*, New York: Oxford University Press, 1999

CRAIG AND DE BÚRCA (2007)
P. Craig and G. de Burca, *EU Law. Text, Cases and Material*, 4th ed., Oxford 2007.

CHRISTOFOROU (2004)
T. Christoforou, The regulation of genetically modified organisms in the European Union: The interplay of science, law and politics, *CMLRev* 2004, pp. 637-709.

CURTIN (1992)
D.M. Curtin, 'The Decentralized Enforcement of Community Law Rights, Judicial Snakes and Ladders', in: D. Curtin and D. O' Keeffe (eds), *Constitutional Adjudiciation in European Community and National Law, Essays for the Hon. Mr Justice T.F. O' Higgins*, Dublin 1992, pp. 33-49.

CURTIN (2007)
D.M. Curtin, 'Holding (Quasi) Autonomous EU Administrative Actors to Public Account', *European Law Journal* 2007, pp. 523-541.

CURTIN AND MORTELMANS (1994)
D.M. Curtin and K.J.M. Mortelmans, 'Application and Enforcement of Community Law by the Member states: Actors in Search of a Third Generation Script', in: D.M. Curtin and T. Heukels (eds.), *The Institutional Dynamics of European Integration, Liber Amicorum Henry G. Schermers*, Dordrecht/ Boston/ London 1994, pp. 423-466.

DANNECKER AND JANSEN (2004)
G. Dannecker and O. Jansen (eds), *Competition Law Sanctioning in the European Union. The EU-Law Influence on the National Law System of Sanctions in the European Area*, The Hague 2004.

DAVID (2003)
A. David, *Inspektionen im Europäischen Verwaltungsrecht*, Berlin 2003.

DEHOUSSE (1999)
R. Dehousse, 'Towards a Regulation of Transnational Governance? Citizen's Rights and the Reform of Comitology Procedures', in: C. Joerges and E. Vos (eds), *EU Commitees: Social Regulation, Law and Politics*, Oxford-Portland 1999, p. 109-127.

DEHOUSSE (2002)
R. Dehousse, 'Misfits: EU Law and the Transformation of European Governance', in: C. Joerges and R. Dehousse (eds), *Good Governance in Europe's Integrated Market*, Oxford 2002, pp. 207-229.

DE LANGE (2003)
F. de Lange, 'Beyond Greenpeace, Courtesy of the Aarhus Convention', in: H. Somsen et al. (eds), *The Yearbook of European Environmental Law*, Vol. 3, Oxford 2003, pp. 227-248

DELICOSTOPOULOS (2003)
J.S. Delicostopoulos, 'Towards European Procedural Primacy in National Legal Systems', *European Law Journal* 2003, pp. 599-613.

DE SADELEER, ROLLER AND DROSS (2005)
N. de Sadeleer, G. Roller and M. Dross (eds), *Access to Justice in Environmental Matters and the Role of NGOs; Empirical Findings and Legal Appraisal*, Groningen 2005.

DINGEMANS AND WIDDERSHOVEN (2005)
R.P.B.A. Dingemans and R.J.G.M.Widdershoven, 'De Schutznormleer in communautair perspectief: het Duitse debat', *NTB* 2005, pp. 327-337.

DIRKZWAGER (1999)
N. Dirkzwager, 'The Shifting Boundaries of European and National Enforcement: a Case Study of Customs Law', in: J.A.E. Vervaele (ed), *Compliance and Enforcement of European Community Law*, The Hague 1999, pp. 253-246.

DODDS-SMITH (2000)
I. Dodds-Smith, 'Data protection and abridged applications for marketing authorizations in the pharmaceutical industry', in: R. Goldberg and J. Lonbay (eds.), *Pharmaceutical Medicine, Biotechnology, and European Law*, Cambridge 2000, pp. 93-136.

DOUGAN (2000)
M. Dougan, 'Minimum Harmonization and the Internal Market', *CMLRev* 2000, pp. 853-885.

DOUGAN (2002)
M. Dougan, Enforcing the Single Market: 'The Judicial Harmonisation of National Remedies and Procedural Rules', in: C. Barnard and J. Scott (eds), *The Law of the Single European Market: Unpacking the Premises*, Oxford and Portland, Oregon 2002, pp. 153-180.

EILMANSBERGER (2004)
T. Eilmansberger, 'The Relationship between Rights and Remedies in EC Law: In Search of the Missing Link', *CMLRev* 2004, p. 1199-1246.

FAVRE (1989)
Favre, David S., *International trade in endangered species*, Dordrecht 1989.

FRANK (2003)
S. Frank, *A New Model for European Medical Device Regulation. A Comparative Legal Analysis in the EU and in the USA*, Groningen 2003.

FRANCHINI (2004)
C. Franchini, 'European Principles Governing National Administrative Proceedings', *Law and Contemporary Problems 2004*, pp. 184-190.

GARSTECKI (2006)
T. Garstecki, 'Implementation of Article 16, Council Regulation (EC) No 338/97 in the 25 Member States of the European Union', *A TRAFFIC Europe Report for the European Commission*, Brussels, 2006.

GIL IBANEZ (1999)
A.J. Gil Ibanez, *The Administrative Supervision and Enforcement of EC Law. Powers, Procedures and Limits*, Oxford 1999.
GROUSSOT (2006)
X. Groussot, *General principles of Community Law*, Groningen 2006.
GUTMAN (2006)
K. Gutman, Case C-66/04, Smoke Flavourigs; case C-436/03, SCE; and Case C-217/04, ENISA, *The Columbia Journal of European Law*, winter 2006/2007, pp. 147-187.
HANCHER (2000)
L. Hancher, 'EC competition law, pharmaceuticals and intellectual property: recent developments', in: Richard Goldberg and Julian Lonbay (eds), *Pharmaceutical Medicine, Biotechnology, and European Law*, Cambridge 2000, pp. 76-92.
HARDING (1996)
C. Harding, 'Models of Enforcement', in: C. Harding and B. Swart (eds) *Enforcing European Community Rules. Criminal Procedures, Administrative Procedures and Harmonization*, Aldershot 1996, p. 22-42.
HARDING (1997)
C. Harding, 'Member State Enforcement of European Community Measures: The Chimera of 'Effective' Enforcement', *MJ* 1997, pp. 5-24.
HARLOW (2002)
C. Harlow, *Accountability in the European Union*, Oxford 2002.
HATJE (1998)
A. Hatje, *Die gemeinschaftrechtliche Steuerung der Wirtschaftverwaltung*, Baden-Baden 1998.
HERVEY (2001)
T. K. Hervey, 'Regulation of GM Products in a Multilevel System of Governance', *RECIEL* 2001, pp. 321-333
HETZER (2004)
W. Hetzer, 'National Criminal Prosecution and European Tendering of Evidence. Perspectives of the European Anti-Fraud Office (OLAF)', *European Journal of Crime, Criminal Law and Criminal Justice*, 2004 p. 166-183.
HILL (2007)
Andrew Hill, United Kingdom: *Dramatic increase in seizures of counterfeit medicines, Managing intellectual property 2007*, available at: http://www.managingip.com/Article.aspx?ArticleID=1445827andTitle=Dramatic%20increase%20in%20seizures%20of%20counterfeit%20medicines.
HOFMANN (2004)
J. Hofmann, *Rechtsschutz und Haftung im Europäischen Verwaltungsverbund*, Berlin 2004.

HOFMANN AND TÜRK (2007)
H.C.H. Hofmann and A. Türk, 'The Development of Integrated Administration in the EU and its Consequences', *ELJ* 2007 p. 253-271.
JACOBS (2004)
F.G. Jacobs, 'The Evolution of the European Legal Order', *CMLRev* 2004 p. 303-316.
JAEGER (1999)
Marc Jaeger, 'Are the various judicial remedies interconnected?', in: R. Iglesias, G. Carlos et al, *Mélanges en homage a Fernand Schockweiler*, Baden Baden 1999, pp. 233-243, translated by the CVCE, http: //www.ena.lu/mce.swf?doc=7041andlang=2.
JANS (2006)
J.H. Jans, 'Over kanonskogels, bretels en andere ongelofelijke verhalen...', *SEW* 2006, pp. 419-424.
JANS (2006)
J.H. Jans, 'Did Baron von Munchhausen ever Visit Aarhus? Some Critical Remarks on the Proposal for a Regulation on the Application of the Provisions of the Aarhus Convention to EC Institutions and Bodies', in: Richard Macrory (ed) *Reflections on 30 Years of EU Environmental Law: A High Level of Protection?*, Groningen 2006, p. 475-490.
JANS, DE LANGE, PRECHAL AND WIDDERSHOVEN (2007)
J.H. Jans, R. de Lange, S. Prechal and R.J.G.M. Widdershoven, *Europeanisation of Public Law*, Groningen, 2007.
JANSEN AND LANGBROEK (2007)
O.J.D.M. Jansen and P. Langbroek (eds), *Defence Rights during Administrative Investigations*, Antwerpen-Oxford 2007.
JONES AND THOMPSON (2002)
B. Jones and K.Thompson, 'Administrative Law in the United Kingdom', in: R. Seerden and F. Stroink (eds) *Administrative Law of the European Union, its Member States and the United States, A Comparative Analysis*, Antwerp 2002, pp. 199-258.
KAKOURIS (1997)
C.N. Kakouris, 'Do the Member States possess judicial procedural 'autonomy'?',*CMLRev* 1997, p. 1389-1412.
KAPTEYN AND VERLOREN VAN THEMAAT (2003)
Kapteyn and VerLoren van Themaat; Hoofdredactie: P.J.G. Kapteyn, L.A. Geelhoed, K.J.M. Mortelmans en C.W.A. Timmermans, *Het recht van de Europese Unie en van de Europese Gemeenschappen*, 6th edn, Deventer 2003.
KEESSEN (2006)
A.M. Keessen 'Ambtshalve toepassing van Gemeenschapsrecht' *NTER* 2006, pp. 55-64.

KEESSEN (2007)

A.M. Keessen, 'Reducing the Judicial Deficit in Multilevel Environmental Regulation: The Example of Plant Protecting Products' *EELRev 2007*, pp. 26-36. Also published in: A. Follesdal, R.A. Wessel and J. Wouters (eds), *Multilevel Regulation and the EU. The Interplay between Global, European and National Normative Processes*, Leiden 2008, pp. 323-344.

KLIP (1999)

A. Klip, 'Integrated Protection of the Community's Financial Interests: Shift from 'State-State' Approach towards Verticalisation of the Procedure?', in: J.A.E. Vervaele (ed), *Transnational Enforcement of the Financial Interests of the European Union, Developments in the Treaty of Amsterdam and the Corpus Iuris*, Antwerpen/Groningen/Oxford 1999, pp. 95-107.

KLIP AND VERVAELE (2001)

A.H. Klip and J.A.E. Vervaele, 'Suprationational rules governing cooperation in administrative and criminal matters', in: J.A.E. Vervaele and A.H. Klip (eds), *European Cooperation between Tax, Customs and Judicial Authorities*, The Hague 2001, pp. 7-48.

KOCH (2005)

C. Koch, 'Locus standi of private applicants under the EU Constitution: preserving gaps in the protection of individuals' right to an effective remedy', *ELRev* 2005, pp. 511-527.

KRÄMER (1993)

L. Krämer, *European Environmental Law, Casebook*, London 1993.

LADEUR (1999)

K. Ladeur, 'Towards a Legal Concept of the Network in European Standard-Setting', in: C. Joerges and E. Vos (eds), *EU Committees: Social Regulation, Law and Politics*, Oxford-Portland 1999, pp. 151-170.

LANGBROEK AND JANSEN (2007)

P. Langbroek and O.J.D.M.L. Jansen, 'The juridical backgrounds of OLAF investigations', in: Oswald Jansen and Philip Langbroek (eds), *Defence rights during Administrative Investigations. A comparative study into defence rights during administrative investigations against EU fraud in England and Wales, Germany, Italy, the Netherlands, Romania, Sweden and Switzerland*, Antwerpen 2007, pp. 27-50.

LASOK (1998)

D. Lasok, *The Trade and Customs Law of the European Union*, 3rd edition, London 1998.

LAVRANOS (2006)

N. Lavranos, MOX Plant Dispute – Court of Justice of the European Communities, *EUConst.* 2006, pp. 456-469.

LAZOWSKI (2007)

A. Lazowski, 'And then they were twenty-seven... A legal appraisal of the sixth Accession Treaty', *CMLRev.* 2007, pp. 401-430.

LEEBRON (1996)
D.W. Leebron, 'Lying Down with Procrustus: An Analysis of Harmonization Claims', in: J. Bhagwati and R. Hudec (eds), *Fair Trade and Harmonization*, Volume 1, Cambridge: MIT Press 1996, pp. 41-118.

LENAERTS AND VANHAMME (1997)
K. Lenaerts and J. Vanhamme, 'Procedural Rights of Private Parties in the Community Administrative Process', *CMLRev* 1997, pp. 531-569.

LENAERTS AND ARTS (1999)
K. Lenaerts and D. Arts, *Europees procesrecht*, 2e druk, Antwerpen/Apeldoorn, 1999.

LENAERTS AND VERHOEVEN (2000)
K. Lenaerts and A. Verhoeven, 'Towards a Legal Framework for Executive Rule-Making in the EU? The Contribution of the New Comitology Decision', *CMLRev* 2000, pp. 645-686.

LENAERTS (2004)
K. Lenaerts, '"In the Union we Trust": Trust-enhancing Principles of Community Law', *CMLRev* 2004, pp. 317-343.

LENAERTS (2006)
K. Lenaerts, D. Arts and I. Maselis, *Procedural Law of the European Union*, 2nd edn, London 2006.

LENAERTS (2007)
K. Lenaerts, 'The Rule of Law and the Coherence of the Judicial System of the European Union', *CMLRev* 2007, pp. 1625-1659.

LIISBERG (2006)
J.B. Liisberg, 'The EU Constitutional Treaty and its distinction between legislative and non-legislative acts – oranges into apples?', *Jean Monnet Working paper* 01/06, 2006.

LISMAN (2004)
J. Lisman, 'Voorbij goed en kwaad, Off label mag, maar niet zomaar', *Pharmaceutisch weekblad*, 2004, pp. 895-899.

LISMAN (2006)
J. Lisman, 'De toelating van geneesmiddelen, Hoe effectief is ons systeem?', in: Vereniging voor Gezondheidsrecht, Geneesmiddelen en Recht, *Preadvies 2006*, Den Haag 2006.

LONBAY (2000)
Julian Lonbay, 'Free movement of healthcare professionals', in: Richard Goldberg and Julian Lonbay (eds.), *Pharmaceutical Medicine, Biotechnology, and European Law*, Cambridge 2000, pp. 45-75.

LUCHTMAN (2007)
M.J.J.P. Luchtman, *Grensoverschrijdende sfeercumulatie, Over de handhavingssamenwerking tussen financiële toezichthouders, fiscale autoriteiten en justitiële autoriteiten in EU-verband*, Nijmegen 2007.

LUGT (1999)
M. Lugt, *Enforcing European and National Food Law in the Netherlands and England*, Den Haag, 1999.

MEIJ (1997)
A.W.H. Meij, 'Article 215 (92) EC and Local Remedies', in: T. Heukels and A. McDonnell, *The Action for Damages in Community Law*, The Hague, London, Boston 1997.

MENG (1994)
W. Meng, *Extraterritoriale Jurisdiktion im öffentlichen Wirtschaftsrecht*, Berlin, Heidelberg, New York 1994.

MONTFORTS AND KEESSEN (2007)
M.H.M.M. Montforts en A.M. Keessen, 'Openbaarheid van milieu-informatie bij registratie (dier) geneesmiddelen', *RIVM Rapport 60150006/2007*, 2007.

MONTFORTS ET AL (2007)
M.H.M.M. Montforts, H.F.M.W. van Rijswick, A.A. Freriks, A.M. Keessen, S. Wuijts, 'De relatie tussen productregistratie en waterkwaliteitsregelgeving: geneesmiddelen, diergeneesmiddelen en veevoederadditieven', *RIVM Report 601500003/2006*, 2006.

NESSLER (2000)
V. Neßler, 'Der transnationale Verwaltungsakt – Zur Dogmatik eines neuen Rechtsinstitutes', NVwZ 1995, pp. 863-866.

NOWAK (2000)
C. Nowak, 'Das Verhältnis zwischen zentralem und dezentralem Individualrechtschutz im Europäischen Gemeinschaftsrecht – Verwirspiel zwischen Wechselwirking und Beziehungslosigkeit', *EuR 2000*, pp. 724-742.

ORTLEP AND WIDDERSHOVEN (2005)
R. Ortlep en R.Widdershoven, 'Europa en de strafrechtelijke handhaving van milieurecht', in: Chris Backes et al (eds), *Lex Dura Sed Lex, Opstellen over de handhaving van omgevingsrecht*, Deventer 2005, pp. 159-176.

OSTROVSKY (2007)
A.A. Ostrovsky, 'Up Against a Wall: Europe's Options for Regulating Biotechnology through Regulatory Anarchy', *European Law Journal* 2007, pp. 110-134.

PRECHAL ET AL (2005)
S. Prechal, R.H. van Ooik, J.H. Jans, K.J.M. Mortelmans, 'The Consequences of the 'Europeanisation of the law for the organisation of the Judiciary in the Netherlands', *Report for the Raad voor de Rechtspraak (Dutch Council for the Judiciary)*, 2005.

PRECHAL (1998)
S. Prechal, 'Community Law in National Courts: The Lessons from Van Schijndel', *CMLRev* 1998, pp. 681-706.

PRECHAL (2005)
S. Prechal, 'Adieu a la Directive?', *European Constitutional Law Review* 2005, pp. 481-494.

PRECHAL (2005A)
S. Prechal et al., *'Europeanization' of the Law: Consequences for the Dutch Judiciary*, Report for the Raad voor de Rechtspraak, The Hague 2005.

PRECHAL (2008)
S. Prechal, 'Protection of Rights: How Far?', in: Sacha Prechal and Bert van Roermund (eds), *The Coherence of EU Law, The Search for Unity in Divergent Concepts*, Oxford 2008, pp. 155-182.

RASMUSSEN (2000)
H. Rasmussen, 'Remedying the Crumbling EC Judicial System', *CMLRev* 2000, p. 1071-1112.

REEVES (2002)
R. Reeves, *Policing International Trade in Endangered Species: The CITES Treaty and Compliance*, London 2002.

RUFFERT (1997)
M. Ruffert, 'Rights and Remedies in European Community Law: A Comparative View', *CMLRev* 1997, pp. 307-336.

RUFFERT (2001)
M. Ruffert, 'Der transnationale Verwaltungsakt', *Die Verwaltung* (2001), pp. 453-487.

RUTTEMAN (1975)
J. Rutteman, 'De toelating van bestrijdingsmiddelen: terug naar 1975?' *MenR* (2002), pp. 312-317.

SANDS (1996)
P.Sands, 'Is the Court of Justice an Environmental Tribunal?', in: Han Somsen (ed) *Protecting the European Environment: Enforcing EC Environmental Law*, London 1996, pp. 23-36.

SANDS AND KLEIN (2001)
P. Sands and P. Klein, *Bowett's Law of International Institutions*, fifth edn., London, 2001.

SCHMIDT-ASSMANN (2004)
E. Schmidt-Aßmann, *Das allgemeine Verwaltungsrecht als Ordnungsidee, Grundlagen und Aufgaben der verwaltungsrechtlichen Systembildung*, 2nd edn, Berlin/ Heidelberg 2004.

SCHMIDT-ASSMANN AND SCHÖNDORF-HAUBOLT (2005)
E. Schmidt-Aßmann and B. Schöndorf-Haubolt (Hrg), 'Der Europaische Verwaltungsverbund', Berlin/ Heidelberg 2005.

SCHRÖDER (2002)
M. Schröder, 'Administrative Law in Germany', in: René Seerden and Frits Stroink (eds) *Administrative Law of the European Union, its Member States and the United States, A Comparative Analysis*, Antwerp 2002, pp. 91-144.

SCHWARZE (2004)

J. Schwarze, 'Judicial Review of European Administrative Procedure', *Law and Contemporary Problems* 2004, pp. 85-106.

SEERDEN AND STROINK (2002)

R. Seerden and F. Stroink, 'Administrative Law in the Netherlands', in: René Seerden and Frits Stroink (eds) *Administrative Law of the European Union, its Member States and the United States, A Comparative Analysis*, Antwerp, 2002.

SHAPIRO (1999)

Martin Shapiro, 'Implementation, Discretion and Rules', in: J.A.E. Vervaele, *Compliance and Enforcement of European Community Law*, The Hague 1999, pp. 27-34.

SHERLOCK (1996)

A. Sherlock, 'The Protection of Rights in the Enforcement and Application of Community Rules and Procedures', in: Ch. Harding and B. Swart, C. Harding and B. Swart (eds) *Enforcing European Community Rules. Criminal Procedures, Administrative Procedures and Harmonization*, Aldershot 1996, pp. 43-61.

SOMMER (2003)

Julia Sommer, *Verwaltungskooperation am Beispiel administrativer Informationsverfahren im Europaischen Umweltrecht*, Berlin: Springer, 2003.

SOMSEN (1996)

H. Somsen, Editor's Preface, Han Somsen (ed.) *Protecting the European Environment: Enforcing EC Environmental Law*, London 1996, pp. ix-xii.

SOMSEN (2000)

H. Somsen, 'The Private Enforcement of Member State Compliance with EC Environmental Law: an Unfulfilled Promise?', in: *Yearbook of Environmental Law* (1) Oxford 2000, pp. 311-360.

SUTHERLAND REPORT (1992)

P. Sutherland et al, 'The Internal Market after 1992: Meeting the Challenge', Report to the EEC Commission by the High Level Group on the Operation of Internal Market ("Sutherland Report"), 1992.

SWART (1999)

B. Swart, 'The Shifting Boundaries of European and National Enforcement; Some Comments on the National Dimension', in: J.A.E. Vervaele, *Compliance and Enforcement of European Community Law*, The Hague 1999, pp. 321-334.

SYDOW (2004)

G. Sydow, *Verwaltungskooperation in der Europäischen Union, Zur horizontalen und vertikalen Zusammenarbeit der europäischen Verwaltungen am Beispiel der Productzulassungsrecht*, Tübingen 2004.

TIMMERMANS (2004)

C. Timmermans, 'The European Union's Judicial System', *CMLRev* 2004, pp. 393-405.

TRIDIMAS (2000)
T. Tridimas, *The General Principles of EC Law*, Oxford 2000.
TRIDIMAS (2003)
T.Tridimas, 'Knocking on Heaven's Door: Fragmentation, Efficiency and Defiance in the Preliminary Reference Procedure', *CMLRev* 2003 pp. 9-50.
TREBILCOCK AND HOWSE (2005)
M.J. Trebilcock and R. Howse, The Regulation of International Trade, 3rd edn, London/New York 2005.
USHER (2003)
J.A. Usher, 'Direct and Individual Concern – An Effective Remedy or a Conventional Solution', *E.L. Rev.* 2003, pp. 575-600.
VAN DE GRONDEN (1998)
J.W. van de Gronden, *De implementatie van het EG-milieurecht door Nederlandse, decentrale overheden. De EG-rechtelijke eisen voor de omzetting, inkadering, toepassing en handhaving van EG-milieurechtrichtlijnen en -verordeningen door provincies, gemeenten en waterschappen*, Deventer 1998.
VAN DER MEULEN (2003)
B.M.J. van der Meulen, 'Marktautoriteiten, een aanzet tot interne rechtsvergelijking', in: *Toezicht op markten, VAR reeks*, The Hague 2003, pp. 13-130.
VAN DER MEULEN (2007)
B.M.J. van der Meulen, 'Niets nieuws is goed nieuws, Aansprakelijkheid voor falend toezicht', *O&A* 2007, pp. 19-26.
VAN DER MEULEN AND FRERIKS (2006)
B.M.J. van der Meulen and A.A. Freriks, 'Millefeuille. The emergence of a multi-layered controls system in the European food sector', *Utrecht Law Review* 2006, p. 156 – 176.
VAN GERVEN (1996)
W. van Gerven, 'Bridging the Unbridgeable: Community and National Tort Laws after Francovich and Brasserie', *ICLQ* 1996, pp. 507-544.
VAN GERVEN (2000)
W. van Gerven, 'Of Rights, Remedies and Procedures', *CMLRev* 2000 pp. 501-536.
VAN GERVEN (2005)
W. van Gerven, *The European Union – A Policy of States and People*, Oxford 2005.
VAN HOEK (2006)
A. van Hoek, 'Private Enforcement and the Multiplication of Legal Orders', in A. van Hoek et al (eds), *Multilevel Governance in Enforcement and Adjudication*, Antwerpen 2006, pp. 313-337.

VAN KREVELD (2007)
A. van Kreveld, *Gekweekt met de vangkooi, Verkenning naar illegale praktijken in de handel in wilde Europese vogels in Nederland*, 2007, available at: www.vogelbescherming.nl.
VAN OOIK (1999)
R. van Ooik, *De keuze der rechtsgrondslag voor besluiten van de Europese Unie*, Deventer 1999.
VAN OOIK AND VANDAMME (2005)
R. H. van Ooik and T.A.J.A. Vandamme, Schorsing van Europese regelgeving in Nederland, Kanttekening bij de Nevedi-uitspraak van de rechtbank, *SEW* 2005, pp. 60-69.
VAN OOIK (2007)
R. van Ooik, 'The Euorpean Court of Justice and the Division of Competence in the Euroepan Union, in: D. Obradovic and N. Lavranos (eds), *Interface between EU Law and National Law*, Groningen 2007, pp. 13-42.
VAN RIJN (1993)
T.P.J.N. van Rijn, 'Administrative Application and Enforcement of Community Law: Internal Control by the Commission', in: J.A.E. Vervaele (ed), *Administrative Law Application and Enforcement of Community Law in the Netherlands*, Deventer/ Boston 1993, pp. 143-160.
VAN RIJSWICK (1996)
H.F.M.W. van Rijswick, 'Grensoverschrijdende handel in bedreigde dier- en plantesoorten', in: G.A. Biezeveld et al, *Strafrechtelijke aanpak van grensoverschrijdende milieucriminaliteit, capita selecta, Publicaties van de Vereniging voor Milieurecht* 1995-3, Zwolle 1996.
VELDKAMP (1999)
A. Veldkamp, 'The Shifting Boundaries of European and National Enforcement: Three Case Studies', in J.A.E. Vervaele, *Compliance and Enforcement of European Community Law*, The Hague 1999, pp. 285-300.
VELDKAMP (1998)
A.M.E. Veldkamp, 'Overbrengen van afvalstoffen: (trans)nationale uitvoering en handhaving, Deventer, 1998.
VERHEIJ (1995)
N. Verheij, 'Internationale administratieve bijstand en Nederlands bestuursrecht', in: J.W. van der Hulst (ed), *Administratieve bijstand in de EG*, Arnhem 1995, pp. 89-96.
VERVAELE (1992)
J.A.E. Vervaele, *Fraud against the Community; The Need for European Fraud Legislation*, Deventer 1992.

VERVAELE (1995)
J.A.E. Vervaele, 'Horizontale, verticale en diagonale samenwerking tussen administratieve organen, Horizontale, verticale en diagonale samenwerking tussen administratieve organen', in: J.W. van der Hulst (ed), *Administratieve bijstand in de EG*, Arnhem 1995, pp. 5-17.
VERVAELE (1999)
J.A.E. Vervaele, 'Community Regulation and Operational Application of Investigative Powers, the Gathering and Use of Evidence with Regard to the Infringement of EC Financial Interests, in: J.A.E. Vervaele (ed.), *Transnational Enforcement of the Financial Interests of the European Union. Developments in the Treaty of Amsterdam and the Corpus Juris*, Antwerp-Oxford 1999, pp. 53-91.
VERVAELE (1999 A)
J.A.E. Vervaele, 'Shared Governance and Enforcement of European Law: From Comitology to a Multi-level Agency Structure?', in: C. Joerges and E. Vos (eds) *EU Commitees: Social Regulation, Law and Politics*, Oxford-Portland 1999, pp. 138-147.
VERVAELE (1999 B)
J.A.E. Vervaele, 'Towards an Independent European Agency to Fight Fraud and Corruption in the EU?', *European Journal of Crime, Criminal Law and Criminal Justice*, 1999, pp. 331-346.
VERVAELE (1999 C)
J.A.E. Vervaele, 'Transnational Cooperation of Enforcement Authorities in the Community Area', in: J.A.E. Vervaele (ed) *Compliance and Enforcement of European Community Law*, The Hague 1999, pp. 361-390.
VESTERDORF (2003)
B. Vesterdorf, 'The Community court system ten years from now and beyond: challenges and possibilities' *ELRev* 2003, pp. 303 – 323.
VOGELEZANG-STOUTE (2003)
E.M.Vogelezang-Stoute, *Bestrijdingsmiddelenrecht. Een rechtsvergelijking*, Deventer 2004.
VOS (1999)
E. Vos, 'EU Committees: the Evolution of Unforeseen Institutional Actors in European Product Regulation', in: Christian Joerges and Ellen Vos (eds), *EU Commitees: Social Regulation, Law and Politics*, Oxford-Portland 1999, pp. 19-50.
VOS (2002)
E. Vos, 'Van BSE tot Europese Autoriteit voor Voedselveiligheid: het Europese recept voor Voedselveiligheid en consumentenvertrouwen', *SEW* 2005, pp. 117-127.
WARD (2000)
A. Ward, *Judicial Review and the Rights of Private Parties in EC Law*, Oxford 2000.

WATTEL (2004)
P.J. Wattel, 'Köbler, CILFIT and Welthgrove: We can't go on meeting like this', *CMLRev* 2004, p. 177-190.
WEATHERILL (1995)
S. Weatherill, *Law and Integration in the European Union*, Oxford, 1995.
WEATHERILL (2002)
S. Weatherill, 'Pre-emption, Harmonisation and the Distribution of Competence to Regulate the Internal Market', in: C. Barnard and J. Scott (eds), *The Law of the Single European Market. Unpacking the Premises*, Oxford-Portland 2002, pp. 41-74.
WEATHERILL AND BEAUMONT (1999)
S. Weatherill and P. Beaumont, *EU Law. The Essential Guide to the Legal Workings of European Law*, 3rd edn, London 1999.
WEILER (1999)
J.H.H. Weiler, 'The Constitution of the Common Market Place: Text and Context in the Evolution of the Free Movement of Goods', in: P. Craig and G. De Burca (eds), *The Evolution of EU Law*, New York 1999, pp. 349-376.
WEILER (2000)
J.H.H. Weiler, 'Epilogue: Towards a Common Law of International Trade', in: J.H.H. Weiler (ed), *The EU, the WTO and the NAFTA, Towards a Common Law of International Trade?*, Oxford 2000, pp. 201-232.
WIDDERSHOVEN (1996)
R.J.G.M. Widdershoven, 'Naar een bestuursrechtelijk Ius Commune in Europa', in: *Preadvies Europees recht en het Nederlands bestuursrecht*, Alphen aan den Rijn 1996, pp. 97-200.
WIDDERSHOVEN (1999)
R.J.G.M. Widdershoven, 'Enforcement of EC Regulations by Private Organizations: a Public Law Wolf in Private Law Sheep's Clothing?', in J.A.E. Vervaele (ed), *Compliance and Enforcement of European Community Law*, The Hague 1999, pp. 235-246.
WIDDERSHOVEN (1999 A)
R.J.G.M. Widdershoven, 'The Role of National Administrative Law in Transnational Enforcement Cooperation', in: J.A.E. Vervaele, *Transnational Enforcement of the Financial Interests of the European Union, Developments in the Treaty of Amsterdam and the Corpus Iuris*, Antwerpen/Groningen/Oxford 1999, pp. 131-150.
WIDDERSHOVEN (2002)
R.J.G.M. Widdershoven, 'European Administrative Law', in: René Seerden and Frits Stroink (eds), *Administrative Law of the European Union, its Member States and the United States*, Antwerpen-Groningen 2002, pp. 277-285.

WIDDERSHOVEN (2004)
R.J.G.M. Widdershoven, 'Rechtsbescherming in het milieurecht in Europees perspectief', *MenR* 2004, pp. 530-540.
WIDDERSHOVEN (2004 A)
R.J.G.M. Widdershoven, Rechtsbeginselen in het Europese Recht, in: Raymond J.N. Schlössels et al (eds), *In beginsel, Over aard, inhoud en samenhang van rechtsbeginselen in het bestuursrecht*, Deventer: Kluwer, 2004, pp. 293-328.
WIDDERSHOVEN (2005)
R.J.G.M. Widdershoven, 'The principle of Loyal Cooperation, Lawmaking by the European Court of Justice and the Dutch Courts', in: F.A.M. Stroink and E.C.H.J. van der Linden (eds), *Judicial Lawmaking and Administrative Law*, Antwerpen/ Oxford, 2005, pp. 3-35.
WILLEMSEN (2005)
P.A. Willemsen, *De grenzen van de rechtsstrijd in het bestuursrechtelijk beroep en hoger beroep in rechtsvergelijkend perspectief*, Deventer 2005.
WOLDENDORP (2002)
H.E. Woldendorp, 'Procedurele aspecten van Europese inbreukprocedures op het terrein van het milieubeheer', *MenR* 2002, pp. 130-136.
ZWEIGERT AND KÖTZ (1998)
K. Zweigert and H. Kötz, *Introduction to Comparative Law*, 3rd edn, Oxford 1998.

Table of Cases

European Court of Justice

Case C-9/56 *Meroni* [1958] ECR 133

Joined Cases 42 and 49/59 *Snupat* v *High Authority* [1961] ECR 53

Case 25/62, *Plaumann and Co* v *Commission*, [1963] ECR 95

Case 26/62 *Van Gend en Loos* [1963] ECR 1

Joined Cases 28/62, 69/62 and 30/62 *Da Costa* v *Nederlandse Belastingadministratie* [1963] ECR 31

Case 8-11/66 *Cimenteries Cementbedrijven et al* v *Commission* [1967] ECR 75

Case 120/67 *Upjohn* v *The Licencing Authority established by the Medicines Act* [1968] ECR I-223

Case 11/70 *Internationale Handelsgesellschaft* v *Einfuhr und Vorratstelle für Getreide und Futtermittel* [1970] ECR 1125

Case 22/70 *Commission* v *Council* [1971] ECR I-263

Case C-25/70 *Einfuhr- und Voratstelle für Getreide und Futtermittel* v *Köster, Berodt and Co.* [1970] ECR 1161

Case 5/71 *Aktien-Zuckerfabrik Schöppenstedt* v *Council* [1971] ECR 975

Case 72/74 *Union syndicale-Service public européen and others* v *Council* [1975] ECR 401

Case 104/75 *De Peijper* [1976] ECR 613

Case 33/76 *Rewe-Zentralfinanz and Rewe-Zentral* v *Landwirtschaftskammer für das Saarland* [1976] ECR 1989

Case 45/76 *Comet* v *Produktschap voor Siergewassen* [1976] ECR 2043

Case 106/77 *Amministrazione delle Finanze dello Stato* v *Simmenthal* [1978] ECR 629

Case 120/78, *Rewe-Zentral AG v. Bundesmonopolverwaltung für Branntwein (Cassis de Dijon)* [1979] ECR p. 649

Case 251/78 *Denkavit* [1979] ECR 3369

Case 543/79 *Birke* v *Commission and Council* [1981] ECR 2669

Joined Cases 789 and 790/79 *Calpak SpA and Societá Emiliana Lavorazione Frutta SpA* v *Commission* [1980] ECR 1949

Case 32/80 *Officier van Justitie* v *Kortmann* [1981] ECR 250

Case 60/81 *IBM* v *Commission* [1981] ECR 2639

Case 283/81 *CILFIT* v *Ministro della Sanitá* [1982] ECR 3415

Case 307/81 *Alusuisse* v *Council and Commission* [1982] ECR 3463

Case 11/82 *Piraiki Patraiki* v *Commission* [1985] ECR 207

Case 191/82 *Fediol* v *Commission* [1983] ECR 2913

Case 199/82 *Amministrazione delle Finanze dello Stato* v *San Giorgio* [1983] ECR 3595.

Case 216/82 *Universität Hamburg* v *Hauptzollamt Hamburg-Kehrwieder* [1983] ECR 2771

Case 13/83 *Parliament* v *Council* [1985] ECR 1513

Case 118/83 *CMC* v *Commission* [1985] ECR 2325

Case 294/83 *Les Verts* v *European Parliament* [1986] ECR 1339

Case 199/84 *Procuratore della Repubblica* v *Migliorini* [1985] ECR 3317

Case 165/84 *Krohn* [1986] ECR 768
Case 222/84 *Johnston* [1986] ECR 1651
Joined Cases 133 to 136/85 *Rau* v *BALM* [1987] ECR 228
Case 314/85 *Foto Frost* [1987] ECR 4199
Case 81/86 *De Boer Buizen* v *Council and Commission* [1987] ECR 3677
Joined Cases C-97, 99, 193 and 215/86 *Asteris and Others* v *Commission* [1988] ECR 2181
Case 222/86 *Heylens* [1987] ECR 4097
Case 302/86 *Commission* v *Denmark (Danish bottles)* [1988] ECR 4607
Joined Cases 106-120/87 *Asteris II* [1988] ECR 5538.
Case C-308/87 *Grifoni* v *Commission* [1990] ECR I1203
Case C-354/87 *Weddel* v *Commission* [1990] ECR I-3847
Case C-2/88 *Zwartveld* [1990] ECR I-3365
Case C-68/88 *Commission* v *Greece (Greek maize)* [1989] ECR 2965
Case C-125/88 *Nijman* [1989] ECR 3533
Case C-131/88 *Commission* v *Germany* [1991] ECR I-825
Joined Cases C-143/88 and C-92/90 *Zuckerfabrik Süderditmarschen* [1991] ECR 415
Case C-351/88 *Commission* v *Germany* [1991] ECR I-256
Case C-361/88 *TA Luft* [1991] ECR I-2567
Case C-59/89 *Commission* v *Germany* [1991] ECR I-2607
Case C-63/89 *Assicurance du Crédit* [1991] ECR I-1799
Joined Cases C-104/89 and C-37/90 *Mulder II* [1992] ECR I-3061
Case C-182/89, *Commission* v *France (Bolivian Wildcat Skins)* [1990] ECR I-4337
Case C-309/89 *Codorniu* v *Council* [1994] ECR I-1853
Case C-340/89 *Vlassopoulou* [1991] ECR I-2357
Case C-358/89 *Extramet Industrie* v *Council* [1991] ECR I-2501
Joined Cases C-6 and 9/90 *Francovich and Bonifaci* v *Italy* [1991] ECR I-5357
Joined Cases C-87/90 to C-89/90 *Verholen and Others* [1991] ECR I-3757
Case C-240/90 *Germany* v *Commission (Mutton)* [1992] ECR I-5383
Case C-269/90 *Hauptzollamt München Mitte* v *Technische Universität München* [1991] ECR I-5469
Case C-295/90 *European Parliament* v *Council* [1992] ECR I-4193
Case C-97/91 *Oleifici Borelli* v *Commission* [1992] ECR I-6313
Case C-146/91 *KYDEP* v *Council and Commission* [1994] ECR I-4199
Case C-212/91 *Angelopharm* v *Freie Hansestadt Hamburg* [1994] ECR I-171
Case C-325/91 *France* v *Commission* [1993] ECR I-3283
Case C-188/92 *Textilwerke Deggendorf* v *Deutschland (TWD)* [1994] ECR I-833
Joined Cases C-46 and 48/93 *Brasserie du Pecheur* v *Germany*, *R* v *Secretary of State ex parte Factortame* [1996] ECR I-1029
Case C-312/93 *Peterbroeck* v *Belgian State* [1995] ECR I-4599

Joined Cases C-430/93 and C-431/93 *Van Schijndel and Others* [1995] ECR I-4705
Case C-465/93 *Atalanta Fruchthandelsgesellschaft and others* v *Bundesamt für Ernährung und Forstwirtschaft* [1995] ECR I-3761
Opinion 2/94 [1996] ECR I-3425
Case C-5/94 *Hedley Lomas* [1996] ECR I-2553
Joined Cases C-178/94, C-179/94, C-188/94, C-189/94 and C-190/94 *Dillenkofer* [1996] ECR I-4845
Case C-194/94 *CIA Security* [1996] ECRI-2201
Case C-201/94 *The Queen* v *The Medicines Control Agency, ex parte Smith and Nephew Pharmaceuticals and Primecrown* v *The Medicine Control Agency* [1996] ECR I-5819
Case C-202/94 *Criminal proceedings against Godefridus van der Feesten* [1996] ECR I-355
[1996] ECR I-1029
Case C-10/95 *Asociación Española de Empresas de la Carne (Asocarne)* v *Raad* [1995] ECR I-4149
Case C-68/95 *T. Port GmbH and Co* v *Bundesanstalt für Landwirtschaft und Ernährung* [1996] ECR I-
6065.
Case C-72/95 *Kraaijeveld* [1996] ECR I-5403
Case C-29/95 *Pastoors and Trans-Cap* [1997] ECR I-285
Case C-178/95 *Wiljo* [1997] ECR 585
Case C-265/95 *Commission* v *France (Spanish strawberries)* [1998] ECR I-963
Case C-282/95 P *Guérin automobiles* v *Commission* [1997] ECR I-1503
Case C-298/95 *Commission* v *Germany* [1996] ECR I-6747
Case C-321/95 P *Stichting Greenpeace Council (Greenpeace International) and Others* v *Commission* [1998] ECR I-1651
Case C-338/95 *Wiener* [1997] ECR I-6495
Case C-390/95 P *Antillean Rice Mills* v *Commission* [1999] ECR I-769
Case C-408/95 *Eurotunnel and Others* v *Sea-France* [1997] ECR I-6315
Case C-10/96 *Ligue royale belge pour la protection des oiseaux and Société d'études ornithologiques v. Région Wallonne* [1996] ECR I- 6775
Case C-22/96 *European Parliament* v *Council* [1998] ECR I-3231
Case C-100/96 *The Queen* v *Ministry of Agriculture, Fisheries and Food, ex parte British Agrochemicals Association* [1999] ECR I-1499
Case C-129/96 *Inter-Environnement Wallonie* [1997] ECR I-7411
Case C-213/96 *Outokumpu Oy* [1998] ECR I-1801
Case C-274/96 *Bickel* [1998] ECR I-7637
Case C-348/96 *Calfa* [1999] ECR I-11
Case C-368/96 *Generics* [1998] ECR I-7967
Case C-386/96 P *Dreyfus* v *Commission* [1998] ECR I-2309
Case C-400/96 *Criminal proceedings against Jean Harpegnies* [1998] ECR

I-5121
Case C-404/96 P *Glencore Grain* v *Commission* [1998] ECR I-2435
Case C-95/97 *Région Wallone* v *Commission* [1997] ECR I-5245
Case C-70/97 P *Kruidvat* [1998] ECR I-7183
Case C-178/97 *Banks* [2000] ECR I-2005
Case C-180/97 *Regione Toscana* v *Commission* [1997] ECR I-8973
Case C-209/97 *Commission* v *Council* [1999] ECR I-8067
Case C-288/97 *Regione Autonoma Friuli-Venezia Giulia* v *Commission* [1999] ECR II-2575
Case C-310/97 P *Commission* v *AssiDomän Kraft et al* [1999] ECR I-5363
Case C-378/97 *Wijsenbeek* [1999] ECR I-6207
Case C-387/97 *Greece* v *Commission* [2000] ECR I-5047
Case C-435/97 *WWF* [1999] ECR I-5613
Case C-95/98 *Rhone-Poulenc* [1999] I-04835
Case C-151/98 P *Pharos* v *Commission* [1999] ECR I-8157
Case C-287/98 *Linster* [2000] ECR I-6917
Case C-306/98 *The Queen* v *Minister of Agriculture, Fisheries and Food and Secretary of State for the Environment ex parte Monsanto* [2001] ECR I-3279
Case C-352/98 P *Laboratoires Parmaceutiqus Bergaderm and Goupil* v *Commission* [2000] ECR I-5291.
Case C-376/98 *Germany* v *Parliament and Council (Tobacco Advertising)* [2000] ECR I-8419
Case C-473/98 *Toolex Alpha* [2000] ECR I-5681
Case C-1/99 *Kofisa Italia* [2001] ECR I-207
Case C-6/99 *Association Greenpeace France and Others* v *Ministere de l'Agriculture et de la Peche and Others* [2000] ECR I-1651
Case C-74/99 *British American Tobacco (Investments) and Imperial Tobacco* [2000] ECR I-8599
Case C-120/99 *Italy* v *Council* [2001] ECR I-7997
Case C-199/99 P *Corus UK* v *Commission* [2003] ECR I-11177
Case C-226/99 *Siples* [2001] ECR I-277
Case C-239/99 *Nachi Europe* [2001] ECR I-1197
Case C-424/99 *Commission* v *Austria* [2001] ECR I-9285
Case C-510/99 *Tridon* [2001] ECR I-7777
Case C-23/00 P *Council* v *Boehringer* [2002] ECR I-1873
Case C-50/00 P *Union de Pequenos Agricultores* v *Council (UPA)* [2002] ECR I-6677
Case C-94/00 *Roquette Freres* [2002] ECR I-9011
Case C-112/00 *Eugen Schmidberger* v *Austria* [2003] ECR I-05659
Case C-142/00 P *Commission* v *Nederlandse Antillen* [2003] ECR I-3483
Case C-172/00 *Ferring* v *Eurim Pharma* [2002] ECR I-6891
Case C-210/00 *Käserei Champignon Hofmeister* [2002] ECR I-6453
Case C-336/00 *Austria* v *Martin Humber* [2002] ECR I-7699

Case C-378/00 *Commission* v *Parliament and Council (LIFE)* [2003] ECR I-937
Case C-13/01 *Safalero* v *Prefetto di Genova* [2003] ECR I-8679
Case C-15/01 *Paranova* [2003] ECR I-4175
Case C-106/01 *Novartis* [2004] ECR I-4403
Case C-113/01 *Paranova* [2003] ECR I-4243
Case C-189/01 *Jippes and Others* [2001] ECR I-5689
Case C-213/01 P *T. Port* v *Commission* [2003] ECR I-2319
Case C-236/01 *Monsanto* [2003] ECR I-8105
Case C-322/01 *Deutscher Apothekerverband eV* v *0800 DocMorris and Jacques Waterval* [2003] ECR I-14887
Case C-491/01 *The Queen* v *Secretary for Health, ex parte British American Tobacco (Investments) and Imperial Tobacco* [2002] ECR I-11453
Case C-93/02 P *Biret* v *Council* [2003] ECR I-10497
Case C-112/02 *Kohlpharma* [2004] ECR I-3369
Case C-127/02 *Landelijke Vereniging tot Behoud van de Waddenzee and Nederlandse Vereniging tot Bescherming van Vogels* v *Staatssecretaris van Landbouw, Natuurbeheer en Visserij* [2004] ECR I-7405
Case C-174/02 *Streekgewest Westelijk Noord-Brabant* [2005] ECR I-85
Case C-216/02 *Österreichischer Zuchtverband für Ponys, Kleinpferde und Spezialrassen* [2004] ECR I-10683
Case C-222/02 *Peter Paul* [2004] ECR I-9425
Case C-258/02 P *Bactria Industriehygiene-Service Verwaltungs* v *Commission* [2003] ECR I-1505
Case C-263/02 P *Jégo Queré* v *Commission* [2004] ECR I-3425
Case C-293/02 *Jersey Produce Marketing Organisation* v *States of Jersey and Jersey Potato Export Marketing Board (Jersey Potatoes)* [2005] ECR I-9543
Case C-304/02 *Commission* v *France* [2005] ECR I-6263
Case C-443/02 *Schreiber* [2004] ECR I-7275
Case C-39/03 P *Commission* v *Artegodan* [2003] ECR I-7885
Case C-74/03 *SmithKline Beecham plc* v *Laegemiddelstyreisen* [2005] ECR I-595
Case C-111/03 *Commission* v *Sweden* [2005] ECR I-8789
Case C-131/03 P *Reynolds and Others* v *Commission* [2006] ECR I-7795
C-132/03 *Ministero della Salute* v *Coordinamento delle asscociazioni per la difesa dell'ambiente e dei diritti degli utenti e dei consumatori (Codacons)* [2005] ECR I-4167
Case C-176/03 *Commission* v *Council* [2005] ECR I-7879
Case C-198/03 P *Commission* v *CEVA and Pfizer* [2005] ECR I-6357
Case C-210/03, *Swedish Match* [2004] ECR I-11893
Joined Cases C-211/03, C-299/03 and C-316/03 to C-319/03 *HLH Warenvertriebs, Orthica* v *Bundesrepublik Deutschland* [2005] ECR I-5141
Case C-239/03 *Commission* v *France (Etang de Berre)* [2004] ECR I-9325
Case C-245/03 *Merck Sharp and Dohme* [2005] ECRI-237

Case C-287/03 *Commission* v *Belgium* [2005] ECR I-3761
Case C-364/03 *Commission* v *Greece* [2005] ECR I-6159
Case C-416/03 *Commission* v *Greece* OJ 2005 C-106/7
Case C-422/03 *Commission* v *the Netherlands* OJ 2005 C 6/16
Case C-436/03 *SCE* [2006] I-03733
Joined Cases C-453/03, C-11/04, C-12/04 and C-194/04 *ABNA and others* [2005] ECR I-10423
Case C-459/03 *Commission* v *Ireland (MOX Plant)* [2006] ECR I-4635
Case C-461/03 *Gaston Schul* [2005] ECR I-10513
Case C-495/03 *Intermodal* [2005] ECR I-8151
Case C-511/03 *Ten Kate Holding Musselkanaal and Others* [2006] ECR I-8979
Case C-547/03 P *Asian Institute of Technology (AIT)* v *Commission* [2006] ECR I-845
Case C-15/04 *Koppensteiner* v *Bundesimmobliliengesellschaft* [2005] ECR I-4855
Case C-66/04 *Smoke Flavourings* [2005] I-10553
Case C-114/04 *Commission* v *Germany* [2005] ECR I-0000
Case C-122/04 *Commission* v *Parliament and Council* [2006] ECR I-2001
Joined Cases C-154/04 and C-155/04 *The Queen on the application of Alliance for Natural Health and Nutrilink* v *Secretary of State for Health and the Queen, on the application of National Association of Health Stores and Health Food Manufacturers* v *Secretary of State for Health and National Assembly for Wales* [2005] ECR I-6451
Case C-217/04 *ENISA* [2006] I-03771
Case C-310/04 *Spain* v *Council* [2006] ECR I-7285
Case C-316/04 *Stichting Zuid-Hollandse Milieufederatie* v *College voor de toelating van bestrijdingsmiddelen (ZHM I)* [2005] ECR I-9759
Case C-344/04 *The Queen, on the application of International Air Transport Association and European Low Fares Airline Association* v *Department for Transport* [2006] ECR I-403
Joined Cases C-346 and 529/03 *Giuseppe Atzeni and Others* v *Regione Autonoma della Sardegna* [2006] ECR I-1875
Case C-380/04 *Bactria* v *Commission* [2004] ECR I-0000
Case C-417/04 P *Regione Siciliana* v *Commission* [2006] ECR I-3881
Case C-482/04 P *SNFSA* v *Commission* OJ 2006 C143/20
Case C-28/05 *G.J. Dokter et al* v *Minister van Landbouw, Natuur en Voedselkwaliteit* [2006] ECR I-5431
Case C-138/05 *Stichting Zuidhollandse Milieufederatie* v *College voor de toelating van bestrijdingsmiddelen (ZHM II)* [2006] ECR I-8339
Case C-174/05 *Stichting Zuid-Hollandse Milieufederatie, Stichting Natuur en Milieu* v *College voor de toelating van bestrijdingsmiddelen* [2006] ECR I-2443
Case C-232/05 *Commission* v *France* [2006] ECR I-10071

Case C-243/05 P *Agraz, SA and Others* v *Commission* [2006] ECR I-10833
Case C-255/05 *Commission* v *Italy* [2007] ECR I-5767
Case C-282/05 P *Holcim* v *Commission* [2007] ECR I-6441
Case C-326/05 P *Industrias Chimicas del Valles* v *Commission* [2007] ECR I-6557
Case C-361/05 *Commission* v *Spain* [2007] ECR I-71
Case C-423/05 *Commission* v *France* [2007] I-47
Case C-431/05 *Merck Genericos-Produtos Farmaceuticos* v *Merck and Co and Merck, Sharp and Dohme* [2007] ECR I-0000
Case C-432/05 *Unibet* v *Justitiekanslern* [2007] ECR I-2271
Joined Cases C-439/05 P and C-454/05 P *Land Oberosterreich and Austria* v *Commission* [2007] ECR I-7141
Case C-440/05 *Commission* v *Council* [2007] ECR I-9097
Case C-441/05 *Roquette Freres* v *Ministre de l'Agriculture, de l'Alimentation, de la Peche et de la Ruralité* [2007] ECR I-1993
Case C-201/06 *Commission* v *France* [2008] ECR I-0000
Joined Cases C-260/06 and C-261/06 *Criminal proceedings against Daniel Escalier and Jean Bonnarel* [2007] ECR I-9717
Case C-361/06 *Feinchemie Schwebda and Bayer Crop Science* v *College voor de toelating van bestrijdingsmiddelen* [2008] ECR I-0000
Case 452/06 *The Queen on the application of Synthon* v *Licensing Authority of the Department of Health* [2008] ECR I-0000
Case C-236/07 P (R) *Sumitomo Chemical Agro Europe* v *Commission* [2008] ECR I-0000
C-237/07 *Janecek* [2008] ECR I-0000
Case C-76/08 R *Commission* v *Malta* [2008] ECR I-0000
C-132/05 *Parmigiano Reggiano* [2008] ECR I-0000

Court of First Instance

Case T-113/89 *Nefarma* v *Commission* [1990] ECR II-816
Case T-28/90 *Asia Motor France and Others* v *Commission* [1992] ECR II-2285
Case T-74/92 *Ladbroke* v *Commission* [1995] ECR II-115
Joined Cases T-480 and 483/93 *Antillean Rice Mills and Others* v *Commission* [1995] ECR II-2305
Case T-481 and 484/93 *Exporteurs in Levende Varkens and Others* v *Commission* [1995] ECR II-2653
Case T-585/93 *Greenpeace and Others* v *Commission* [1995] ECR II-2205
Case T-99/94 *Asociación Espanalo de Empresas de la Carne (ASOCARNE)* v *Council* [1994] ECR II-71
Case T-154/94 *Comité des Salines de France* v *Commission* [1996] ECR II-1377
Case T-95/96 *Gestevisión Telecinco* v *Commission* [1998] ECR II-3407
Case T-105/96 *Pharos* v *Commission* [1998] ECR KK-285
Case T-122/96 *Federolio* v *Commission* [1997] ECR II-1559

Joined Cases T-125/96 and T-152/96 *Boehringer* v *Council and Commission* [1999] ECR II-3427
Case T-127/98 *UPS Europe* v *Commission* [1999] ECR II-2633
Case T-135/96 *UEAPME* v *Council* [1998] ECR II-2335
Joined Cases T-172, 175 and 177/98 *Salamander AG* v *Parliament and Council* [2000] ECR II-2487
Case T-199/96 *Bergaderm and Goupil* v *Commission* [1998] ECR II-2805
Case T-13/99 *Pfizer Animal Health SA* v *Council* [2002] ECR II-3305
Case T-52/99 *T. Port* v *Commission* [2001] ECR II-981
Case T-69/99 *DSTV* v *Commission* [2000] ECR II-4309
Case T-70/99 *Alpharma* v *Council* [2002] ECR II-3495
Case T-212/99 *Intervet* v *Commission* [2002] ECR II-1445
Case T-326/99 *Nancy Fern Olivieri* v *Commission and EMEA* [2003] ECR II-6053
Joined Cases T-74/00, T-76/00, T-83/00 to T-85/00, T-132/00, T-137/00 and T-141/00 *Artegodan and Others* v *Commission* [2002] ECR II-4945
Case T-123/00 *Dr Karl Thomae* [2002] ECR II-5193
Case T-174/00 *Biret International* v *Council* [2002] ECR II-17
Joined Cases T-344 and 345 /00 *CEVA and Others* v *Commission* [2003] ECR II-229
Joined Cases T-377/00, T-379/00, T-390/00, T-260/01 and T-272/01 *Philip Morris International and Others* v *Commission* [2003] ECR 2639
Case T-177/01 *Jégo Queré* v *Commission* [2003] ECR II-2365
Case T-226/01 *CAS Succhi di Frutta* v *Commission* [2006] ECR II-2763
Case T-304/01 *Julia Abad Perez and Others, Confederacion de Organizaciones de Agricultores y Ganaderos and Unió de Pagesos* v *Council and Commission* [2006] ECR II-4857
Case T-306/01 *Ahmed Ali Yusuf and Others* v *Council* [2005] II-03533
Case T-315/01 *Yassin Abdullah Kadi and Others* v *Council* [2005] II-03649
Case T-213/02 *SNFSA Commission* [2004] ECR II-3047
Case T-392/02 *Solvay Pharmaceuticals* v *Council* [2003] ECR II-4555
Case T-228/02 *Organisation des Modjahedines du people d'Iran* v *Council* [2006] ECR II-4665
Case T-138/03 *E.R. and others* v *Council and Commission* [2006] ECR II-4923
Case T-141/03 *Sniace SA* v *Commission* [2005] ECR II-1197
Joined Cases T-366/03 and T-235/04 *Land Oberosterreich and Austria* v *Commission* [2005] ECR II-4005
Case T-37/04 *Regiao autonoma dos Acores* v *Council* [2008] ECR II-0000
Case T-94/04 *European Environmental Bureau (EEB) and Others* v *Commission* [2005] ECR II-4919
Case T-229/04 *Sweden* v *Commission* [2007] ECR II-2437
Joined Cases T-236/04 and T-241/04 *European Environmental Bureau, Stichting Natuur en Milieu* [2005] ECR II-04945

Case T-395/04 *Air One* v *Commission* [2006] ECR II-1343
Case T-216/05 *Mebrom* v *Commission* [2007] ECR II-1507
Case T-31/07 R *Du Pont de Nemours and Others* v *Commission* [2007] ECR II-2767
Case T-350/07 R *FMC Chemical SPRL, Arysta Lifesciece, Belchim Crop Protection, FandN Agro Slovenkso, FandN Agro Ceska republika, FandN Agro Polska and FMC Corp* v *Commission* [2007] ECR II-0000
Case T-475/07 R *Dow AgroSciences and Others* v *Commission* [2008] ECR II-0000

European Court of Human Rights

ECtHR 21 February 1984 *Oztürk* v *Germany* Series A 73 No 9/1982/55/84
ECtHR 17 December 1996 *Saunders* v *UK* Series A No 43/1994/490/572
ECtHR 24 Sept. 2002 *Posti and Rahko* v *Finland* Case 27824/95
ECtHR *Bosphorus Airlines* v *Ireland* (2006) 42 EHRR 1

The Netherlands

Hoge Raad (Supreme Court)
21 May 2002, NJ 2002, 404

Rechtbanken (District Courts)
26 May 2004 *Holland International Bird Trading* (Rechtbank Roermond), 03/718 and 03/719 Wet K1, unpublished

Raad van State (Council of State)
22 August 2001, AB 2001/310
18 December 2002, AB 2003/276, JGR 2003/1
18 June 2003, JGR 2003/23
12 November 2003, LJN: AN 7892, available at: www.rechtspraak.nl.
11 February 2004, LJN AO3387, not reported
01 July 2004, AB 2005/19, JGR 2004/41
21 July 2004, AB 2005/19
18 December 2004, AB 2003,276
23 February 2005, JGR 2005/22
28 April 2005, JGR 2005/23

College van Beroep voor het bedrijfsleven (Trade and Industry Appeals Tribunal)
17 January 1992 *Italrille tegen de minister van LNV*, MenR 1993/2, p. 134
19 April 2005, AWB 04/300 32010.

Table of Legislation

Council Directive 79/117 prohibiting the placing on the market and the use of plant protection products containing certain active substances, OJ 1978 L33/36

Council Directive 79/409/EEC on the conservation of wild birds, OJ 1979 L 103/1

Council Decision 84/133/EEC introducing a Community system for the rapid exchange of information on dangers arising from the use of consumer products, OJ 1984 L 70/16

Council Directive 85/374/EEC on the approximation of the laws, regulations and administrative provisions of the Member States concerning liability for defective products, OJ 1985 L210/29

Council Directive 90/220 on the deliberate release of genetically modified organisms into the environment, OJ 1990 L117/15

Directive 90/642 on the fixing of maximum levels for pesticide residues in and on certain products of plant origin, including fruit and vegetables, OJ 1990 L 350/71

Council Directive 91/414 EC concerning the placing of plant protection products on the market, OJ 1991 L 230/1

Council Directive 92/43/EEC on the conservation of natural habitats and of wild fauna and flora, OJ 1992 L 206/7

Council Regulation 2913/92 establishing the Community Customs Code, OJ 1992 L 302/1

Commission Regulation 3600/92 laying down the detailed rules for the implementation of the first stage of the programme of work referred to in Article 8(3) of Directive, 91/414 OJ 1992 L 366

Council Regulation 339/93 on checks for conformity with the rules on product safety in the case of products imported from third countries, OJ 1993 L 40/1

Commission Regulation 2454/93 laying down provisions for the implementation of Council Regulation 2913/92 establishing the Community Customs Code, OJ 1993 L 253/1

Decision 3052/95 of the European Parliament and of the Council, establishing a procedure for the exchange of information on national measures deviating from the principle of the free movement of goods within the Community, OJ 1995 L 321/1

Council Regulation 338/97 on the protection of species of wild fauna and flora by regulating trade therein, OJ 1997 L 61/1

Council Regulation 515/97 on mutual assistance between the administrative authorities of the Member States and cooperation between the latter and the Commission to ensure the correct application of the law on customs and agricultural matters, OJ 1997 L82/1

Directive 98/8/EC of the European Parliament and of the Council, concerning the placing of biocidal products on the market, OJ 1998 L 123/1

Council Regulation 2679/98 on the functioning of the internal market in relation to the free movement of goods among the Member States, OJ 1998 L 337/8
Directive 99/45 concerning the approximation of the laws, regulations and administrative provisions of the Member States relating to the classification, packaging and labelling of dangerous preparations, OJ 1999 L 200/1
Council Decision 1999/468, laying down the procedures for the exercise of implementing powers conferred on the Commission, OJ 1999 L 184/23
Regulation 141/2000 of the European Parliament and the Council on orphan medicines, OJ 2000 L 18/1
Commission Regulation 450/2000 laying down the detailed rules for the implementation of the second and third stages of the work programme referred to in Article 8 (2) of Council Directive 91/414/EEC, OJ 2000 L 55/25
Directive 2001/95 EC of the European Parliament and of the Council on general product safety, OJ 2002 L11/4
Regulation 1049/2001 of the European Parliament and of the Council regarding public access to documents held by institutions of the European Community, OJ 2001 L 145/43
Directive 2001/18/EC of the European Parliament and of the Council on the deliberate release into the environment of genetically modified organisms and repealing Council Directive 90/220, OJ 2001 L 106/1.
Directive 2001/82 of the European Parliament and the Council on the Community Code relating to medicinal products for veterinary use, OJ 2001 L 311/1
Directive 2001/83/EC of the European Parliament and the Council on the Community Code relating to medicinal products for human use, OJ 2001 L311/67
Commission Decision 2002/204 on the operation of the registers for recording information, OJ 2002 L 65/20
Regulation 178/2002 laying down the general principles and requirements of food law, establishing the European Food Safety Authority and laying down procedures in matters of food safety, OJ 2002 L 31/1
Council Decision 2002/628/EC concerning the conclusion, on behalf of the European Community, of the Cartagena Protocol on Biosafety, OJ 2002 L 201/48
Council Decision 2002/811 and Council Decision 2002/812 on the summary information format, OJ 2002 L 280/37
Directive 2003/4/EC of the European Parliament and of the Council on public access to environmental information and repealing Council Directive 90/313/EEC, OJ 2003 L 41/26
Directive 2003/35/EC of the European Parliament and of the Council providing for public participation in respect of the drawing up of certain

plans and programmes relating to the environment and amending with regard to public participation and access to justice Council Directives 85/337/EEC and 96/61/EC, OJ 2003 L 156/17
Proposal for a Directive of the European Parliament and of the Council on access to justice in environmental matters, COM (2003) 624 final
Council Regulation 1383/2003 concerning customs action against goods suspected of infringing certain intellectual property rights and the measures to be taken against goods found to have infringed such rights, OJ 2003 L 196/7
Regulation 1829/2003 of the European Parliament and of the Council on genetically modified food and feed, OJ 2003 L 268/1
Regulation 1830/2003 of the European Parliament and of the Council concerning the traceability and labelling of genetically modified organisms and the traceability of food and feed products produced from genetically modified organisms and amending Directive 2001/18/EC, OJ 2003 L 268/24
Regulation 1946/2003/EC of the European Parliament and the Council on transboundary movements of genetically modified organisms, OJ 2003, L 287/1
Commission Regulation 65/2004 establishing a system for the development and assignment of unique identifiers for GMOs OJ 2004 L 10/5
Commission Decision 2004/204 on guidance notes for the environmental risk Assessment, OJ 2004 L 200/22
Decision 2004/387/EC of the European Parliament and of the Council on interoperable delivery of pan-European e-Government services to public administrations, businesses and citizens (IDABC), OJ 2004 L 181/25
Commission Regulation 641/2004 containing detailed rules for the implementation of Regulation 1829/2003, OJ 2004 L 102/14
Regulation 726/2004 laying down Community procedures for the authorisation and supervision of medicinal products for human and veterinary use and establishing a European Medicines Agency, OJ 2004 L 136/1
Regulation 850/2004 of the European Parliament and of the Council on persistent organic pollutants and amending Directive 79/117/EEC, OJ 2004 L 158/7
Regulation 882/2004 of the European Parliament and of the Council on official controls performed to ensure the verification of compliance with feed and food law, animal health and animal welfare rules 2004, OJ L 165/1
Council Decision 2005/370/EC on the conclusion, on behalf of the EC, of the Convention on access to information, public participation in decision-making, and access to justice regarding environmental matters, OJ 2005 L124/1, deposited with the United Nations

Regulation 396/2005 of the European Parliament and of the Council on maximum residue levels of pesticides in or on food and feed of plant and animal origin and amending Council Directive 91/414, OJ 2005 L 70/1

Council Decision 2006/957/EC on the conclusion, on behalf of the European Community, of an amendment to the Convention on access to information, public participation in decision-making and access to justice in environmental matters, OJ 2006 L 386/46

Commission Regulation 865/2006 laying down detailed rules concerning the implementation of Council Regulation 338/97/EC, OJ 2006 L 166/1

Regulation 1367/2006 of the European Parliament and of the Council on the application of the Aarhus

Convention on Access to Information, Public Participation in Decision-Making and Access to Justice in Environmental Matters to Community institutions and bodies, OJ 2006 L 264/13

Regulation 1907/2006 of the European Parliament and the Council concerning the Registration, Evaluation, Authorisation and Restriction of Chemicals (REACH), establishing a European Chemicals Agency, amending Directive 1999/45/EC and repealing Council Regulation (EEC) No 793/93 and Commission Regulation (EC) No 1488/94 as well as Council Directive 76/769/EEC and Commission Directives 91/155/EEC, 93/67/EEC, 93/105/EC and 2000/21/EC, OJ 2006 L 396/1

Commission Regulation 658/2007 concerning financial penalties for infringement of certain obligations in connection with marketing authorizations granted under Regulation 726/2004 of the European Parliament and of the Council, OJ 2007 L 155/10

(Amended) Proposal for a Regulation of the European Parliament and the Council concerning the placing of plant protection products on the market COM 2008 (93) final